INTERMEDIATE

The Education Center

The IDEA MAGAZINE FOR TEACHERS.
MAILBOX.

2004–2005
YEARBOOK

The Education Center, Inc.
Greensboro, North Carolina

The Mailbox® 2004–2005 Intermediate Yearbook

Managing Editor, *The Mailbox* Magazine: Peggy W. Hambright

Editorial Team: Becky S. Andrews, Kimberley Bruck, Karen P. Shelton, Diane Badden, Debra Liverman, Karen A. Brudnak, Sarah Hamblet, Hope Rodgers, Dorothy C. McKinney

Production Team: Lisa K. Pitts, Margaret Freed (COVER ARTIST), Pam Crane, Rebecca Saunders, Jennifer Tipton Cappoen, Chris Curry, Sarah Foreman, Theresa Lewis Goode, Ivy L. Koonce, Clint Moore, Greg D. Rieves, Barry Slate, Donna K. Teal, Tazmen Carlisle, Irene Harvley-Felder, Amy Kirtley-Hill, Kristy Parton, Cathy Edwards Simrell, Lynette Dickerson, Mark Rainey

ISBN 1-56234-660-1
ISSN 1088-5552

The Education Center, Inc.
P.O. Box 9753
Greensboro, NC 27429-0753

Look for *The Mailbox® 2005–2006 Intermediate Yearbook* in the summer of 2006. The Education Center, Inc., is the publisher of *The Mailbox*®, *Teacher's Helper*®, *The Mailbox*® BOOKBAG®, and *Learning*® magazines, as well as other fine products. Look for these wherever quality teacher materials are sold, or call 1-800-714-7991.

Contents

Seasonal Ideas & Reproducibles

Autobiographical Trivia Wheels

Here's a unique **getting-acquainted** activity your students will "wheel-y" enjoy! Enlarge the templates shown, making each wheel eight inches in diameter. Next, distribute the materials listed and guide students through the steps below to make the trivia wheels. Then invite each child to share his completed project with the class. *Darrin Praska—Gr. 6, Meeker Elementary, Ames, IA*

Materials for each student: scissors, brad, red pen, blue pen, crayons, white copy of wheel B, copy of wheel A in one color for boys and another color for girls

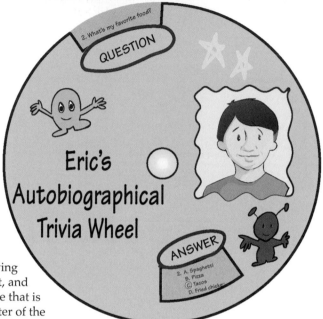

Steps:
1. Create ten questions about yourself, with two for each of the following difficulty levels: easy, somewhat easy, somewhat difficult, difficult, and challenging. Then write four answer choices for each question: one that is correct and three that are incorrect. Use a blue pen to circle the letter of the correct answer. Have your teacher check your work.
2. Cut out both wheels. Decorate one side of the colorful wheel.
3. Place the decorated wheel atop the white one. Align the windows.
4. Use a red pen to copy your first question on the white paper in the window at the top edge of the decorated wheel. Copy the four corresponding answer choices on the white paper in the window near the bottom edge. Use a blue pen to circle the letter of the correct answer.
5. Turn the top wheel clockwise to add the remaining questions and answers.
6. Remove the top wheel and color each question and answer set a different color.
7. Stack the colorful wheel atop the white one. Push the brad through the center of both wheels and fasten it in place.

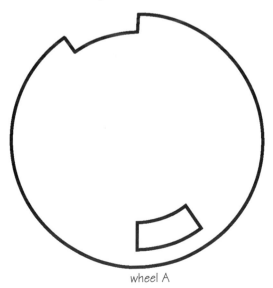

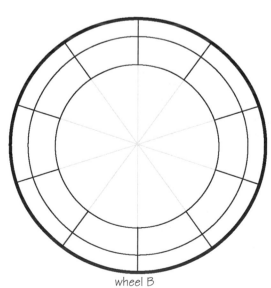

wheel A   wheel B

Get-to-Know-Me Bags

This **getting-to-know-you** activity is in the bag! Have each child use markers, scissors, glue, and colorful paper scraps to decorate a lunch-size paper bag to represent herself. Also have her write on an index card a paragraph about her goals for the school year and place it inside the bag. Direct the student to take her bag home and fill it with five objects—photographs, awards, ribbons, or magazine cutouts—that represent her personal interests, talents, and family. The next day, set aside time for students to share their get-to-know-me bags with the class. *Joann Toomey—Gr. 4, James H. Boyd School, Huntington, NY*

All About Me

My favorite color is _____.
My favorite food is _____.
My favorite ice-cream flavor is _____.
My favorite TV show is _____.
My favorite type of music is _____.
My favorite movie is _____.
My proudest moment was _____
_____.
Three words I would use to describe school are _____,
_____, and _____.

Dual-Purpose Survey

Discover what your students' interests are outside of the classroom with a **getting-to-know-you** survey that becomes a revealing exercise at open house! Create a survey, such as the one shown, for each child to complete. Also prepare an adult version, replacing the words *me, my,* and *I* with *my child* or *my child's*. At open house, have each parent or guardian complete the adult version and compare it to the one his child completed. Don't be surprised if a parent says he learned something new about his child! *Brooke Beverly—Gr. 5, Julia Bancroft School, Auburn, MA*

Me Too!

Help students identify classmates who have similar interests and attributes with this fun **getting-acquainted** game! Have each child write her first and last name on a slip of paper. Collect the slips in a container. Next, direct each student to draw a gameboard grid similar to the one shown. Have the student label each blank space with a generalized descriptor about herself. For example, she should write "I have visited Maine" instead of "I visited Maine in January." If students have trouble thinking of 24 different descriptors, allow repeats (in different columns).

To play, draw a slip from the container and read the name aloud. Also call out the letter at the top of one of the gameboard's columns. Instruct the child whose name was drawn to share one of her descriptors from that column. Have each student with that descriptor on her gameboard cover it with a marker and then stand. Repeat the process until one player covers a row horizontally, vertically, or diagonally. *Jeanne Maloney—Gr. 4, Bells Elementary, Turnersville, NJ*

M	E	T	O_1	O_2!
I have a sister.	I have blue eyes.	I like malls.	I like to read.	I have red hair.
I have blue eyes.	I have visited Disney World.	I have visited Maine.	I have red hair.	I like chocolate.
I like to sing.	I have a cat.	FREE	I have a brother.	I like spelling.
I have a bike.	I saw Shrek.	I play on a soccer team.	I like pizza.	I wear braces.
I have a dog.	I like computer games.	I like Harry Potter books.	I love school.	I saw Finding Nemo.

Cereal Box Math

Celebrate Better Breakfast Month in September with a **problem-solving** activity that can make students more nutrition-savvy! Ask parents to send in empty cereal boxes until there is one box for each pair of students. After distributing the boxes, point out that the nutrition information is usually found in a box on the side panel. Use data from a nutrition facts box to create a word problem. Next, have each set of partners use its nutrition facts box to create five similar problems. Check students' work. Then give each twosome scissors, glue, markers, and a 12" x 18" sheet of construction paper. Instruct the partners to cut out a large paper cereal bowl and spoon and glue the cereal's nutrition facts box to it as shown. Have the pair write the cereal's name on the spoon handle; also have the pair write its favorite problem next to the nutrition facts box on the bowl and the answer on the bowl's back. Pin the completed cutouts to a bulletin board titled "Nutritious Math" to create a self-checking center!

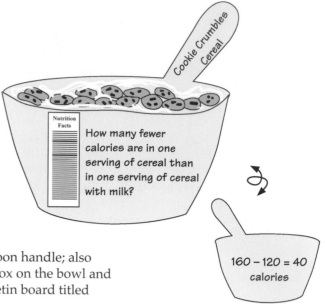

How many fewer calories are in one serving of cereal than in one serving of cereal with milk?

160 – 120 = 40 calories

September Journal Topics

Slip into September with **writing prompts** that are perfectly suited for the season!

• What's the weirdest thing you've ever eaten or seen anyone eat on ice cream? Explain where you were and what you were doing at the time.

• The first Miss America was crowned in Atlantic City, New Jersey, on September 8, 1921. Should this competition continue to be held? Why or why not?

• Which embarrasses you more: arriving at an event early or late? Why?

• September 10 is Swap Ideas Day. Explain what you think would happen if baseball player Barry Bonds and computer software expert Bill Gates could swap ideas.

• Which would you prefer to receive as a gift: cash or a gift certificate to your favorite store? Explain.

• September 11 is Patriot Day. Describe three events you think should be part of this year's observance.

• Samuel Johnson, born on September 18, 1709, created the first great dictionary of the English language. Define three words that Johnny Appleseed might have wanted to be in the dictionary.

• What would your life be like if the telephone had never been invented? Explain.

• Suppose that every baseball, football, and soccer field turned blue overnight. How do you think people would feel: afraid, excited, angry, confused? Explain.

• What do you think the proverb "The grass always looks greener on the other side" means?

The reproducibles on pages 9–12 were written by Ann Fisher of Toledo, OH.

Supercool School

Suzie and Skooter are super excited about attending their new school! Read their comments. If a comment is a fact, color it yellow. If it is an opinion, color it orange.

To New Squirrel School

1. The new teacher, Ms. Nutts, lives on Oak Street.

2. Ms. Nutts's class will be the best one this year!

3. There are 25 more students in school this year than last year.

4. Social studies is the easiest subject.

5. The principal's name is Mr. Bush E. Tail.

6. Mr. Tail is taller than Ms. Nutts.

7. Ms. Nutts will probably be a good math teacher.

8. The new cafeteria is painted an ugly color.

9. This year we will have to learn 30 spelling words every week.

10. Mr. Tail wears the coolest clothes.

11. The new library is across the hall from Ms. Nutts's room.

12. The school's mascot should be a giant acorn.

Bonus Box: On the back of this page, write two facts and two opinions about your own school.

Batter Up!

September is National Little League Month! Read the sports story Homer Runn wrote about his team's last game. Cross out each boldfaced verb. Above it, write a verb that is more vivid. Then copy the improved story on another sheet of paper and staple it to this one.

Tigers Beat Lions to Win City Title!

Freddy Frost, the coach of the Tigers, **said,** "We did it! We finally **won** the city championship! I thought this day would never come!" His players **stood** around him, **talked,** and clapped.

The game began well for the Lions. In the first inning, Sluggin' Sally **hit** a ball deep into left field for a triple. She **ran** home on a single by Sprinting Sammy. That was to be the team's only run.

The Tigers **had** the rest of the game. Shortstop Smitty **made** two home runs. Catcher Connie crossed home plate all three times she was on base.

One of the game's greatest plays **was** in the seventh inning. The Lions had runners on first and second with their top hitter, Babs Ruth, up to bat. Pete Pitcher **threw** a high fastball that Babs **hit** hard. But the ball **went** straight to Smitty's glove. Smitty quickly tossed it to the second baseman, who shot it to first base. The double play **ended** the Lions' last threat.

With this win, the Tigers can now **say,** "We are ter-r-r-rifically great!"

Bonus Box: On the back of this page, draw a picture that could help readers picture your favorite part of this sports story.

Note to the teacher: Students may need to use a thesaurus to complete this page.

Swimming in School Supplies

It sure takes a lot of supplies to get a whole school of fish ready for school! The order has arrived. Make sure it is correct by writing the letter on each fish next to its matching word form in the box. Then solve the riddle.

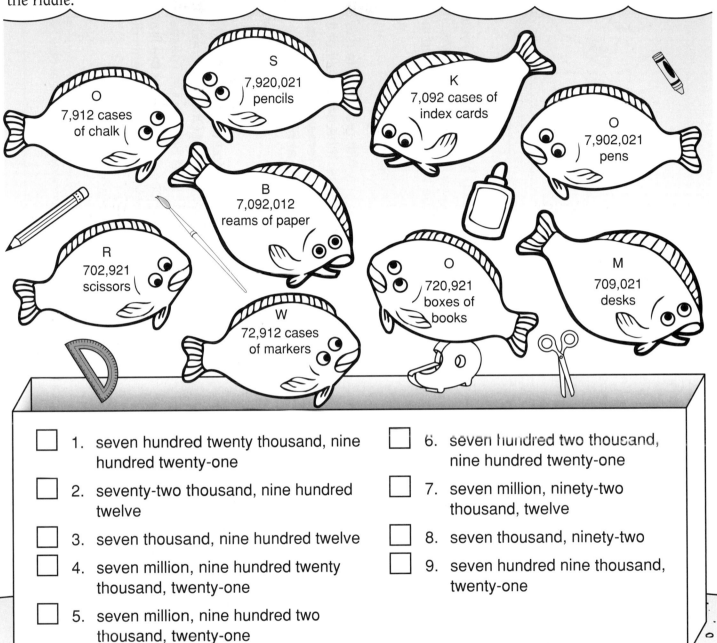

O
7,912 cases of chalk

S
7,920,021 pencils

K
7,092 cases of index cards

O
7,902,021 pens

B
7,092,012 reams of paper

R
702,921 scissors

O
720,921 boxes of books

M
709,021 desks

W
72,912 cases of markers

☐ 1. seven hundred twenty thousand, nine hundred twenty-one

☐ 2. seventy-two thousand, nine hundred twelve

☐ 3. seven thousand, nine hundred twelve

☐ 4. seven million, nine hundred twenty thousand, twenty-one

☐ 5. seven million, nine hundred two thousand, twenty-one

☐ 6. seven hundred two thousand, nine hundred twenty-one

☐ 7. seven million, ninety-two thousand, twelve

☐ 8. seven thousand, ninety-two

☐ 9. seven hundred nine thousand, twenty-one

Why was the hungry halibut so eager to go to school?

To answer the riddle, write the letter of each answer above in its matching blank below.

He heard there were __ __ __ __ __ __ __ __ __ !
7 3 1 8 2 5 6 9 4

Bonus Box: Use the following digits to form the greatest six-digit number you can: 6, 2, 9, 8, 9, 1. Then write the number's word form.

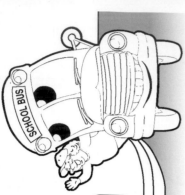

Riders 'n' Drivers

School bus drivers must know where to stop, how many students to pick up, and where to drop them off. Solve the problems below by writing numbers in the blanks provided. Some problems will be solved using numbers from an earlier problem.

Example: Mr. Loudhorn picks up 14 students at his first stop and 19 at his second stop. If he drops off 10 students at one school, how many will he take to other schools? $14 + 19 - 10 = 23$ students

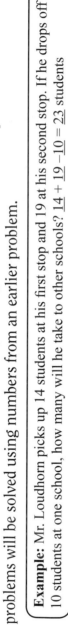

1. Two dozen children got on Ms. Smiley's bus at its first stop. If 7 more climbed on before the bus pulled away, how many students in all boarded her bus?

_____ + _____ = _____ students

2. Mr. Jolly's bus takes 87 students to three different schools. If 19 students go to Green School and 36 go to Brown School, how many go to Gray School?

_____ − _____ − _____ = _____ students

3. From Monday through Thursday, Mr. Jolly takes the same number of students to Green School. On Friday, he takes 8 fewer students there. By Friday, how many students will he have taken to Green School?

_____ + _____ + _____ + _____ + _____ = _____ students

4. Mr. Honker picks up 56 students. Ms. Tooter picks up 82. Ms. Beeper picks up half as many as Ms. Tooter. How many riders do the three drivers pick up in all?

_____ + _____ + _____ = _____ riders

5. Mr. Penta drives only fifth graders. He has 88 riders at the beginning of his route. If he drops half of them at Orange School and half of the remaining students at Red School, how many will he drop at Blue School?

_____ − _____ = _____ students

6. Ms. Quad drives only fourth graders. On Monday, she dropped off 24 students at Orange School, 35 at Red School, and 27 at Blue School. On Tuesday, she dropped off the same number of students at the first two schools but 9 fewer at the third. How many students did Ms. Quad drop off on Tuesday?

_____ + _____ + _____ = _____ students

Bonus Box: Suppose that there are 23 fifth graders at Orange School and 37 at Red School. If there are twice as many fifth graders at Blue School as Orange School and Mr. Penta's bus holds 98 students, can it carry all of these fifth graders? Explain.

©The Education Center, Inc. • *The Mailbox*® • TEC44014 • Aug./Sept. 2004 • Key p. 306

Celebrate the Season

October

Classy Scarecrow

Harvest bushels of **expository writing** with an activity that has students creating a class scarecrow! Ask students to bring in a pillowcase and old clothes suitable for dressing a scarecrow. Also collect shredded paper or newspaper to use as stuffing. Next, have students share what they know about the purpose of scarecrows. Afterward, help students stuff the pillowcase and clothes with paper to make a scarecrow and prop it in a corner of your classroom. Then have each student write a paragraph that not only explains how to make a scarecrow but why and where it can be used. *Mary Maxey—Gr. 4, Orange Grove Intermediate, Orange Grove, TX*

How to Make a Scarecrow
To make a scarecrow, collect a pillowcase and an old long-sleeved shirt, a pair of overalls, some boots, a hat, and lots of paper for stuffing!

Candy Timeline

Whet your students' appetites for sweet treats with a **timeline** all about candy! First, type up important dates in candy history, such as those shown. Then pair students and give each pair a sheet of light-colored construction paper and markers. After assigning each duo one timeline event, instruct the twosome to design a poster that illustrates the candy and label it with the date. If desired, ask the partners to research additional facts about the candy and include them on the poster. Allow early finishers to create posters about concurrent historical events for a parallel timeline. Collect the posters and tape them to lengths of yarn in order. Then display the timeline(s) along a wall titled "Candy History: How Sweet It Is!" *Nicole Miner—Gr. 4, Painted Sky Elementary, Albuquerque, NM*

Candy	Year Introduced
Candy corn	1800s
Tootsie Roll candy	1896
Hershey's milk chocolate bar	1900
Hershey's Kisses candy	1906
Peppermint Life Savers candy	1912
Baby Ruth bar	1920
Bit•O•Honey candy	1925
Reese's peanut butter cups	1928
Snickers bar	1930
Tootsie Roll Pops candy	1931
Red Hots candies	1932

Candy corn
1800s

Leaf Haiku Book

Follow up a fall study of **poetry** with a bookmaking project that is "unbe-leaf-ably" unique! Have students brainstorm words that describe fall, and record them on the board. Next, review with students how to write a haiku poem (three lines: five syllables, seven syllables, five syllables). Then have each child use the words on the board to help him write a haiku poem about autumn. After you check the poems, give each poet a 6" x 9" piece of fall-colored construction paper on which to draw a leaf. Instruct him to cut out the shape and copy his poem on it. Collect the cutouts and punch a hole near the left edge of each one. Then put all the leaves on a binder ring to make a leaf book that everyone will enjoy! *Angela Basel—Gr. 4, St. Paul's Lutheran School, Chicago Heights, IL*

Red is the one hue
Out of all the leaves I see
That I like the best.

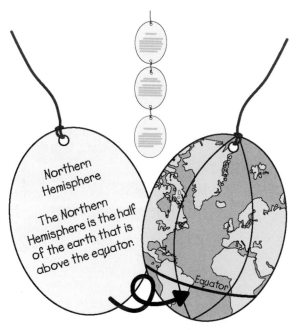

Northern Hemisphere

The Northern Hemisphere is the half of the earth that is above the equator.

Equator

Geography Mobiles

Celebrate National Geography Awareness Week in November with a mobile-making project that sharpens students' **vocabulary** skills! Provide each child with a list of geography terms, an oval shape for each term, scissors, yarn, and access to a hole puncher. Next, instruct the student to write a term and its definition on one side of each oval and draw an illustration on the other. After she has defined and illustrated each term, have her hole-punch the top and bottom of each oval except one. Direct her to hole-punch that one only at the top. Then have each student tie her cutouts together to create a hanging mobile whose lowermost oval is the one with no bottom hole. How geographic! *adapted from an idea by Thomas Fitzmaurice—Gr. 5, John F. Kennedy Intermediate, Deer Park, NY*

Mayflower Queries

Invite inquisitive students to learn more about the *Mayflower* with this shipshape Thanksgiving **research** project. Ask your media specialist to gather resources on the *Mayflower* and Pilgrims. Then write on the board the questions shown and divide students into groups of four. Instruct each group member to research a different question and then report the findings to his group (see the key on page 306). Conclude by grouping together the students who researched the same question and having them create a visual aid that reflects their research to share with the class. *Starin Lewis, Phoenix, AZ*

Mayflower

96.5 feet long
26 feet wide

oak planks

Questions

1. What did the ship look like? What kinds of materials were used to build it?
2. Who owned and operated the ship? What was the ship normally used for?
3. How many passengers were on the ship? What was it like living on the ship?
4. What happened to the ship after it left the Plymouth Colony?

Seasonal Journal Topics

Rake in spectacular journal writing during October and November with these seasonal **writing prompts.**

October Topics

- List ten words a squirrel might use to describe fall.

- Suppose that fall leaves were pink, blue, and purple this fall instead of yellow, orange, and red. Do you think people would be horrified, feel surprised, be pleased, or not react at all? Explain.

- To celebrate National Food Bank Week in October, design a campaign that is sure to make almost everyone you know give canned food items to a local food bank.

- Explain in four steps how to carve a pumpkin into a simple jack-o'-lantern.

- How are candy apples and cotton candy alike? Different?

- Best friends (even the animal kind) come in all shapes and sizes. Describe what you like most about your closest friend.

- Imagine that you were the *Pinta* sailor who spotted land on October 12, 1492. What were you thinking just before you saw land? Just after?

- Name two things you like to cook in a microwave. Describe how you would cook them without a microwave.

- Do you think a fifteen-year old is too old to trick-or-treat on Halloween? Why or why not?

- Could you make your Halloween candy last until Christmas? Why or why not?

November Topics

- November is Family Stories Month. Describe one of the funniest adventures your family has ever had.

- November is Peanut Butter Lover's Month. Which kind of peanut butter do you prefer: creamy or crunchy? Explain.

- If there were major electrical blackouts in several large cities throughout the country on election day, do you think the elections would be canceled? Why or why not?

- Which would be easier for you to give up: drinking sodas or eating junk food? Explain.

- If you could change one thing about fall weather, what would it be? Explain.

- Pop-Tart toaster pastries were created on November 19, 1965. Would you recommend Pop-Tart pastries as a good breakfast food? Why or why not?

- If you could build a float for the Macy's Thanksgiving Day Parade event, what would it be like?

- Suppose a Pilgrim from the first Thanksgiving traveled forward in time to your family's holiday dinner. Describe the three things you think would surprise him the most.

- On November 29, 1775, Silas Deane became the first person to use invisible ink. Do you think he wrote something funny or serious? Explain.

- Which annoys you more: having to remove gum from the bottom of your shoe, finding the cookie jar empty when you're hungry, or spilling food on your clothes at breakfast and having to change before school? Explain.

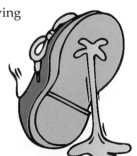

The reproducibles on pages 16–19 were written by Ann Fisher of Toledo, OH.

Fall Weigh-In

It's time for pumpkins, squash, turkeys, and more to get weighed!
Convert the weights below. Use a calculator. The first one in each
section has been done for you.

How many ounces?

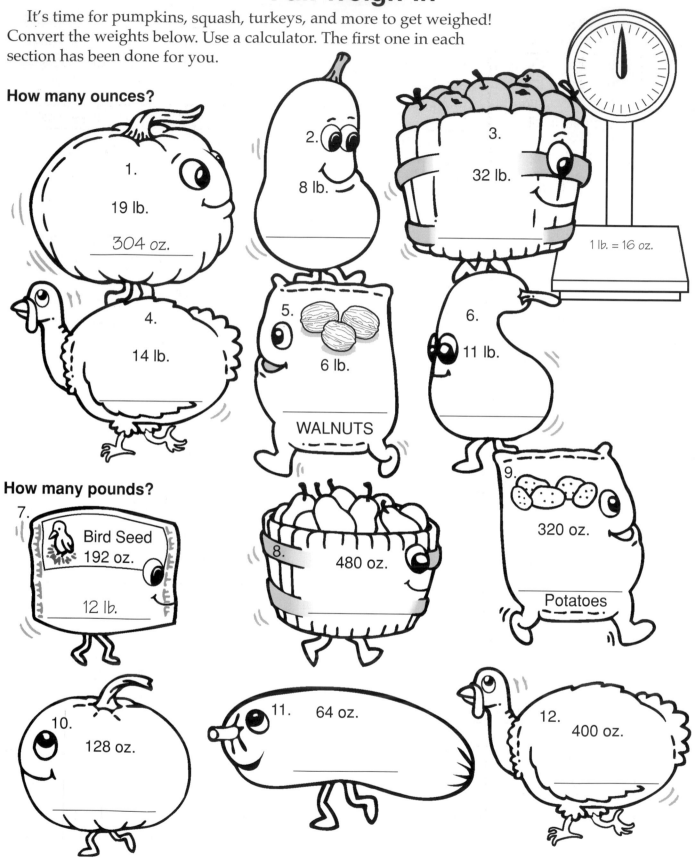

1. 19 lb.
   304 oz.

2. 8 lb.

3. 32 lb.

4. 14 lb.

5. WALNUTS
   6 lb.

6. 11 lb.

1 lb. = 16 oz.

How many pounds?

7. Bird Seed
   192 oz.
   12 lb.

8. 480 oz.

9. 320 oz.
   Potatoes

10. 128 oz.

11. 64 oz.

12. 400 oz.

Bonus Box: What is the average weight of the first six items in ounces? In pounds?

Trick-or-Treat!

What kinds of treats are in each trick-or-treater's bag? Use the guess-and-check strategy to find out! Keep track of your guesses on each chart below (see the example). If you need more space, staple another sheet of paper to this page.

Rick has 7 packages with 20 treats in all.

__15__ Gummy Ghouls

__2__ Candy Creeps

__3__ Popcorn Pythons

	pkgs.	treats	pkgs.	treats	pkgs.	treats
Gummy Ghouls (5 per pkg.)	2	10	2	10	3	15
Candy Creeps (2 per pkg.)	3	6	4	8	1	2
Popcorn Pythons (1 per pkg.)	2	2	2	2	3	3
Totals	7	18	8	20	7	20

	pkgs.	treats	pkgs.	treats	pkgs.	treats	pkgs.	treats
Gummy Ghouls (5 per pkg.)								
Candy Creeps (2 per pkg.)								
Popcorn Pythons (1 per pkg.)								
Totals								

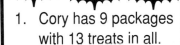

1. Cory has 9 packages with 13 treats in all.

____ Gummy Ghouls

____ Candy Creeps

____ Popcorn Pythons

2. Rita has 15 packages with 25 treats in all.

____ Gummy Ghouls

____ Candy Creeps

____ Popcorn Pythons

	pkgs.	treats	pkgs.	treats	pkgs.	treats	pkgs.	treats
Gummy Ghouls (5 per pkg.)								
Candy Creeps (2 per pkg.)								
Popcorn Pythons (1 per pkg.)								
Totals								

	pkgs.	treats	pkgs.	treats	pkgs.	treats	pkgs.	treats
Gummy Ghouls (5 per pkg.)								
Candy Creeps (2 per pkg.)								
Popcorn Pythons (1 per pkg.)								
Totals								

3. Hal has 11 packages with 33 treats in all.

____ Gummy Ghouls

____ Candy Creeps

____ Popcorn Pythons

Bonus Box: Owen has 30 packages with 100 treats in all. What kinds of treats did he get? Show your work on the back of this page.

Harvest Time

The fall crops are ripe and ready to harvest! Write ten sentences about harvest time on the lines below. To create each sentence, pluck a subject from one tree and a verb that agrees with it from the other. Then add other words to make the sentences more interesting. Happy harvesting!

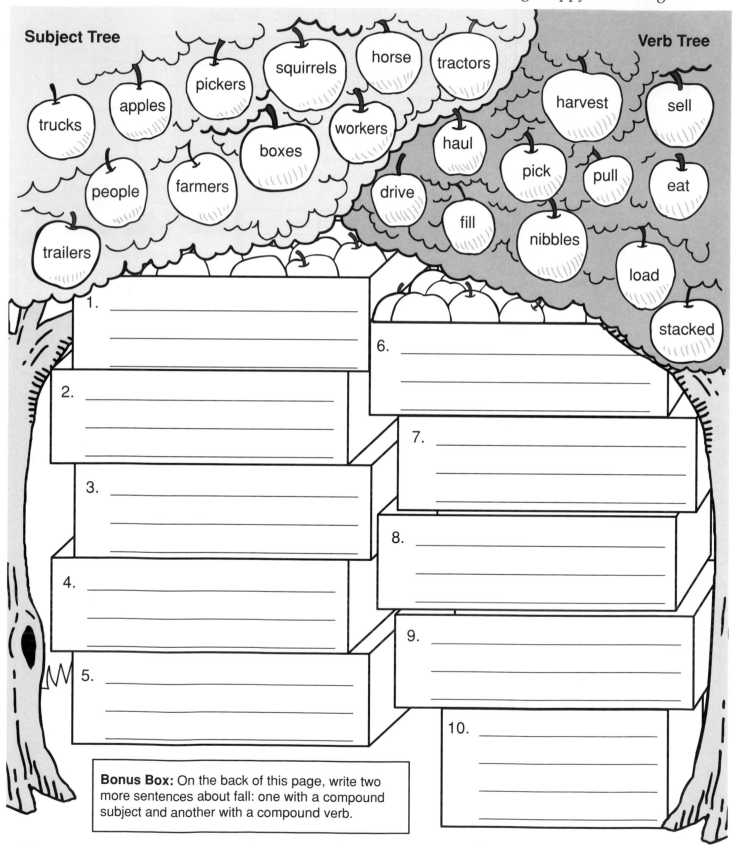

Subject Tree

trucks · apples · pickers · squirrels · horse · tractors · workers · boxes · people · farmers · trailers

Verb Tree

harvest · sell · haul · pick · pull · eat · drive · fill · nibbles · load · stacked

1. _____

2. _____

3. _____

4. _____

5. _____

6. _____

7. _____

8. _____

9. _____

10. _____

Bonus Box: On the back of this page, write two more sentences about fall: one with a compound subject and another with a compound verb.

A Thanksgiving to Remember

Have you ever had a holiday dinner you won't forget? Tabby Kat has! Read her story. Circle each homophone that has not been used correctly. Then write the correct word on the line below. The first one has been done for you.

Last year (four) Thanksgiving, my family flew in a plain to my Ant Kitty's home. That's write! We flew right up too her front door. You sea, my aunt and uncle have an airstrip in they're front yard.

Aunt Kitty had a big dinner ready when wee arrived. I new she had been working hard. She still had flower on her hands and face. I followed my knows to the kitchen, where I saw ten dozen fresh rolls and 20 pounds of mashed potatoes. The turkey was the biggest turkey I'd ever scene! Next, I peaked into the pantry and found 25 huge pumpkin pies.

"Okay," Aunt Kitty and Uncle Allie announced, "It's time to eat!" We all scrambled to there big table.

Just as we got ready to take our first bites, we herd a loud noise. A jumbo jet made an emergency landing inn the front yard! Uncle Allie went to help.

When he came back, he brought 158 passengers with him. They joined our Thanksgiving feast. Like I said before, that was won huge turkey! (We eight every bite.) And believe it ore not, there was a peace of pie for everyone!

1. ____for____   11. _____
2. _____   12. _____
3. _____   13. _____
4. _____   14. _____
5. _____   15. _____
6. _____   16. _____
7. _____   17. _____
8. _____   18. _____
9. _____   19. _____
10. _____   20. _____

Bonus Box: On the back of this page, write a different ending for the story above. Use at least two homophones.

Foolish Fables

Strengthen **narrative-writing** skills with a fun-to-do activity that has students creating absurd Hanukkah tales! Start by reading aloud one or more stories from *The Jar of Fools: Eight Hanukkah Stories From Chelm* by Eric A. Kimmel, a collection of retellings of the Fools of Chelm stories. Next, help students brainstorm foolish situations that could jump-start similar tales. Record the suggestions on the board. Then challenge each child to write a story about one of the listed topics. Expect some chuckles during sharing time!

Motke Fool and the Cinnamon-Scented Oil

3-D "Christ-math" Tree

Decorate your classroom for the holidays with this creative **measurement** project! Give students the materials listed and guide them through the steps shown to make "tree-rific" decorations! *Christy Morejon—Grs. 1–8 Art, The Chapel School, Bronxville, NY*

Materials for each student: 9" x 12" sheet of green construction paper, compass, pencil, ruler, scissors, glue, 1" gold gift bow (or yellow star cutout), colorful sequins or glitter, fishing line, paper clip

Steps:

1. Using the compass, draw an eight-inch circle on the green paper. Cut out the circle and fold it in half twice.
2. Using the ruler, draw a margin line one-fourth inch away from each folded edge.
3. Using the compass, draw a curved line, starting at the left fold one-half inch below the vertex and stopping at the right margin line. Cut along this line.
4. Draw a second curved line, starting at the right fold one inch below the vertex and stopping at the left margin line. Cut along this line.
5. Continue drawing curved lines one-half inch apart in this manner, alternating the sides at which the lines start and stop, until five more lines (1½, two, 2½, three, and 3½ inches from the vertex) have been drawn and cut.
6. Unfold the circle and place it pencil side down on a flat surface. Using one hand, hold down the circle's outer edge. With the other hand, gently pull the circle upward from its centermost fold.
7. Punch a hole in the tree's top with one end of the paper clip. Then tie a loop of fishing line through the hole to make a hanger.
8. Glue sequins and glitter to the tree to represent ornaments. Affix the bow to the top of the tree.

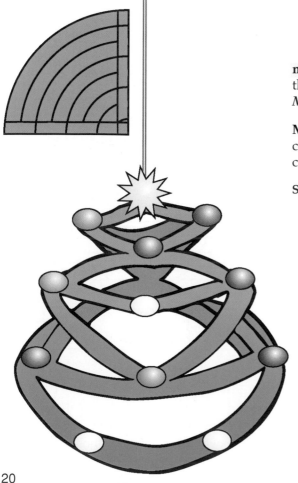

Motion-Filled Scenarios

To celebrate Sir Isaac Newton's birthday (January 4), season your **science** lesson plans with holiday scenarios that represent his three laws of motion! Review the laws with students. Then read aloud each scenario shown. Have students match each law to a different scenario. Then challenge groups of students to create similar scenarios and share them with the class! *Leigh Cody, Needwood Middle School, Brunswick, GA*

One Christmas Eve, Santa's sleigh was filled with so many gifts that his eight reindeer could not pull it. So the jolly old fellow added two extra reindeer, Clyde and Bubba, to the team! It took the combined force of ten powerful animals to pull Santa's sleigh up into the starlit sky. *(second law)*

As the sleigh moved forward, faster and higher, no one noticed that a brown stuffed bear fell off the back of the sleigh. Now some little child will be very disappointed! *(third law)*

The children living in the house at Santa's first stop left oats and berries on the roof for Santa's reindeer. Once the animals saw the treats, they raced toward them and stopped so quickly that Santa flew forward, bumping his head on the front of the sleigh. Obviously, he had forgotten to fasten his seat belt! *(first law)*

January

New Year's Resolution Record

New Year's resolutions are fun to make but easily forgotten! This **holiday project** helps students not only remember their resolutions throughout the year but keep track of them as well! Give each child the materials listed and guide her through the steps shown to make a booklet in which to record what she does each month. By year's end, she'll know whether she reached her goal! *Marcia Barton, Prairieville, LA*

Materials for each student: 2 sheets of 8½" x 11" white paper, scissors, pencil, 2 pieces of 3½" x 5" colorful construction paper, tape, glue, crayons or markers

Steps:
1. Accordion-fold one white sheet into four equal sections. Fold the resulting strip in half from left to right. Then unfold the strip and cut it in half along the fold to make two four-section strips.
2. Repeat the process with the second white sheet.
3. Tape three of the strips end to end to make one 12-section-long strip; then refold it. Discard the extra strip.
4. To make a cover, glue one colorful piece of paper to the top of the folded strip and the other to the bottom.
5. Write your resolution on the booklet's front cover. Label the top of each inside page with a different month.
6. Decorate the cover.

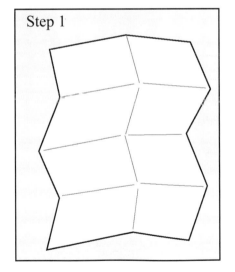

Step 1

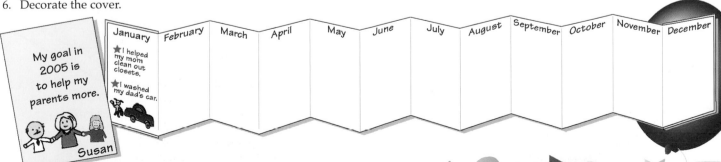

Seasonal Journal Topics

Reserve a spot in your December and January lesson plans for these must-use **writing prompts!**

December Topics

- Twenty percent of all ties bought are given as holiday gifts. Describe a tie you think Santa would like to get from Mrs. Claus.

- If someone gave you a real gingerbread house, would you eat it? Or would you use it as a holiday decoration? Explain.

- Walt Disney was born on December 5, 1901, and died on December 15, 1966. Who is your favorite Disney character? Why?

- Your mom wants to know how the ribbon and wrapping paper on your family's gifts got torn. You know that your grandmother's cat is to blame. What will you do?

- Marie Grosholtz Tussaud, born on December 7, 1761, was the creator of a famous waxwork museum. Who should the museum make its next life-size image of? Explain.

- Which member of your family is the best peacemaker (the one who tries to help everyone get along)? Explain.

- How could you convince your great-aunt not to give your family a poinsettia plant for the holidays without hurting her feelings?

- December 12–18 is Tell Someone They're Doing a Good Job Week. To whom would you say this? Why?

- Margaret Chase Smith, born December 14, 1897, was the first woman to be elected to both houses of Congress. How long do you think it will be before a woman is elected president of the United States? Explain.

- List five things you think Santa Claus does to relax after Christmas. Also list five resolutions you think he might make for the new year.

January Topics

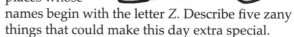

- January is Oatmeal Month. Describe the funniest way you've ever seen someone eat or use oatmeal.

- Z Day, celebrated on January 1, is a day to recognize the people and places whose names begin with the letter Z. Describe five zany things that could make this day extra special.

- Describe five very unusual uses for a Frisbee disk.

- If you had a chance to sit around all day doing nothing, would you enjoy it? Or would you be bored? Explain.

- Suppose that an animal you are watching at the zoo could ask you a question. What do you think it would ask? Explain.

- How do you feel when you go to a dentist's office: scared, relaxed, confident, or nervous? Explain.

- What if a snowman you built suddenly came to life for an hour? Describe the things you would do together.

- If a doctor said that you could no longer eat hamburgers, pizza, and ice cream, what three foods would you eat instead? Why?

- Suppose that the sidewalk you are on suddenly opens up to reveal a secret door. Would you go through the door? Why or why not?

- How are calendars and books alike? Different?

The reproducibles on pages 23–26 were written by Ann Fisher of Toledo, OH.

Hanukkah Happenings

Hannah and her mother have lots to do for a special dinner for Hanukkah.
So they wrote out a schedule! Find out how long they will work at each task.
Write your answer in minutes or in hours and minutes. The first one has been
done for you.

Schedule	Time
Task	
1. Make and eat potato latkes for breakfast from 7:05 A.M. to 7:49 A.M.	44 min.
2. Make a grocery list from 7:50 A.M. to 8:16 A.M.	
3. Drive to the store and shop for groceries from 8:17 A.M. to 9:39 A.M.	
4. Drive home and put the groceries away from 9:40 A.M. to 10:15 A.M.	
5. Get out the menorah and put the candles in it from 10:16 A.M. to 10:45 A.M.	
6. Put out other Hanukkah decorations from 10:46 A.M. to 11:49 A.M.	
7. Prepare and eat lunch from 11:50 A.M. to 1:09 P.M.	
8. Set the table for dinner from 1:10 P.M. to 1:47 P.M.	
9. Make dreidels and wrap them for the guests from 1:48 P.M. to 3:57 P.M.	
10. Fill lamps with oil from 3:58 P.M. to 4:26 P.M.	
11. Visit with guests and read the story of Hanukkah from 4:27 P.M. to 5:19 P.M.	
12. Prepare, serve, and clean up after dinner from 5:20 P.M. to 7:48 P.M.	

Bonus Box: How much time passed from the time Hannah
and her mother started preparing potato latkes until they
finished serving and cleaning up after dinner?

Trim the Tree!

Tina and Tyler Tinsel need help trimming their tree. Find the correct plural form of each noun on an ornament. Write the correct form in the blank on the garland. Color the ornament of each word used. Some ornaments will not be colored.

backpacks

moose

mice

boxes

1. one shirt, three _____

2. one diary, two _____

shirts

3. one watch, four _____

4. one football, five _____

bookshelfs

watchs

footballies

5. one pet mouse, three pet _____

monkies

6. one toy moose, two toy _____

monkeys

watches

backpackies   7. one backpack, six _____

diaries

8. one new bookshelf, four new _____

bookshelves

box's

shirties

9. one windup monkey, five windup _____

mooses

10. one box of chocolates, two _____ of chocolates

footballs

diarys

mouses

Bonus Box: Write the singular form of each of the following plurals: children, teeth, geese, dresses, babies.

Deck the Halls!

Noelle is shopping for holiday decorations. At Deci Mall, prices are in decimals, not dollars and cents! To find out how much the items cost, add together the values of the letters that spell each one's name.

Example: B + E + L + L = 2.34 + 9.001 + 3.45 + 3.45 = 18.241

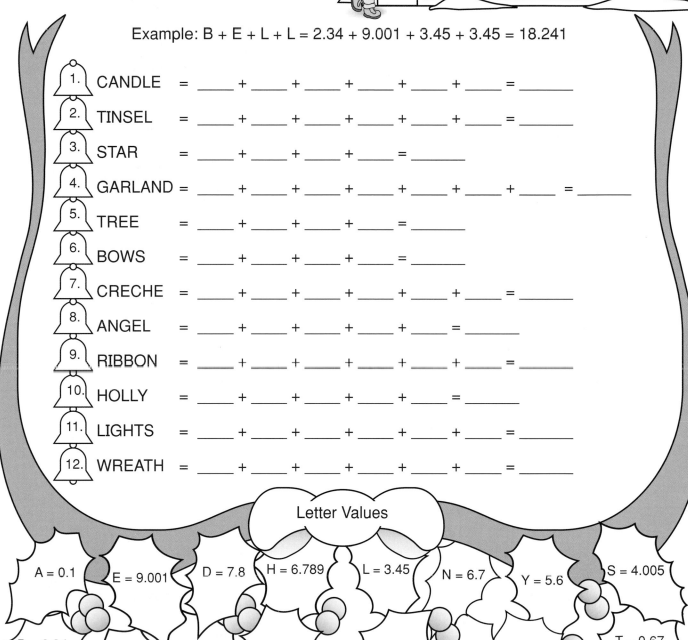

1. CANDLE = ___ + ___ + ___ + ___ + ___ + ___ = ___
2. TINSEL = ___ + ___ + ___ + ___ + ___ + ___ = ___
3. STAR = ___ + ___ + ___ + ___ = ___
4. GARLAND = ___ + ___ + ___ + ___ + ___ + ___ + ___ = ___
5. TREE = ___ + ___ + ___ + ___ = ___
6. BOWS = ___ + ___ + ___ + ___ = ___
7. CRECHE = ___ + ___ + ___ + ___ + ___ + ___ = ___
8. ANGEL = ___ + ___ + ___ + ___ + ___ = ___
9. RIBBON = ___ + ___ + ___ + ___ + ___ + ___ = ___
10. HOLLY = ___ + ___ + ___ + ___ + ___ = ___
11. LIGHTS = ___ + ___ + ___ + ___ + ___ + ___ = ___
12. WREATH = ___ + ___ + ___ + ___ + ___ + ___ = ___

Letter Values

A = 0.1　E = 9.001　D = 7.8　H = 6.789　L = 3.45　N = 6.7　Y = 5.6　S = 4.005

B = 2.34　R = 10.23　K = 0.19　G = 4.5　P = 0.706　I = 1.2　O = 8.09　T = 0.67　C = 5.06　W = 2.034

Bonus Box : Which has a higher cost at the Deci Mall: a poinsettia or a stocking?

Martin's Mark in History

What was Dr. Martin Luther King Jr.'s life like? Read the sentences below to find out. Then use context clues to help you answer each question or complete each statement. Write the letter of your answer in the blank. Some letters will not be used.

1. Young Martin's dad preached sermons at church and visited the sick. What job did his dad have? _____

2. Martin started college at age 15. He graduated from college when he was 19. What kind of student was Martin? _____

3. Martin studied the teachings of Mahatma Gandhi. He learned to react in a peaceful way when someone treated him badly. So when people did not like his protests and bombed his home, Martin _____

4. Rosa Parks was arrested in Montgomery, Alabama, when she refused to give up her seat on a bus to a white person. To protest her arrest, Martin _____

5. The movement to improve the bus laws in Montgomery, Alabama, finally led to the law being changed. This meant that Martin's protest had been _____

6. Martin did not want his four children growing up with laws that kept blacks and whites separate. In one of his speeches, he said, "I have a dream that… _____

7. During his lifetime, Martin Luther King Jr. received Time magazine's Man of the Year award and the Nobel Peace prize. Why did he get these awards? _____

8. Martin Luther King Jr. was killed in 1968. In 1986, Congress passed a law to honor him in a special way. What did this law do? _____

A. moved to another city.
B. my four little children will one day live in a nation where they will not be judged by the color of their skin but by the content of their character."
C. created a national holiday in his name
D. He tried to solve problems peacefully.

E. asked blacks not to ride any city bus.
F. ordered his writings to be locked away.
G. my family will move."
H. He had a lot of friends.
I. stopped giving speeches.
J. successful.

K. pastor
L. bright
M. dangerous
N. poor
O. convinced his supporters to remain peaceful.

Bonus Box: Think of three adjectives that best describe the difference you think Martin Luther King Jr.'s life made on history. Include the words in a paragraph you write on the back of this page.

26   ©The Education Center, Inc. • *The Mailbox®* • TEC44016 • Dec./Jan. 2004–5 • Key p. 306

February

Honest Abe Bank

Getting students to eagerly research a fact about Abraham Lincoln for this nifty **art project** is something you can bank on! Give each child the materials listed and guide her through the steps below to make a piggy bank. Then have her research a fact about Lincoln and display it in a creative way somewhere on her bank. Now Abe's ready to be filled with coins! *Colleen Dabney, Williamsburg, VA*

Materials for each student: clean, empty Pringles can with plastic lid, primer paint, paintbrush, light tan or peach paint, black acrylic paint, scissors, 6" square of black craft foam, ruler, 6" square of black felt, 3½" circle of black felt, two 25 mm wiggle eyes, craft glue, black permanent marker

Steps:
1. Set the lid aside. Paint the outside of the Pringles can with primer. Allow the paint to dry.
2. Paint the top three inches of the can with black paint to make the hat. Paint the rest of the can with light tan or peach paint. Allow the paint to dry.
3. Cut a six-inch circle from the black foam. From the center of this circle, remove a three-inch circle to make the hat's brim. Slide the brim down the can until it is just above where the two paint colors meet.
4. Cut out a beard and eyebrows from the felt square.
5. Glue the felt cutouts and wiggle-eyes to the can. Use the marker to draw a nose and mouth.
6. Cut a one-inch slit in the center of the lid. Glue the felt circle to the lid's top and outer sides. Trim the circle to fit if necessary. Then cut a slit in the felt to match the one in the lid. Attach the lid to the can.

I was the sixteenth president of the United States.

Symmetrical Signatures

Welcome the Chinese New Year with a signature dragon whose body parts really stretch students' **symmetry** skills! Draw a large dragon's head on a sheet of poster board. Color the drawing; then cut it out and mount it on a wall. Next, give each child a 12" x 18" sheet of colorful construction paper, scissors, markers, and glue, along with colorful paper scraps, glitter, and various other art materials. Then guide students through the steps below to make the dragon's symmetrical body parts. Once the parts are finished, tape them behind the dragon's head and add a tail, legs, and a spiny back! *Richard McCoy, Laquey Middle School, Laquey, MO*

Steps:
1. Fold the sheet of construction paper in half lengthwise. Trim the paper's corners to round the edges. Then unfold the paper and trace the fold line with a marker.
2. Using large letters, print your name with a pencil in the space above the traced line. Be sure the letters touch the line.
3. Print the reflection of the letters in the space below the line. Then trace the letters with a marker.
4. Decorate the spaces around and between the letters with symmetrical drawings, sprinkles of glitter, or colorful cutouts.

Cupid's Gift Store

"Sale-ebrate" Valentine's Day with a **math** activity that could make cash registers ring! Ask parents to provide zany items related to the holiday. Attach to each item an index card that names the item in a unique way and lists a price and tax amount. Display the items around the room; then invite students to move from item to item calculating the final cost of each one to the nearest cent. The next day, announce that the items are now on sale at one-fourth off the original price. Have each child recalculate each item's cost with the discount. After checking the answers, award the items as prizes! *Dawn Murray, Freehold, NJ*

Cupid's Chocolates
$4.99 + 6% tax = ?

March

Irish Blessing Box

It won't take the luck of the Irish to inspire students to write **poetry** for these blessing boxes! Make a copy of a pyramid net on heavy paper for each child. Also, share several traditional Irish blessings with the class. Then have each child write a poem containing a similar blessing. Next, give each student a copy of the pyramid net, scissors, markers, a length of green ribbon or yarn, and access to a hole puncher. Instruct her to copy her edited poem on the net's base. Then have her cut out the net, decorate its triangles, and fold each triangle upward along the base to form a box. Once she punches small holes near the tops of the triangles and weaves ribbon through them to close the box's top, it's ready to fill with small treats for someone special! *Kelli Higgins, P.L. Bolin Elementary, East Peoria, IL*

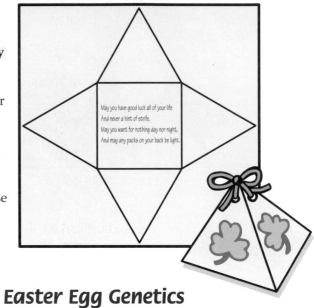

May you have good luck all of your life
And never a hint of strife.
May you want for nothing day nor night,
And may any packs on your back be light.

Easter Egg Genetics

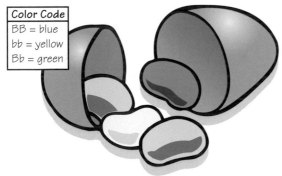

Color Code
BB = blue
bb = yellow
Bb = green

There's a sweet reward for completing this "eggs-ceptional" **science** activity! Make and display a poster of the color code chart shown. Also obtain jelly beans and enough colorful plastic Easter eggs for each child to have a blue, green, or yellow egg (or one whose halves are two different colors), plus an extra egg for you. Fill each egg with four candies that match the color combinations on the chart below. Then draw a 2 x 2 grid on the board and display an egg. Explain that each egg half represents the genetic input of one parent and that the candies inside the egg represent the possible offspring of those parents.

Next, follow the steps shown to demonstrate how to find the color of the egg's candies. When finished, open the egg and check its contents by the chart. Then give each child an egg and guide her through the same steps to identify the colors of her egg's candies. After students check their answers, invite them to eat the jelly beans as you collect the eggs to use again next year! *Amani Abuhabsah, Shields School, Chicago, IL*

Color of Halves	Kind of Candies Inside the Egg
blue x blue	4 blue
blue x yellow	4 green
yellow x yellow	4 yellow
yellow x green	2 green, 2 yellow
blue x green	2 blue, 2 green
green x green	1 blue, 2 green, 1 yellow

Steps:
1. Draw arrows at the top and side of the grid's boxes as shown.
2. Write the letters of the color code of each egg half above and along the side of the grid as shown.
3. Fill in the grid, using the arrows as a guide. Write two letters in each box.
4. Record the possible color combinations as shown.

	B	b
B →	BB	Bb
b →	Bb	bb

green x green =
1 blue
2 green
1 yellow

28

Seasonal Journal Prompts

Bid winter goodbye and welcome spring with these top-notch **writing prompts!**

February Topics

- Gregory Groundhog is proud of the new clothes he will wear when he comes out of his hole to predict the weather. Describe his outfit from head to toe.

- February is the shortest month of the year. If all months had only 28 days, we would need another month in our year! What would you name this month? Explain.

We almost didn't make it!

- Charles Lindbergh, the first person to fly solo across the Atlantic Ocean without stopping, was born on February 4, 1902. If his plane had been able to talk after it landed safely in Paris, France, what do you think it would have said?

- If you notice that your teacher has marked an answer on your math test right when it should have been marked wrong, what would you do? Explain.

- Valentine's Day comes in the middle of the month. Would you rather have this holiday come earlier or later in the month instead? Why or why not?

- Some people are cat lovers. Others prefer dogs. Some people do not like pets of any kind! How does your best friend feel about pets? Explain.

- Which would be easier for you to do: admit you are wrong, clean your room, do your homework, or help a grouchy neighbor clean out her garage? Why?

- February is Library Lovers' Month. What kind of books would your dad check out of the library? Your mom? Explain.

- When do you eat more snack foods: right after school, while watching TV, or before going to bed? Explain.

- If you were the main chef at the White House, what would you have on tonight's dinner menu for the president and first lady? Explain.

March Topics

- Congratulations! You are in charge of this year's kite-flying contest at a local park. Describe one type of kite that you will not allow to be in the contest because it would have an unfair advantage.

- You have just found an envelope with $50.00 in it on a bench at a shopping mall. What will you do?

- How are balloons and airplanes alike? How are they different? Explain.

- Two friends will be at your house any minute to work with you on a school project. You have just caught your little sister using fingerpaint on the poster board you bought for the project. What will you do?

- Leonard Leprechaun wants to put his gold coins in something other than a metal pot. Should he put them in a suitcase, a backpack, or a strongbox? Why?

- Describe something nice you could do for someone without that person knowing you did it.

- What are you like when you first wake up in the morning: happy, grumpy, talkative, or quiet? Explain.

- If there were a law allowing only one form of printed material to exist, which would you rather it be: newspapers, magazines, or books? Why?

- Explain what you think the following proverb means: The pen is mightier than the sword.

- Pretend that you are at a concert watching your favorite music group perform. Before doing the last song, the lead singer invites you onto the stage. Explain what happens next.

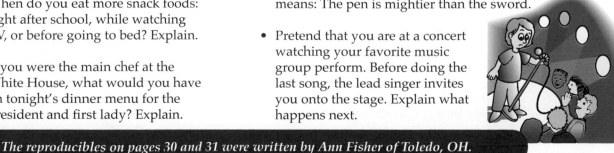

The reproducibles on pages 30 and 31 were written by Ann Fisher of Toledo, OH.

A Hearty Party

Gus Groundhog is planning a Valentine's Day party for his friends. Help him by solving each division problem and finding the matching answer on a balloon. Color each balloon after you write its answer in an answer blank. Some balloons will not be colored.

 1. Gus is buying 96 heart-shaped veggie burgers packed in 4 boxes. How many burgers are in each box? _____ burgers

 2. Heart-shaped buns for the burgers come in packages of 6. How many packages does Gus need for 96 burgers? _____ packages

 3. Gus wants to order heart-shaped oatmeal cookies. How many dozen should he order to have 96 cookies? _____ dozen

 4. Gus needs 80 ounces of beets to make his famous beet juice punch. Since there are 16 ounces in a pound, how many pounds of beets should Gus buy? _____ pounds

5. Streamers come in rolls that are 20 feet long. How many rolls does Gus need if he wants 160 feet of streamers? _____ rolls

6. Balloons are sold in packages of 15. If Gus uses 75 balloons, how many packages will he need? _____ packages

7. If Gus spends $14.00 for 4 packages of paper plates, how much is each package? _____ per package

8. Gus has 3 packages of napkins. If there are 108 napkins in all, how many napkins are in each package? _____ napkins

9. Gus's friends want to play games for 1 hour. If Gus plans 5 different games, how long can each game be played? _____ minutes

10. As a special treat, Gus plans to serve 98 chocolate-covered mini carrots. How many plates will he need if he puts 7 mini carrots on each dessert plate? _____ plates

Balloons shown: 8, 36, 18, 24, $3.50, 16, 12, 8, 5, 5, $3.40, 14

Bonus Box: If Gus spends $14.40 on 6 boxes of invitations, what is the price of each box?

Presidential Puzzlers

George Washington

Thomas Jefferson

Directions: To solve each puzzle, you will need to put together several clues. Use the chart to keep track of the facts. For each puzzle, make Xs in the column to mark off the presidents that do not match each clue. The boxes for Clue A of Puzzle 1 have been marked for you.

⭐ **1 Who was the first president to have no vice president?**

A. His ordinal number (the number that tells the order, such as *first, second,* and *third*) is not divisible by 3.
B. The sum of the digits in the year he took office is less than 20.
C. He did not serve more than 4 years.
D. The sum of the digits in this president's last year of office is greater than the sum of the digits of the year in which he began his term.

⭐ **2 Who was the first president to be born in a log cabin?**

A. This president served for more than 4 years.
B. His last year in office is not divisible by 5.
C. The sum of the digits of his first year in office is 1 more than the sum of the digits of his last year in office.
D. The total number of letters in his first and last names is a prime number.

⭐ **3 Which two of the first ten presidents died on July 4?**

A. One of these presidents served for 4 years; the other served for 8 years.
B. The ordinal numbers of both presidents are prime numbers.
C. The first president was not one of them.
D. The sum of the digits of the year in which one of these presidents took office is 10.

Number	President	Term in Office	Puzzle Number		
			1	2	3
1	George Washington	1789–1797			
2	John Adams	1797–1801			
3	Thomas Jefferson	1801–1809	X		
4	James Madison	1809–1817			
5	James Monroe	1817–1825			
6	John Quincy Adams	1825–1829	X		
7	Andrew Jackson	1829–1837			
8	Martin Van Buren	1837–1841			
9	William H. Harrison	1841	X		
10	John Tyler	1841–1845			

Bonus Box: The difference between the sums of the digits of the year in which this president took office and when he left office is a two-digit number.

Lenny's Shenanigans

Oh, no! Lenny Leprechaun is up to his tricks again! This time, he has removed some of the prepositions from the paragraph below. Fill in the blanks with the prepositions on the coins.

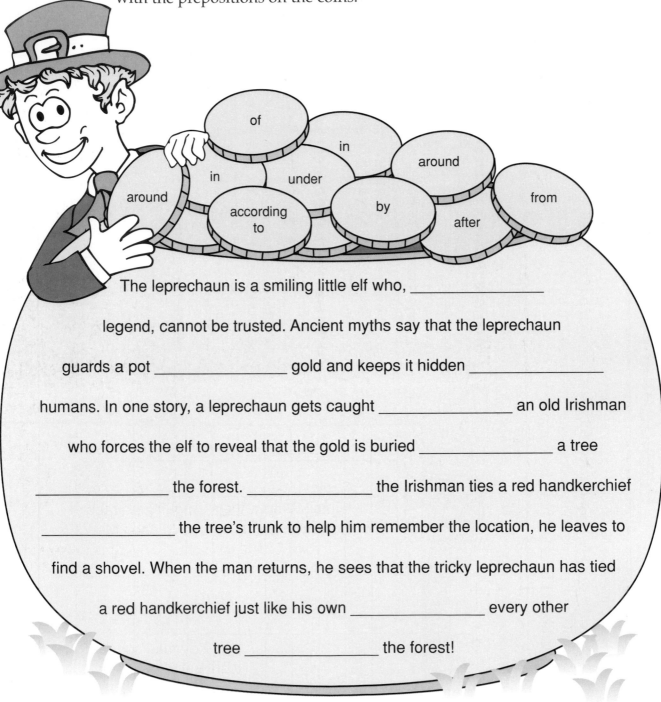

of

in

around

in

under

according to

by

around

after

from

The leprechaun is a smiling little elf who, _____

legend, cannot be trusted. Ancient myths say that the leprechaun

guards a pot _____ gold and keeps it hidden _____

humans. In one story, a leprechaun gets caught _____ an old Irishman

who forces the elf to reveal that the gold is buried _____ a tree

_____ the forest. _____ the Irishman ties a red handkerchief

_____ the tree's trunk to help him remember the location, he leaves to

find a shovel. When the man returns, he sees that the tricky leprechaun has tied

a red handkerchief just like his own _____ every other

tree _____ the forest!

Now go back through the story and underline each prepositional phrase in green. Circle the preposition or compound preposition and draw a box around the object of the preposition.

Bonus Box: On the back of this page, write a story about another trick Lenny could play on someone. Use at least five prepositional phrases in your story. Underline the phrases in your favorite color.

©The Mailbox® • TEC44017 • Feb./Mar. 2005 • Key p. 307 • written by Dee McGraw, Bolles School, Jacksonville, FL

"Hoppy" Easter!

Eddie and Edie eat jelly beans every year when they dye Easter eggs! Maybe that is why they used jelly bean colors on their biggest egg. To see the colors, decide what part of speech the underlined word or words in each sentence are. Then color that section of the egg by the code.

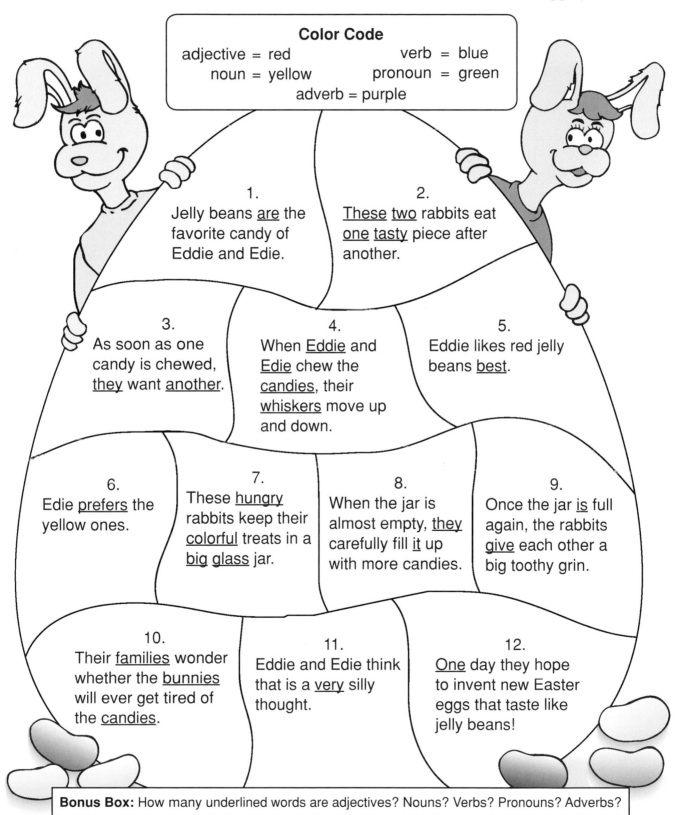

Color Code

adjective = red   verb = blue

noun = yellow   pronoun = green

adverb = purple

1. Jelly beans <u>are</u> the favorite candy of Eddie and Edie.

2. <u>These</u> <u>two</u> rabbits eat <u>one</u> <u>tasty</u> piece after another.

3. As soon as one candy is chewed, <u>they</u> want <u>another</u>.

4. When <u>Eddie</u> and <u>Edie</u> chew the <u>candies</u>, their <u>whiskers</u> move up and down.

5. Eddie likes red jelly beans <u>best</u>.

6. Edie <u>prefers</u> the yellow ones.

7. These <u>hungry</u> rabbits keep their <u>colorful</u> treats in a <u>big</u> <u>glass</u> jar.

8. When the jar is almost empty, <u>they</u> carefully fill <u>it</u> up with more candies.

9. Once the jar <u>is</u> full again, the rabbits <u>give</u> each other a big toothy grin.

10. Their <u>families</u> wonder whether the <u>bunnies</u> will ever get tired of the <u>candies</u>.

11. Eddie and Edie think that is a <u>very</u> silly thought.

12. <u>One</u> day they hope to invent new Easter eggs that taste like jelly beans!

Bonus Box: How many underlined words are adjectives? Nouns? Verbs? Pronouns? Adverbs?

©The Mailbox® • TEC44017 • Feb./Mar. 2005 • Key p. 307

Note to the teacher: Each child will need crayons or colored pencils to complete this page.

Funny Photos

Invite a chuckle or two during April, National Humor Month, with this **alliteration** activity! Ask each child to bring in a photo of herself that could elicit a laugh. Have the student tape her photo to a colorful paper rectangle and leave room for a caption. Next, review with the class that *alliteration* is the repetition of one initial sound several times in a phrase. Then direct each child to write an alliterative caption to add to her photo. Invite her to share her photo and caption with the class. The faster the captions are read, the funnier they will be! For more fun, display the photos and invite students to vote on the funniest photo and caption!

Don't drop a dunked doughnut on designer denims!

Baseball Buddies

Boost students' **descriptive-writing** skills with the help of these bouncy buddies! Have each child find a colorful picture of his favorite baseball team's logo. Next, give him the materials listed and guide him through the steps shown to make a character that represents his team. Have him write on the back of his character's head a paragraph describing the logo and then share the description with the class. *adapted from an idea by Jennifer L. Kohnke, Nature Ridge Elementary, Bartlett, IL*

Materials: enlarged copy of the baseball pattern on page 67; two 1" x 9" strips of white construction paper; markers; scissors; glue; sheet of notebook paper; access to colorful paper scraps, yarn, and reference materials

Steps:
1. Trace the baseball pattern onto the notebook paper. Cut out the tracing and glue it to the back of the baseball cutout.
2. Use markers to add facial features to the cutout.
3. To make the character's legs, accordion-fold each white strip of paper; then unfold the strips and glue them to the bottom of the cutout.
4. Use the paper scraps and yarn to make the character's shoes and cap.

The logo

Cinco de Mayo Math

Spice up your May 5 math lesson with some peppery **numeration** practice! Model how to create problems whose answers consist only of fives (see the examples); then divide students into groups of five. Have each group member create a math problem similar to those you modeled and have a group mate check her work. Next, give each group scissors, a 40-inch length of string or yarn, and access to a hole puncher. Give each child in the group a different-colored five-inch paper square (red, green, light green, yellow, or orange) to cut into the shape of a chili pepper. For reproducible patterns, go to www.themailboxcompanion.com. Have each group member write her math problem on her cutout's front and the answer on the back; then have her punch a hole below the cutout's stem. Instruct the group to thread its peppers onto the string one at a time, knotting the string after each addition, to simulate a hand-strung rope of foods called a *ristra*. Finally, direct the groups to trade ristras and pull off one peppery problem at a time from the bottom for each group member to solve. Olé!

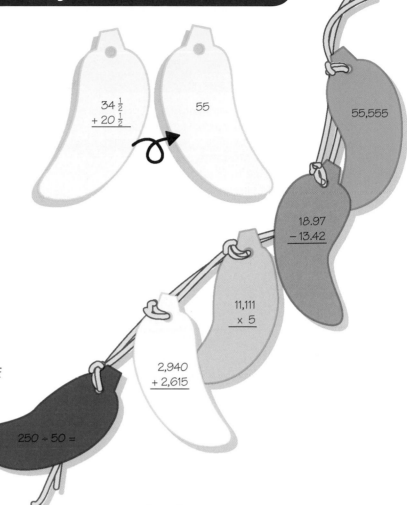

Mother's Day Memory Jar

Make Mother's Day memorable with these **student-made gifts!** Obtain a small baby food jar (without the lid) for each child. Give each student a jar, a four-inch fabric circle trimmed with pinking shears, fabric paints, a rubber band, a hole-punched cutout of a red heart, 12 colorful two-inch paper squares, and a 24-inch length of ribbon, lace, rickrack, or yarn. Then guide students through the steps shown to make gifts their moms are sure to cherish. *Ruth Menzer, Haskins Elementary, Pratt, KS*

Steps:
1. Use the paint to write "Mother's Day Memory Jar" on the outside of your jar. Allow to dry.
2. Use the paint to decorate the center of your fabric circle. Allow to dry.
3. Write on each paper square a message thanking your mom for something she has done. Fold the squares and put them inside the jar.
4. Center the decorated circle over your jar's mouth. Then place the rubber band around your jar's neck to hold the circle in place.
5. Sign your name on the heart cutout and thread it onto the ribbon. Tie the ribbon around the jar's neck so that it covers the rubber band.

35

Seasonal Journal Prompts

Make your April and May lesson plans blossom beautifully with this fresh bouquet of **journal prompts!**

April Topics

- Would you rather have someone play an April Fool's Day joke on you at school or at home? Explain.

- Where would you prefer to receive an award: in your classroom, on stage in front of your whole school, or at a special event in your town? Explain.

- Do you ever look forward to rainy days? Why or why not?

- In your opinion, what is the best day of the week? Explain.

- What would you do if you suddenly realized you could speak and understand every language now spoken in the world?

- It has been said that actions speak louder than words. What do you think this means?

- How are golf balls and boiled eggs alike? How are they different?

- Suppose it is up to you to plan your school's lunches from now until school is out. What kinds of foods will you serve: junk foods, healthy foods, or some of both? Explain.

SCHOOL MENU
sloppy joes
french fries
green beans
applesauce
milk

- If you had to live where there was only one kind of weather, which type would you prefer: hot and sunny, hot and rainy, cold and sunny, cold and rainy? Why?

- What is your least favorite kind of rain gear: umbrella, poncho, raincoat, or boots? Explain.

May Topics

- May 1 is Mother Goose Day. Who is your most favorite nursery rhyme character? Why is this character so special to you?

- What would you do if someone praised you for doing a good deed that you really did not do?

- When you have two things to do and one is easier to do than the other, which do you do first: the easier one or the harder one? Why?

- May 8 is No Socks Day. Would you mind not wearing socks for a day? Why or why not?

- Do you prefer a birthday cake that is homemade or one made at a bakery? Explain.

- How is a whistle like a trumpet? How is it different?

- Which would your mother prefer getting on Mother's Day: a gift bought at a store or something you made? How do you know?

- Have you always lived in the same house, or has your family moved often? How do you feel about this?

- Which upsets you more: finding the jar of peanut butter empty when you want a quick snack, spilling ketchup on a white shirt or blouse, or not getting to go to the movies with your friends? Explain.

- What do you think the proverb "Many hands make light work" means?

The reproducibles on pages 37 and 38 were written by Ann Fisher of Toledo, OH.

Is Jerry Jesting?

Why is everyone so tired on April 1?

Is the king's jester joking? Or is he being serious? Since it's April Fool's Day, you can't be sure!

Directions: Look at each pair of entry words and guide words. Decide whether the first entry word, second entry word, both entry words, or neither entry word could be found on a dictionary page with those guide words. Circle the letters or numbers in the appropriate column to show your answer. The first one has been done for you.

Entry Words	Guide Words	Entry Words Found on a Page With Those Guide Words			
		1st Word	2nd Word	Both	Neither
1. ribbon, rich	rhyme–riddle	al	th	(fi)	sc
2. clap, club	clown–clue	gh	ng	lk	rd
3. direct, distant	dictionary–dish	we	us	me	is
4. lace, likely	laugh–lot	ch	ed	es	mo
5. gorilla, ground	goose–grouse	ze	we	ve	re
6. hundred, human	humor–hungry	st	cr	bl	sh
7. slice, stylish	smile–style	ha	go	pu	lo
8. command, comfort	comedy–commercial	up	wi	ni	ch
9. tilt, ticket	tickle–tightrope	mo	sa	tr	ha
10. gasoline, gumdrop	funny–girl	Ma	ro	pa	he
11. jiffy, jug	joke–juggler	ja	ju	jo	je
12. preen, prime	prank–prize	the	one	day	low
13. music, mighty	merry–museum	dr	ch	pl	sn
14. gander, gallon	game–gimmick	sh	th	br	at
15. silver, simple	silly–sit	47	03	31	88

To answer Jerry's question, write the circled answers above in the numbered blanks below.

Because ___ ___ ___ ___ ___ fi ___ ___ ___ a ___ ___ ___ - ___ ___ r ___ !
      3   9 5   11 6   1 8 14 4   7 2 15   12 10 13

Bonus Box: Would the word *jester* appear on a page whose guide words are *jelly* and *jewel*? Explain your answer on the back of this page.

Earth Day Decisions

Do your part to keep our earth healthy! Cut out the puzzle pieces below. Decide whether the action written on each piece is helpful or harmful to the earth. Arrange the pieces inside the correct frame. Then glue the pieces in place.

Helpful Actions   **Harmful Actions**

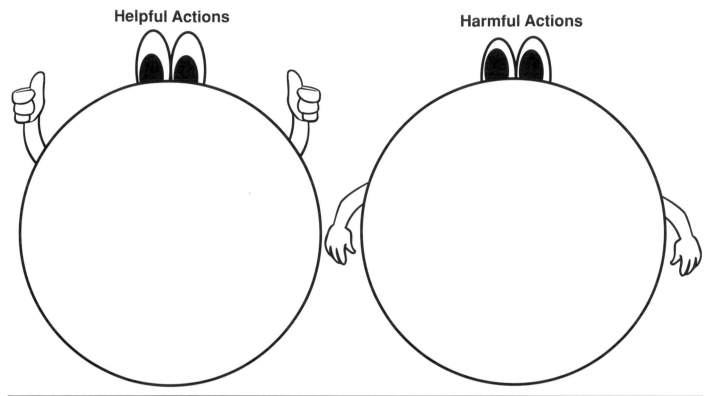

Bonus Box: On the back of this page, list five ways that you and your family are helping to keep the earth healthy.

©The Mailbox® • TEC44018 • April/May 2005 • adapted from an idea by Colleen Dabney, Williamsburg, VA • Key p. 307

Note to the teacher: Each student will need scissors and glue to complete this page.

Shoe-Size Statistics

Archie Goodfoot is buying new shoes for each athlete playing a sport at Fit Feet sports center. He needs to know the mean, median, mode, and range of each team's shoe sizes. Use a calculator to help him get the data. Round your answers to the nearest tenth.

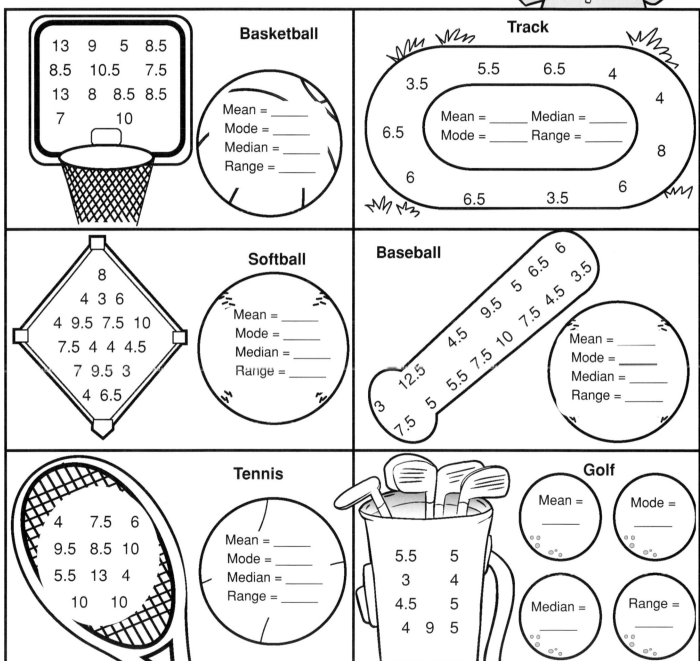

Basketball

13   9   5   8.5
8.5   10.5   7.5
13   8   8.5   8.5
7   10

Mean = _____
Mode = _____
Median = _____
Range = _____

Track

3.5   5.5   6.5   4
6.5   4
6   8
       6.5   3.5   6

Mean = _____ Median = _____
Mode = _____ Range = _____

Softball

8
4 3 6
4 9.5 7.5 10
7.5 4 4 4.5
7 9.5 3
4 6.5

Mean = _____
Mode = _____
Median = _____
Range = _____

Baseball

6
6.5
5
9.5   5   3.5
4.5   7.5 4.5
12.5   5.5 10
3   5
7.5

Mean = _____
Mode = _____
Median = _____
Range = _____

Tennis

4   7.5   6
9.5   8.5   10
5.5   13   4
10   10

Mean = _____
Mode = _____
Median = _____
Range = _____

Golf

5.5   5
3   4
4.5   5
4   9   5

Mean = _____
Mode = _____
Median = _____
Range = _____

Bonus Box: Record the shoe size of six classmates and your own. Find the mean, median, mode, and range of the sizes. Is your shoe size above or below the mean?

©The Mailbox® • TEC44018 • April/May 2005 • written by Karen Turner, Tompkinsville, KY • Key p. 307

Note to the teacher: Each student will need a calculator to complete this page.

Art's Cards

Art D. Sign has a small business making and selling Mother's Day cards. Use the graphs to answer the questions and find out how his business is doing.

Card Designs

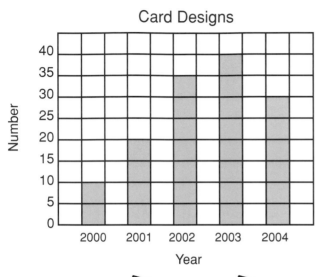

1. What is the greatest number of designs Art made in a single year? _____

2. In what year did Art make 30 kinds of cards? _____

3. How many kinds of cards did Art make in all in 2002 and 2003? _____

4. In what year did Art have the biggest increase from the year before? _____

5. In what year did Art make five more designs than the year before? _____

6. In what years did Art sell more silly cards than serious cards? _____

7. In 2002, how many silly cards and serious cards did Art sell in all? _____

8. In which two years were the sales of serious cards the same? _____ and _____

9. In what year was the greatest difference between the number of silly cards sold and the number of serious cards sold? _____

10. What was the only year Art sold more of both kinds of cards than the year before?

_____

Serious and Silly Cards Sold

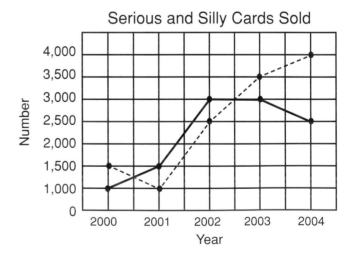

serious ———
silly - - - - - -

Bonus Box: Ask your classmates whether they like to buy silly cards or serious cards for Mother's Day. On the back of this page, make a bar graph to show your results.

Gold-Star Thanks
Recognizing volunteers

Give a deserving parent helper gold-star recognition with this simple-to-do idea. Using yellow paper, make one more than a class supply of the star pattern on page 43. Provide each child with a star. On the star, have him write a note thanking the volunteer for all she has done for the class this year. When he's finished, have him outline the star's edges with gold glitter glue. When the glue is dry, tape all of the stars together end to end as shown. Label the extra star with a title similar to the one shown and tape it to the front of the chain; then accordion-fold the chain. Present the appreciation card to the valuable volunteer the next time she stops by. If there are additional people you wish to honor, just make more copies of the star!

We Thank Our Lucky Stars for You!

Thank you for helping us box up the cans of food we collected at Christmas.

Thank you for going with us on our class trip to the museum.

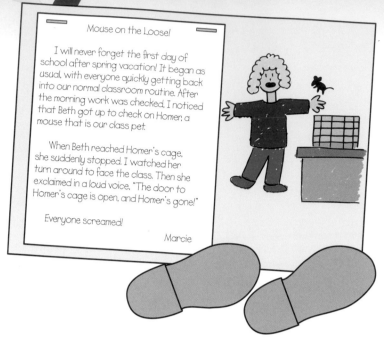

Mouse on the Loose!

I will never forget the first day of school after spring vacation! It began as usual, with everyone quickly getting back into our normal classroom routine. After the morning work was checked, I noticed that Beth got up to check on Homer, a mouse that is our class pet.

When Beth reached Homer's cage, she suddenly stopped. I watched her turn around to face the class. Then she exclaimed in a loud voice, "The door to Homer's cage is open, and Homer's gone!"

Everyone screamed!

Marcie

Strolling Down Memory Lane
Reflective writing

Wind down the school year with this student-pleasing writing activity, which becomes an attractive display! Have each child write an essay about what she thinks was the most memorable event of the school year. Once she is finished, instruct her to staple the essay to construction paper and add illustrations. Post the completed projects on a bulletin board titled "Making Our Way Down Memory Lane." Next, have each writer trace her feet on colorful construction paper and cut out the tracings. Then arrange the cutouts around the board's perimeter to make an eye-catching border!

Colleen Dabney, Williamsburg JCC Public Schools, Williamsburg, VA

Complimentary Bookmarks
Bookmark project

Wrap up the year with a meaningful activity! Instruct students to sit in a circle and have each child label a colorful paper strip with her name. Direct her to pass her strip to the left. Have each student write on the strip a compliment to its owner. Then, on your signal, have the student pass the strip to the left. Repeat until each child has written a compliment on every classmate's strip. Collect and laminate the strips. Then punch a hole near the top of each one and add a ribbon. Present each completed bookmark to its namesake and watch her smile in appreciation!

You are a great speller! Destiny You are kind.
I like the way you draw horses.

adapted from an idea by Amanda Steele, Timberline Elementary, Aurora, CO

Helping Hands

This helping-hand coupon entitles you to one FREE car wash.

Helping Hands
Father's Day gift

This Father's Day, encourage students to help out around the house with a booklet-making idea that makes a nifty gift! Give each child five sheets of unlined paper and have him trace his hand once on each sheet. Instruct him to cut out the tracings, stack them, and then staple the cutouts along one side to make a booklet. After he labels the cover as shown, have him write on each remaining cutout a coupon for a task he could do for his dad or for someone who is a father figure. Send the completed books home knowing that they will make Father's Day extra special!

Seasonal Journal Prompts
June Topics

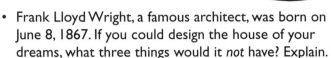

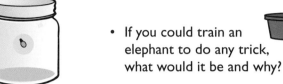

- Pretend you are a firefly that a child has caught. How would you convince him or her to let you go?

- Frank Lloyd Wright, a famous architect, was born on June 8, 1867. If you could design the house of your dreams, what three things would it *not* have? Explain.

- Imagine that there is a horse hitched to a golden chariot outside your house. If you could keep the horse for the entire summer, what would you do?

- If everything you touched turned to cheese, would you be happy or sad? Explain.

- If you could train an elephant to do any trick, what would it be and why?

- What would you do if you were craving ice cream but there was none at your house? Explain.

- Pretend that your principal wants to have school from January to September, with October, November, and December off in place of summer vacation. Is this a good idea? Why?

- If a dog could choose what it does during the summer, what do you think it would do? Explain.

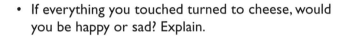

Star Pattern
Use with "Gold-Star Thanks" on page 41.

Name _____

Road Trip!

Read the sentences.
Underline each adjective in red. Do not include *a, an,* and *the.*
Underline each adverb in blue.

1. The Smiths traveled safely from Illinois to California along old Route 66 with their camping trailer.

2. In Missouri, they saw a large drive-in movie theater. People can sit there silently in their cars to watch a movie.

3. In Kansas, they slowly crossed the famous Rainbow Arch Bridge.

4. In Oklahoma, they stopped briefly to see a big blue whale of concrete. It used to be part of an old water park.

5. In Texas, they drove west across the flat plain to Cadillac Ranch. There they saw a row of ten cars buried nose-down in the dirt.

6. In New Mexico, they quickly shopped for Route 66 souvenirs at two roadside stores.

7. At Grand Canyon Caverns in Arizona, they eagerly took an elevator ride down to tour the cool, limestone caves.

8. After a nice visit to Route 66 Territory Museum in California, they turned around and headed home.

Note to the teacher: Each student will need two crayons (red and blue) to complete this page.

The Spelling Bee

Unscramble each set of letters to spell a summertime word.

1. CAATOINV = __ __ __ __ __ __ __
                    1

2. CEBHA = __ __ __ __ __
                 2

3. UECABBRE = __ __ __ __ __ __ __ __
                       3

4. IBRD GNIHCWTA = __ __ __ __ - __ __ __ __ __ __ __ __
                           4

5. ECI MEARC = __ __ __ __ __ __ __ __
                      5

6. EIRFKROSW = __ __ __ __ __ __ __ __ __
                    6

7. TSELAACDNS = __ __ __ __ __ __ __ __ __ __
                            7

8. LABESLAB = __ __ __ __ __ __ __ __
                        8

9. ARTSOEABDK = __ __ __ __ __ __ __ __ __ __
                       9

10. PCIMANG = __ __ __ __ __ __ __
                         10

11. TOAINBG = __ __ __ __ __ __ __
                        11

12. LLEESSSAH = __ __ __ __ __ __ __ __ __
                          12

13. INSGWMIM OLOP = __ __ __ __ __ __ __ __ __ __ __ __
                              13

14. STUNNA = __ __ __ __ __ __
                       14

15. GNIHTAB ITSU = __ __ __ __ __ __ __ __ __ __
                            15

Why does Honey Bee like to spell so much?

To solve the riddle, match the numbered letters above to the blanks below.

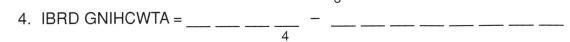

__ __   __ __ __ __ __   __ __ __   __ __ __ __
10 15   13 1 9 2 7   12 2 5   6 2 2 8

" __ - __ __ __ __ - __ __ __ __ __ __ " !
  4 10 7 15 10 14 11 3 10 7 12 2 4

The Dog Days of Summer

Read the chart below.
Record each day's temperature on the thermometer. The first one is done for you.
Then answer the questions.

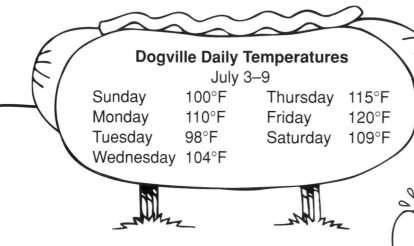

Dogville Daily Temperatures
July 3–9

Sunday	100°F	Thursday	115°F
Monday	110°F	Friday	120°F
Tuesday	98°F	Saturday	109°F
Wednesday	104°F		

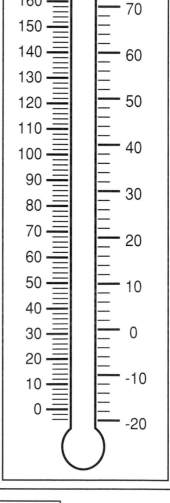

1. What was the hottest day in Dogville for the week? _____

2. What was the coolest day in Dogville for the week? _____

3. What is the difference in temperature between Tuesday and Wednesday?

   _____

4. About how many degrees Celsius was it on Sunday? _____

5. What was the average daily temperature for the week? _____

6. On Sunday, July 10, the temperature was 50°C. Record this temperature on the thermometer.

7. How much hotter was it on Friday than on Tuesday? _____

8. Which is warmer: 100°F or 100°C?

   _____

Sunday
100°F ➡

Bonus Box: What is the temperature for problem 6 in degrees Fahrenheit?

Major-League Mix-Up

Only four problems below are correct.

Rework each problem to find the six that are wrong. Use the space provided.

Then find the jersey number below that matches the correct product of each incorrect
   problem and cross off its number. One number will not be crossed off.

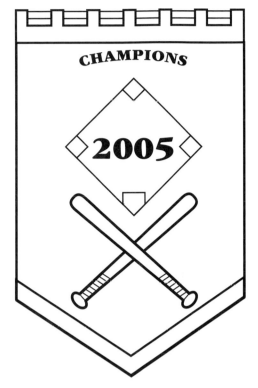

1)
```
    25
  x 14
   100
 +  25
   125
```

2)
```
    53
  x 23
   159
 + 760
   619
```

3)
```
    21
  x 19
   189
 + 210
   399
```

4)
```
     67
   x 36
   3642
 + 18210
  21,852
```

5)
```
     56
   x 43
    168
 + 2240
   2,408
```

6)
```
     29
   x 18
    232
 +  290
    522
```

7)
```
    19
  x 12
    38
 +  19
    57
```

8)
```
     42
   x 40
     42
 + 1680
  1,722
```

9)
```
     35
   x 26
    183
 +  700
    883
```

10)
```
     37
   x 22
     74
 +  740
    814
```

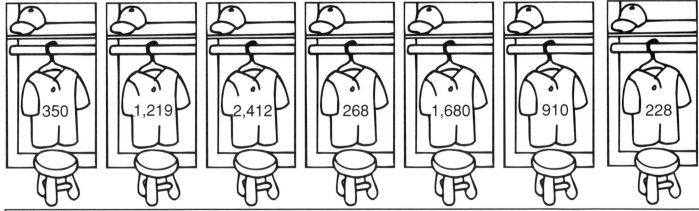

350   1,219   2,412   268   1,680   910   228

Bonus Box: To find out how many home runs Mickey Mantle hit during his baseball career, multiply the jersey number that is not crossed off by two.

Make Way for a Fabulous First Day!

Fantastic Activities for the First Day of School

Get the school year off to a smooth start with this fine flock of first-day activities!

Puzzle Piece Icebreaker

This simple icebreaker will help students fit in right away! Before school starts, send each child a special letter that tells a little bit about yourself. Along with the letter, enclose a puzzle piece with instructions to bring it on the first day of school (or to open house if it is held before school starts). On the back of each puzzle piece, write "You are an important piece of the puzzle!" As each student arrives, have him fit his piece into a puzzle that is completed except for the pieces that were mailed! *Jean Kowalski, Lincoln Elementary, Alpena, MI*

School Supply Notice

Help parents avoid spending money on unnecessary school supplies by sending a note that lists what you *really* need! In advance, prepare a supply list that specifies sizes and amounts. If desired, include pictures of the items photocopied from store flyers. Mail the list as soon as possible after receiving your class roster. (If you know at the end of the year which students will be assigned to you, ask their current teachers to place the lists in the report cards so parents can take advantage of summer sales.) Parents will certainly appreciate the note! *Julie Kwoka—Gr. 5, George M. Southard Elementary, Lockport, NY*

School Supplies for Ms. Waddler's Class

2 quill pens (black ink only)
3-ring binder
five 2-pocket folders
loose-leaf paper
#2 pencils
three 200-page spiral notebooks

Get-to-Know-the-Teacher Test

Give your students a chance to get to know you better with this first-day team-building activity! In advance, write 20 statements about yourself that may or may not be true. Plan to read them aloud to the class. As each statement is read, ask students whether they think the statement is true or false. For example, say, "I have a dog named Thunder. True or false?" Have students raise their hands to show their guesses. Then, if the statement is false, share the correct answer. For example, say, "False. Actually, I have a cat named Storm!" Follow up by having each child write a similar true-or-false statement about herself to share with the class. What a fun way for students to discover shared interests! *Elizabeth Wladkowski—Gr. 4, Aborn Elementary, Lynn, MA*

Parent-Friendly Brochure

Impress parents with a beginning-of-the-year brochure that communicates important classroom information in a user-friendly way! When designing the brochure, arrange its information in chunks. For example, have a section that includes a brief paragraph introducing yourself, one that describes your homework policy, one that lists classroom rules and consequences, and one that suggests ways to contact you. Parents are much more apt to read an eye-catching brochure than a multiparagraphed letter! *Dulcy Leigh Wells, Dan McCarty Middle School, Fort Pierce, FL*

Important Info at a Glance

Wouldn't planning for your new class be easier if you had important student information recorded on a single sheet of paper? Make it happen with this useful tip! Program a basic form such as a checklist with students' names. Above each column, add a heading for each category you wish to include, such as medical needs (glasses, allergies), special services received, standardized test scores, subject-area grades from the previous year, etc. Then fill in the columns using data from students' cumulative folders. You'll soon see that grouping students, arranging seating, and managing other aspects of your curriculum is much more doable! *Suanne Ciavaglia—Gr. 4, Maryvale Intermediate School, Cheektowaga, NY*

Class Introductions Book

Get more miles out of first-day introductions by creating a book that will help students who join your class later in the year get to know their classmates more quickly! On the first day of school, have each student write a paragraph introducing himself to the class. Explain that the paragraph could include things such as the child's favorite subject and activities as well as information about his family and pets. Collect the paragraphs after students share them. Then ask each child to bring in a picture of himself. Attach each child's photo to his paragraph and bind the pages into a class book. When a new student is added to your class, allow him to take the book home to look at overnight. He'll return the next day no longer feeling that his classmates are strangers! *Colleen Dabney, Williamsburg JCC Public Schools, Williamsburg, VA*

Hi! I'm Davie Duck. I like to swim in the marshes and eat bugs.

Buzz Into Summer
Terrific end-of-the-year ideas

KID-CONSTRUCTED CENTERS

Liven up the last days of school by having students construct learning centers for next year's class! Provide students with supplies, directions, and copies of any patterns or reproducibles needed to prepare and color the centers. After you laminate the centers for durability, have students cut out and assemble each one. Then set up the new centers and allow your students to use them for a day. You'll be building toward a new and successful school year before it even gets started!

Melinda Pieart, Hawthorne Christian Academy, Hawthorne, NJ

HANDY TIPS

Allow this year's class to welcome next year's class by offering some friendly advice! During the last week of school, have each child trace both of her hands on construction paper and cut out the tracings. Direct her to label each hand with a piece of advice for the new class. Then, at the beginning of the next school year, display the cutouts on a bulletin board titled "Handy Tips for a Great School Year." No doubt your new class will appreciate the counsel!

Always do your homework.

Wait until you're called on to speak.

Carrie Roux, Henry Wilson School, Manchester, NH

VOLUNTEER HOLIDAY

Recognize your classroom volunteers with a special end-of-the-year event planned and given by your students. If possible, read aloud Dr. Seuss and Jack Prelutsky's book *Hooray for Diffendoofer Day!* to inspire creativity. After the class brainstorms a theme for the event, divide students into five groups and assign each group a different one of the tasks below. All those attending the event are sure to sense sincere appreciation!

Jennifer Garbett, Daly Elementary, Hamilton, MT

Group 1: Decide on a name for the event; plan the date, time, and place; and make the necessary arrangements.
Group 2: Make the decorations.
Group 3: Make the invitations.
Group 4: Plan the entertainment.
Group 5: Plan the refreshments.

CLASSROOM DISPLAYS

Look Who's Coasting Into Ms. Bray's Room!

Welcome your students with a giant roller coaster display they'll love! Create a track by affixing black masking tape to a wall outside your classroom. Then write each child's name on a colorful copy of a car pattern from page 64 and place it on the track. Everyone will be ready to ride into an exciting new school year!

Kathy Bray—Gr. 4, West School, Carlinville, IL

REACH FOR THE MOON!

Kelsey   Mahmoud
Allie   Steven
Antwon
Marco
Jamal   Cara
Davis
LaVonne
Kyle
Ben   Nya

Even If You Miss, You'll Land Among the Stars!

Kara
Read at least one book each week.
Turn in my homework every day.
Study hard for tests.

Inspire your students to reach for the moon with a dazzling goal-setting display! Cover a board with black paper and spray-paint it lightly with silver or gold paint. Use colored chalk to draw a moon and other heavenly bodies. Have each child add glitter to the edge of a yellow paper star, label it with her goals for the year (or first grading period), and add it to the display. What a star-studded way to start the school year!

Dana Sanders—Grs. 3–5, Kingston Elementary, Cartersville, GA
Gratsiela Sabangan, Grs. 4–6, Three Angels School, Wichita, KS

DISPLAYS

"Bee" a Good Citizen!

"Bee-lieve in yourself."

"Bee" kind to others.

Put materials where they "bee-long."

"Bee-gin" the day in a positive way.

"Bee-have" in class.

Promote good citizenship with a buzzing display! Have each child write an original "bee-" phrase on an enlarged flower or bee pattern copied from page 64 and decorate it. Collect the cutouts. Each week, display a different selection of cutouts on the board. Your room will buzz with positive reminders about being a good citizen!

Cathy Ogg
Happy Valley Elementary
Elizabethton, TN

Check out the ease of assigning student helpers in this simple display! Cover a board with red and black sheets of construction paper to make a giant checkerboard. Add white paper strips labeled with classroom jobs. Give each child a colorful paper circle to personalize and decorate. To assign daily or weekly jobs, simply pin a student's circle to a square!

Donna G. Pawloski—Gr. 4
Primos Elementary
Primos, PA

It's YOUR Turn!

Austin — Line Leader
Kelly — Plants
Davis — Bookshelves
Ikube — Collect Papers
Sean — Assignments
Anya — P. E. Equipment
Kenan — Supplies
Mia — Library Helper
Sara — Messenger
Zach — Lunch Count
Reed — Windows
Paula — Boards

Watch fall trees burst into color with this beautiful parts-of-speech display! On a green and blue background, arrange a different bare tree cutout for each part of speech you wish students to review. Have each child write a word that represents one of the parts of speech on a colorful leaf cutout and attach it to the correct tree. What a "tree-rific" review!

Jessica Reis—Gr. 5, Taconic Hills Central School, Craryville, NY

Use a "cents-ible" monthly display to keep students in the know! Enlarge and decorate copies of the piggy bank and coin patterns on page 65. Add a laminated calendar grid labeled with test dates, field trips, project due dates, etc. Each month, give each child a copy of a blank calendar to update as needed. Then watch your investment in students' accountability grow!

Andrea Wohl—Gr. 5, Washington School, Westfield, NJ

DISPLAYS

A
Vote
for
Reading
Is a
Vote
for
Success!

Use an election-theme wall display to promote reading for Children's Book Week in November! Enlarge and decorate the donkey and elephant patterns on page 65. Have each child write a brief summary of a favorite book on a balloon cutout and add it to the display. Near the display, place a ballot box in which each student casts his vote for the best book featured. Will it be a landslide victory?

adapted from an idea by Cyndi Smith—Gr. 6, Fairview Elementary, Carthage, MO

Gobble up the chance to showcase students' writing talents! Surround a large turkey cutout with mounted examples of students' stories, summaries, essays, poems, paragraphs, or whatever type of writing you wish to display. Everyone will be talking turkey for sure!

CLASSROOM

Holiday ⭐ "Poet-tree"

*Christmastime is here.
It's my favorite time of year.
Are those bells I hear?
Maybe Santa Claus is near!*
by Jay

Trim a holiday tree with decorative student rhymes! Mount a green tree cutout and attach a fringed, light-gray paper garland. Have each student create a festive paper ornament on which to copy a holiday poem he has written. Then hang the ornaments on the tree using colorful lengths of yarn. Simply "tree-rific"!

Brandi Lampl
J. W. Arnold Elementary
Jonesboro, GA

Create a wonderful display that can satisfy students' curiosity! Share examples of things students might be curious about, such as why the sky is blue or how deep the ocean is. Ask each child to write on a colorful index her own "I wonder…" statement and research the answer. Have her also create a cutout of a frosty friend and decorate it with colorful markers and paper scraps. Then post each snowman along with its matching card on a blue and white background for a crisp winter display!

Marsha Townsend—Gr. 4, Schuylkill Valley Elementary, Leesport, PA

DISPLAYS

Recognize hardworking students by accumulating a huge mass of snowflakes! Each time a student earns an A on a test, project, or other assignment, have her label a snowflake cutout with her name and the assignment for which she earned the good grade. Then have her decorate the cutout and add it to the board next to a Poly-Fil hill. Prepare for an avalanche!

Jenelle Triplett—Gr. 5
Plain City Elementary
Plain City, OH

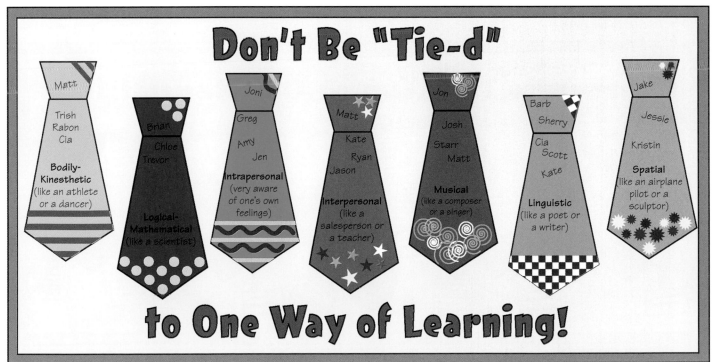

Which learning styles best suit your students? To find out, label each of seven different necktie cutouts with a different learning style and then mount them all on a board. Discuss the different multiple intelligences with students. Then invite each child to sign the necktie of each learning style that describes how he learns!

adapted from an idea by Bridget McKenna James—Gr. 5, Sterling Elementary, Warrensburg, MO

CLASSROOM

Don't Forget!

Elephants don't forget, right? With the help of this friendly fellow, your students should have no trouble remembering important dates, upcoming tests, and special activities! Enlarge the elephant pattern on page 66 and mount it on a wall along with items such as special notices, the weekly lunch menu, and a calendar of important dates. Allow your classroom helpers to add to or update the display as needed!

Natalie McGregor, Grenada Upper Elementary, Grenada, MS

Characters That Tug at Our Heartstrings

Some book characters touch our hearts in a special way. Help students remember such characters with this heartwarming display! Give each child two index cards. On one card, have her write a paragraph about a character she will never forget. On the other card, direct her to write the title of the book in which the character appears and the author's name. Have her also cut out a red heart shape and write her name on it. Mount the cutouts on the board. Then use a piece of string to attach each of the child's index cards to her cutout.

Colleen Dabney, Williamsburg, VA

DISPLAYS

The Braggin' Dragon

Instead of puffing smoke, this dragon just wants to brag about your students' good work! Enlarge the dragon pattern on page 66 and post it on a wall. Every week or so, invite each child to choose an example of his work to mount and display. That should keep the dragon happy!

Brooke Blake, Wentworth Elementary, Wentworth, NH

Make your students' hunger for knowledge obvious with this eye-catching display! Cover a board with colorful paper and tall tree cutouts, each labeled with a different core subject. Glue small animal bedding (or shredded paper resembling sawdust) to the lower sides and bottom of each tree trunk. Near the bedding, mount copies of the beaver pattern from page 66, each labeled with a different child's name. Passersby will admire how eagerly your class is gnawing at knowledge!

Natalie McGregor, Grenada Upper Elementary, Grenada, MS

We're Team Players

on and off the Field!

Students will eagerly step to the plate to contribute to this inspiring wall display! Have each volunteer label a white poster board square with an encouraging character-building statement related to a particular position on a baseball field: batter, pitcher, first baseman, etc. Arrange the ten labeled squares around a diamond on a large green poster board baseball field, placing each square near the field position it represents. Then, using the patterns on page 67, have students surround the playing field with cutouts of baseballs and baseball gloves that they have colored and then labeled with their names. When it comes to developing character, your students' batting averages will be outstanding!

Lisa Wildschuetz
John Weldon Elementary
St. Charles, MO

Pitcher
Pitch in and help others every chance you get.

Third Baseman
No matter what happens in life, there is always someone who can help you find the way home.

Poetry was never prettier than with this springtime display! Brainstorm with students different words and ideas about spring. Next, write the poem pattern below on the board. Have each student write a draft of a sensory poem using the pattern; then have her copy her poem onto a sheet of springtime stationery. Finally, have each child make a butterfly to add to the display by filling a small clear plastic bag with paper confetti and attaching to its twisted middle a colorful plastic clothespin with pipe cleaner antennae.

Kelli Higgins
P. L. Bolin Elementary
East Peoria, IL
and Angie Regan
Brandon, MS

Poem Pattern

I see _____.
I hear _____.
I touch _____.
I smell _____.
I taste _____.

Spring's Just Fluttering By!

DISPLAYS

Inspire students to flavor their writing with pinches of figurative language with a tantalizing display of the right ingredients! Glue sheets of white paper labeled with definitions of different figurative language terms to colorful construction paper recipe cards. Arrange the cards on a bulletin board along with an enlarged and colored copy of the chef pattern on page 67. Then, when students spice up their writing, add their samples to the board. Bon appétit!

Heather Kime Markland
Chatham Park Elementary
Havertown, PA

Support and appreciate current and past members of the military with a heartfelt Memorial Day display! Have each student write a letter to an unknown serviceperson, expressing thanks for what that person has done or is doing for our country. Then have each child copy his edited letter onto a large index card, glue it to a larger white paper heart, and decorate its outer edges with patriotic designs.

Natalie McGregor
Grenada Upper Elementary
Grenada, MS

Ms. Alford's Shining Stars

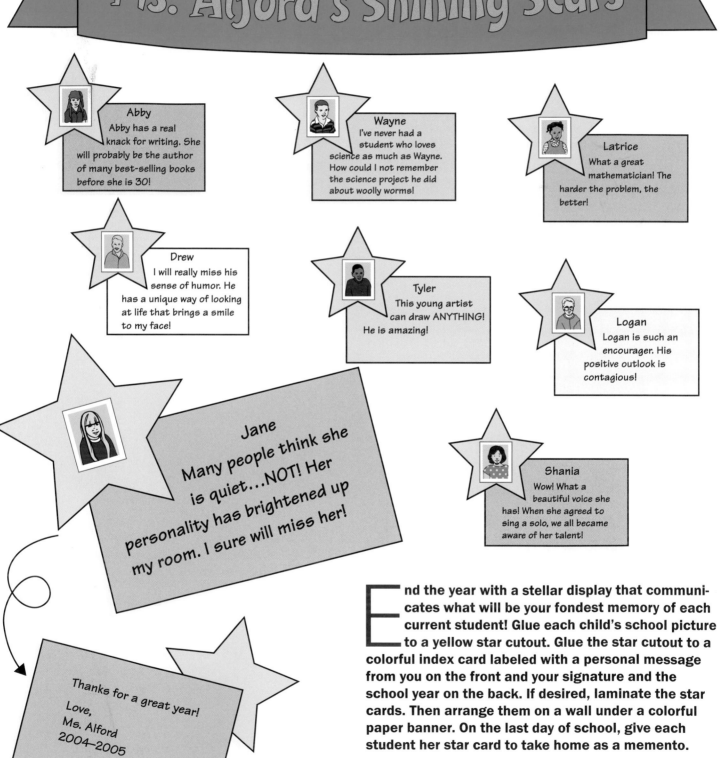

Abby
Abby has a real knack for writing. She will probably be the author of many best-selling books before she is 30!

Wayne
I've never had a student who loves science as much as Wayne. How could I not remember the science project he did about woolly worms!

Latrice
What a great mathematician! The harder the problem, the better!

Drew
I will really miss his sense of humor. He has a unique way of looking at life that brings a smile to my face!

Tyler
This young artist can draw ANYTHING! He is amazing!

Logan
Logan is such an encourager. His positive outlook is contagious!

Jane
Many people think she is quiet...NOT! Her personality has brightened up my room. I sure will miss her!

Shania
Wow! What a beautiful voice she has! When she agreed to sing a solo, we all became aware of her talent!

Thanks for a great year!
Love,
Ms. Alford
2004–2005

End the year with a stellar display that communicates what will be your fondest memory of each current student! Glue each child's school picture to a yellow star cutout. Glue the star cutout to a colorful index card labeled with a personal message from you on the front and your signature and the school year on the back. If desired, laminate the star cards. Then arrange them on a wall under a colorful paper banner. On the last day of school, give each student her star card to take home as a memento.

Debbie Alford, Garnett Elementary Center, Garnett, KS

DISPLAYS

Leaves on tree:
- *Tuck Everlasting* by Natalie Babbitt
- *Because of Winn-Dixie* by Kate DiCamillo
- *Holes* by Louis Sachar
- *Sarah, Plain and Tall* by Patricia MacLachlan
- *Number the Stars* by Lois Lowry
- *Bridge to Terabithia* by Katherine Paterson
- *Junebug* by Alice Mead
- *Just Juice* by Karen Hesse
- *Wringer* by Jerry Spinelli
- *The Barn* by Avi

S-T-R-E-T-C-H YOUR IMAGINATION WITH READING!

Whet students' appetites for summer reading with this inviting display! Several weeks before school ends, cover a board with cloud-print fabric or white cloud cutouts on blue background paper. Add an enlarged and colored copy of the giraffe pattern on page 68. Near the board, place a supply of the leaf pattern on page 68 copied on green paper. Have students label the leaves with book titles they recommend and staple them above the giraffe's head. On the last day of school, invite each child to take home a leaf or two to remind him of the books he can read during the summer!

Patty Hamilton, Harbor Creek Youth Services, Erie, PA

High Fives for the Flag and the Fourth

I can worship as I please.

I don't have a dictator as a leader.

I can vote when I am 18 years old.

My family can own a home.

I can get a free education.

Being an American means that I am free to do things that I could not do if I lived in another country.

Celebrate Flag Day and the Fourth of July with this patriotic red, white, and blue display! Have each child trace her hand three times on white paper with a red or blue crayon and cut out the tracings. In each hand's center, have her write a sentence explaining what it means to be an American. On each finger, have her write an example of a freedom she enjoys. Arrange the cutouts on a wall to form a large wreath. Be sure Old Glory is flying nearby!

Cheryl Stewart, Rawlinson Road Middle School, Rock Hill, SC

Coaster Car Patterns
Use with the display on page 52.

Bee and Flower Patterns
Use with "'Bee' a Good Citizen!" on page 53.

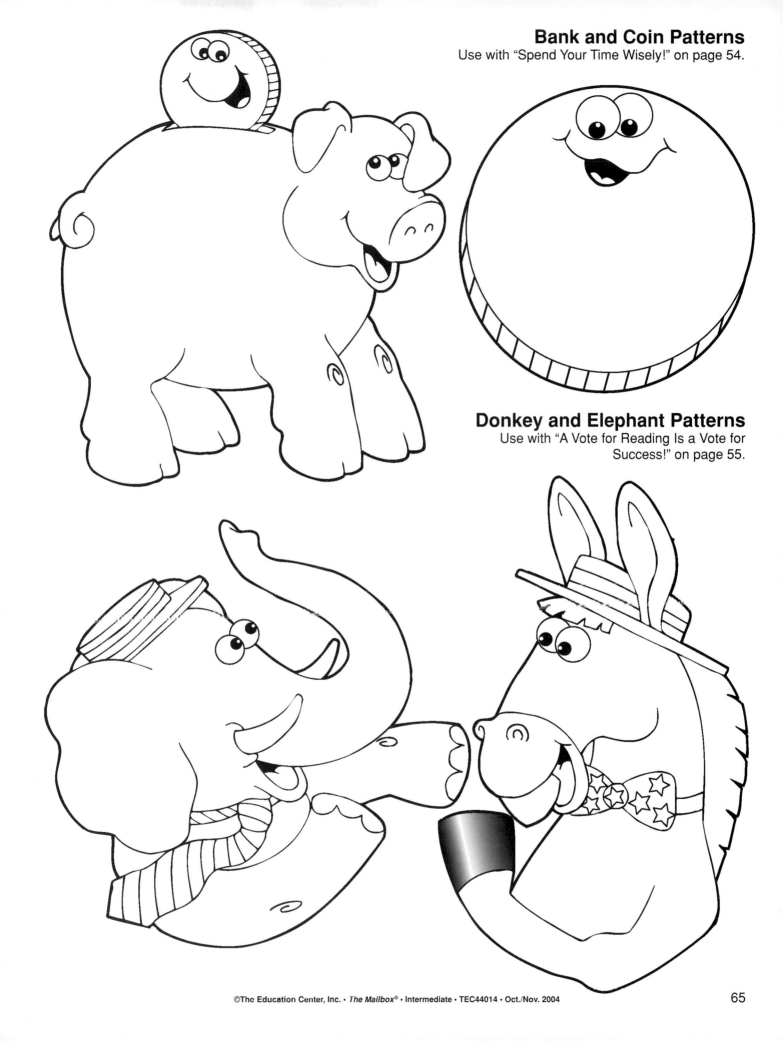

Bank and Coin Patterns
Use with "Spend Your Time Wisely!" on page 54.

Donkey and Elephant Patterns
Use with "A Vote for Reading Is a Vote for Success!" on page 55.

Elephant Pattern
Use with "Don't Forget!" on page 58.

Beaver Pattern
Use with "We're Hungry for Knowledge!" on page 59.

Dragon Pattern
Use with "The Braggin' Dragon" on page 59.

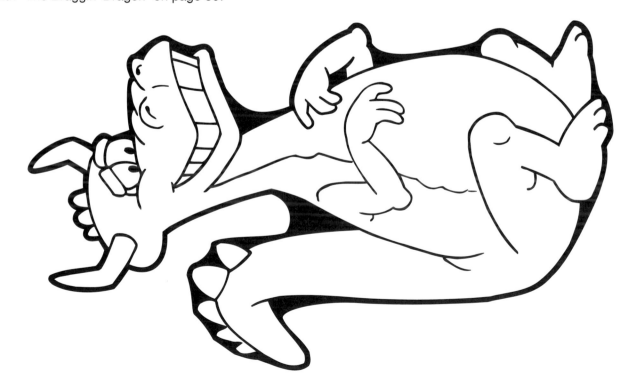

Baseball and Baseball Glove Patterns
Use with "We're Team Players on and off the Field!" on page 60, "Baseball Buddies" on page 34, "Adverb All-Stars" on page 269, and "Catch-It Folders" on page 292.

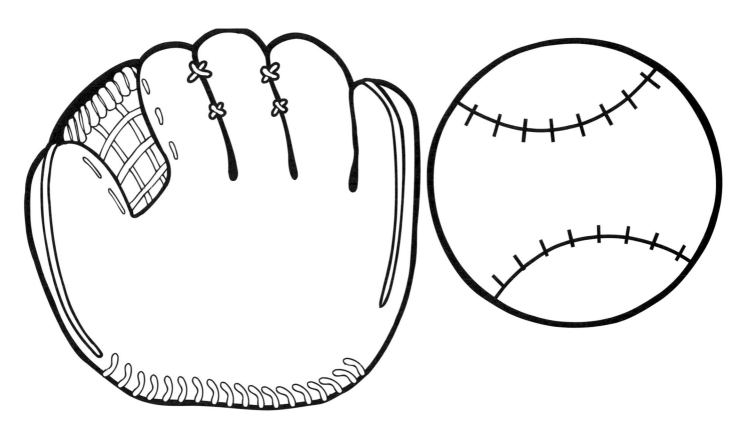

Chef Pattern
Use with "Spice Up Your Writing!" on page 61.

Giraffe and Leaf Patterns

Use with "S-T-R-E-T-C-H Your Imagination With Reading!" on page 63.

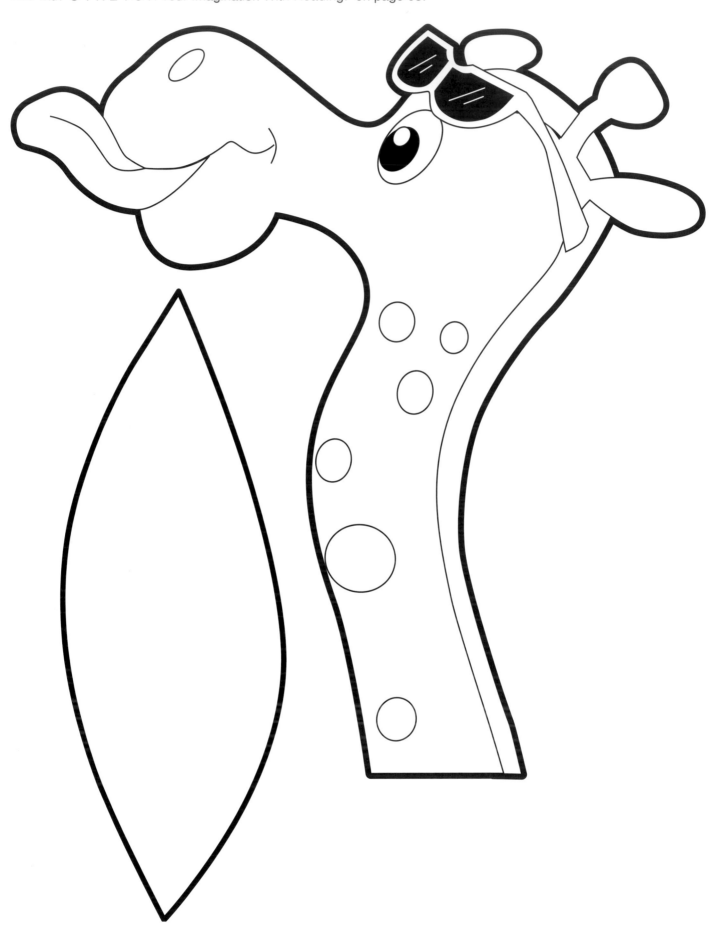

Language Arts Units

High-Flying Sentences

Watch students' skills with sentence structure soar with this sky-high collection of activities on simple, compound, and complex sentences!

by Julia Ring Alarie, Williston, VT

Simply Delicious!
Writing simple sentences

Whet students' appetites for writing simple sentences with this tasty activity. Begin by reviewing with students that a simple sentence has one complete thought but can include compound subjects, predicates, and phrases. Afterward, ask each child to list the foods she would most like to eat for breakfast, lunch, and dinner. Next, direct her to write a simple descriptive sentence about each of her favorite foods. Then give the student a sheet of 9" x 12" construction paper and have her fold it in thirds. Instruct her to copy her sentences in each section, as shown, and decorate it to create her own menu of favorites. Display the menus with the title "Simply Delicious Sentences!"

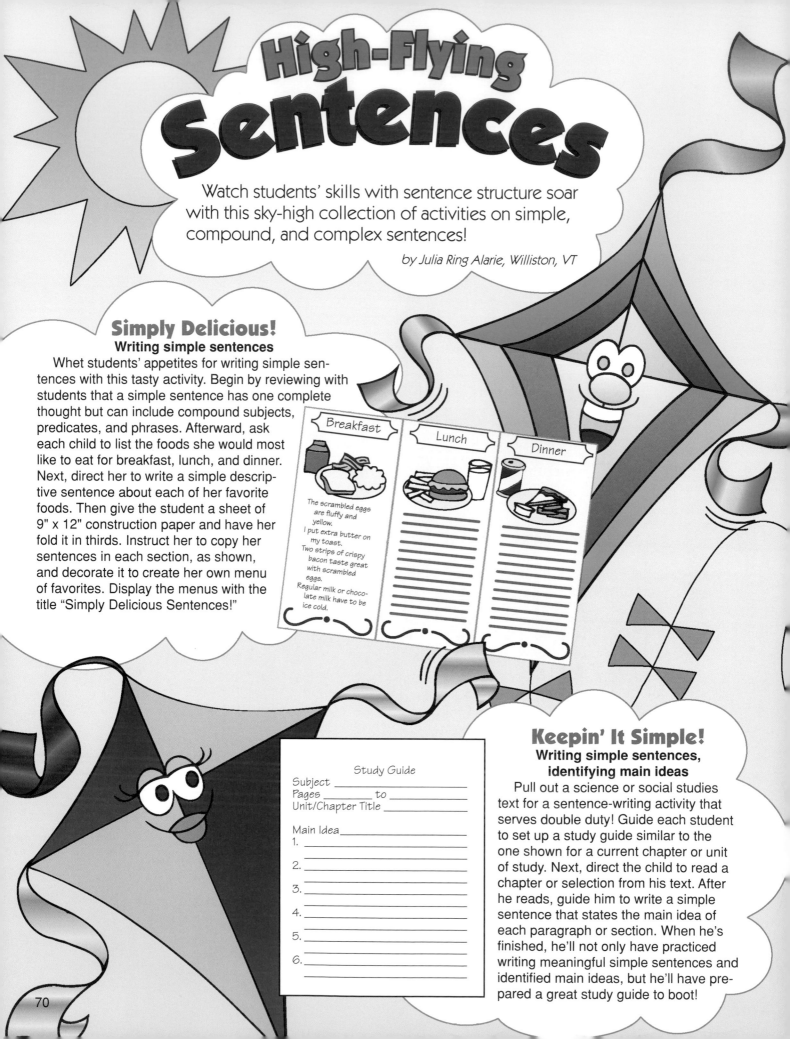

Breakfast

The scrambled eggs are fluffy and yellow.
I put extra butter on my toast.
Two strips of crispy bacon taste great with scrambled eggs.
Regular milk or chocolate milk have to be ice cold.

Lunch

Dinner

Study Guide

Subject _____
Pages _____ to _____
Unit/Chapter Title _____

Main Idea_____
1. _____
2. _____
3. _____
4. _____
5. _____
6. _____

Keepin' It Simple!
Writing simple sentences, identifying main ideas

Pull out a science or social studies text for a sentence-writing activity that serves double duty! Guide each student to set up a study guide similar to the one shown for a current chapter or unit of study. Next, direct the child to read a chapter or selection from his text. After he reads, guide him to write a simple sentence that states the main idea of each paragraph or section. When he's finished, he'll not only have practiced writing meaningful simple sentences and identified main ideas, but he'll have prepared a great study guide to boot!

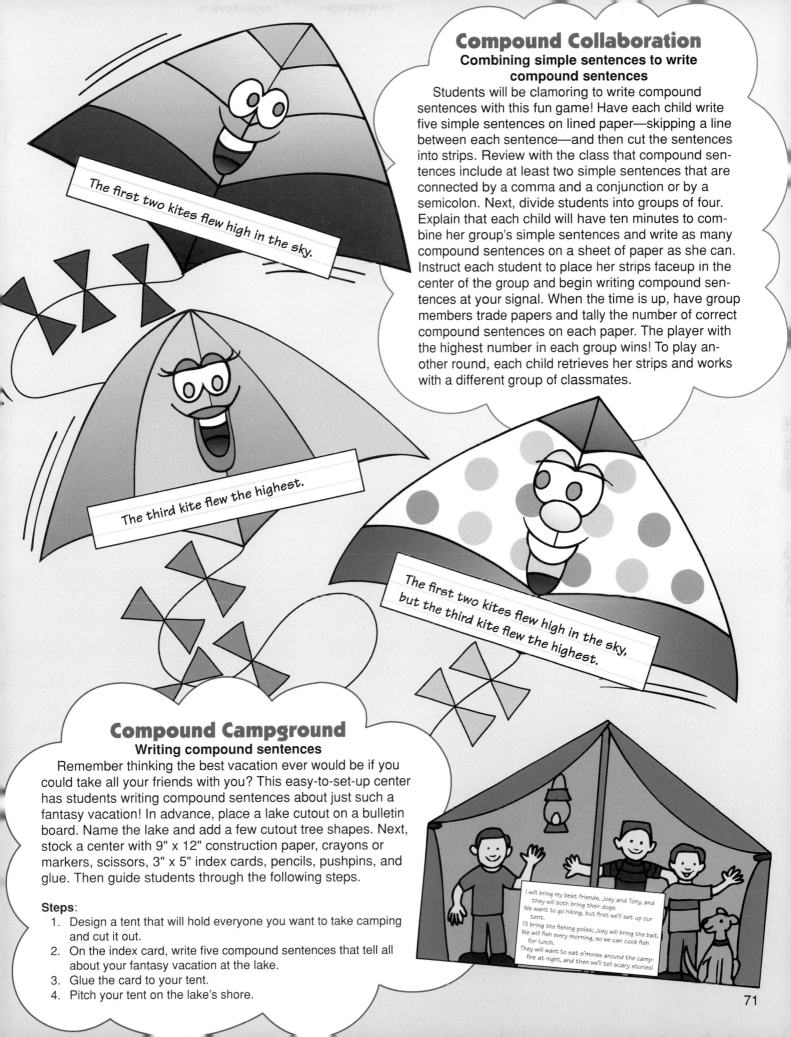

Compound Collaboration
Combining simple sentences to write compound sentences

Students will be clamoring to write compound sentences with this fun game! Have each child write five simple sentences on lined paper—skipping a line between each sentence—and then cut the sentences into strips. Review with the class that compound sentences include at least two simple sentences that are connected by a comma and a conjunction or by a semicolon. Next, divide students into groups of four. Explain that each child will have ten minutes to combine her group's simple sentences and write as many compound sentences on a sheet of paper as she can. Instruct each student to place her strips faceup in the center of the group and begin writing compound sentences at your signal. When the time is up, have group members trade papers and tally the number of correct compound sentences on each paper. The player with the highest number in each group wins! To play another round, each child retrieves her strips and works with a different group of classmates.

The first two kites flew high in the sky.

The third kite flew the highest.

The first two kites flew high in the sky, but the third kite flew the highest.

Compound Campground
Writing compound sentences

Remember thinking the best vacation ever would be if you could take all your friends with you? This easy-to-set-up center has students writing compound sentences about just such a fantasy vacation! In advance, place a lake cutout on a bulletin board. Name the lake and add a few cutout tree shapes. Next, stock a center with 9" x 12" construction paper, crayons or markers, scissors, 3" x 5" index cards, pencils, pushpins, and glue. Then guide students through the following steps.

Steps:
1. Design a tent that will hold everyone you want to take camping and cut it out.
2. On the index card, write five compound sentences that tell all about your fantasy vacation at the lake.
3. Glue the card to your tent.
4. Pitch your tent on the lake's shore.

I will bring my best friends, Joey and Tony, and they will both bring their dogs.
We want to go hiking, but first we'll set up our tent.
I'll bring the fishing poles; Joey will bring the bait.
We will fish every morning, so we can cook fish for lunch.
They will want to eat s'mores around the campfire at night, and then we'll tell scary stories!

When _____, it sounds like _____.

When Dad does the dishes, it sounds like he's playing the cymbals. Crash! Crash! Clink!

Complex Sentences Made Simple

Writing complex sentences

Liven up the writing of complex sentences with this creative auditory exercise. First, review with students that a complex sentence is made up of one independent clause and at least one dependent clause. Next, write on the board the complex sentence template shown. Then direct each student to use the template to write ten different complex sentences. Allow time for each student to share his favorite sentence with the class and accompany it with the matching sound effect!

My cat, Tabby, likes to stay outside!

because she likes to hunt.

Get to the Point!

Using complex sentences to enhance or clarify meaning

Show students that adding dependent clauses can create complex sentences that really get to the point! In advance, copy the sentences below on the board. Then pair students and give each twosome ten 1" x 4½" strips of construction paper, scissors, and glue. Have the partners cut one end of each strip into a point. Next, instruct each duo to copy the first sentence on the board onto a sheet of lined paper. Then direct the partners to write on a strip a dependent clause that will enhance or clarify the sentence and glue the strip in place as shown. Have pairs repeat the process with each remaining sentence. Now that's getting to the point!

1. My cat, Tabby, likes to stay outside.
2. Fergus chased Tabby into the woods.
3. There used to be more trees in the woods.
4. Did you see the new park?
5. Some of the equipment is missing.
6. Let's go to the park.
7. My cousin might come too.
8. Tabby hasn't come home.
9. We can look for Tabby.
10. We'll find Tabby.

Complete the Compounds!

Box Kite Bob is confused. Why? The compound sentences below are not complete! To finish each one, find the simple sentence on each kite that best completes each sentence below and write it on the line. Color each kite as you use its sentence.

My brother is younger than I am

I want a new bike for my birthday

but she won't do it if you are watching.

and this will be my first time on a horse.

Brad is the best writer in class

We may go to the mountains

and Elly is my calico cat.

I asked my dad if I could drive the car

I have visited Vermont

but I have never played a video game.

1. I taught my dog Fifi a new trick, _____.

2. _____, but I haven't been to the capital.

3. _____; he moved here from Dallas.

4. You may not believe this, _____.

5. _____; he's in first grade.

6. Ally is my poodle, _____.

7. _____, or we may go to the beach.

8. _____, so I have been dropping hints.

9. I'm going horseback riding Friday, _____.

10. _____, but he said no.

Bonus Box: Write two new compound sentences on the back. Then rewrite them as four simple sentences.

©The Mailbox® • TEC44017 • Feb./Mar. 2005 • Key p. 308

Whose Note Is It?

Kathy Kite's kids left notes for her, but they forgot to sign them! To help her sort the notes, label each kite shape below with the correct child's name.

Simple Sid always uses simple sentences.

Compound Carla always uses compound sentences.

Complex Conrad always uses complex sentences.

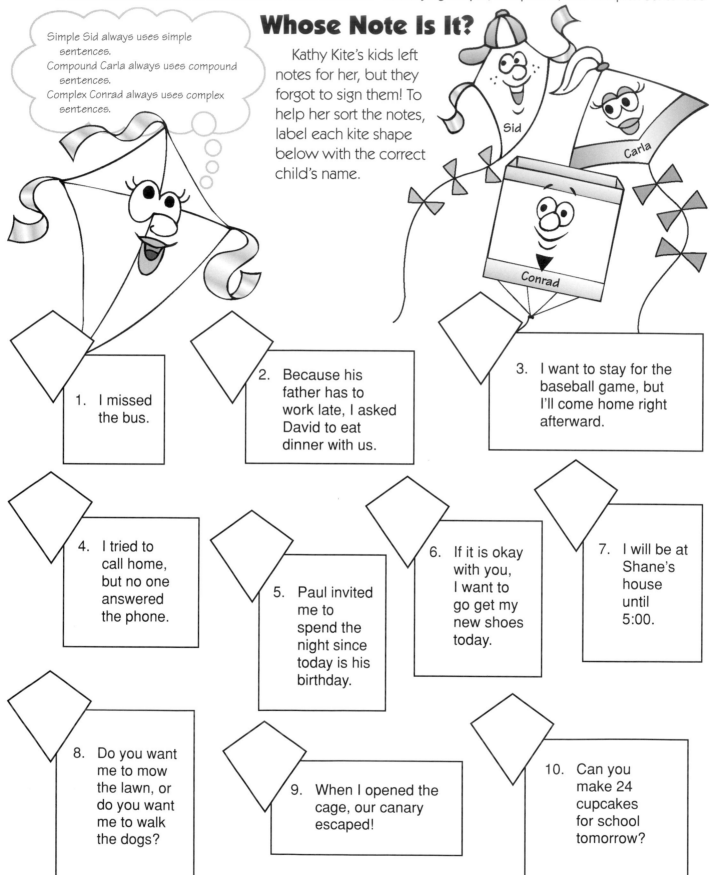

1. I missed the bus.

2. Because his father has to work late, I asked David to eat dinner with us.

3. I want to stay for the baseball game, but I'll come home right afterward.

4. I tried to call home, but no one answered the phone.

5. Paul invited me to spend the night since today is his birthday.

6. If it is okay with you, I want to go get my new shoes today.

7. I will be at Shane's house until 5:00.

8. Do you want me to mow the lawn, or do you want me to walk the dogs?

9. When I opened the cage, our canary escaped!

10. Can you make 24 cupcakes for school tomorrow?

Bonus Box: On the back of this page, write a note about your afterschool plans. Include one simple, one compound, and one complex sentence.

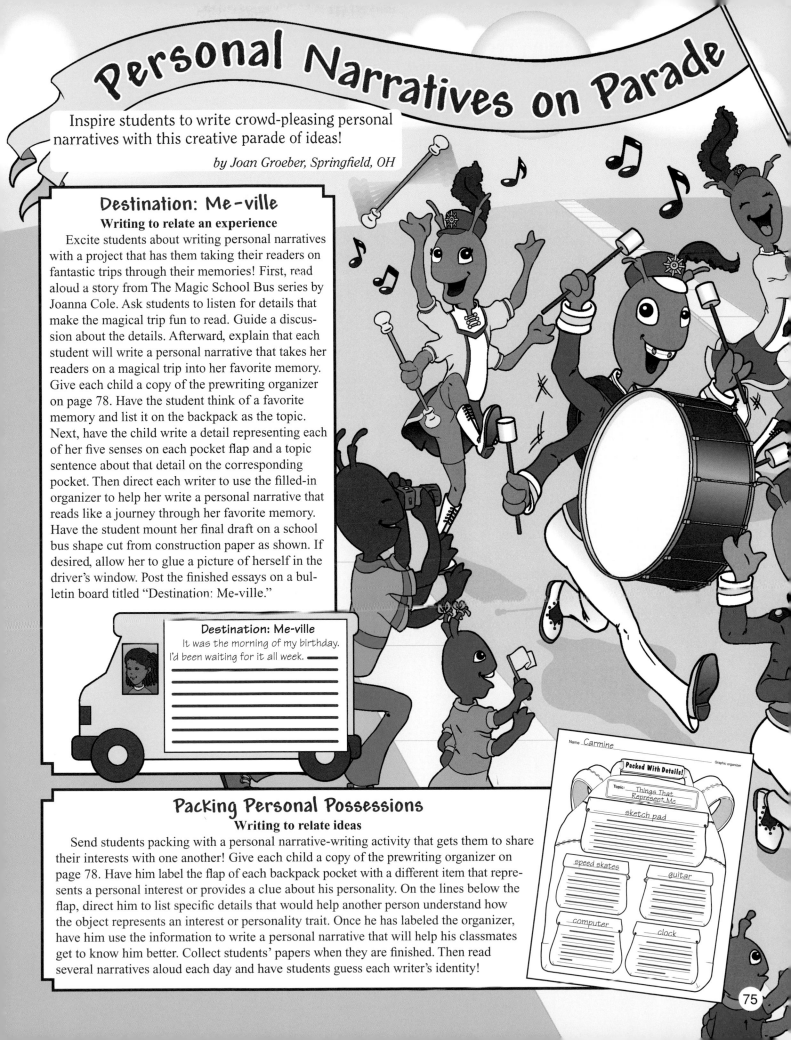

Personal Narratives on Parade

Inspire students to write crowd-pleasing personal narratives with this creative parade of ideas!

by Joan Groeber, Springfield, OH

Destination: Me-ville
Writing to relate an experience

Excite students about writing personal narratives with a project that has them taking their readers on fantastic trips through their memories! First, read aloud a story from The Magic School Bus series by Joanna Cole. Ask students to listen for details that make the magical trip fun to read. Guide a discussion about the details. Afterward, explain that each student will write a personal narrative that takes her readers on a magical trip into her favorite memory. Give each child a copy of the prewriting organizer on page 78. Have the student think of a favorite memory and list it on the backpack as the topic. Next, have the child write a detail representing each of her five senses on each pocket flap and a topic sentence about that detail on the corresponding pocket. Then direct each writer to use the filled-in organizer to help her write a personal narrative that reads like a journey through her favorite memory. Have the student mount her final draft on a school bus shape cut from construction paper as shown. If desired, allow her to glue a picture of herself in the driver's window. Post the finished essays on a bulletin board titled "Destination: Me-ville."

Destination: Me-ville
It was the morning of my birthday. I'd been waiting for it all week.

Packing Personal Possessions
Writing to relate ideas

Send students packing with a personal narrative-writing activity that gets them to share their interests with one another! Give each child a copy of the prewriting organizer on page 78. Have him label the flap of each backpack pocket with a different item that represents a personal interest or provides a clue about his personality. On the lines below the flap, direct him to list specific details that would help another person understand how the object represents an interest or personality trait. Once he has labeled the organizer, have him use the information to write a personal narrative that will help his classmates get to know him better. Collect students' papers when they are finished. Then read several narratives aloud each day and have students guess each writer's identity!

Name Carmine

Graphic organizer

Packed With Details!

Topic: Things That Represent Me

sketch pad

speed skates   guitar

computer   clock

Heralding Personal Heroics
Writing to recollect an event

Have your students ever thought of themselves as heroes to others? Ask this question to motivate each child to write a personal narrative about a time when she may have been someone's hero. Explain that everyday heroes are people who do things for others or help them just because it is the right thing to do. Further explain that everyday heroes expect no recognition or reward. Help students brainstorm everyday deeds that can be heroic. For example, sharing a lunch with a classmate who forgot hers or visiting an elderly neighbor who is lonely may be considered heroic. Ask each student to think about a time when she did something similar. Give each child a copy of page 78. Direct her to list the heroic thing she did on the topic lines and explain on the first pocket why she did it. Next, instruct her to label each remaining pocket with something that happened as a result of her action. Then have the student use the information to help her write about the event. Compile the completed narratives into a class newsletter titled "The Heroic Herald." Be sure to send the newsletter home so parents can read about these unsung heroes!

The Heroic Herald

On my birthday, my mom had packed the best lunch ever! I could hardly wait to eat it. Then I saw Jan. She looked sad. She had forgotten her lunch.

Recipe for a Delightful Day
Writing to help the reader imagine an experience

Whet students' appetites for writing personal narratives by having them cook up recipes for a day that's perfect in every way! Display a cookbook recipe and discuss its format. Next, ask each student to list the ingredients (important details) and the amount of each one that he'd need to make what he considers to be a perfect day. Then guide the student to write a personal narrative that tells how and in what order he would mix the ingredients to make the day progress toward the happy ending he desires. Encourage the writer to sprinkle his narrative with dashes of humor and pinches of surprise. After the child adds a mouthwatering title, have him copy his final draft on paper cut in the shape of a large recipe card. After students share their narratives with the class, display them on a bulletin board titled "Recipes for a Great Day!"

A Sunny-Side Up Day

quiet, sandy beach
dozens of waves, begging to be ridden
gallon of sunshine

Aunt Jenny
12 buckets of laughter

Let me tell you how to make the most perfect day ever! Start with the beach and the waves. Then mix in the sunshine. Add an aunt who loves to swim.

Memory Markers
Using sensory details

Give students a chance to commemorate their favorite places by writing personal narratives they display on historical markers! Display a local, state, or national map and ask each child to choose a place on it that is special to him. Invite students to describe markers commemorating historically significant spots that they have seen. Afterward, explain that each child will write a narrative about his memories of his special place and then mount it on the shape of a historical marker. Ask the student to recall what he hears, smells, feels, sees, and tastes when he is in this place. Next, give each child a copy of the prewriting organizer on page 78. Have him list the details and memories associated with each sense on a different pocket. Then direct him to use the information to help him write his narrative. When he is finished, have him cut out the shape of a historical marker from construction paper, decorate it, and glue his essay to it as shown. After students share their narratives with the class, display the markers around the map, using yarn to connect each marker to its correct location.

McGregor Farmhouse
Built 1902
Visiting the McGregor Farmhouse in the fall is always a treat for me. The first thing I smell is smoke coming from its old rock chimney.

Seeing Through Another's Eyes
Writing from a different perspective

What would it be like for students to write personal narratives from other perspectives? Find out with this fun narrative-writing activity! Ask each student to think of her favorite activity to do at home. Explain that she will be describing that activity being performed as seen through the eyes of the family pet, a favorite stuffed animal, or a fly on the wall. To begin, direct the student to have the narrator introduce itself and explain who and what is being observed. Next, instruct the writer to think about how she actually behaves when doing that activity. Have her also consider how these actions might be perceived by a nonhuman observer. Encourage students to include vivid descriptions and humorous observations that the narrator might make about its human subject. On the final draft, have each student include a drawing of the narrator observing her perform the activity. Display the completed narratives on a bulletin board titled "Through Another's Eyes."

I'm Lucky, the family cat. I'm always around when Lauren practices for her dance class. You'll never catch me bending my body in the directions she does. It looks too painful!

Packed With Details!

Topic: _____
_____

Note to the teacher: Use with "Destination: Me-ville" and "Packing Personal Possessions" on page 75, "Heralding Personal Heroics" on page 76, and "Memory Markers" on page 77.

Let Me Think!

When was the last time you felt excited, sad, afraid, angry, or another strong emotion? Complete the sentence in the thought bubble to tell what you felt, when you felt it, and where you were at the time. Next, use the lines provided to describe how that emotion made each part of your body feel. Then, on another sheet of paper, write a narrative that tells how this emotion made you feel from head to toe.

I felt _____
_____

head: _____
_____
_____
_____
_____
_____

hands: _____
_____
_____
_____

heart: _____
_____
_____
_____
_____

legs: _____
_____
_____
_____
_____
_____

stomach: _____
_____
_____
_____
_____

skin: _____
_____
_____
_____
_____

Bonus Box: Think about a time when you felt the opposite of this feeling. How did that emotion make each body part above feel? List the ways on the back of this page.

DEVELOPING EXPOSITORY-WRITING SKILLS

Bring students' expository-writing skills into clearer focus with this picture-perfect collection of ideas!

with ideas by Joan Groeber, Springfield, OH

Step by Step
Writing sequential directions

This simple activity on writing directions includes some mixed-up fun! Begin by having students discuss how a reader would be affected if a set of directions were not written in the correct sequence. Next, divide students into groups of three or four. Assign each group a different topic from the list shown; then have group members work together to write a paragraph that explains how to complete the assigned task. When the group finishes its rough draft, give its members a supply of sentence strips. Instruct each group member to copy a different sentence from the paragraph onto a separate sentence strip. Have her also label the back of the strip with a number that shows her sentence's order in the paragraph. Then direct each group to shuffle its strips and trade them with another group. After students arrange the sentences in an order that satisfies each group member, have them turn the strips over to check the answers!

Topics

making a bed
riding a bike
making a paper airplane
turning a cartwheel
brushing your teeth
making a snowman
cleaning a fishbowl
making an ice-cream sundae

Chronicle the Moments!
Writing to explain events in chronological order

What series of events could be captured if students photographed every action that occurred in a particular place over a ten-minute span of time? Find out with this timely activity! First, have each child picture himself as a photographer in a particular place, such as a theme park, a room in his house, or a vacation spot. Next, instruct the child to choose one event such as wind from an open window blowing a newspaper all over the room and describe in chronological order what happens before, during, and after the event. Then challenge him to write a paragraph (or a multiparagraph paper) explaining when those events occurred as if they had been photographed with a camera. Have students post their paragraphs next to camera cutouts on a board titled "Chronological Camera Bugs." If desired, follow up by asking each student to chronicle five events from a section of his history text in a similar way.

My Lucky Charm
Writing to explain, summarizing

Make expository writing irresistibly alluring with this "charm-ing" activity! Ask each child to think about (or invent) an object she thinks brings her good luck. Next, have her write a multiparagraph paper about the object. Have her identify her lucky charm and explain how she got it in the first paragraph. Instruct her to explain in the next two paragraphs why the object is so important to her and why she thinks it brings her good luck. Have her summarize her thoughts in the concluding paragraph. When she has completed her rough draft, give her a large cutout of a green four-leaf clover. Direct her to write each paragraph in order on a different clover leaf and the selection's title in the center of the clover as shown. After each writer shares her work with the class, post it on a bulletin board titled "Our Lucky Charms."

Switched!
Writing to explain differences, summarizing

Spark students' imaginations with this idea, which is anything but ordinary! First, pair students and have the duos imagine that they are standing close together when an earthquake occurs, forcing each child to collide with her partner. Further explain that after the dust settles, the students realize that their identities have been switched! Next, have each partner list on paper at least five things about herself that are different (number of family members, height, hair color, ability to play basketball or the piano, different house, etc.) and five things that are not different (being right-handed, being good at sports, eye color, etc.). Then have each partner use the list to write a multiparagraph paper that explains the differences and concludes by summarizing how much of a change actually occurred. No doubt there will be an interested audience when it's time to share!

Cause-and-Effect Cubes
Writing to explain cause and effect

Integrating a current unit of study with this expository-writing activity can cause quite an effect! First, collect enough cube-shaped tissue boxes for each child to have a box. Next, guide each child to choose a topic from a current science or social studies unit that represents a cause-and-effect event, such as tornadoes. Instruct the student to research his topic's causes and effects and write a rough draft of a four-paragraph essay. Remind him to introduce his topic in the first paragraph and explain his topic's causes and effects in the second and third paragraphs. In the final paragraph, have him summarize the causes and effects. When he finishes his writing, have him cut out five pieces of light-colored construction paper to fit his cube's top and sides. Instruct him to write his topic on one piece, add an illustration, and then glue the piece to the cube's top. Then have him copy his first, second, third, and fourth paragraphs on the remaining pieces and glue them to the cube as shown. After students share their cubes with the class, arrange the boxes with the uncovered sides facedown to create a tabletop display.

What's the Problem?
Writing to explain a problem and its solution, writing a friendly letter

Promote problem solving with a letter-writing campaign that could produce interesting results! Guide a class discussion about school issues that students would like to see resolved. List the issues on the board. For each problem listed, ask students to suggest ways it could be solved. Next, explain that each child will choose an issue and write about it in a letter addressed to the appropriate person in charge. Review the different parts of a friendly letter with the class; then have each student select an issue and write a letter explaining the problem, who it affects, and how the situation can be improved. After students share their letters with the class, allow the authors to deliver their letters and get the problem-solving process underway!

Now You're Cookin'!

What's the most important thing to do when you're cooking? Follow the recipe! If you don't do things in the right order, you could end up with a mess!

Directions: Read the steps below for making peanut butter fudge. Write a number on each bowl to show the statement's order in the recipe. Then copy the steps in the correct order on another sheet of paper.

 Stir the heated mixture of sugar, milk, corn syrup, and salt until the sugar dissolves.

 When the mixture's temperature reaches 234°F, remove the saucepan from the heat.

 After the fudge cools completely, cut it into one-inch squares.

First, gather a two-quart saucepan, a candy thermometer, and the following ingredients: two cups of sugar, two-thirds cup of milk, a dash of salt, two table-spoons of corn syrup, two tablespoons of margarine, one teaspoon of vanilla, and one-third cup of peanut butter.

 When the mixture cools to 130°F, add the peanut butter and vanilla.

 Once the sugar dissolves, clip the candy thermometer inside the pan. Stir the mixture until the temperature reaches 234°F.

 After adding the peanut butter and vanilla, stir for one minute. Then pour the mixture into a slightly greased pan to cool completely.

 As soon as you remove the saucepan from the heat, add the margarine.

After gathering the ingredients, heat the sugar, milk, corn syrup, and salt in the two-quart saucepan over medium heat.

Once the margarine is added, let it cool to 130°F.

Name ______________________________ Expository writing

Strange School Day

Directions: Notice that the letters at the beginning of each line spell the topic. Using the example as a guide, write sentences on the lines below to explain something weird that's happening at your school today.

Example:
Pets are great friends for boys and girls.
Unless your parents object, think about getting a pet.
Pedigree animals are fine, but mutts are full of love too!
Plenty of shelters have lovable animals looking for good homes.
You'd be surprised by how much a pet adds to your life.

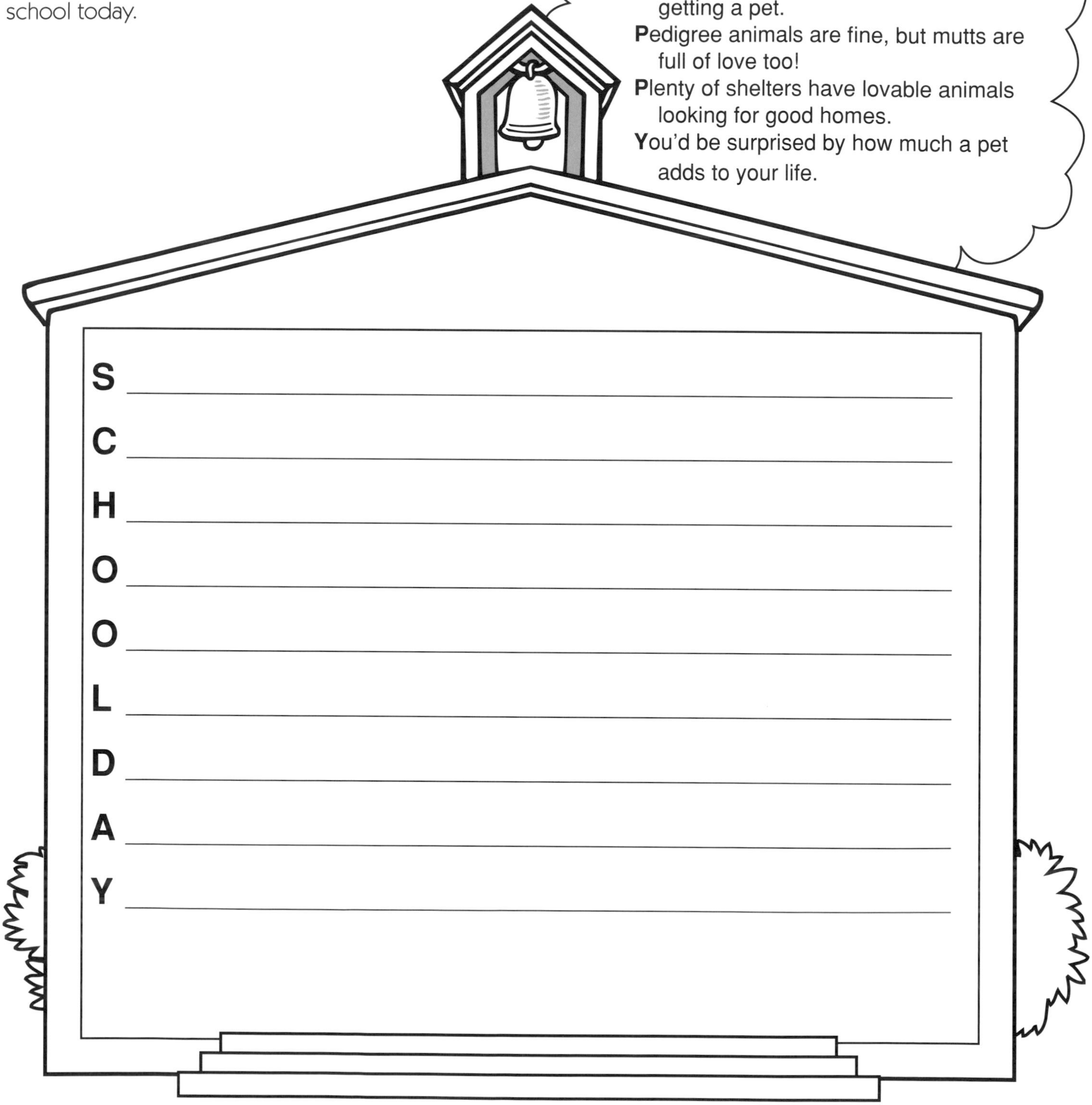

S ______________________________

C ______________________________

H ______________________________

O ______________________________

O ______________________________

L ______________________________

D ______________________________

A ______________________________

Y ______________________________

Bonus Box: Use the method above to write a similar paragraph on the back of this page about a topic of your choice.

Hot on the Trail of Text Features

When your students read, do they ignore text features such as special type, colorful labels, and diagrams that alert them to important information? If so, these creative activities can put your readers on a trail to track down the features with ease!

with contributions by Joan Groeber, Springfield, OH, and Kim Minafo, Cary, NC

The Search Is On!

Identifying text features

Unleash students to hunt for helpful text features with this simple activity. Gather a variety of nonfiction reading materials, including encyclopedias, magazines, and trade books. Next, pair students and give each twosome a copy of page 88. Point out the features and their definitions on the page. Explain that these features help readers focus their reading. Then give each pair a sample of nonfiction text. Have the partners identify any features they find in the text by listing them along with the corresponding page number(s) in the table on page 88. Instruct students to complete the page as directed and discuss how each feature helped them better understand the text. Finally, invite the partners to share with the class which features they found to be most helpful.

Text Feature	Page Number(s)	What I Learned From the Feature
heading	215	the main idea or topic
photograph	215	what the Mexican flag looks like
map	216	where Mexico is located in relation to the United States

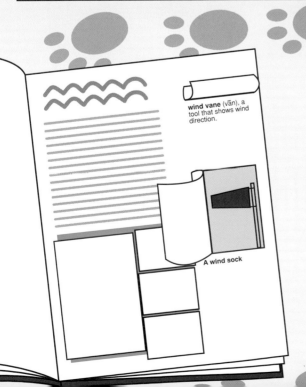

wind vane (vān), a tool that shows wind direction.

A wind sock

Focusing on the Features

Identifying and evaluating text features

Send students on a hunt for text features with this partner activity! Make a copy of page 89 for each pair of students. Then give each twosome scissors and several sticky notes. Instruct the partners to flip through a textbook until they find a variety of text features on two facing pages that they have not yet studied. Have the pair cover each text feature with a sticky note, trimming it to fit if necessary. Next, direct each duo to trade books with another twosome. Then have each set of partners take turns removing one sticky note at a time and discussing how helpful the revealed feature will be in helping them understand the text when they read the page. Once all notes are removed, have the pair read the text together and complete a copy of page 89 as directed. Conclude by having students answer questions such as the following: Were the features that covered the greatest space on the page the most helpful? Which features were the least helpful? How did the features work together to help you better understand the information?

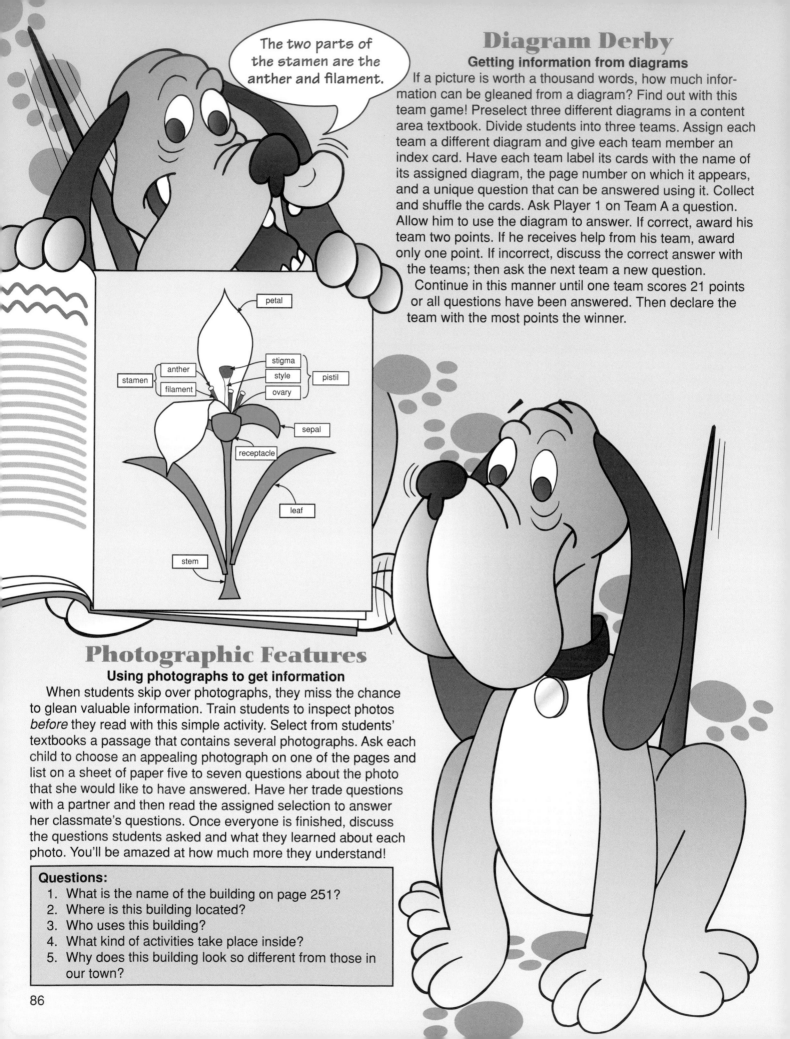

The two parts of the stamen are the anther and filament.

Diagram Derby
Getting information from diagrams

If a picture is worth a thousand words, how much information can be gleaned from a diagram? Find out with this team game! Preselect three different diagrams in a content area textbook. Divide students into three teams. Assign each team a different diagram and give each team member an index card. Have each team label its cards with the name of its assigned diagram, the page number on which it appears, and a unique question that can be answered using it. Collect and shuffle the cards. Ask Player 1 on Team A a question. Allow him to use the diagram to answer. If correct, award his team two points. If he receives help from his team, award only one point. If incorrect, discuss the correct answer with the teams; then ask the next team a new question.

Continue in this manner until one team scores 21 points or all questions have been answered. Then declare the team with the most points the winner.

Diagram labels: petal, stigma, style, ovary, pistil, anther, filament, stamen, sepal, receptacle, leaf, stem

Photographic Features
Using photographs to get information

When students skip over photographs, they miss the chance to glean valuable information. Train students to inspect photos *before* they read with this simple activity. Select from students' textbooks a passage that contains several photographs. Ask each child to choose an appealing photograph on one of the pages and list on a sheet of paper five to seven questions about the photo that she would like to have answered. Have her trade questions with a partner and then read the assigned selection to answer her classmate's questions. Once everyone is finished, discuss the questions students asked and what they learned about each photo. You'll be amazed at how much more they understand!

Questions:
1. What is the name of the building on page 251?
2. Where is this building located?
3. Who uses this building?
4. What kind of activities take place inside?
5. Why does this building look so different from those in our town?

Tallying Special Type
Using boldfaced and italicized type
Narrow the text features hunt to specialized type with this investigative activity. Have each pair of students open a science or social studies text to any chapter. Direct the duo to skim the text and make separate tallies of the boldfaced and italicized words the chapter contains. Then have each twosome dig deeper by identifying the number of tallied words that are defined directly in the text, the number that are defined using context clues, and the number that can only be defined with the book's glossary. Invite the pairs to share their findings with the class and put in a plug for which of these formats they find easiest to use. After everyone has shared, have students vote for the one they prefer!

Boldfaced Words	Italicized Words
ℍℍ I	II

Words defined in text: ℍℍ II
Words defined using context clues: 0
Words defined with glossary: I

Pick Up the Scent!
Using text features to get information
Alert students to the different types of text features they should watch for when reading with this timed game. Preselect a chapter from a content area textbook that contains a variety of text features. Compile a list of questions that can be answered using the text features. Next, give each child or pair of students a copy of the questions. Have the players use their textbooks to answer the questions and then raise their hands as soon as they finish so you can record the time. When everyone is finished, discuss the answers together and award a small treat to the players who picked up the scent (answered the questions) the quickest!

Questions:
1. Look at the cutaway diagram of a caravel on page 116. What are three ways the space below its main deck could be used?
2. Find the map on page 117. Which three explorers' routes does the map show?
3. On page 116, why is the word *isthmus* boldfaced?
4. Why is the question next to the colorful check mark at the bottom of page 116 boldfaced, italicized, and in larger print?
5. What three important pieces of information does the colorful box on page 114 give you?
6. According to the caption for the picture on page 118, who used instruments such as the ones shown? What type of instruments are they?

Finding "Bone-a Fide" Text Features

Directions:
1. Look through the text.
2. List each feature you find and its page number(s) in the table below.

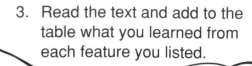

3. Read the text and add to the table what you learned from each feature you listed.

Text Features

heading: title at the top of a page

subhead: title at the beginning of a section

caption: words that describe a picture

special print: special treatment, such as font styles, used to bring attention to words or phrases

chart or table: lists important information in rows and columns

label: identifies part of a picture

timeline: table that shows the chronological order of events within a certain time period

map: image that shows places in and features of a geographic area

photograph: picture that is obtained by photography

illustration: drawing, map, or diagram that shows something

Text Feature	Page Number(s)	What I Learned From the Feature

Closing In on Text Features

Write the name of each text feature you found on a different bone below.

Read the text.

Color the labeled bones by the code.

Code

green = very helpful

yellow = somewhat helpful

red = not helpful

Note to the teacher: Use with "Focusing on the Features" on page 85. Each pair of students will need three crayons (green, yellow, and red) to complete this page.

Frame It!

A Gallery of Poetry Ideas

A Friend...

Accepts me as I am,
Believes in me,
Calls just to say, "Hi!"
Doesn't give up on me,
Encourages me,
Forgives my mistakes,
Gives me support,
Helps me,
Invites me over,
Just hangs out with me,
Keeps me in line,
Loves me just as I am,
Makes a difference in my life,
Never judges me,
Offers advice,
Picks me up when I'm down,
Quiets my fears,
Raises my spirits,
Says nice things about me,
Tells me the truth,
Understands me,
Values my opinion,
Walks beside me,
X-plains things I don't understand,
Yells when I won't listen, and
Zaps me back to reality.

Acrostic

THE ABCS OF FRIENDSHIP
Writing an acrostic poem

What qualities do your students look for in a good friend? To find out, have each child express his thoughts by writing an alphabet acrostic! Have the class discuss friendship and the special attributes that make a person a true friend. Then give each child a copy of the form on page 92. Direct him to write an acrostic on the form by listing or describing for each letter of the alphabet an attribute of a real friend. When finished, each child will have his own personal definition of friendship!

Dr. Morton Tener, Rowan University, Glassboro, NJ

POCKET-SIZE POEMS
Writing different types of poetry

Students can pocket a trio of original poems with this booklet-making activity! Give each child scissors and a copy of page 93. Direct him to cut out the booklet cover and pages and stack them so that the cover is on top. Once he staples the booklet along the side and writes poems according to each page's directions, he'll have a poetry booklet he can decorate any way he wishes.

Mary Christensen
Emmott Elementary
Houston, TX

COLORFUL POETRY
Writing an inventive poem

This poetry-writing activity will reveal your students' true (favorite) colors! Have each child list on scrap paper as many items as she can that are her favorite color. Then instruct her to use her list to write a poem about that color. On the poem's first line, have her write the name of the color. On the second line, have her write two words: one item from her list and an adjective that describes that item. On the third line, have her write three words: a different item from her list and a phrase that identifies or describes that item. Have the student continue adding lines to her poem in this manner, with each line being one word longer than the one before it, until the poem includes all of the items she listed. Then have her trim the poem around the edges, glue it to a matching color of construction paper, and decorate the edges with drawings of the mentioned items. Now that's colorful poetry!

Mary Maxey, Orange Grove Intermediate, Orange Grove, TX

SCAVENGER HUNT
Identifying characteristics of poems and literary devices

Grab a variety of poetry books for a scavenger hunt students won't soon forget! Give each child a copy of the checklist on page 94 and have her staple it to a sheet of lined paper. Then instruct her to search through the poetry books to find a poem that represents each type of poem or characteristic on the checklist. For each example she finds, have her record the following information on her stapled sheet: the title of the book containing the example, the page number where the example can be found, the title of the poem that contains or represents the element, and a one-sentence summary of what that poem is about. Allow students to search for a set amount of time each day over a period of days. Then award the searcher(s) finding the most examples with a small treat!

Donna Patron, George A. Jackson School, Jericho, NY

Name __Irene__   Checklist

Poetry Scavenger Hunt

Check off each example you can find.

- ☑ A poem that rhymes
- ☑ A poem with a one-word title
- ☐ A concrete or shape poem
- ☑ A funny poem
- ☐ A poem with four stanzas
- ☑ A poem with only four lines
- ☑ A limerick
- ☐ A poem about a school subject
- ☑ A poem with onomatopoeia (using a word that sounds like its meaning, such as *buzz*)
- ☐ A poem with a simile (a comparison of two unlike things using *like* or *as*)
- ☑ A poem with alliteration (the repetition of beginning consonant sounds in words)
- ☐ A poem with a hyperbole (an exaggeration)
- ☑ A poem about food
- ☑ A poem about a season of the year
- ☑ A poem about an animal or a pet

Quintain

Falling Up, p. 97 "Kanga Ruby"
It's about a female kangaroo that gets elected queen.

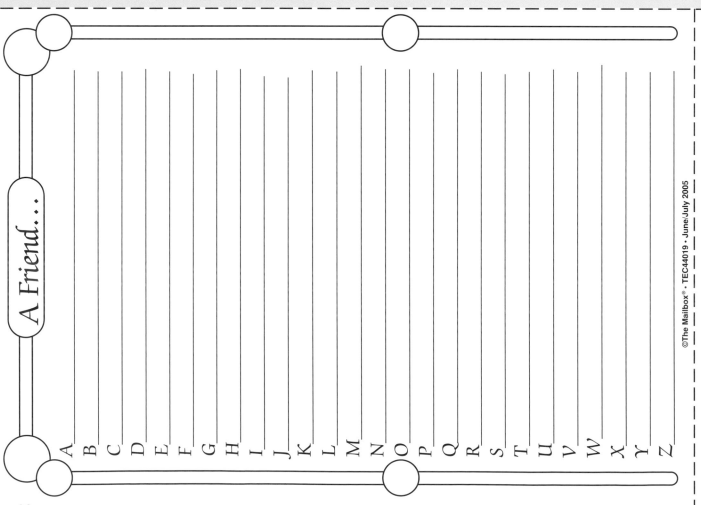

A Friend...

A
B
C
D
E
F
G
H
I
J
K
L
M
N
O
P
Q
R
S
T
U
V
W
X
Y
Z

©The Mailbox® • TEC44019 • June/July 2005

Note to the teacher: Use with "The ABCs of Friendship" on page 90.

Quintain

two syllables

four syllables

six syllables

eight syllables

two syllables

Cinquain

noun

two adjectives that describe the noun ,

three -ing verbs ,

your opinion of the noun

synonym for the noun

Diamante

noun

two adjectives ,

three -ing verbs ,

four nouns

three -ing verbs ,

two adjectives ,

noun

My Poetry Booklet

name

Poetry Scavenger Hunt

Check off each example you can find.

▢ A poem that rhymes

▢ A poem with a one-word title

▢ A concrete or shape poem

▢ A funny poem

▢ A poem with four stanzas

▢ A poem with only four lines

▢ A limerick

▢ A poem about a school subject

▢ A poem with onomatopoeia (using a word that sounds like its meaning, such as *buzz*)

▢ A poem with a simile (a comparison of two unlike things using *like* or *as*)

▢ A poem with alliteration (the repetition of beginning consonant sounds in words)

▢ A poem with a hyperbole (an exaggeration)

▢ A poem about food

▢ A poem about a season of the year

▢ A poem about an animal or a pet

Note to the teacher: Use with "Scavenger Hunt" on page 92.

Capitalization Station

Check out this trainload of fresh new ways to reinforce capitalization skills. It's one stop you'll be glad you made!

by Julia Ring Alarie, Essex Middle School, Essex, VT

Capitalization Collages

Identifying and categorizing capitalized words

Use yesterday's news to turn a review of capitalization rules into creative collages! Begin by helping students brainstorm different instances when capital letters are used. List students' responses on the board (see the examples shown). Next, divide students into groups of two or three. Give each group a newspaper section, scissors, and glue. Challenge group members to find and cut out as many of the listed examples as they can. As students work, write each category at the top of a separate 12" x 18" sheet of colorful construction paper. Give a different sheet to each group and have the group mates glue their examples to it. Then rotate the sheets around the classroom so that each group can add its examples to the appropriate sheet. Display the completed collages on a bulletin board titled "Capitalization in the News!"

All words in titles except articles, short prepositions, and coordinating conjunctions
Titles of magazines, newspapers, movies, books, poems, plays, stories, essays, and works of art and music
Names of businesses and products
Abbreviations of titles and organizations
First word of a sentence
First word in a direct quotation
Names of geographic places, roads, and highways
Names of languages, races, and religions
Words used as names
Days of the week, months of the year, and holidays

Table of Contents Capitalization
Capitalizing titles

This activity is just the ticket to teach students which words in a title need to be capitalized! First, provide each student with a highlighter and a copy of any textbook's table of contents. Point out that a table of contents lists chapter and section titles and that the first and last word of each title is capitalized. Have students highlight each title's beginning and ending words. Next, direct them to highlight any other capitalized words in each title. Explain that every word in a title should be capitalized except short prepositions (of, to, in, on), articles (the, a, an), and coordinating conjunctions (or, but, and). Follow up by having each student write and capitalize three titles of his own on the back of the page, using the highlighted page for help.

Capitalized Conversations
Using capitals in direct quotations

All aboard for an activity that reminds students to capitalize the first word in direct quotations! First, have students cut out pictures of interesting-looking people from old magazines. Collect the pictures. Then divide students into groups of three. Give each group three pictures, glue, a sheet of lined paper, and a colorful 12" x 18" sheet of construction paper. Direct each group member to choose a cutout and a character name. Next, have the group brainstorm a conversation that could take place among its cutout characters. Review with students that the first word in a direct quote must be capitalized. Then instruct the group to record its characters' dialogue on the lined paper, with each child writing the lines of his character. After each group glues its characters and written dialogue to the construction paper, allow it to share its paper with the class. Then post the papers on a bulletin board titled "People Are Talking."

"Hey, Jake and Benji! I've got a surprise for you!" called Dad.

"What is it, Dad?" questioned Jake.

Benji asked, "Yeah, what is it, Dad?"

"Well, it's black and white," Dad hinted, "and has a leash."

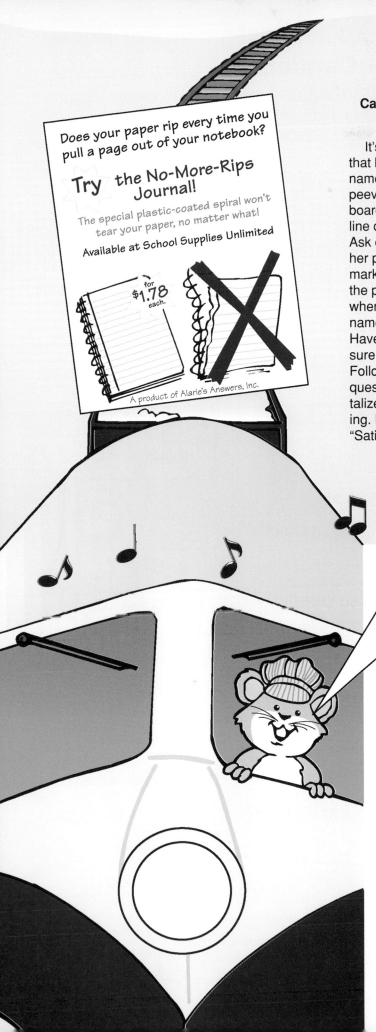

Satisfaction Guaranteed!

Capitalizing business and product names and a letter's heading, salutation, and closing

It's full steam ahead when students create advertisements that have them learning to capitalize business and product names! Begin by asking students to brainstorm frustrating pet peeves or irritating tasks. Record students' responses on the board. Next, announce that a new company is introducing a line of products that are guaranteed to end such annoyances. Ask each child to think of a name for a product that could solve her problem. Then give her a sheet of construction paper and markers for creating a colorful advertisement that not only lists the product's name, manufacturer, and features, but a store where the product could be found. Remind students that the names of businesses and products should be capitalized. Have each child trade her completed ad with a partner to make sure the business and product names are capitalized correctly. Follow up by having each child write a business letter asking a question about her partner's product. Remind students to capitalize each word in the salutation and the first word in the closing. Finally, post the ads and letters on a bulletin board titled "Satisfaction Guaranteed!"

(sung to the tune of "If You're Happy and You Know It")

If it's a special person, place, or thing,
Capitalize it!
If it's a book, song, or magazine,
Capitalize it!
If it names a state or city,
Then forget the itty bitty.
If it names a big committee,
Capitalize it!

Capitalize It!

Reviewing capitalization rules

Looking for a fun way to review capitalization rules? Invite students to create jazzy jingles about the rules to the tunes of familiar songs. Begin by writing on a transparency a verse about capitalization rules and inviting students to sing along with you (see the example shown). Next, divide students into small groups and guide each group to write its own verse about capitalization rules and copy it onto a transparency. After collecting the completed jingles, display them one at a time and lead the class in a rollicking sing-along review!

At a Loss for Capitals

Marvin wrote an essay about his family's beach trip. But he forgot to use capital letters! Read Marvin's essay and circle the words that should be capitalized. Then write the essay correctly on another sheet of paper. Can you find all 45 mistakes?

my trip to the beach

by marvin m. mouse

last june, my family went to long beach. we stayed at the sands hotel on ocean drive. we walked to the beach every day. one day, we were almost the only ones there. so dad said, "this is like having our own private beach!" we ate a lot of great food on the trip. we had cheeseburgers at b. j.'s surfin' grill. the fishnet had great seafood. i loved the cheesy shrimp and grits! we had cheese sticks at dana's diner because mom read about how good it was in *beach life*. friday was our last day at the beach. we went for a ride on a boat called the *luna*. the *luna* had a glass bottom, so we could see the fish swimming under us! after the boat ride, we made sand castles. i heard that there is a sand castle contest at the beach every year on the fourth of july. maybe we can do that next summer!

Bonus Box: On the back of this page, write three sentences about a place you have visited. Include at least seven words that should be capitalized.

Movin' On Down the Track!

Oops! This track isn't ready for a train yet! Help finish the track by writing a complete sentence to answer each question below. Check your answers to make sure you used capital letters correctly.

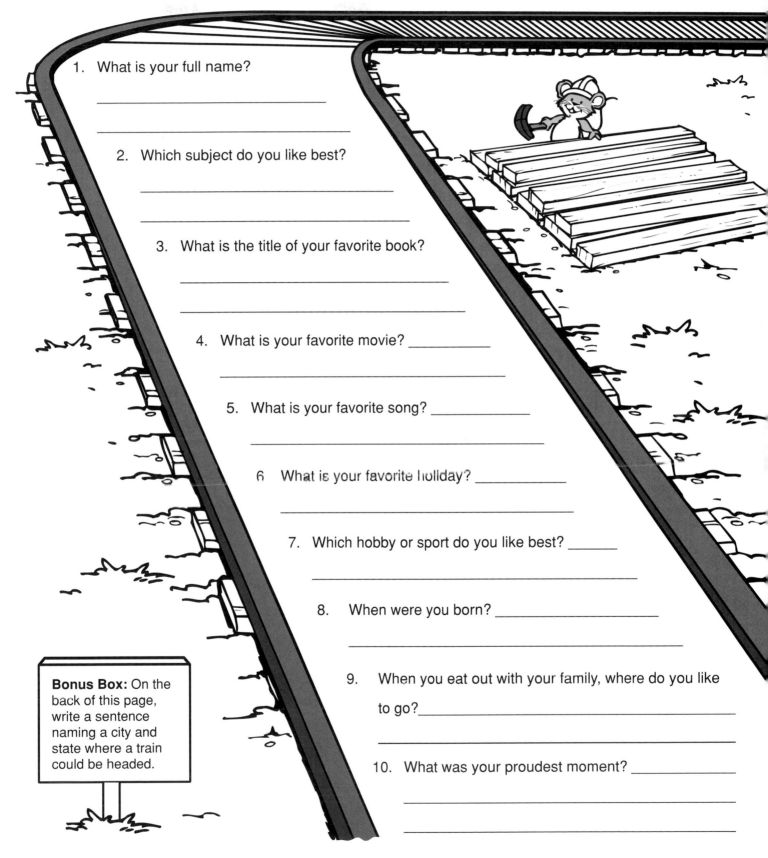

1. What is your full name?

_____

_____

2. Which subject do you like best?

_____

_____

3. What is the title of your favorite book?

_____

_____

4. What is your favorite movie? _____

_____

5. What is your favorite song? _____

_____

6. What is your favorite holiday? _____

_____

7. Which hobby or sport do you like best? _____

_____

8. When were you born? _____

_____

9. When you eat out with your family, where do you like to go?_____

_____

10. What was your proudest moment? _____

_____

_____

Bonus Box: On the back of this page, write a sentence naming a city and state where a train could be headed.

Fishing for Great Comma Activities!

Angling for new ways to give students practice with commas?
Reel in the catch of the day with these creative ideas!
by Julia Ring Alarie, Pierce Memorial School, Huntington, VT

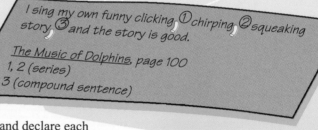

I sing my own funny clicking, ①chirping, ②squeaking
story, ③and the story is good.

The Music of Dolphins, page 100
1, 2 (series)
3 (compound sentence)

Comprehensive Comma Committees
Identifying comma uses

Cast a wide net when it comes to having students
identify different comma uses! Divide students into small groups and declare each
one a Comma Committee. Provide each committee with markers, five 6" x 18" strips
of construction paper, glue, and a handful of uncooked elbow macaroni. Review with
students common ways of using commas: in a series of words or phrases, in compound
sentences, with direct quotations, with direct address, after introductory words or phrases,
in large numbers, in dates and addresses, and to set off appositives and interjections.
Next, assign each committee the task of finding five different examples of comma usage
in their texts, library books, or other classroom materials. Instruct the group to copy each
example without the commas on a paper strip and list the source. Then have the group glue
a macaroni piece on the paper to show the location of each comma, number each one, and
identify its use (see the example). To showcase the strips, display them along with a list of
comma uses on a bulletin board titled "Comma Committee Findings."

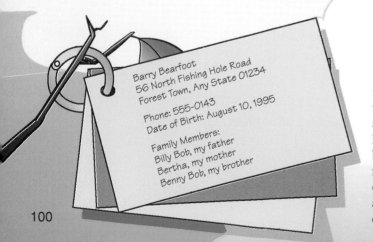

Barry Bearfoot
56 North Fishing Hole Road
Forest Town, Any State 01234

Phone: 555-0143
Date of Birth: August 10, 1995

Family Members:
Billy Bob, my father
Bertha, my mother
Benny Bob, my brother

Addressing Comma Usage
Using commas in dates and addresses

Looking for a practical way for students to review commas
in dates and addresses? Have students make information cards
that you can then use! Review comma placement in dates and
addresses. Then give each student a colorful index card and have
him carefully print on it his name, address, phone number, and
birthdate. If desired, have the student also list his family members,
reminding him to set off appositives with commas. Collect the
cards and alphabetize them. Once you punch a hole in each card
and bind them with a metal ring, you'll have a handy source of
data right at your fingertips!

"Comma-plimentary" Practice
Using commas in direct address

Promote positive interactions *and* proper comma usage with this simple yet memorable activity! Review with students that a noun in direct address is set off from the rest of a sentence with a comma (or commas). Next, give each child a copy of your roster and direct her to write a complimentary sentence to each classmate, setting off the classmate's name with commas. After checking the sentences for appropriateness, have each child copy her compliments onto 2" x 9" strips of colorful construction paper. Collect the strips and sort them by student. Then give each child her set of compliments, a blank strip to use for a cover, a brad, and access to a hole puncher. Have her assemble her strips into a booklet and personalize its cover to create a memento that is destined to become a keepsake!

Bonnie, you are the friendliest bear in the forest!

"Comma-dy" Relief
Using commas in a series

Add humor to your next lesson on using commas in a series with this laugh-out-loud partner activity! Type sentences, such as the ones shown below, on a sheet of paper (do not add commas). Cut the sentences into strips. Then give each twosome a sentence, a sheet of construction paper, and crayons or markers. Instruct the duo to copy its sentence on one side of the construction paper and add intentionally misplaced commas to give the sentence a hilarious meaning. Have the partners illustrate the sentence on the back of the paper. When they are finished, invite each set of partners to read its wacky sentence aloud, share the illustration, and challenge their classmates to write and punctuate the sentence correctly.

I had a potato, a pancake fruit salad, fish ice cream, and some cookies for dinner.

We had cheese pizza nachos cake chocolate bananas ice cream sodas and apple juice at the party.
I got a robot toy dog bed bugs sour candy socks bubble gum CDs and sunglasses for my birthday.
Seth and I both like eating jelly worms dogs skateboarding books video games and camping.
We read a story about a forest stomping giants white-tailed deer miniature houses hiking and pup tents.
I love horses riding my bike my hamster playing cards painting my family and cats.
We saw clowns flying trapeze artists dancing elephants skipping poodles and roaring lions at the circus.
Mom and I saw dancing ladies hats potting soil boxes racing cars parking lots and trees.
I'll never forget the first time I saw a hot dog stand honor guards jumping beans and lightning.

Clearing Up Comma Confusion
Using commas with interjections and appositives

End any confusion your students have about using commas with interjections and appositives with this rousing class game! Review that mild interjections and appositives are set off from the rest of a sentence with commas. Next, have each student write a simple sentence on a piece of paper. Collect the sentences and divide students into teams of four or five. Then appoint a recorder for each team and follow the steps shown.

Steps:

1. Read a student-written sentence aloud. Then say, "Add a mild interjection."
2. Have each team decide how to make the addition and have its recorder write the sentence on paper.
3. Direct a volunteer from each team to copy its sentence on the board. If the sentence is correct, give that team five points. If not, award no points. Then have each volunteer return to his team.
4. Read aloud a different sentence. This time say, "Add an appositive." Then repeat Steps 2 and 3.
5. Continue play in this manner for several rounds. Then declare the team with the most points the winner.

Oh, I forgot to wear my new fishing hat!

Like Bernie, your brother, you'd forget your head if it wasn't attached to your body!

We have commas for every possible need: separating words in a list, setting off introductory words, separating compound sentences…. You name it, we've got it!

Come on down to the Colossal Comma Warehouse!

Comma Commercials
Reviewing rules for comma usage

Bring students' understanding of comma usage into the spotlight with this fun activity. First, tell students that the Prominent Punctuation Production Company (PPPC) has hired them to create compelling comma commercials that advertise a comma's varied and wonderful uses. After reviewing rules for comma usage with students, divide them into small groups. Direct each group to create a one- to two-minute commercial that advertises comma usage. Encourage each group to include a catchy song or ditty, props, art, or sound effects to make its commercial really sell comma usage. When everyone is ready, have each group perform its commercial for the CEO of the PPPC (you) and your board of directors (the rest of the class). If desired, videotape each group's presentation and share the tape with other classes!

Name _____

The Fishin' Is Fine!

It's a perfect day for fishing, and the bear cubs can't wait to throw out their lines! Read each sentence of their conversation. If the sentence is correct, color the bobber in the yes column. If the sentence is not correct, color the bobber in the no column.

	Yes	No
1. Bert, bragged "I've got the best bait ever!"	A	T
2. Bertha asked, "What makes you say that?"	K	I
3. "It cost $5.00 a jar" Bert answered.	E	I
4. "And," Bert added, "it's guaranteed to attract fish."	M	U
5. "Hold on, I'm getting a bite," Bertha said.	D	I
6. Bert checked his line and asked ", Are you sure?"	R	A
7. "I haven't felt a nibble all morning," Bert added.	H	N
8. Bertha squealed "Look at this! I've caught three fish!"	B	F
9. Bert, asked "What bait are you using?"	S	C
10. Bertha replied "Worms from my garden."	R	G
11. "Hmm," Bert said. "I haven't caught any fish with my new bait."	Y	L
12. Bert asked shyly "Could I have one of your worms?"	G	J

The cubs' cousin, Benny, got to the fishing hole late. To find out why he was late, write the uncolored letter for each number in the matching blank.

He lost his " __ __ __ __ - __ __ __ __ " !
              8   3   1 10   5   7 12   9

Bonus Box: Write the incorrect sentences above correctly on another sheet of paper.

In the Spotlight!

Read each sentence below. Add commas where they are needed. Then color the spotlight by the code to show why you added each comma.

1. We finished play practice early so I still had time to ride my bike.

2. Sandra the best singer in the choir will play the lead role.

3. Ty did you find a costume?

4. We read over our lines found our spots on stage and began practice.

5. After practice we had pizza.

6. We have to wear white shirts black pants and black shoes for the final act.

7. Mrs. Jones our drama teacher said we are almost ready to perform.

8. Mrs. Jones I found a costume!

9. During the first act there are nine actors on the stage.

10. Our first show will be November 13 2004.

11. We will perform at the Smith Center on Thursday Friday Saturday and Sunday.

12. The Smith Center is at 2103 Cowan Road Ogden Utah.

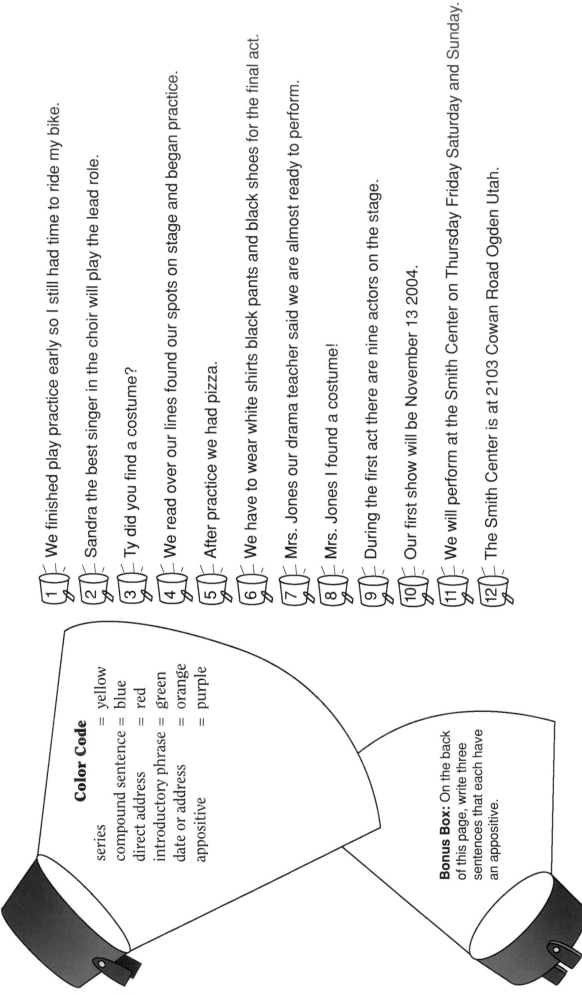

Color Code

series	= yellow
compound sentence	= blue
direct address	= red
introductory phrase	= green
date or address	= orange
appositive	= purple

Bonus Box: On the back of this page, write three sentences that each have an appositive.

MIXING IT UP
With Multiple-Meaning Words

Looking for just the right ingredients to help students understand multiple-meaning words? Try these delectable ideas!

by Julia Ring Alarie, Pierce Memorial School, Huntington, VT

Multiple-Meaning Melodies

Using multiple-meaning words, writing rhymes

Here's lyrical practice with multiple-meaning words that students won't soon forget! Copy on a poster the verse and chorus below and have students sing along with you. Afterward, point out that the word *rest* has two different meanings in the song. After discussing the meanings, divide students into groups of three. Help each trio think of a word that has at least two different meanings (see the list of suggestions). Next, instruct the threesome to compose its own rhyming verse for the song that uses the group's word in two different ways. Give each trio time to practice singing its verse; then have each group perform it for the class. Between verses, lead the whole class in the chorus!

(sung to the tune of "My Bonnie Lies Over the Ocean")

There's no rest from words' multiple meanings.
You might wish they'd just go away.
But words that have more than one meaning
Stay with you the rest of the day!

Chorus
Meanings, meanings,
A word may have multiple meanings.
And then you can
Use it in multiple ways.

Multiple-Meaning Words

arms	kind
bank	like
bark	mean
bat	mine
bit	pen
blow	present
case	rest
date	stick
fair	story
fan	well
file	will
hide	yard
jam	

I'm going to the Champlain Valley <u>Fair</u>.

That's not <u>fair</u>! I want to go too!

Doubleheader Practice

Writing dialogue using multiple-meaning words

Double up on skills practice with an activity that targets multiple-meaning words and writing dialogue! Display a list of the multiple-meaning words at the left. Next, have students cut out magazine pictures of two people or animals that are grouped together. Direct each child to glue a picture and two large speech bubbles to a colorful sheet of paper as shown. Then have her choose a multiple-meaning word from the list and use it to write a sentence in each speech bubble. Explain that each sentence should illustrate a different meaning of the word. Also have her underline the word in each sentence. After students share their work with the class, display the papers on a bulletin board titled "Double-Meaning Dialogues."

City Creates No-Fly Zone

Cold Season Starts Early

Lost Seal Found in Family's Car

Store Owner Complains About Change

Lack of Use Closes Bank

Club Owner Lost at Sea

Organ Found in Abandoned Building

Lawyer Wins Case

Baseball Player Steals Home

Fan Falls at Stadium

Multiple-Meaning Headlines

Using context clues to define multiple-meaning words

Can multiple-meaning words in headlines inspire students to write brief news stories? You bet they can! Pair students and provide each duo with paper and one of the headlines shown. Direct the pair to copy the headline and underline a multiple-meaning word that it contains. Next, have the partners use a dictionary to list two meanings for the word that could explain what the headline means. Then have the duo identify for each meaning a possible who, what, when, where, and why and use the information to write two brief news stories. After students share the stories, bind them into a class book titled "Extra! Extra! What Multiple-Meaning Headlines Really Mean!"

Marketing Multiple-Meaning Words

Exploring multiple-meaning words

Motivate students to explore multiple-meaning words with this billboard activity! Assign each student a different multiple-meaning word (see the list on page 105) and have her use a dictionary to find two or more of the word's meanings. Next, give the child crayons or markers and a 12" x 18" sheet of construction paper. Challenge her to design a mini billboard that proclaims the different meanings of her word. Suggest that she cut her paper into an eye-catching shape and add borders, pictures, or designs that represent her word's definitions. Set aside time for students to share their mini billboards with the class. Then display the projects on a wall titled "Marketing Multiple-Meaning Words."

PUNCH

Drink it instead of soda!
Make holes in paper!
Use it on a boxing bag!

Sorry, Wrong Meaning!

Distinguishing between a word's multiple meanings

Making greeting cards takes on a whole new meaning when multiple-meaning words are involved! Discuss with students possible ways that a multiple-meaning word could cause a misunderstanding. Allow volunteers to share their experiences. Next, explain that each child will create a greeting card that helps someone apologize for a misunderstanding caused by a multiple-meaning word. Then direct each student to select a multiple-meaning word (see the list on page 105) and use it to write a message inside a folded sheet of white paper. Then have her decorate the card using crayons or markers. Who knows? Card companies might try to hire some of your card creators!

You said, "I'll meet you at the bank."
I thought you were saying, "I'll meet you at the river bank."
I waited and waited. Instead, you were saying, "I'll meet you at First State Bank."
I'm so sorry!

I'm Sorry

What's Will leaving us?

"To Pat and Patty I leave this set of pans so that no one will pan their cookies...."

I, Will Wilson, being of sound mind, do declare this to be my true will.

To my cat, Wendy, I leave my set of ceramic mice and a table on which to set them.

Writing Will's Will

Using pairs of multiple-meaning words

Using multiple-meaning words to write the will of a really old fictional character is an activity students will definitely enjoy! Make a long scroll using a 12" x 36" strip of bulletin board paper. Label the top of the scroll with an introductory sentence such as the one shown. Then tell students that old Will Wilson is celebrating his 112th birthday this week and has decided it's finally time to write a will. Explain that Will needs a little help with the writing because he wants each sentence in the will to include a multiple-meaning word that is used in two different ways. Divide students into groups and give each group a list of multiple-meaning words (see the list on page 105). Guide the groups to brainstorm things that Will's will could include. Then have each group write five sentences to put in the will. After each group writes and edits its sentences, have a group member copy them onto the scroll and underline the multiple-meaning words. When all the groups have finished, call them together for a not-so-official reading of Will's will!

Names _____

It's a Race!

Be the first one to taste a cookie fresh from the oven!
Follow the directions to play.

Directions:
1. Each player places a game piece on Start.
2. Player 1 rolls the die and moves his game piece
   that many spaces. He writes two sentences that
   show two different meanings of the word in the
   space. If he cannot write two sentences, he moves
   back two spaces.
3. Player 2 takes a turn in the same manner.
4. Players keep taking turns until one player reaches
   Finish.

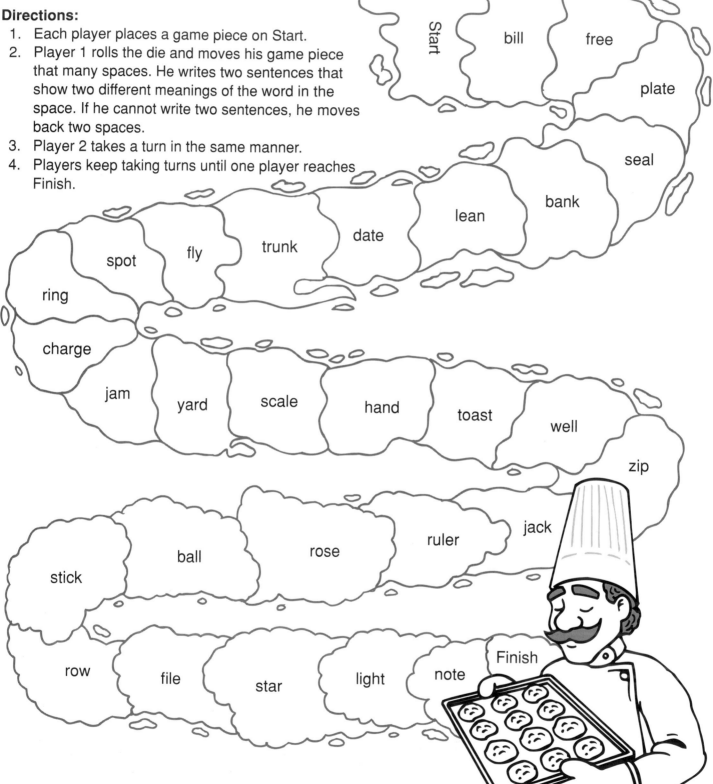

Start, bill, free, plate, seal, bank, lean, date, trunk, fly, spot, ring, charge, jam, yard, scale, hand, toast, well, zip, jack, ruler, rose, ball, stick, row, file, star, light, note, Finish

Note to the teacher: Pair students. Then give each pair a die, paper, pencils, two game pieces, and a copy of this page.

Pour In the Right Chips!

Read each pair of sentences below. Find the word on a chocolate chip that can take the place of both underlined words. Write the word on the line provided. Shade the chip after you use its word. Some chips will not be shaded.

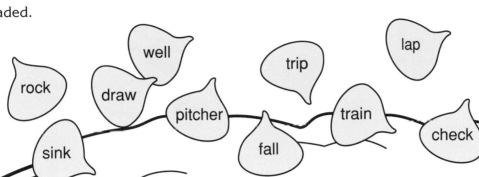

rock   well   draw   trip   lap   bear   pitcher   train   sink   fall   check   break

1. The <u>beast</u> crashed through the brush.
   Ben can't <u>stand</u> the pain of his sprained ankle. _____

2. Sophie is going to <u>teach</u> her dog to catch a tennis ball.
   They took the <u>locomotive</u> all the way to Chicago. _____

3. Chris doesn't feel <u>healthy</u>.
   When the power went out, Toby slept <u>far</u> past the time
   to get up. _____

4. Did you <u>sketch</u> this picture of your dog?
   The game ended in a <u>tie</u>. _____

5. The runner ran a <u>circle</u> around the track.
   Did you see Bowser <u>slurp</u> the water from his bowl? _____

6. Theo bumped the table, causing the lamp to <u>sway</u>.
   This <u>stone</u> is part crystal. _____

7. The <u>baseball player</u> had a perfect game.
   The <u>container</u> is full of tea. _____

8. Dana was careful not to <u>fall</u> over the loose stone.
   Jackson wrote about his summer <u>journey</u> to Texas. _____

9. After dinner, Grace put all of the dishes in the <u>basin</u>.
   Tina watched the coin <u>drop</u> to the bottom of the pool. _____

10. Mr. Jones always asks for the <u>bill</u> when we eat out.
    Before riding, Phil stopped to <u>inspect</u> his bike's tires. _____

Bonus Box: On the back of this page, write a pair of sentences that show two different meanings of *bark*.

Spotting Cause and Effect

Once you spot this collection of creative activities, teaching cause and effect will have an added spark!

by Beth Gress, Highland Central Elementary, Sparta, OH

The Domino Effect

Recognizing cause and effect

Grab a set of dominoes to show students a concrete example of cause and effect! Stand dominoes on their ends, about an inch apart. Allow a volunteer to push over the first domino. Ask the class what caused the event *(the push)* and what was the effect *(the dominoes fell down)*.

Next, read aloud a picture book that shows a cause-and-effect relationship, such as the ones shown. When you finish, tape a row of index cards to the chalkboard and draw an arrow between each card. Then ask students to name an event that happened in the beginning of the book. Invite a volunteer to write the event on the first card. Have students tell what happened to trigger that event or explain what happened as a result of that event. Allow another child to label the second card with the response. Continue the process until a chain of causes and effects (the story's main events) have been listed on the cards. Keep the chain posted somewhere in the classroom as a visual reminder of cause and effect. *Paula Odom—Gr. 4, Bob Hope Elementary, San Antonio, TX*

A mouse is given a cookie. → The mouse asks for a glass of milk. → The mouse is given the milk. → The mouse asks for a straw. →

Books That Show Cause-and-Effect Relationships
If You Give a Mouse a Cookie by Laura Joffe Numeroff
If You Give a Pig a Pancake by Laura Joffe Numeroff
If You Give a Moose a Muffin by Laura Joffe Numeroff
The Runaway Bunny by Margaret Wise Brown
Stone Soup by Marcia Brown

Unlocking Cause and Effect

Using key words to identify cause and effect

Give students the keys they need to unlock cause and effect! Write the following sentence on the board: "We were late because my mom couldn't find the car keys." Invite a volunteer to identify the cause *("…my mom couldn't find the car keys")* and the effect *("we were late…")*. Next, ask the class what key word indicates that the sentence has a cause-and-effect structure *(because)*. Then explain that there are other words that identify cause-and-effect relationships. Write on the board the list shown and review it with the class. Have volunteers use each word or phrase in a sentence.

Next, direct each child to write ten similar sentences using a key word or phrase from the list in each one. When the student finishes, give her two different-colored highlighters and have her trade papers with a partner. Instruct her to read each sentence and highlight the cause in one color and the effect in the other. Then have the student return the paper to its owner. Finally, invite several students to share their sentences with the class and have volunteers identify each one's cause and effect.

Signal Words and Phrases

as a result of	if…then
because of	may be due to
consequently	therefore
effect of	thus
for this reason	

Match!

The moon has no clouds or weather.

There is no water or water vapor on the moon.

Planets reflect the light of the sun or other stars.

Planets shine but do not give off light.

Cause-and-Effect Matchup

Matching a cause to its effect

Causes and effects will meet their match in this small-group game! Write several topics from current units of study on the board. Give each child eight index cards (or four index cards cut in half). Direct the student to write a cause related to one of the topics on one card and its matching effect on another. Have her repeat the process with her remaining cards. Next, instruct her to separate the causes from the effects. Then divide students into groups of four or five. Have each group combine and shuffle its cards and then spread them facedown. To play, guide the group through the directions shown.

Directions:
1. One player turns four cards faceup.
2. All players examine the words to find a matching cause and effect. The first player to spot one says, "Match!" Then he picks up the cards and reads them aloud.
3. If everyone agrees that the match is correct, the player making the match keeps the two cards, and another player turns two more cards faceup. If the cards do not match, the player replaces the cards faceup and the group tries again to make a match.
4. If a match cannot be made with the faceup cards, a player turns two more cards at a time faceup until one can be made.
5. Play continues in this manner until all the cards have been won or time is up. The player with the most cards at the end wins.

Picturing Cause and Effect

Developing cause-and-effect relationships

Help students develop a picture-perfect understanding of cause and effect with this picture strip–producing activity! Have each child cut a picture from an old magazine. Ask her to think of the object or situation shown in the picture as either a cause or an effect. For example, a boy swinging a baseball bat could be used to show why a window has been broken (a cause) or the result of making the baseball team (an effect). Next, give the child a 5½" x 14" strip of paper to divide into two or three sections. Explain that she will use the sections to create a comic strip. Have her glue her magazine picture in one frame, representing either the cause or the effect. In the remaining frame(s), have her illustrate the cause(s) leading up to the event or the subsequent event(s) it caused. If desired, have the child add dialogue to the illustrations. Set aside time for students to share their picture strips with the class. Then post the strips on a bulletin board titled "Picturing Cause and Effect."

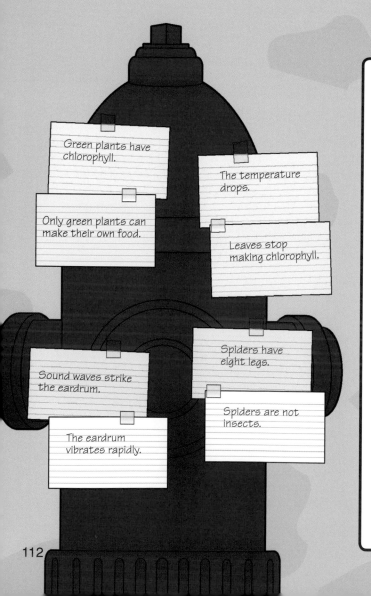

Green plants have chlorophyll.

The temperature drops.

Only green plants can make their own food.

Leaves stop making chlorophyll.

Spiders have eight legs.

Sound waves strike the eardrum.

Spiders are not insects.

The eardrum vibrates rapidly.

Cause-and-Effect Circles

Writing cause-and-effect statements

You'll have students moving in the right circles with this cause-and-effect activity! Divide students into two groups. Give each child in Group 1 two index cards: one blue, one green. Give each child in Group 2 two index cards: one pink, one white. Next, pair each student with another child from his group. Instruct each pair to write two sets of cause-and-effect statements about a current unit of study or a class read-aloud. Direct Group 1's pairs to write their cause statements on the blue cards and their effect statements on the green ones. Instruct Group 2's pairs to write their cause statements on the pink cards and their effect statements on the white ones. Check the cards to make sure the statements are appropriate and not too challenging.

Next, collect the cards from both groups and divide them separately into two sets: effect cards together in one set and cause cards in another. Shuffle each set. Give one pink and one white card to each child in Group 1. Give one blue and one green card to each child in Group 2. Direct the student to hold the cause card in his left hand and the effect card in his right. Then have him rotate through his group to find a match. When he does, have him stay with that child but continue rotating until each has found the match for his other card and the group is standing in a circle ready to read its cards aloud.

Domino Duos

Dana and Damon are trying to tell each other about their busy day. Help them fill in the missing details.

Directions: Read the cause or effect sentence on each domino. Then think of a matching cause or effect statement and write it in the space provided. Make sure your statement makes sense. The first one has been done for you.

1. **Cause**
Dana helped her mom make dinner.

Effect
She got 30 extra minutes of TV time.

2. **Cause**

Effect
Damon had to change his clothes.

3. **Cause**
Everyone in Dana's class turned in the homework.

Effect

4. **Cause**
At the baseball game, Damon hit a home run.

Effect

5. **Cause**

Effect
Dana had wet feet for the rest of the day.

6. **Cause**
Damon finished his homework early.

Effect

7. **Cause**

Effect
Dana made an *A* on her math test.

8. **Cause**

Effect
Damon dropped his food tray at lunch.

Bonus Box: Write a paragraph about your day on the back of this page. Include at least four cause-and-effect statements.

Because of Plants

Directions: Read the passage below about plants. Then highlight each cause phrase in yellow and each effect phrase in green. Use the words in the box to help you.

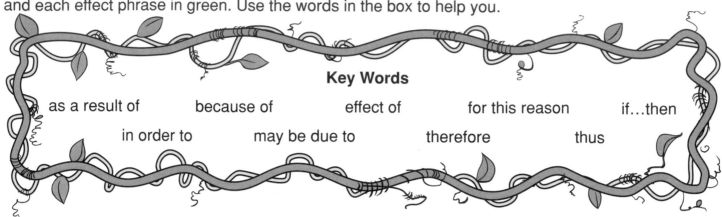

Key Words

as a result of	because of	effect of	for this reason	if…then
in order to	may be due to	therefore	thus	

Plants are needed for life on Earth. They provide food for many living things. We need plants because they are a major part of our food chain. Animals at the bottom of the food chain eat plants. These animals can be eaten by other ones. We eat plants and animals.

Providing food is not the only way plants help us. Most plants make their own food. In order to do this, they use water, sunlight, minerals, and carbon dioxide. The process makes glucose and oxygen. The plant uses the glucose for food and releases the oxygen into the air. Therefore, humans and animals can breathe.

Many plants produce seeds. If the seeds scatter, then new plants can grow. For this reason, many seeds have special parts. Some have small hooks. The hooks stick to animal fur and the seed is moved from one place to another. Other seeds have parts that act like wings. As a result, these seeds can be carried by the wind. Some plants can only release their seeds in extreme heat. One effect of a forest fire is that some pine tree seeds burst from their cones. These features may be due to plants adapting to their climate and setting.

When a plant dies, it breaks down and returns nutrients to the soil. Thus, dying plants help new plants grow.

Note to the teacher: Each student will need a yellow and a green highlighter to complete this page.

Analyze This!

Activities for Analyzing Literary Characters

Theo Mindfulman

Psychoanalyst

Thoroughly examine a character's words, actions, thoughts, and feelings with these creative activities!

by Elizabeth H. Lindsay, Greensboro, NC

Profiling Personalities
Identifying character traits, classifying characters

Pinpoint a character's personality type with this trait-profiling activity! Review that an individual's personality is all of the special traits that make him different from others. Also review that characters are often classified either as *protagonists,* the main characters, or as *antagonists,* characters in opposition to the main characters. Next, brainstorm with the class a list of familiar book characters, helping students choose characters of both types without identifying which type they are. Afterward, pair students and assign each duo a character from the list. Have each twosome complete a copy of page 118 based on its assigned character. When everyone is finished, have the pair fold a sheet of 12" x 18" light-colored construction paper in half and trim it to resemble a file folder. Then direct the duo to cut out the profile, glue it inside the folder, and add an illustration of the character, as shown. After the pairs share their profiles with the class, post them on a display titled "Personality Profiles: Our Professional Opinions!"

I See Your Point (of View)!
Identifying a character's perspective, comparing characters' points of view

This is how I see it.

Instill insight about a character's behavior with this thought-provoking activity! Gather several pairs of inexpensive plastic eyeglasses. Also, discuss with students how a character's thoughts, feelings, words, and actions help the reader understand the character's perspective. Next, have students identify the main characters from a recent story or novel. In addition, select a story event that involves at least two of the main characters; then choose a different student to portray each character. Have each chosen student put on a pair of glasses and retell the event from his character's point of view, using clues from the character's thoughts, feelings, words, and actions for help. Repeat the process using different characters and events. Finally, discuss the different events and perspectives that were portrayed. Guide students to realize that understanding a character's point of view is a key part of comprehending the story.

Character: <u>Brian Robeson</u>
The Prognosis: <u>I predict Brian will face</u>
<u>a winter storm before he is rescued.</u>

A Predictable Prognosis
Making predictions and judgments
about a character's behavior

What's the key to making a good prognosis? Examining all the evidence, of course! Read aloud from a current class novel an event that involves the book's main character. Ask students to listen for details about the character's thoughts, feelings, words, and actions during and after the event. Afterward, discuss with the class what the evidence reveals about the character and whether the character responds as expected. Next, give each student scissors, glue, markers, and two sheets of drawing paper. Challenge each child to select a different story event and predict the character's response to it. To display her prediction, have her create a colorful drawing of a large paper doll. Instruct her to write her predictions of how the character will react on the four body parts shown and then cover them with camouflaged paper flaps. When students are finished, invite each child to share her character's prognosis with the class!

Prescription for Confronting Conflict
Identifying traits that affect a character's response to conflict

Understanding a character's response to conflict is in the bag with this activity! In advance, gather a supply of paper lunch bags. After finishing a story or novel, have the class generate a list of problems faced by the main character; record them on the board. Circle one problem and have students identify traits that helped or could help the character solve it. Invite the class to rate each trait's importance on a scale of one to five, with five being the most important. Explain how each rating can be thought of as the dosage a doctor prescribes for an ailing patient. Next, write each unsolved problem on a different paper bag. Then pair students and give each twosome scissors and a copy of page 119. Have the partners complete the page as directed and then place the completed prescription forms in the appropriate bags. To find out what the doctors ordered, share several prescriptions from each bag with the class!

Little Willy needs to win a race to save his grandfather's farm.

Rx for Confronting Conflict
Patient: <u>Little Willy</u>
Ailment: <u>He needs to win a race</u>
<u>to save his grandfather's farm.</u>
Remedy: <u>Lots of courage</u>

Dosage: <u>Take five teaspoons of</u>
<u>courage daily</u>
Doctor: <u>Brent</u>

See the colorful character analysis poster in this issue!

Can Characters Change?
Recognizing a change in a character

If your students struggle with recognizing how characters change, help is on the way! Using a familiar story, brainstorm with students a list of the main character's traits to record on the board. Have the class identify whether each trait is present at the story's beginning or end. If the trait represents a change, discuss with students the reasons why it changes. Afterward, pair students. Have each twosome list on paper the traits of the main character from a recent class novel and identify those that change. Next, distribute the materials listed and guide each twosome through the steps shown to chart the observed change. Then invite the partners to present their completed projects to the class. Yes, characters can change!

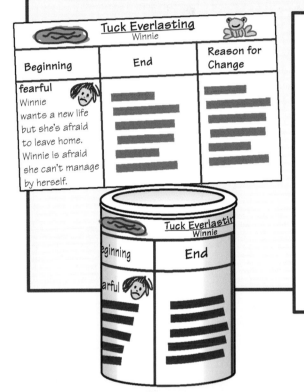

Materials for each pair: 12" x 18" sheet of light-colored construction paper, ruler, scissors, colored pencils or markers, transparent tape, large cylinder (such as an oatmeal container)

Steps:
1. Cut the construction paper so that it will completely cover the container when taped.
2. Write the book's title and the main character's name across the top of the page. Divide the paper into three sections. Label each section as shown. Add illustrations around the title.
3. In the chart's first section, write a trait the character possesses at the beginning of the book. Include two examples to support your idea. Draw a picture or symbol to represent the trait.
4. In the chart's second section, repeat Step 3, using a trait the character shows at the end of the book.
5. In the third section, explain why the change occurs.
6. Wrap the paper around the container and secure the ends with tape.

What's the Diagnosis, Doc?
Analyzing the causes of a character's actions

Give a character's motives a thorough checkup with this simple small-group activity. After reading a class story or novel, divide students into groups of four. Give each group a sheet of paper on which to draw a chart such as the one shown. Next, direct each group to record four important story events that the main character encounters and her reaction to each one. Then instruct the group to analyze why the character reacts to the first event the way she does. Have one groupmate record the group's diagnosis on the chart. Repeat the process for each remaining event, using a different recorder each time. Conclude by inviting each group to share one of its carefully examined diagnoses with the class.

File Folder Pattern

Use with "Profiling Personalities" on page 115.

Personality Type

☐ Protagonist

☐ Antagonist

Explanation (supporting details from the

story): _____

_____

_____

_____

_____

_____

_____

Character name: _____

Male ☐   Female ☐   Age ☐

Physical traits: _____

_____

_____

Habits: _____

_____

Behaviors: _____

_____

Attitudes and feelings: _____

_____

Hopes, dreams, and goals: _____

_____

©The Education Center, Inc. • *The Mailbox*® • TEC44016 • Dec./Jan. 2004–5

Problem-Solving Prescriptions

Problems are a part of life, even for a book character! Use character traits to treat a patient's ailment (solve the character's problem).

Directions for each form:
1. Write the name of the patient.
2. Describe an ailment the patient faces.
3. For a remedy, list a trait (medicine) the patient uses or could use to treat the ailment.
4. Rate the medicine, using a scale from 1 to 5 (with 5 being the most important). For the dosage (solution), write a sentence using the rating number to explain how much and when to take the medicine.
5. Write your name as the doctor.

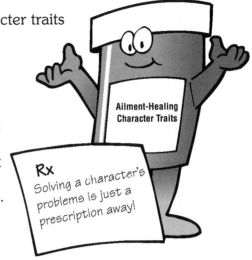

Ailment-Healing Character Traits

Rx
Solving a character's problems is just a prescription away!

Rx for Confronting Conflict

Patient: _____

Ailment: _____

_____

Remedy: _____

_____

Dosage: _____

_____

Doctor: _____

Rx for Confronting Conflict

Patient: _____

Ailment: _____

_____

Remedy: _____

_____

Dosage: _____

_____

Doctor: _____

Rx for Confronting Conflict

Patient: _____

Ailment: _____

_____

Remedy: _____

_____

Dosage: _____

_____

Doctor: _____

Rx for Confronting Conflict

Patient: _____

Ailment: _____

_____

Remedy: _____

_____

Dosage: _____

_____

Doctor: _____

Bonus Box: Think of a problem you could have this week. On another sheet of paper, write your own prescription for solving it.

Note to the teacher: Use with "Prescription for Confronting Conflict" on page 116.

Making an Authors' Quilt

Sew up students' interest in authors with this creative project!

adapted from an idea by Patricia Altmann, Yonkers, NY

Materials for each pair of students: copy of page 121, four 6" squares of light-colored cotton cloth, access to fabric markers and research materials

Getting Started

Enlist parent volunteers to donate materials and to sew the quilt. Gather books by well-known authors who have written at least three books. Then introduce the project to the class. Explain that pairs of students will read books by famous authors and illustrate fabric squares to make a quilt.

Reading the Books

Pair students of similar reading levels. Allow the pair about four weeks to read three books by the same author. As soon as the first book is finished, give the pair a copy of page 121. Direct the partners to complete section 2 together. As they finish each remaining book, have them complete sections 3 and 4 in the same way. Explain that the sketches should show what the pair plans to illustrate on its fabric squares. Point out that the first square should include the author's name and that each remaining square should include the author's name and a book title.

Researching the Author

When students have finished reading, have each pair use research materials to complete section 1 on page 121.

Illustrating the Fabric Squares

After students complete page 121, give each pair four fabric squares and markers. Direct the partners to refer to the sketches to draw a colorful illustration on each square.

Step 1

Step 2

Step 3

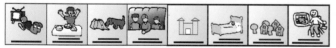

Step 4

Step 5

Making the Quilt

Provide parent volunteers with the materials and directions shown below to assemble the quilt. If there is an odd number of four-section strips (see Step 1), add blank fabric squares to even out the row. Or ask the volunteers to design their own squares. While the quilt is being made, ask each student to write a letter to the author whose books he read. In his letter, have the child share his reactions to the books, tell about the quilt project, and ask the author a question. When the quilt is finished, allow students who have received replies to stand next to the quilt and share their letters with the class.

Materials: 45" x 60" crib-size quilt batting, 45" x 60" cotton fabric for the quilt back, blanket binding, cotton thread, access to a sewing machine, cotton yarn, large gauge needle

Steps:

1. Sew each set of four squares into a strip.
2. Sew two strips together to make a row of eight.
3. Sew each row of eight together, as shown, to complete the quilt top.
4. Layer the backing fabric, batting, and quilt top. Trim excess batting and backing fabric so that the layers are the same size. Sew the blanket binding around the quilt's edges.
5. At the intersection of each four-square section, use the needle and the yarn to make a stitch down and up through all three layers. Tie the knot twice and trim the ends.

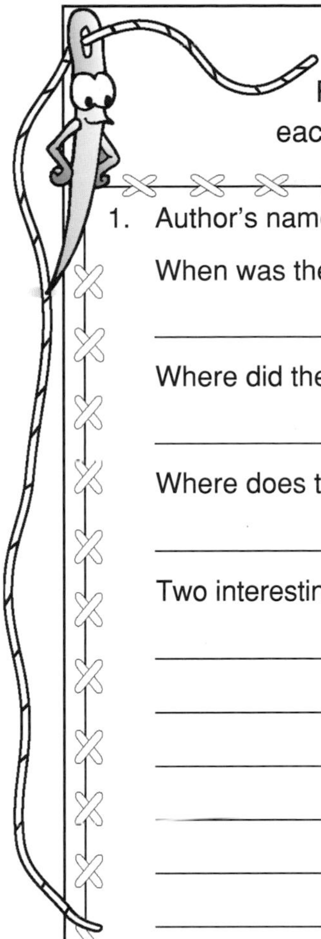

Piecing It Together

Fill in the information for each section below. Draw something in
each box that represents the book or its author.

1. Author's name: _____

   When was the author born?

   _____

   Where did the author go to school?

   _____

   Where does the author live?

   _____

   Two interesting things about the author:

   _____
   _____
   _____   [sketch]
   _____
   _____
   _____
   _____   sketch

2. Book's title: _____

   Setting: _____

   Main character(s): _____

   _____

   Problem to be solved: _____

   _____

   How problem is solved: _____

   _____

   _____
   _____   [sketch]
   _____
   _____
   _____
   _____   sketch

3. Book's title: _____

   Setting: _____

   Main character(s): _____

   _____

   Problem to be solved: _____

   _____

   How problem is solved: _____

   _____

   _____
   _____   [sketch]
   _____
   _____
   _____   sketch

4. Book's title: _____

   Setting: _____

   Main character(s): _____

   _____

   Problem to be solved: _____

   _____

   How problem is solved: _____

   _____

   _____
   _____   [sketch]
   _____
   _____
   _____   sketch

Note to the teacher: Use with "Making an Authors' Quilt" on page 120.

Reading Fluency: The

Getting students front-row seats at this award-winning show is sure to increase their reading fluency!

Kim Minafo, Dillard Drive Elementary School, Raleigh, NC

Clearly Fluent Readers
Developing fluency with reading tools

Is there a simple tool that can help your students become more fluent readers? You bet! Give each student a clear overhead transparency, a wipe-off marker, two paper clips, and a copy of a short reading passage. Direct him to paper-clip his transparency atop the passage as shown. Next, have him skim the passage and use the wipe-off marker to underline any unfamiliar words. When he is finished, instruct him to discuss with a partner the pronunciations and meanings of the underlined words. Then have him read his passage again, this time placing marks to show where pauses or breaks in the text are appropriate. After he reads through the passage several more times to establish fluency and make any additional adjustments, have him share his markings with his partner. Once he cleans his transparency, it's ready to store for future use!

Bravo!

Once upon a time...

PLAYBILL

Homework
Oh, homework, why do you take so long?
Don't you know I want to play?
Oh, homework, I don't think you belong
On such a wonderful day.

Line-by-Line Fluency
Using poetry to practice fluency

With a poem in your pocket, you can teach fluency without missing a beat! Make two copies of the same entertaining poem for each pair of students. Direct the partners to cut apart one copy of the poem line by line and then place both the cut and uncut copies in a resealable bag. Next, read the poem aloud to the class. Also discuss with students the importance of rhythm and help them determine the poem's beat. Then instruct each duo to read the uncut copy of the poem aloud to each other and use it as a guide to arrange the cut pieces in the correct order. When they are finished, have one student pick up the poem's first line and read it aloud while his partner softly counts the beats. Then have the second student pick up the poem's second line and read it aloud while the first partner softly counts the beats. Once the pairs have practiced reading the entire poem with the correct rhythm, guide the whole class to read the poem together and clap to the beat. It's as easy as 1, 2, 3!

Hottest Ticket in Town!

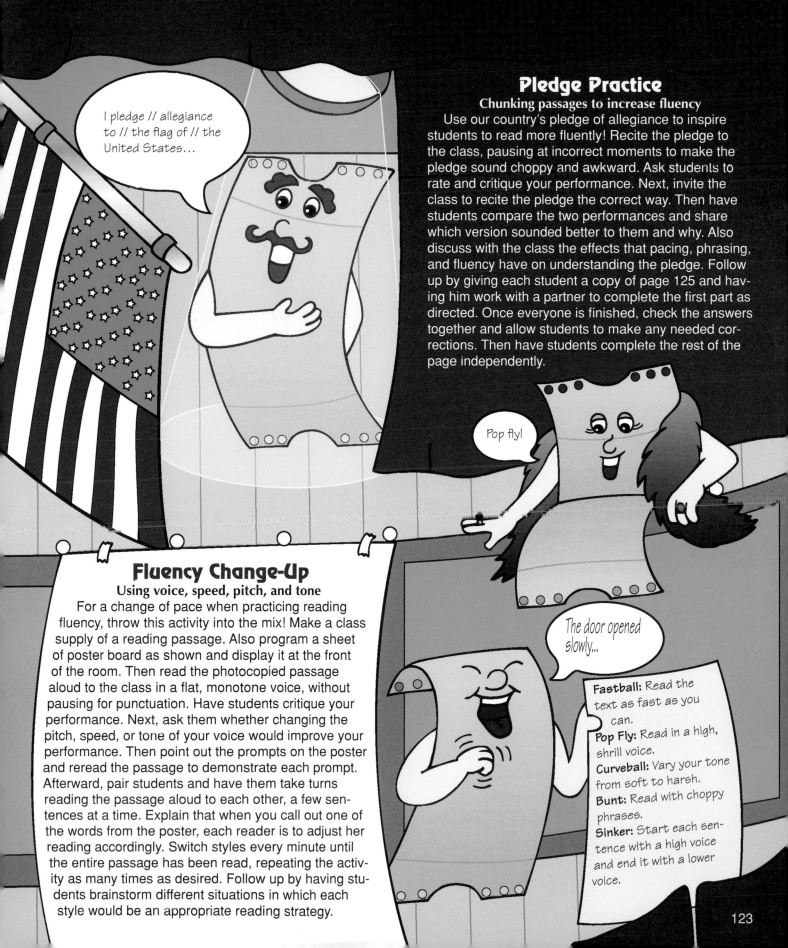

Pledge Practice
Chunking passages to increase fluency

Use our country's pledge of allegiance to inspire students to read more fluently! Recite the pledge to the class, pausing at incorrect moments to make the pledge sound choppy and awkward. Ask students to rate and critique your performance. Next, invite the class to recite the pledge the correct way. Then have students compare the two performances and share which version sounded better to them and why. Also discuss with the class the effects that pacing, phrasing, and fluency have on understanding the pledge. Follow up by giving each student a copy of page 125 and having him work with a partner to complete the first part as directed. Once everyone is finished, check the answers together and allow students to make any needed corrections. Then have students complete the rest of the page independently.

Fluency Change-Up
Using voice, speed, pitch, and tone

For a change of pace when practicing reading fluency, throw this activity into the mix! Make a class supply of a reading passage. Also program a sheet of poster board as shown and display it at the front of the room. Then read the photocopied passage aloud to the class in a flat, monotone voice, without pausing for punctuation. Have students critique your performance. Next, ask them whether changing the pitch, speed, or tone of your voice would improve your performance. Then point out the prompts on the poster and reread the passage to demonstrate each prompt. Afterward, pair students and have them take turns reading the passage aloud to each other, a few sentences at a time. Explain that when you call out one of the words from the poster, each reader is to adjust her reading accordingly. Switch styles every minute until the entire passage has been read, repeating the activity as many times as desired. Follow up by having students brainstorm different situations in which each style would be an appropriate reading strategy.

123

Rainbow Reading Assessment

Assessing oral reading

Here's a colorful tip to help you manage oral-reading assessments! On your class roster, randomly color-code students into groups of four or five. Each day, pick a different color group to evaluate. Begin by reading aloud from any student text; then pause and call, "Time out!" Explain that when students hear this prompt, each child should pick up reading where you stopped, reading aloud in a quiet voice that can only be heard by the person closest to her. While students are reading softly to their partners, move around the room, listening to individual readers from the selected color group. As you do so, write a brief progress note for each child's records or an encouraging note to place on her desk. After a few minutes say, "Time in!" to signal students to stop reading aloud so the lesson can continue as before. Assessing oral reading has never been so simple!

Laugh-Out-Loud Practice

Practicing pacing, intonation, and expression

Students will be eager to practice fluency skills if you use laugh-out-loud limericks! Ask your librarian to gather limerick books for your class. Then select a limerick to read aloud to the class. Discuss with students the limerick's rhyming pattern *(aabba)* and the rhythm and speed at which to read it. Next, have each child choose a limerick from a book, or invite her to write an original limerick of her own. Then divide students into groups and have each group practice reading its limericks aloud, focusing on fluency, tone, and expression. Finally, have each group member read her limerick aloud while the rest of the group taps to the beat. Once students are comfortable performing their limericks, send the groups to a neighboring classroom to show off their skills! For more practice, have each child complete a copy of page 126 as directed.

Chunking sentences to improve fluency

Marks of Fluency

Stella found some poems about famous American symbols. But she needs your help to read them. Use a colored pencil to divide each poem into phrases that make it easier to read and understand.

1. These men are carved in stone high above the fruited plain, and visitors come to see them from California to Maine.

2. Sweet bell of freedom, now old and worn, you cracked just as our nation was born. Years after repair, you cracked again. How you are now is how you'll remain.

3. Just beside the harbor's door stands a statue tall and sure. She welcomes the tired, the weak, and the poor. She lights the way to our country's shore.

4. A declaration told the king that freedom waited in the wings. It told him why and made it clear that England's flag would not fly here.

What famous American symbol is each poem above about?

1. _____

2. _____

3. _____

4. _____

Bonus Box: On the back of this page, write your own poem about a famous American symbol. Then practice reading it aloud to a friend.

©The Mailbox® • TEC44018 • April/May 2005 • Key p. 309

Note to the teacher: Use with "Pledge Practice" on page 123. Each student will need a colored pencil to complete this page.

Performing Lloyd's Laugh Lines

The big show is only days away, and Lloyd is having trouble with his lines!
His friend Larry is helping him practice so he'll get lots of laughs.

There is always // music in my ear. And // sometimes I hear it real // clear. But when I do not, I remove the // big clot of wax that's // been there all year!

Try it this way: There is always music in my ear. // And sometimes I hear it real clear. // But when I do not, // I remove the big clot // of wax that's been there all year!

Help Larry divide the rest of Lloyd's lines correctly. Then practice reading them aloud with a partner.

1 My younger brother wanted a pet. He said he'd take anything that he could get. But when I brought him a snake, the kid started to quake and fell to the ground in a sweat!

2 Consider yourself quite a fan? Let me tell you about my neighbor, Dan. He went opening day and decided to stay. Four months later, he's still in the stands!

3 Mrs. Wilson just visited Mars. She brought us all back candy bars that are made by wee folk who sell eggs with six yolks and carry their children in jars!

4 I once knew a man who had eyes that got larger each time he told lies. They started off small, but in no time at all, they'd grown to 50 times the normal size!

5 My sister plays music each spring. She's loud and she makes my ears ring. She's a rock and roll star, and I'm sure she'll go far, so long as she learns how to sing!

Let's Work Out!

Exercises for Improving Speaking Skills

WORKOUT WARMUP
Practicing enunciation and articulation

Grab a whistle for a tongue twister activity that will warm up students' speaking skills! Make a copy of the tongue twister cards on page 129. Cut the cards apart; then divide the class into two even groups. If necessary, join a group in order to have an even number in each group. Have one group stand in an outward-facing circle. Then give each child in the circle a tongue twister card. Next, pair students by directing each child not in the circle to face a student in the circle. Tell each pair that it will have one minute to take turns trying to say the tongue twister to each other three times in a row without making any mistakes. When time is up, blow the whistle. Direct the partner in the inner circle to pass the card to her right and the partner in the outer circle to move one person to his right. Once students have new partners, they'll have a new tongue twister to say. Continue practicing in this manner until each child is facing his original partner.

127

How strong are your students' speaking skills? Give them a hearty workout with the following activities and reproducibles!

ideas by Beth Gress, Highland Central Elementary, Sparta, OH, and
Simone Lepine, Gillette Road Middle School, Cicero, NY

EXERCISING THE FUNNY BONE
Identifying and evaluating incorrect speaking techniques

Ask your librarian to supply you with several appropriate joke books for kids. Next, make five copies of the joke on page 129. Also make one copy of the reading directions on page 129. Cut the directions apart and staple one strip to each joke copy. Next, enlist five outgoing volunteers. Give each volunteer a copy of the joke and have him practice it out of earshot of his classmates before reading it to them in the assigned way. After each child reads, have the class explain what was wrong with the delivery and what could be done to improve it. For example, if a reader speaks too softly, students could suggest that he speak loudly enough for everyone to hear. After all five readers have been evaluated, enlist a new volunteer to read the joke using the proper techniques. Follow up by having each child choose a joke from one of the joke books and practice reading it to a partner before sharing it in front of the class. Who knows—you may discover the next David Letterman!

> Read very softly so that everyone has a hard time hearing you.
>
> **Joke**
> A teacher saw a boy walking down the street with a monkey. She told the boy he should take the monkey to the zoo. "Good idea," the boy replied, and off he went. The next day the teacher saw the boy again, and he still had the monkey with him. "I thought I told you to take the monkey to the zoo," the teacher said. "I did," answered the boy, "and today I'm taking it to the movies!"

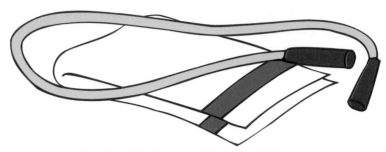

SHAPING UP SPEAKING SKILLS
Practicing correct speaking techniques

Exercise students' speaking skills by providing opportunities to perform! First, display this issue's speaking tips poster and discuss it with the class. Next, give each child a chance to practice her speaking skills in front of a friend or family member by having her make and complete a contract. Give each student scissors, glue, and a copy of page 130. Have her cut out the hand weights and glue them back to back. Then go over the directions and assign both a due date and a number of exercises for students to fill in. When each child has completed her workout and turned in her hand weight, she'll be ready to speak in front of the whole class or school by doing one of the tasks below!

- Explain to the class the correct solution to a daily math problem.
- Read aloud a journal entry in front of the class.
- Perform either a monologue by a book character, a skit that re-creates a scene from a book, or a TV commercial or radio advertisement that promotes a book.
- Make the morning announcements or lead the "Pledge of Allegiance" over the school intercom.
- Introduce a guest speaker at a school assembly.

Three free throws.

Sam's shop stocks short spotted socks.

Friendly Frank flips fine flapjacks.

We surely shall see the sun shine soon.

Fat frogs fly past fast.

Sly Sam slurps Sally's soup.

Old oily Ollie oils old oily autos.

The 2:22 train tore through the tunnel.

Twelve twins twirled 12 twigs.

Betty better butter Bonnie's bread.

Brad's big black bath brush broke.

Listen to the local lad yodel.

Joke and Reading Directions
Use with "Exercising the Funny Bone" on page 128.

Five Ways to Read the Joke

HA! HA! HA!

Joke
A teacher saw a boy walking down the street with a monkey. She told the boy he should take the monkey to the zoo. "Good idea," the boy replied, and off he went. The next day the teacher saw the boy again, and he still had the monkey with him. "I thought I told you to take the monkey to the zoo," the teacher said. "I did," answered the boy, "and today I'm taking it to the movies!"

Read very softly so that everyone has a hard time hearing you.

Read at a normal pace, but do not pause at the end of a sentence or anywhere else in the passage.

Read loudly at a very fast pace.

Read in a monotone voice, with no expression at all.

Read in an acceptable way, but shuffle your feet and sway back and forth. Keep your eyes on the paper and do not look at anyone.

Hand Weight Patterns

Use with "Shaping Up Speaking Skills" on page 128.

Speaking Skills Workout

How strong are your speaking skills? Follow the directions to give them a good workout!

Directions:

1. Complete _____ of the seven exercises by _____.
   date

2. As you complete an exercise, color its box.

3. For each exercise, have the listener sign his or her name on the signature page next to the letter of the matching exercise. Also have the person rate how well you did.

Exercises

A	Tell a parent about your school day.
B	Explain how to wrap a gift or tie a shoe.
C	Tell how to get from home to school and back.
D	Tell about a movie you watched with your family.
E	Tell about a current news event.
F	Explain why it is important for kids to do chores.
G	Tell about an embarrassing moment.

Trainer's Signature

Exercise	Signature	Rating
A		
B		
C		
D		
E		
F		
G		

Rating Scale

1 = Good job but needs more practice!
2 = Great job—understood every word!
3 = Excellent job—sounds like a pro!

Ten "Pen-tastic" Ways to Improve Journal Writing

Give your journal-writing program a boost with ten terrific tips
that can inspire in your students a lifelong love of writing!

by Daniel Kriesberg, Bayville, NY

1. Take advantage of tiny bits of time. Even if a busy class schedule leaves you with only ten minutes once a week or five minutes here and there for impromptu writing, giving students a small amount of time to write is better than none at all. Train your students to whip out their journals and begin writing whenever you say, "Journal time!"

2. Use a class journal to model journal writing. Teach students how to write in a journal by using chart paper. Ask students to call out entries one at a time for you to record. Or invite each child to come up and write his entry on the chart paper. As this is being done, explain your expectations or model one of the other tips on these pages.

3. Display and discuss the journals of other writers. Inspire students to write in their journals by showing them your own journal or one published by a famous author or scientist. Or ask friends or family members if you can share excerpts from their journals. Then discuss the different topics people write about or the writing styles they use.

4. Encourage visits to online journal sites. Suggest that students visit Web sites you have preapproved to see how some people have used journals, diaries, and letters to record memories about hiking the Appalachian Trail or traveling the Oregon Trail.

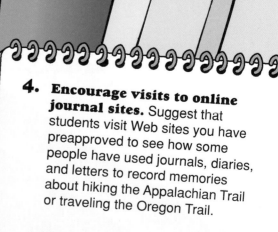

5. Share inspirational picture books. Motivate students by sharing picture books that inspire journal writing, such as *I'm in Charge of Celebrations* by Byrd Baylor and *An Island Scrapbook: Dawn to Dusk on a Barrier Island* by Virginia Wright-Frierson.

6. Suggest that students occasionally make lists. Post a list of topics such as the following: animals I have seen, places I have been, goals I'd like to reach, jokes I like, sports I play, books I have read. Then have each writer complete an entry using single words or short phrases instead of complete sentences or paragraphs.

7. Challenge students to go beyond a simple accounting of a day's events. Gently push students to dig deeper and use richer descriptions when they write in their journals. Begin by having each writer describe an everyday object such as a spoon, using as much detail as possible. The next day, ask the writer to add to her description. Then have her go back a third time and write even more. Help students understand that the closer they look, the more they will find to write about!

8. Take students outside to sharpen their senses. Have them sit under a tree and watch younger children at recess or notice insects crawling on the ground. Students could even listen to all the sounds around them or look for shapes in the clouds. Return to the same spot often so students can observe the changes that occur.

9. Permit students to add sketches and illustrations to their journals. Accept the fact that words are not the only way to record memories, thoughts, or observations. Allowing students to include drawings—even colorful ones—in their journals helps them become better observers.

10. Allow items to be glued to the pages. If a child understands that he can add personal items such as small mementos, maps, photographs, or ticket stubs to a journal, he is more likely to turn it into a treasured keepsake.

MATH UNITS

"Fin-tastic" Ways to Practice Multiplication Facts

$2 \times 3 = 6$

$1 \times 3 = 3$

$3 \times 5 = 15$

$5 \times 10 = 50$

$0 \times 4 = 0$

$4 \times 2 = 8$

$2 \times 8 = 16$

Dive into a refreshing pool of activities that are perfect for practicing multiplication facts and can be adapted for other facts as well!

What Time Is It?

Practicing multiplication facts is just a tick away with this timely activity! Announce that several times during the school day you will ask, "What time is it?" Explain that when this happens, you will call on someone to find the product of the two numbers the hands on the classroom clock are pointing to (or are closest to). For example, at 9:15 A.M., the clock's hands point to 9 and 3, so a student would say, "Nine times three equals 27." At first, ask the question two or three times each hour. Then taper off to several times a week. With digital clocks, have students multiply the hour by the minute's tens-place digit and then by its ones-place digit. So what time is it? *Rebecca McCright—Gr. 5, Henderson Elementary, Midland, TX*

Nine times three equals 27.

Rollin' With the Facts

What do multiplication flash cards, a die, index cards, plus a small group of students add up to? Piles of fun facts practice! Begin by drawing a different die face on each of six index cards. Arrange the flash cards in six piles and place an index card atop each pile. Next, have a child roll the die and take a flash card from the rolled number's pile. Direct the child to read the card aloud and say its product. If correct, allow the player to keep the card. If incorrect, instruct him to place the card at the bottom of that number's pile. Then have the next player roll the die and take his turn. If there are no more cards in the rolled number's pile, a player loses his turn. When all cards have been claimed, declare the player with the most cards the winner! *Sharyn Jontz, Winter Park, FL*

Multiplication War

Declare all-out war on multiplication facts with this competitive card game! Pair students. Have each player stack ten flash cards, equation side up, in front of her. Instruct Player A to place her top card in the middle of the table, read its fact, and say its product. Player B turns the card over to check the answer. Player B takes her turn in a similar manner. The player whose card has the greater product gets to keep both cards. If the cards' products are equal, have the players declare war by stacking four cards each in the center of the table and using only the products of the fourth cards to break the tie. Direct both players to return those cards to the bottom of their piles. Then continue play in the manner described until all of the cards have been captured. Declare the player with more cards the winner! *Stacy Shaener—Grs. 4–5, Riverside Elementary, Greenwich, CT*

I get both cards because my product is greater!

$6 \times 5 = 30$

Magic-Number Multiplication

Make practicing multiplication facts magical with this "cap-tivating" game! Ask parents to send in clean caps from plastic jugs and bottles. Label each cap's top with a number from 0 to 12. Give each child a handful of caps to place number side down on his desk. Direct him to pick up any cap and use it as the magic number by which he multiplies each of the other caps' numbers (see the example). After practicing in this way several times, pair students. Make sure that partners have the same number of caps. At your signal, have each partner repeat the steps he practiced. Award a point to the first player in each pair who multiplies the facts correctly. Play several rounds. Then declare the player with more points in each pair the winner! *Amber Jenkins—Gr. 4, Smith Elementary, Richmond, TX*

Magic number: 12

$12 \times 6 = 72$
$12 \times 3 = 36$
$12 \times 10 = 120$
$12 \times 7 = 84$

$7 \times 1 = 7$

Clapping for Multiples

Give your students practice with multiplication tables one clap at a time! Direct each student to stand behind his chair. Name a number from 1 to 12. Then have children count off beginning with 1. When a student reaches a number that is a multiple of the original number named, direct him to clap one time instead of naming the multiple. For example, if you named the number 6, the children who reach 6, 12, 24, and so on should each clap one time. Continue having each student call out a number or clap until 12 times the number has been reached. If a child incorrectly names a number or claps, have her sit down. Play as many rounds as desired, changing the original number named each time. *Irene Taylor, Fort Ann, NY*

1 2 3 4 5 CLAP

"Tower-ful" Facts

Strengthen students' skills with multiplication facts by using a tower of blocks from a Jenga game! Label each block's sides and ends with the product of a different multiplication fact. Have students build one or more towers (one with 18 stories, two with nine stories, or three with six stories). To play, have one player call out a fact whose product is not written on the tower's top layer. Have the player on his left locate the block with the matching answer, remove it, and stack it carefully on the top of the tower to start a new layer. Continue having students take turns in this manner until the tower falls. Declare the last player to take a turn without making the tower fall the winner! *Kim Brown—Gr. 4, Mounds, OK*

135

Swimmin' to School

Freddy doesn't know the way to his new school. Show him the path by using a blue crayon to color the bubble of each correct multiplication fact. Then answer the riddle by writing the letter found inside each colored bubble in order on the lines below.

6 x 9 = 54 **R**	8 x 6 = 48 **E**	3 x 9 = 27 **A**	4 x 8 = 32 **L**

8 x 9 = 78 **S**	7 x 7 = 42 **U**	4 x 7 = 21 **P**	8 x 8 = 65 **E**	6 x 7 = 48 **R**	5 x 8 = 40 **L**
9 x 9 = 81 **A**	12 x 12 = 144 **T**	10 x 10 = 100 **N**	4 x 9 = 36 **I**	6 x 6 = 36 **F**	4 x 6 = 24 **Y**

7 x 5 = 35 **S**	3 x 8 = 26 **B**	4 x 4 = 18 **O**	0 x 8 = 8 **R**	3 x 7 = 24 **E**

3 x 3 = 6 **D**	4 x 5 = 20 **T**	8 x 7 = 56 **I**	9 x 7 = 63 **C**

under-the-Sea School

What did Freddy say about his first day at the school?

It was ___ ___ ___ ___ ___ ___   "___ ___ ___ - ___ ___ ___ ___ ___ ___ ___ !"

Bonus Box: Replace each incorrect answer in the uncolored bubbles above with the correct answer.

Staying on Track With Decimals

Keep your students on track with basic decimal concepts with these record-setting games and activities!

by Terry Healy, Eugene Field Elementary, Manhattan, KS

Dealing With Decimals
Reading and writing decimals

Reading and writing decimals is in the cards with this simple activity! Remove all face cards and 10s from a deck of cards. Stack the red and black cards in separate piles. Explain that the black cards will represent whole numbers and the red cards decimals. Copy on the board (leaving out the numbers) the place-value charts shown. Draw four cards (two from each pile) and record in one chart the greatest (or least) possible value they represent. Next, erase the numbers from the chart. Then divide students into two teams and assign each team a chart.

To play, have Player A on Team 1 draw four cards and arrange them on the chalk tray to form the greatest (or least) number possible for the chart. Have Player A on Team 2 read the number and write it in his team's chart. If correct, award his team points equal to the number formed. If incorrect, give Player A on Team 1 a chance to score. Then have Player B on Team 2 draw four cards and repeat the procedure. When everyone has had a turn, total the points, and declare the team with more points the winner!

ninety-six and twenty-one hundredths

Team 1

Tens	Ones .	Tenths	Hundredths
9	6.	2	1

Team 2

Tens	Ones .	Tenths	Hundredths

RACE-O
Ordering decimals

It'll be a race to the finish when students play this decimal-ordering game! Write the decimals shown on separate paper slips and place them in a container. Also write these headings on the board: "0.000 to 0.200," "0.201 to 0.400," "0.401 to 0.600," "0.601 to 0.800," "0.801 to 0.900." Next, draw a slip and write its number on the board. Have students determine where the number should be written. Repeat until every number has been recorded correctly under a column. Then return the slips to the container.

To play, have each student draw a 5 x 6 gameboard grid and title it as shown. (For a pattern, go to www.themailboxcompanion.com.) Direct each student to program her gameboard's *R* column using any numbers from the 0 to 0.200 column. Explain that there are more numbers than boxes. After students have programmed their *A, C, E,* and *O* columns with numbers from each of the remaining number columns in order, erase the board and draw a slip from the container. Call out the slip's decimal and instruct each player who has that number on her gameboard to cover it with a marker. Continue calling numbers until a player covers five spaces in a row on her board.

0.05	0.11	0.01	0.12	0.16
0.09	0.19	0.21	0.24	0.203
0.319	0.35	0.38	0.399	0.41
0.42	0.444	0.51	0.59	0.594
0.599	0.62	0.67	0.68	0.703
0.749	0.781	0.79	0.801	0.82
0.843	0.86	0.873	0.89	0.894

R	A	C	E	- O
0.11	0.21	0.41	0.67	0.82
0.01	0.203	0.444	0.68	0.86
0.05	0.319	0.59	0.703	0.894
0.12	0.24	0.51	0.79	0.89
0.09	0.35	0.42	0.749	0.801

Rounding Relay
Rounding decimals

All you need for this decimal-rounding game are three empty paper towel tubes, a die, and a paper bag. Cover each towel tube baton with the same color of paper. Label one baton "Ones," another "Tenths," and the third "Hundredths." Then put the batons in the bag and draw a place-value chart on the board with the headings shown. Create a decimal to record in the chart by rolling a die four times and recording, in turn, each number rolled. Review with students how to round the decimal to the nearest whole number, tenth, and hundredth.

	Ones .	Tenths	Hundredths	Thousandths
O	6.	1	5	4
	6			
H	2.	5	6	6
	2.	5	7	
T	4.	2	1	5
	4.	2		

To play, divide students into two teams. Have Player A on Team 1 roll the die four times to create a decimal and record it in the chart. Next, direct Player A on Team 2 to pull a baton from the bag and read its label aloud. Have him round the recorded decimal to the announced place value and code it with "O," "T," or "H." If correct, award his team a point. If incorrect, give Player B on Team 1 a chance to score. Then draw a dividing line to separate the rounds and have Player B on Team 2 roll the die for the next turn. When everyone has had a turn, declare the team with more points the winner.

0.7 and 0.70—they're equivalent!

Equitable Decimals
Finding equivalent decimals

Make equivalent decimals crystal clear with this easy-to-do activity! Display a transparency of a 10 x 10 grid. Use a wipe-off marker to color one square on the grid. Explain that it represents one hundredth, or one of 100 parts. Finish coloring an entire column or row. Explain that it represents one tenth, or one of ten parts. Point out that one tenth equals ten hundredths and write "0.1 = 0.10" on the board. Then copy the decimal sets shown on the board.

Next, divide students into groups of four. Assign each group a different set of decimals. Then give each group colored markers and three 10 x 10 grids. (For a pattern, go to www.themailboxcompanion.com.) Have three group members color one grid each to represent a different decimal in their set. Have the fourth group member check the group's work and prepare to share with the class which equivalent decimal on the board matches each groupmate's grid. When everyone is finished, have each group share its grids and identify the matching equivalents.

Set 1: 0.1, 0.2, 0.3
Set 2: 0.4, 0.5, 0.60
Set 3: 0.7, 0.80, 0.9
Set 4: 0.10, 0.20, 0.50
Set 5: 0.30, 0.40, 0.6
Set 6: 0.70, 0.8, 0.90

Reveal the Route!

Boomer and Nellie need to know the route they will be running. To show it to them, decide whether the decimals in each box are equivalent. If they are, color the box.

Equivalent decimals show the same amount.

To make an equivalent decimal, add a zero to (or remove one from) the end of a decimal.

Start   **Finish**

0.250 0.25	0.7 0.70	0.705 0.75	0.9 0.99	0.50 0.5
0.80 0.08	0.20 0.2	0.606 0.66	0.0 0.0	0.03 0.030
0.330 0.33	0.450 0.45	0.61 0.6	0.75 0.77	0.540 0.54
0.08 0.080	0.205 0.250	0.012 0.12	0.07 0.070	0.80 0.8
0.63 0.630	0.10 0.1	0.602 0.6020	0.750 0.75	0.065 0.65

Bonus Box: Write at least one equivalent decimal below one of the numbers in each uncolored box above.

Vaulting Into Decimals

Matching word and number forms of decimals

Help Vinnie and Vonda run to the pole. Cut out the shoe prints at the bottom of the page. Match each number to its word form. Then tape each number at the top of its corresponding word form to create a flap.

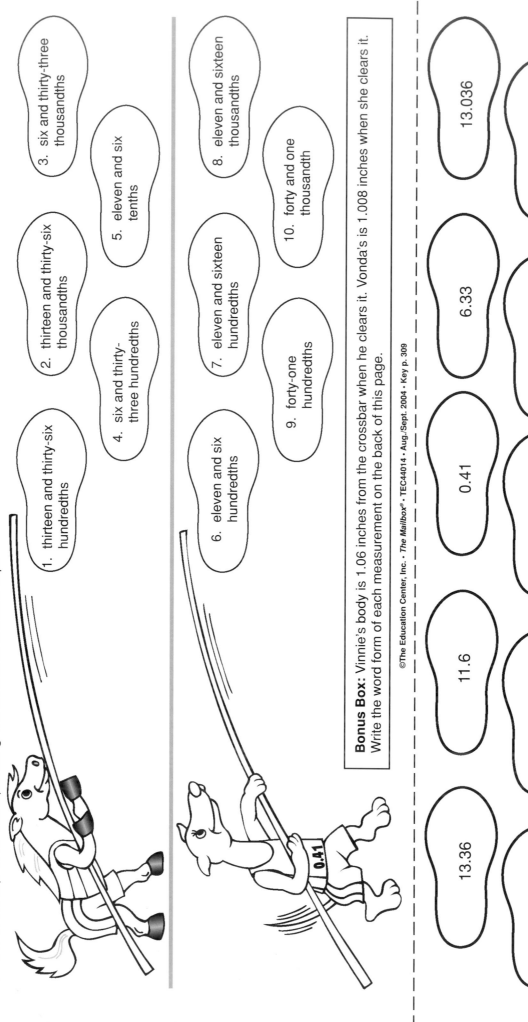

1. thirteen and thirty-six hundredths

2. thirteen and thirty-six thousandths

3. six and thirty-three thousandths

4. six and thirty-three hundredths

5. eleven and six tenths

6. eleven and six hundredths

7. eleven and sixteen hundredths

8. eleven and sixteen thousandths

9. forty-one hundredths

10. forty and one thousandth

Bonus Box: Vinnie's body is 1.06 inches from the crossbar when he clears it. Vonda's is 1.008 inches when she clears it. Write the word form of each measurement on the back of this page.

©The Education Center, Inc. • *The Mailbox®* • TEC44014 • Aug./Sept. 2004 • Key p. 309

11.6   0.41   6.33   13.036

13.36   11.06   11.16   11.016   6.033

40.001

Note to the teacher: Each student will need scissors and tape to complete this page.

Name _____

Decimal Dilemma

Hattie and Hal are stumped and need your help. Circle the decimal and its matching letter in each box on the track as directed. Then write the circled letters in order in the blanks below. If your answers are correct, the letters will spell the riddle's answer.

| 1. Greatest 0.403 0.430 D T | 2. Least 0.3 0.030 E H | 3. Greatest 1.94 1.49 E A | 4. Least 0.55 0.505 R Y | 5. Least 3.441 3.451 D B |

20. Greatest 2.23 2.32 S T

19. Least 19.25 19.52 N L

18. Greatest 31.13 30.13 I H

17. Least 0.008 0.080 O D

16. Greatest 665.02 665.20 R P

15. Least 0.040 0.004 G E

14. Greatest 73.4 74.39 O H

13. Least 101.3 100.3 H T

12. Least 0.002 0.02 T S

11. Greatest 0.7 0.07 E R

6. Greatest 31.92 31.209 I A

7. Greatest 0.593 0.539 D N

8. Least 0.011 0.010 L N

9. Least 0.03 0.30 T L

10. Greatest 3.791 3.971 N G

Why did Hattie and Hal think learning about decimals was so hard?

$\overline{\hspace{0.4cm}}_{1} \overline{\hspace{0.4cm}}_{2} \overline{\hspace{0.4cm}}_{3} \overline{\hspace{0.4cm}}_{4} \quad \overline{\hspace{0.4cm}}_{5} \overline{\hspace{0.4cm}}_{6} \overline{\hspace{0.4cm}}_{7} \overline{\hspace{0.4cm}}_{8} \overline{\hspace{0.4cm}}_{9}$,

$\overline{\hspace{0.4cm}}_{10} \overline{\hspace{0.4cm}}_{11} \overline{\hspace{0.4cm}}_{12}$

$\overline{\hspace{0.4cm}}_{13} \overline{\hspace{0.4cm}}_{14} \overline{\hspace{0.4cm}}_{15} \quad \overline{\hspace{0.4cm}}_{16} \overline{\hspace{0.4cm}}_{17} \overline{\hspace{0.4cm}}_{18} \overline{\hspace{0.4cm}}_{19} \overline{\hspace{0.4cm}}_{20}$!

Bonus Box: If Hattie finished a race in 30.02 seconds and Hal finished it in 30.12 seconds, who won: Hattie or Hal? Explain your answer.

Jazzed Up About Multiplying Decimals

You'll have something to toot about when you use these activities to liven up lessons about multiplying by decimals!

by Shawna Graham, Degan Elementary, Lewisville, TX

Razzle-Dazzle Decimals

Determining the number of decimal places in a product

Assess in a flash whether students know how many decimal places should be in a product with this dazzling activity! Give each child four index cards and access to glitter glue in various colors. Direct him to decorate each card with a different number from 1 to 4. Next, write a problem such as 4.5 x 7 on the board. Have each student hold up the card that tells the number of decimal places the product should have. A quick glance will let you know who needs more help with this concept. Repeat the activity, using a problem such as 2.06 x 0.45. Continue in this manner until there are ten or more problems on the board for each child to solve independently on paper. Have students keep the cards at their desks to use during future impromptu razzle-dazzle reviews!

The product will have four decimal places!

2.06
x 0.45

Decimal Flip-Flap Book

Multiplying hundredths by whole numbers

This multiplying-decimals activity will cause quite a flap! Give each child scissors, glue, markers, a 12" x 18" sheet of construction paper, and access to store fliers and a die. Then guide students through the steps below to create their own flip-flap books about multiplying with money.

Steps:

1. Cut pictures of five items and their prices from a store flyer and set them aside.
2. Fold the construction paper into twelfths. Create six flaps by cutting along the folds of one side to the center. Glue one item and its price atop the first flap.
3. Roll the die to determine how many of the item will be bought. Record the number rolled below the price. Then lift the flap. Above the fold line, write and solve a multiplication problem that represents the purchase. Below the fold line, write one or two sentences summarizing the purchase.
4. Repeat Step 3 for the next four flaps.
5. Label the outside of the last flap "Total Amount of My Purchases." Then lift the flap. Above the fold line, find the total amount of the five purchases. Below the fold line, write a statement summarizing the shopping trip.

$ 9.90
10.95
3.44
2.25
+ .86
$27.40

The total cost of my five items is $27.40.

$1.98 x 5
$3.65 x 3
$0.86 x 4
$0.75 x 3
$0.43 x 2

The Pyramid Challenge
Multiplying decimals by whole numbers, decimals, and mixed numbers

To be the first to reach the top of these towering pyramids, students will have to multiply some decimals! Give each student scissors, glue, a marker, a ruler, and two different-colored sheets of 12" x 18" light-colored paper. Guide the child through the steps shown to make a gameboard; then pair students. Have one partner be the contestant and the other the host. At the host's signal, direct the contestant to begin solving the bottom row of problems on his partner's gameboard from left to right. Have the host use a stopwatch or the second hand of the classroom clock to time him. Once the contestant finds the product, have him lift the door and check the answer. If correct, he immediately starts solving the problem on the next door. If not, the host records the time and the players switch roles. Continue in this manner until both players have solved the problem at the top of each pyramid. The player with less time wins!

Steps:

1. Turn one sheet vertically. Mark the center of its top edge. Draw lines that connect the center with each bottom corner. Cut along the lines to form a triangle.
2. Draw four 1½-inch squares about an inch apart and an inch above the bottom edge. Three inches above this row, draw a row of three 1½-inch squares. Three inches above this row, draw a row of two 1½-inch squares. Two inches above this row, draw one 1½-inch square. Cut along three sides of each square to make a door.
3. Repeat Step 1 with the other sheet. Glue it behind the first pyramid at the edges.
4. Write on each door a multiplication problem that has at least one decimal factor. Write the product in the corresponding door opening.
5. Label the gameboard "The Pyramid Challenge."

Four Corner Flip Out
Reviewing the multiplication of decimals

Looking for a way to review multiplying decimals that students will flip over? This one fills the bill! Have each child create a multiplication problem for the following categories: whole number by a decimal, decimal by a decimal, mixed decimal by a whole number, mixed decimal by a decimal. Also have her create a related word problem. Have the student check her work with a calculator. Next, direct her to fold each corner of an 8½-inch square of white paper to the center to form four triangular flaps. Then have her write one of her four problems atop each flap and the corresponding answer inside the flap. Instruct her to write her word problem on the inner part of the square and the answer on the back. When she is finished, have her trade papers with a classmate and solve her partner's problems. Or place the problems at a center for easy self-checking practice!

143

Jazzy Disc Jockey

Jazzy Jack tells jokes on his radio show between each tune. To find the answers to his last two jokes, solve the problems. Then use each riddle's code to tell you what to write in each numbered blank.

What is a computer's favorite kind of music?

Code	
S = 0.90	I = 0.36
O = 0.84	C = 0.18
D = 16.6	- = 35.5

1. 8.3 x 2 = _____

2. 0.9 x 0.4 = _____

3. 1.5 x 0.6 = _____

4. 0.6 x 0.3 = _____

5. 7.1 x 5 = _____

6. 2.8 x 0.3 = _____

" ___ ___ ___ ___ ___ ___ "
  1   2   3   4   5   6

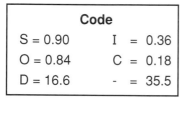

What musical instrument goes "ting-a-ling-a-ling, ting-a-ling-a-ling"?

7. 1.23 x 5 = _____

8. 6.38 x 2.1 = _____

9. 0.8 x 0.9 = _____

10. 6 x 0.4 = _____

11. 9.5 x 6 = _____

12. 3 x 0.9 = _____

13. 0.17 x 5 = _____

14. 7.25 x 4 = _____

15. 20.4 x 1.3 = _____

16. 8.02 x 9 = _____

Code
A = 0.72
P = 2.7
O = 29.00
N = 26.52
A = 6.15
S = 13.398
H = 0.85
E = 72.18
X = 2.4
O = 57.0

___ " ___ ___ ___ ___ - ___ ___ ___ ___ ___ "
7   8   9   10   11   12   13   14   15   16

Bonus Box: On the back of this page, list the answers to problems 1–16 in order from greatest to least.

The Fractions Speedway

Keep students' basic fraction skills on course with these action-packed maneuvers!

by Melissa Bryan, Valley Forge Middle School, Wayne, PA

Rarin' to Reduce!

Identifying and writing fractions in simplest form

You'll cause a race to the starting line with this simplifying-fractions activity! On chart paper, list simplified fractions such as those shown. Next, give each child a large handful of small different-colored manipulatives, such as gram unit cubes, color tiles, or Unifix cubes. Announce any manipulative color. Have each student find what fraction of his manipulatives is that color and then mentally reduce that fraction to its simplest form. If his simplified fraction is listed in the chart, have him write its unsimplified form in the matching row. Discuss any fractions students could not list on the chart and why (fractions were already in simplest form or represented an uncommon fraction, such as $\frac{2}{11}$). Repeat the process four times to generate as many different equivalent fractions as possible. Then display the chart as a ready reference.

Fractions	Simplest Form
$\frac{2}{4}, \frac{3}{6}, \frac{4}{8}, \frac{5}{10}, \frac{6}{12}$	$\frac{1}{2}$
$\frac{2}{6}, \frac{3}{9}, \frac{4}{12}$	$\frac{1}{3}$
$\frac{4}{6}, \frac{6}{9}$	$\frac{2}{3}$
$\frac{2}{8}, \frac{3}{12}$	$\frac{1}{4}$
$\frac{6}{8}, \frac{9}{12}$	$\frac{3}{4}$
$\frac{2}{10}$	$\frac{1}{5}$

Fraction Bow Ties

Comparing fractions

Refuel students' understanding of comparing fractions with a shortcut method that will have them looking quite dapper! Demonstrate the bow tie method using the fractions and directions shown. Then give each child a loop of masking tape and a large, colorful bow tie cutout. Instruct the student to write on her cutout two fractions with numerators and denominators less than ten and then tape the bow tie to her clothing. Next, have her walk around and copy ten problems from her classmates' bow ties onto a sheet of paper. Afterward, instruct her to return to her seat and compare the fractions using the shortcut method. When she's done, have her compare the fractions on her own bow tie. After you check it, have her pin the cutout to a bulletin board titled as shown. Once all of the bow ties are in place, students can check their ten problems by looking at the board!

$$24 \; \frac{3}{4} \bowtie \frac{7}{8} \; 28$$
$$24 < 28$$
$$\text{so} \; \frac{3}{4} < \frac{7}{8}$$

The Bow Tie Method
1. Multiply the first fraction's denominator by the second fraction's numerator. Record the product on the right.
2. Multiply the second fraction's denominator by the first fraction's numerator. Record the product on the left.
3. Compare the two products. Write "<," ">," or "=" between the fractions.

Dapper Comparisons

<	>	=

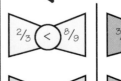

$\frac{2}{3} < \frac{8}{9}$ $\frac{3}{6} > \frac{2}{12}$ $\frac{3}{4} = \frac{9}{12}$

$\frac{2}{4} < \frac{5}{8}$ $\frac{5}{11} > \frac{3}{8}$ $\frac{1}{5} = \frac{2}{10}$

Of all the students in our class, ¹⁴/₂₄ are boys.

This is equivalent to ⁷/₁₂.

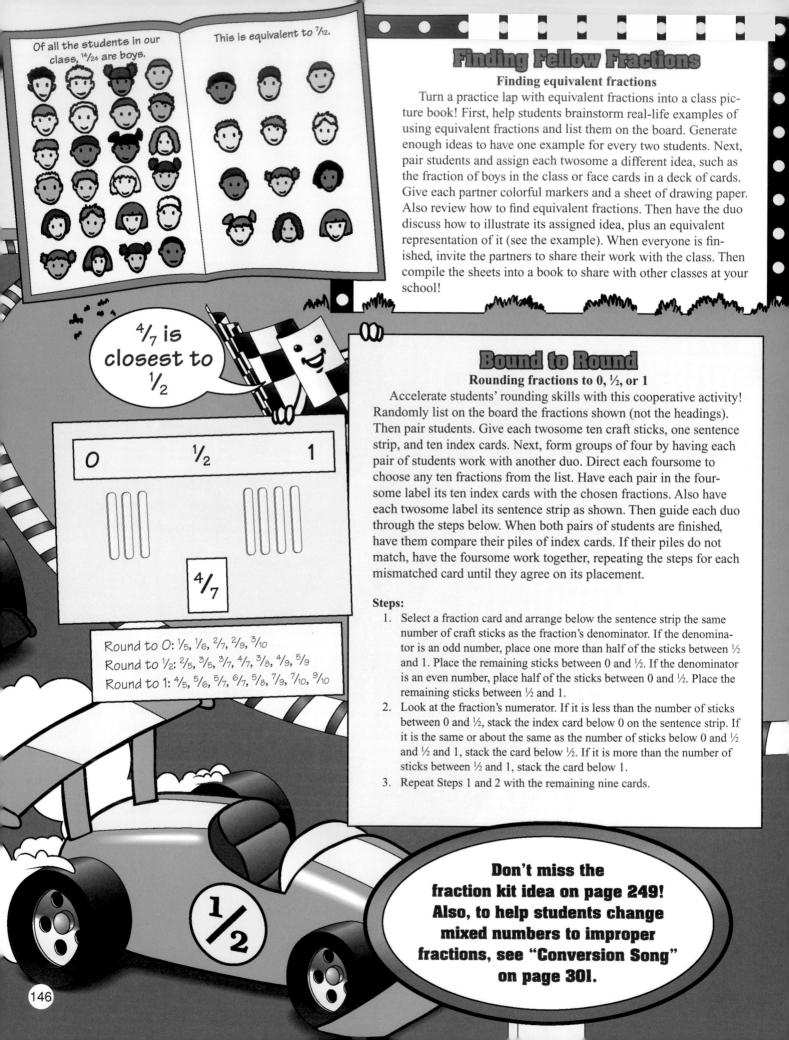

Don't miss the fraction kit idea on page 249! Also, to help students change mixed numbers to improper fractions, see "Conversion Song" on page 301.

Finding Fellow Fractions

Finding equivalent fractions

Turn a practice lap with equivalent fractions into a class picture book! First, help students brainstorm real-life examples of using equivalent fractions and list them on the board. Generate enough ideas to have one example for every two students. Next, pair students and assign each twosome a different idea, such as the fraction of boys in the class or face cards in a deck of cards. Give each partner colorful markers and a sheet of drawing paper. Also review how to find equivalent fractions. Then have the duo discuss how to illustrate its assigned idea, plus an equivalent representation of it (see the example). When everyone is finished, invite the partners to share their work with the class. Then compile the sheets into a book to share with other classes at your school!

⁴/₇ is closest to ½

| 0 | ½ | 1 |

⁴/₇

Round to 0: ¹/₅, ¹/₆, ²/₇, ²/₉, ³/₁₀
Round to ½: ²/₅, ³/₅, ³/₇, ⁴/₇, ³/₈, ⁴/₉, ⁵/₉
Round to 1: ⁴/₅, ⁵/₆, ⁵/₇, ⁶/₇, ⁵/₈, ⁷/₉, ⁷/₁₀, ⁹/₁₀

Bound to Round

Rounding fractions to 0, ½, or 1

Accelerate students' rounding skills with this cooperative activity! Randomly list on the board the fractions shown (not the headings). Then pair students. Give each twosome ten craft sticks, one sentence strip, and ten index cards. Next, form groups of four by having each pair of students work with another duo. Direct each foursome to choose any ten fractions from the list. Have each pair in the foursome label its ten index cards with the chosen fractions. Also have each twosome label its sentence strip as shown. Then guide each duo through the steps below. When both pairs of students are finished, have them compare their piles of index cards. If their piles do not match, have the foursome work together, repeating the steps for each mismatched card until they agree on its placement.

Steps:
1. Select a fraction card and arrange below the sentence strip the same number of craft sticks as the fraction's denominator. If the denominator is an odd number, place one more than half of the sticks between ½ and 1. Place the remaining sticks between 0 and ½. If the denominator is an even number, place half of the sticks between 0 and ½. Place the remaining sticks between ½ and 1.
2. Look at the fraction's numerator. If it is less than the number of sticks between 0 and ½, stack the index card below 0 on the sentence strip. If it is the same or about the same as the number of sticks below 0 and ½ and ½ and 1, stack the card below ½. If it is more than the number of sticks between ½ and 1, stack the card below 1.
3. Repeat Steps 1 and 2 with the remaining nine cards.

Sweet Tooth Fractions

Jill E. Bean just loves working at her grandfather's candy shop. She keeps track of the candy in the jars. Her weekly candy count is due today. Help her complete this sweet task!

Write a fraction that shows each amount of candy.

1. white gumballs _____
2. swirled mints _____
3. marbled gumballs _____
4. striped sticks _____
5. striped mints _____
6. round lollipops _____

Draw and color the candies to show each amount.

7. $\frac{3}{7}$ of the sour stars are purple.

8. $\frac{2}{15}$ of the jelly beans are green.

9. $\frac{3}{10}$ of the fruit chewies are yellow.

10. $\frac{7}{9}$ of the gummy twirls are red.

Bonus Box: On the back of this page, write fractions that show the uncolored candies for problems 7–10.

Winning "Ap-pie-tites"

Yippee! The annual pie-eating contest is today! Who will win? To find out, color each pie or find the equivalent fraction to show how much the group member ate. Then list each group's fractions and matching group members' names in order from greatest to least!

1st Place

Group 1

Jill	$\frac{2}{8}$	
Bob	$\frac{4}{8}$	
Harry	$\frac{3}{8}$	
Lilly	$\frac{1}{8}$	
Ann	$\frac{7}{8}$	

Group 2

Ryan	$\frac{1}{4}$	
Emma	$\frac{6}{8}$	
Erin	$\frac{1}{2}$	
Jack	$\frac{2}{3}$	
Kelly	$\frac{5}{6}$	

Group 3

Jake	$\frac{2}{3} = \frac{}{24}$	
Billy	$\frac{5}{8} = \frac{}{24}$	
Abby	$\frac{1}{6} = \frac{}{24}$	
Kim	$\frac{3}{4} = \frac{}{24}$	
Katie	$\frac{1}{2} = \frac{}{24}$	

Group 1

	Name	Fraction
Winner		
2nd place		
3rd place		
4th place		
5th place		

Group 2

	Name	Fraction
Winner		
2nd place		
3rd place		
4th place		
5th place		

Group 3

	Name	Fraction
Winner		
2nd place		
3rd place		
4th place		
5th place		

Bonus Box: Find out who came in first, second, and third among the three winners. On the back of this page, list the fractions of these three people in order from greatest to least.

Rita's Recipes

When Rita cooks, she changes the ingredient amounts to improper fractions. She just borrowed a pie recipe from her mom. Help her change the amounts.

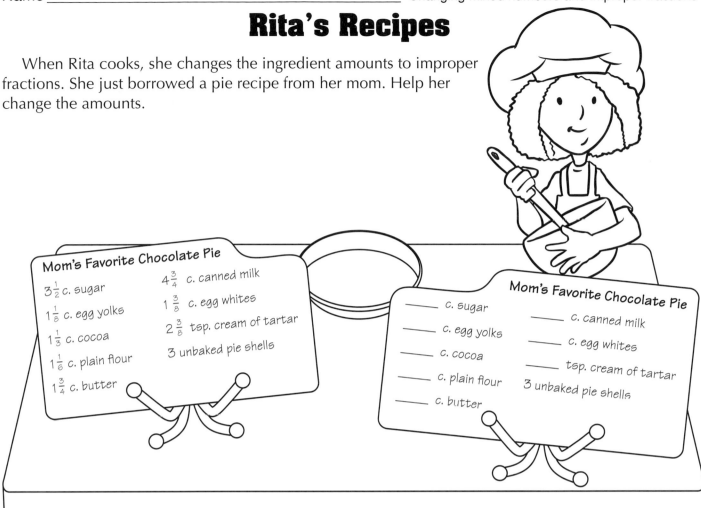

Mom's Favorite Chocolate Pie

$3\frac{1}{2}$ c. sugar

$1\frac{1}{8}$ c. egg yolks

$1\frac{1}{3}$ c. cocoa

$1\frac{1}{6}$ c. plain flour

$1\frac{3}{4}$ c. butter

$4\frac{3}{4}$ c. canned milk

$1\frac{3}{8}$ c. egg whites

$2\frac{3}{8}$ tsp. cream of tartar

3 unbaked pie shells

Mom's Favorite Chocolate Pie

_____ c. sugar

_____ c. egg yolks

_____ c. cocoa

_____ c. plain flour

_____ c. butter

_____ c. canned milk

_____ c. egg whites

_____ tsp. cream of tartar

3 unbaked pie shells

Uh-oh! Rita's mom lost her copy of a muffin recipe, so she borrowed Rita's. Help her change the improper fractions to mixed numbers so she can make the muffins.

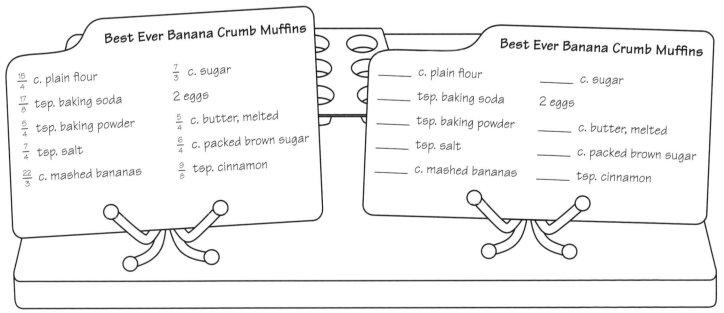

Best Ever Banana Crumb Muffins

$\frac{15}{4}$ c. plain flour

$\frac{17}{8}$ tsp. baking soda

$\frac{5}{4}$ tsp. baking powder

$\frac{7}{4}$ tsp. salt

$\frac{22}{3}$ c. mashed bananas

$\frac{7}{3}$ c. sugar

2 eggs

$\frac{5}{4}$ c. butter, melted

$\frac{6}{4}$ c. packed brown sugar

$\frac{9}{8}$ tsp. cinnamon

Best Ever Banana Crumb Muffins

_____ c. plain flour

_____ tsp. baking soda

_____ tsp. baking powder

_____ tsp. salt

_____ c. mashed bananas

_____ c. sugar

2 eggs

_____ c. butter, melted

_____ c. packed brown sugar

_____ tsp. cinnamon

Bonus Box: On the back of this page, list ten ingredients for a prize-winning cake recipe. Write the amount of each ingredient as an improper fraction. Then rewrite each improper fraction as a mixed number.

Math With Life Savers Candy

Satisfy your need for a math activity that covers a wide range of math skills. With this sweet treat, students will be estimating, writing fractions, practicing the addition of fractions, finding elapsed time, and calculating mean, median, and mode!

by William C. Luke, C. R. Clements Intermediate School, Copperas Cove, TX

Getting started: Obtain a paper towel (or napkin) for each child and enough regular rolls of Life Savers candy (the size with 11 candies per roll) for each child to have two rolls. Save half of the rolls for the end of the activity. Also make a copy of page 151 for each student.

Introducing the activity: Tell students that they will each be using a roll of Life Savers candy and many different math skills for this activity. Next, give each child a copy of page 151. Read the page with students. Explain that each child should use the page to record his answers for each part of the activity. Then divide students into groups of four and give each child a paper towel and a roll of Life Savers candy.

Completing the activity: Guide each group through the steps below. Have each group member write his answers on his recording sheet as directed for each step. If desired, have students graph their data. Then celebrate the end of the activity by giving each child a second roll of Life Savers candy to snack on!

Steps:
1. Estimate and record the number of candies you think are in your roll.
2. Unwrap your candies and place them on your paper towel. Count and record the actual number of candies.
3. Group your candies by color. Count and record the number of candies of each color.
4. Write a fraction for each candy color to tell what part of the roll each color represents.
5. Use those fractions to write an addition sentence that represents the number and color of candies in your roll. The sum should equal one whole.
6. Estimate and record the number of minutes you think it will take to dissolve one piece of candy in your mouth.
7. Choose a color of candy to test. Be sure each group member chooses a different color. Record the color you will test.
8. Put the piece of candy in your mouth and record the starting time. Allow the candy to dissolve without biting it. When your candy is dissolved, record the stopping time. Then find and record the elapsed time.
9. Record in the chart the candy color you tested and your test results. Share your test results with your group. Then collect similar data from your group members and record it in the chart.
10. Find the mean, median, and mode of your group's test data.

Math With Life Savers Candy

Use your roll of Life Savers candy to help you answer the questions.

1. Estimated number of candies in my roll: _____

2. Actual number of candies in my roll: _____

3. Number of candies of each color: _____

_____

_____

4. Fraction of candies for each color: _____

_____

5. Addition sentence with fractions that represents my roll of candies: _____

_____

6. Estimated number of minutes needed to dissolve one piece of candy in my mouth: _____

7. Color of candy I will test: _____

8. My starting time: _____ My stopping time: _____ Elapsed time: _____

9. Test results from my group:

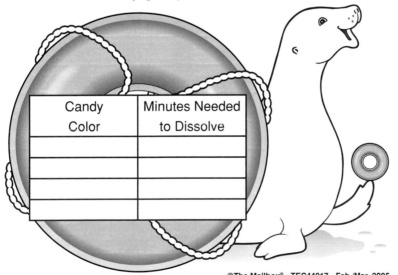

Candy Color	Minutes Needed to Dissolve

10. Mean: _____

11. Median: _____

12. Mode: _____

©The Mailbox® • TEC44017 • Feb./Mar. 2005

Estimation Strategies on the Loose

File Folder Estimation
Using front-end estimation, rounding, and compatible numbers

Open and close the file on estimation practice with an activity that turns old file folders into self-checking center activities! Cut windows with flaps in the front side of a file folder and add directions along the bottom edge as shown. Label each flap with a different problem. In the opening under each flap, write the numbers to estimate that problem. Number the problems and then write the answers on the folder's back. In a similar way, make folders for rounding numbers and compatible numbers. Place the folders at a center along with pencils and paper. Then invite individual students or pairs of students to practice estimation strategies till their hearts are content!

On a Roll With Estimation
Using front-end estimation and rounding

Grab a die for a fun activity that combines estimation skills and logical thinking! Instruct each child to draw a 2 x 2 array of boxes on a sheet of paper. Announce a goal that requires students to reach an estimated sum, difference, or product using front-end estimation or rounding (see the example). Next, roll a die and have each student write the number rolled in one of the boxes on his paper. (To get a number from zero to nine, roll a decahedron die or pull a number tile from a bag.) Explain that once a child writes a number in a box, he cannot move it. Repeat this process three more times and then have the student add, subtract, or multiply according to the goal. Determine who has the closest estimate and invite that child to roll the die for the next round. If there are multiple winners, have each qualifier pick a number between one and 20 to see who gets closest to a number you secretly selected. After each round, discuss other possible solutions. To play a more challenging round, have students use 3 x 3 arrays!

Goal: Front-end estimated sum of 70

Roll 1	Roll 2	Roll 3	Roll 4
☐2	☐2	32	32
+☐☐	+4☐	+4☐	+41
			70

Front-End Estimation

1. 69 + 73	2. 51 + 11	3. 74 + 88	4. 96 − 38	5. 424 − 143	6. 87 + 55
7. 69 × 73	8. 46 × 27	9. 59 × 49	10. 18 × 63	11. 77 × 73	12. 54 × 8
13. 407 ÷ 81	14. 213 ÷ 43	15. 11)94 10)90	16. 25)112	17. 509 ÷ 57	18. 86 ÷ 22

Solve each estimation problem using front-end estimation.
Write your estimates on another sheet of paper.
If you need help on a problem, look under the flap for a hint.
When you have completed the problems, check your work using the key on the back of the folder.

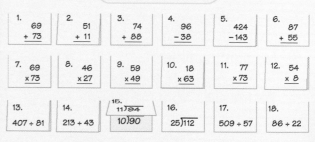

1. 130	7. 4,200	13. 5
2. 60	8. 800	14. 5
3. 150	9. 2,000	15. 9
4. 60	10. 600	16. 5
5. 300	11. 4,900	17. 10
6. 130	12. 400	18. 4

152

ideas by Jennifer Otter, Oak Ridge, NC

attach zeroes

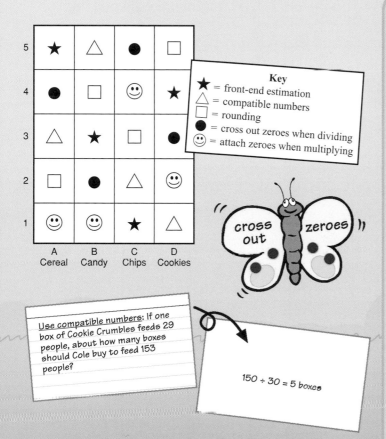

Key
★ = front-end estimation
△ = compatible numbers
▢ = rounding
● = cross out zeroes when dividing
☺ = attach zeroes when multiplying

cross out zeroes

Use compatible numbers: If one box of Cookie Crumbles feeds 29 people, about how many boxes should Cole buy to feed 153 people?

150 ÷ 30 = 5 boxes

Divvying Up the Strategies
Using estimation strategies to write and solve word problems

Guarantee that students will practice different estimation strategies with the help of a simple grid! Create a grid, such as the one shown, that uses a different symbol for each strategy to be practiced. Below each lettered column, write a different food item; then gather a matching empty food container for each listed food item.

Next, divide students into groups that contain one student for each strategy and give each group a diffcrent food container. Give each group member an index card and assign her a different box in that food item's column on the grid. Have her write on the front of her index card a word problem about her group's assigned food using her assigned estimation strategy. Have her solve the problem on the card's back, fold the card in half, and then place it in her group's food container. For example, if a student is assigned to box (D, 1), she would create a problem about cookies that uses compatible numbers (see the example). Then invite each group to trade containers with another group and solve the problems its members find inside!

Estimation Puzzles
Using front-end estimation, rounding, and compatible numbers

Make practicing estimation strategies more fun with this puzzle-making activity! Write on a 4 x 4 grid 24 estimation problems (eight with front-end estimation, eight with rounding, and eight with compatible numbers) so that each problem is next to its solution (see the example). Or have each child create his own problems on a sheet of paper and then copy them onto a grid. Be sure each problem has a unique solution. Next, make two copies of each puzzle. Give each child scissors, the copies of his puzzle, and an envelope. Direct the student to cut one puzzle apart; put its 16 pieces in his envelope along with the other copy, folded for use as a key; and trade puzzles with a partner. Then give each child glue and a colorful sheet of construction paper and have him assemble his partner's puzzle by matching each problem with its solution. Finally, direct him to glue the completed puzzle to the colorful paper so it can be displayed on a bulletin board titled "We're Not Puzzled by Estimation!"

FE = front-end estimation
R = rounding
CN = compatible numbers

compatible numbers

	FE 76 x 18		CN 49 x 5		R 33 x 48	
		700		250		1,500
FE 17 x 19	R 85 x 58		FE 104 x 19		CN 12 + 13 + 11 + 12	
100	5,400		1,000		40	
	R 26 x 13	300	FE 97 x 46	3,600	CN 97 x 46	5,000
R 56 x 11	R 104 x 19		R 102 ÷ 19		FE 56 x 11	
600	2,000		5		500	
	FE 33 + 48	70	CN 74 ÷ 25	3	FE 26 x 13	200
CN 213 ÷ 7	R 17 x 19		FE 85 x 58		R 76 x 18	
30	400		4,000		1,600	
	CN 59 x 7	420	CN 4 + 6 + 7 + 3 + 8 + 2 + 9 + 1 + 5	45	CN 52 ÷ 5	10

What's for Homework?

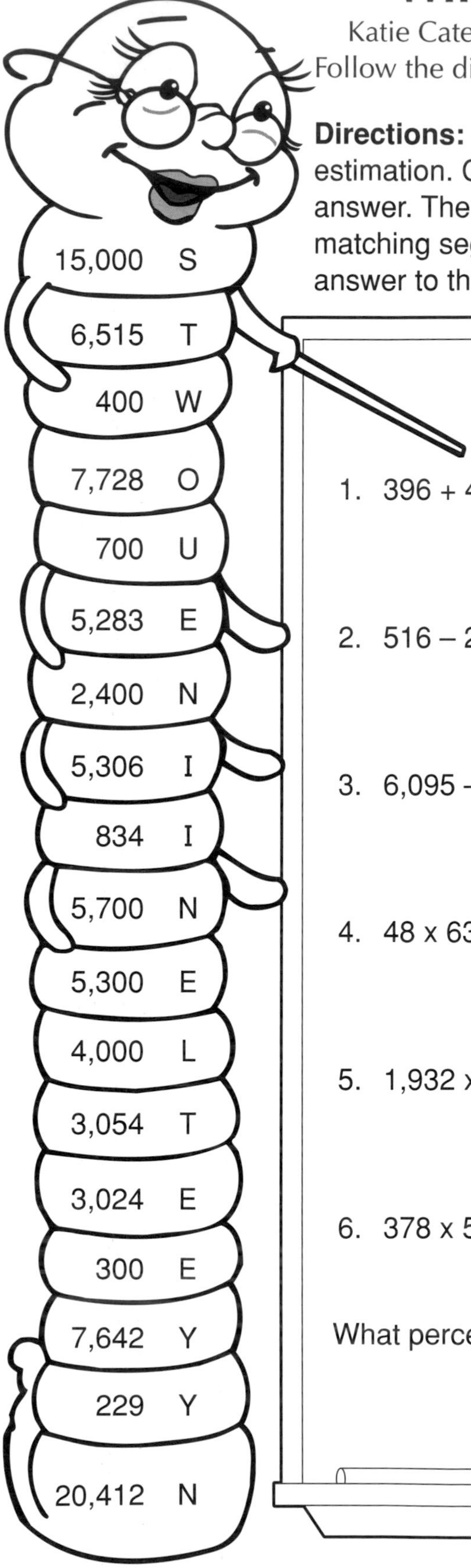

Katie Caterpillar gave her students only one question for homework today. Follow the directions to help them find the correct answer.

Directions: Estimate the answer to each problem using front-end estimation. Color the segment of Katie's body that has the matching answer. Then find the exact answer to each problem and color the matching segment. The letters on the uncolored segments will spell the answer to the homework question.

15,000	S
6,515	T
400	W
7,728	O
700	U
5,283	E
2,400	N
5,306	I
834	I
5,700	N
5,300	E
4,000	L
3,054	T
3,024	E
300	E
7,642	Y
229	Y
20,412	N

Front-End Estimate   **Exact Answer**

1. 396 + 438

2. 516 − 287

3. 6,095 − 789

4. 48 x 63

5. 1,932 x 4

6. 378 x 54

What percent of the earth's vegetation do arthropods eat each year?

____ ____ ____ ____ ____ ____ ____

Bonus Box: Which front-end estimate above is closest to the exact answer? Furthest from the exact answer?

©The Mailbox® · TEC44018 · April/May 2005 · Key p. 310

Butterflies Around the World

The owl butterfly can be found in South America. But where can its friends be found? To find at least one place for each friend, use compatible numbers to solve each problem. Then draw a line to connect each problem's butterfly with the place on the map that has the corresponding answer.

1.

Queen Cracker
302 ÷ 53

____ ÷ ____ = ____

2.

Duke of Burgundy
71 x 59

____ X ____ = _____

3.

The Wizard
21 x 49

____ X ____ = _____

4.

Queen Alexandra's
Birdwing
83 ÷ 18

____ ÷ ____ = ____

5.

Regent Skipper
457 ÷ 89

____ ÷ ____ = ____

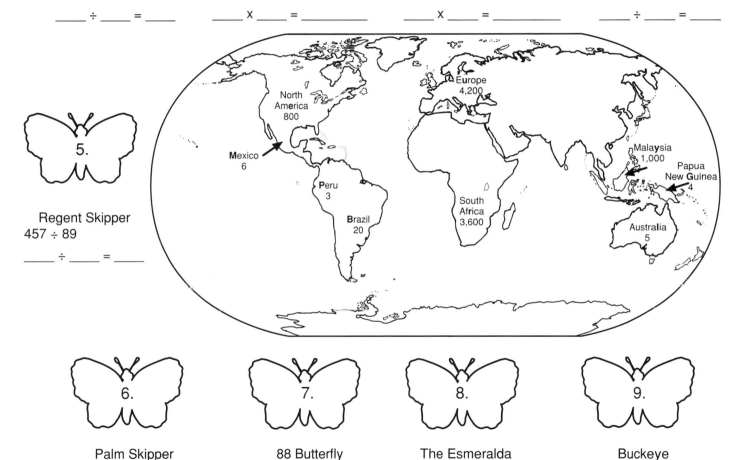

6.

Palm Skipper
120 x 29

____ X ____ = _____

7.

88 Butterfly
239 ÷ 12

____ ÷ ____ = ____

8.

The Esmeralda
63 ÷ 21

____ ÷ ____ = ____

9.

Buckeye
38 x 19

____ X ____ = _____

The smallest butterfly is about as wide as your thumbnail! To learn its name, write the boldfaced letter of each matching answer on the map in the matching numbered blank below.

The w _____ st _____ _____ n   _____ _____ _____ _____   _____ _____ _____ _____
         800   800   3,600   3   1,000   4   6   1,000   20   5   4,200   800

Bonus Box: On the back of this page, use compatible numbers to write a multiplication problem whose product is greater than 500. Then write a division problem whose quotient is less than 500.

Sensible Snacking

Connie's kids want a quick snack! Since it is close to dinnertime, she will give each child only one leaf. Which leaf will each caterpillar get? Follow the directions to find out!

Directions: Use compatible numbers to estimate each sum or difference. Then match each leaf to a caterpillar by writing the letter next to each leaf in a different speech bubble blank.

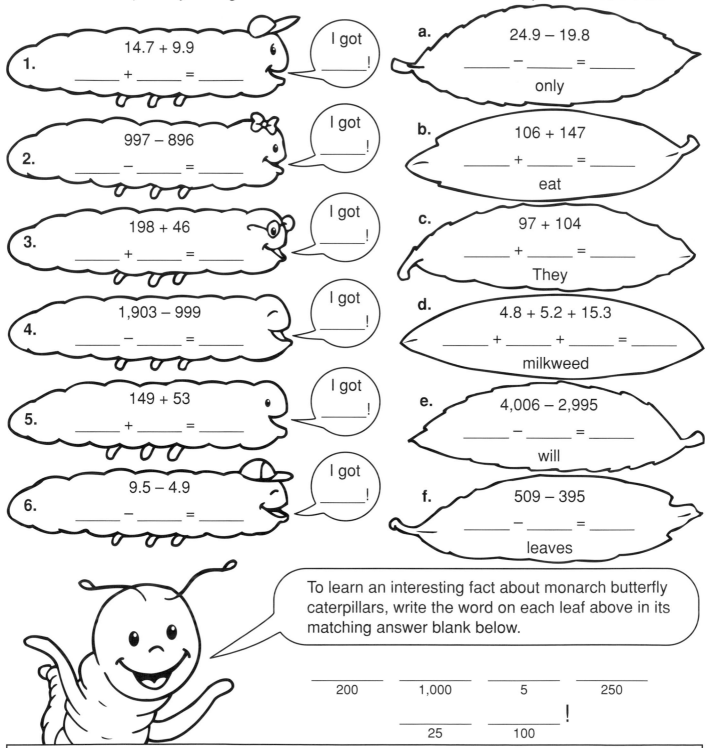

1. 14.7 + 9.9
_____ + _____ = _____

I got _____!

a. 24.9 – 19.8
_____ – _____ = _____
only

2. 997 – 896
_____ – _____ = _____

I got _____!

b. 106 + 147
_____ + _____ = _____
eat

3. 198 + 46
_____ + _____ = _____

I got _____!

c. 97 + 104
_____ + _____ = _____
They

4. 1,903 – 999
_____ – _____ = _____

I got _____!

d. 4.8 + 5.2 + 15.3
_____ + _____ + _____ = _____
milkweed

5. 149 + 53
_____ + _____ = _____

I got _____!

e. 4,006 – 2,995
_____ – _____ = _____
will

6. 9.5 – 4.9
_____ – _____ = _____

I got _____!

f. 509 – 395
_____ – _____ = _____
leaves

To learn an interesting fact about monarch butterfly caterpillars, write the word on each leaf above in its matching answer blank below.

_____ _____ _____ _____
200   1,000   5   250

_____ _____ !
25   100

Bonus Box: Some caterpillars eat 86,000 times their birth weight in 24 days! If you had weighed 9.8 pounds at birth and had eaten like these caterpillars, about how much would you have eaten when you were 24 days old?

Star-Spangled Coordinate Graphing

Make students' understanding of coordinate graphing shine even brighter with this sparkling collection of out-of-this-world activities!

by Melissa H. Bryan, Valley Forge Middle School, Wayne, PA

(4,4) (6,8) (2,10) (10,0)

©The Education Center, Inc. • *The Mailbox®* • TEC44015 • Oct./Nov. 2004

Coordinated Footsteps

Identifying ordered pairs of whole numbers on a grid

Discover how a few small steps on a classroom floor grid can lead to a giant leap in students' understanding of coordinate graphing! Enlarge and make ten copies of the footprint pattern shown. After cutting out the footprints and labeling them with the letters *A–J,* affix masking tape to your classroom floor to form a 10 x 10 grid. Use a marker to number the axes from 0 to 10. Place the cutouts on the grid at different intersections. Call on one student to provide the ordered pair that identifies a particular footprint's location. Call on another student to take that number of steps on the grid across and up from zero to check the answer. Repeat until every letter's location has been correctly identified. Continue in this manner, rearranging the cutouts on the grid as needed, until every child has had a turn. Conclude by having each student describe on paper how to determine a point's coordinates on a grid.

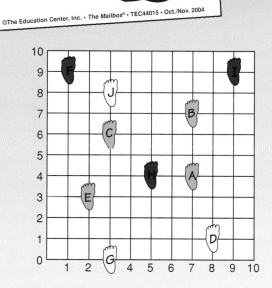

Crater Coordinates

Locating ordered pairs of whole numbers on a grid

This coordinate-graphing activity will have students smiling at the man in the moon! Have students bring in clean, empty egg cartons until there are three cartons for each child. Next, direct each student to cut off the lids and arrange the carton bottoms to form a 6 x 6 grid as shown. Explain that the grid represents the moon's craters. Then give each student a handful of two-color counters. Explain that the counters represent moon rocks that can rest in the moon's craters. Call out the following ordered pairs one at a time, and have each student place a counter red side up in the matching crater of her grid: (1, 3), (2, 2), (2, 6), (3, 1), (3, 4), (4, 1), (4, 4), (5, 2), (5, 6), (6, 3). If students place counters in the correct craters, they'll see a smiling face (the man in the moon). Follow up by having each child create and record the matching ordered pairs for a different design that a partner can try to re- create!

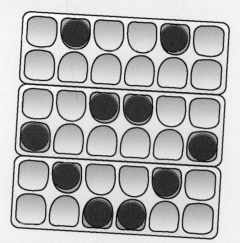

157

Where in the World Should I Plot My Points?

Plotting and identifying ordered pairs of whole numbers on a graph

Make plotting and identifying ordered pairs of numbers a "marshmallow-ific" experience with this Geoboard activity! Label each of 25 index cards with a different ordered pair from (0, 0) to (4, 4). Also wrap the first row and column of each student's Geoboard with rubber bands to create axes. Then give each child a Geoboard and eight mini marshmallows (four white, four colored). Have her place a white marshmallow on any four neighboring pegs. Next, draw a card and announce its ordered pair. If a child has a marshmallow on that peg, have her replace it with a colored marshmallow. Continue calling out ordered pairs in this manner until one child has replaced all four white marshmallows with colored ones and calls out, "Four points plotted!" Instruct her to state the coordinates of her pairs. If they match, allow her to be the next caller!

Decoding Messages From Space

Plotting ordered pairs of whole numbers on a grid

Help students get the point about plotting ordered pairs of numbers with a banner-making activity! Divide students into groups of four or five. Give each group member a 10 x 10 grid. Instruct him to number the grid's axes from 0 to 10. Next, have the group choose a word with the same number of letters as people in its group. Have each group member illustrate a different letter of the word by plotting successive points on his grid and listing the matching ordered pairs below the grid as shown. After group members check each other's work, have them tape their grids together to form a banner that spells their word. Then invite the groups to read each other's words!

(1, 1), (1, 2), (1, 3), (1, 4), (1, 5), (1, 6), (1, 7), (1, 8), (1, 9), (1, 10), (2, 9), (3, 8), (4, 7), (5, 6), (6, 7), (7, 8), (8, 9), (9, 10), (9, 9), (9, 8), (9, 7), (9, 6), (9, 5), (9, 4), (9, 3), (9, 2), (9, 1)

(2, 1), (2, 2), (2, 3), (2, 4), (2, 5), (2, 6), (3, 4), (3, 7), (4, 4), (4, 8), (5, 4), (5, 9), (6, 4), (6, 8), (7, 4), (7, 7), (8, 6), (8, 5), (8, 4), (8, 3), (8, 2), (8, 1)

(2, 9), (3, 9), (4, 9), (5, 1), (5, 2), (5, 3), (5, 4), (5, 5), (5, 6), (5, 7), (5, 8), (5, 9), (6, 9), (7, 9), (8, 9)

(2, 1), (2, 2), (2, 3), (2, 4), (2, 5), (2, 6), (2, 7), (2, 8), (2, 9), (3, 5), (4, 5), (5, 5), (6, 5), (7, 5), (8, 5), (9, 9), (9, 8), (9, 7), (9, 6), (9, 5), (9, 4), (9, 3), (9, 2), (9, 1)

Seeing Stars

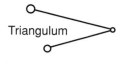
Triangulum

Dr. Luke Stargazer fell on his way to work this morning. Now he's having trouble plotting and identifying the constellations he needs for a lecture. Help him out!

Directions: For problems 1–3, plot a point for each ordered pair. Connect the points on each grid, in order, to draw three different constellations. For problems 4–6, identify each constellation by writing the letter for each ordered pair in its matching blank.

☆1 (8, 10), (8, 9), (9, 7), (9, 5),
(8, 4), (7, 4), (5, 4), (4, 6),
(3, 6), (2, 6), (1, 5), (2, 4),
(4, 1), (5, 1), (5, 0), (4, 0),
(4, 1)

☆2 (0, 9), (1, 9), (3, 8), (4, 7),
(4, 5), (8, 5), (9, 7), (4, 7)

☆3 (6, 1), (6, 2), (4, 4), (4, 6),
(3, 6), (3, 7), (2, 7), (2, 8)

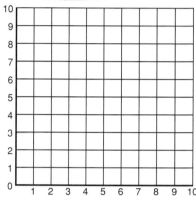

☆4 __ __ __ __ __ __
(2, 9) (3, 3) (1, 6) (6, 2) (5, 8) (1, 0)

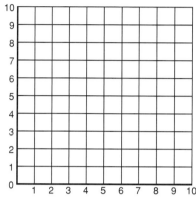

☆5 __ __ __
(2, 3) (4, 7) (8, 0)

__ __ __ __ __ __
(1, 8) (4, 7) (7, 9) (7, 9) (6, 3) (0, 2)

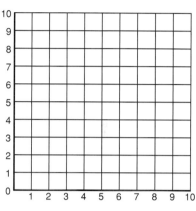

☆6 __ __ __ __ __ __ __
(1, 5) (4, 1) (5, 8) (7, 3) (1, 1) (4, 5) (4, 1)

Bonus Box: To find out another name for the constellation in problem 6, write the letters for the following ordered

pairs: _____ _____ _____ _____ _____ _____ .
         (1, 5) (8, 9) (8, 1) (4, 1) (1, 1) (7, 5)

GETTING THE SCOOP ON CONGRUENCY

Hankering for fresh new ways to teach congruent shapes? Satisfy that craving with the use-it-now ideas dished up on the following pages!

ideas by Shawna Graham, Degan Elementary, Lewisville, TX

1. the two spoons
2. the trays
3. the wooden slats on the table
4. the checked squares of basket liner

Can you find **4** sets of congruent objects in this picture?

Can you find ___ sets of congruent objects in this picture?

Can you find ___ sets of congruent objects in this picture?

CONGRUENCY POCKETS
Identifying congruent objects

Dip into congruent shapes with this three-pocketed idea! Give each student a magazine, three index cards, a 12" x 18" sheet of construction paper, scissors, glue, and access to a stapler. Have him fold his paper in half (to 6" x 18") and then into thirds (to 6" x 6"). Then instruct him to unfold the thirds and staple together the two open sides and inner folds to create three open-top pockets. Next, have him cut out three magazine pictures that show two or more congruent objects each and glue each one to a different pocket. Have him label each pocket with the question shown, filling in the number of congruent objects illustrated in each picture. Then direct him to list those objects on an index card and place it in the corresponding pocket. Finally, invite students to trade pockets and identify the objects in their partners' pictures!

CONGRUENT CONSTRUCTIONS
Using transformations to make and match congruent shapes

Build students' understanding of congruency by having them construct the shapes they'll use to play a matching game! Make and display the chart shown. Then review with students how to make a translation (slide), a reflection (flip), and a rotation (turn). Next, divide students into groups of four. Give each group four different pattern blocks, four index cards, scissors, markers, a resealable plastic bag for storing the game cards, and a die. Instruct the group to cut its four cards in half to make eight cards and to make Xs in the bottom corners of each card, as shown, so players will know how to orient the cards during the game. Then have each group member choose a pattern block and trace it onto a card. After she colors the tracing, have her roll the die to determine from the chart which type of colorful tracing to make on a second card. Once each group member completes the second card, invite the group to sit in a circle, turn its eight cards facedown in the middle of the circle, and challenge each other to a game of Congruency Concentration!

Roll	Transformation
1 or 2	translation
3 or 4	reflection
5 or 6	rotation

CHECK IT OUT!

Recognizing congruent shapes

Find out how well students understand congruency with this simple game! Draw two shapes on a transparent grid; then divide students into three teams and display the grid on an overhead projector. Next, say, "Check it out!" Prompt team members to decide whether the displayed shapes are congruent. As soon as a team decides on an answer, it calls out, "Checked it!" If the answer is incorrect, discuss why; then wipe off the shapes and draw two more. If the answer is correct, award that team one check mark and call on any team member to prove the answer. For example, the child could measure the shapes with a ruler or trace one shape onto another transparency and place the tracing atop the second shape to see if they match. If the student proves his team's answer, award his team a second check mark. Play several rounds; then declare the team with the most check marks the winner!

These rectangles are not congruent because one is three centimeters by four centimeters and the other is three centimeters by five centimeters.

Team 1
✓✓

Team 2
✓

Team 3
✓✓✓

CONGRUENT QUILTING

Using congruent polygons to create a tessellation

How can students discover which regular polygons tessellate? By creating a colorful paper quilt! Review with students that a tessellation is a shape that can be traced and transformed with no gaps or overlaps, using either a translation, reflection, or rotation. Next, divide the class into groups of four students. Give each group a handful of different pattern blocks and a large sheet of paper. Allow students three minutes to explore which shapes will tessellate *(squares, triangles, and hexagons)*. Then give each student a six-inch square of white paper and crayons or markers. Instruct him to decorate the square with a colorful tessellated design, using tracings of one or more pattern blocks to represent one or more transformations. Attach the completed squares to a large sheet of black bulletin board paper. Mount the display on a wall and title it "Congruent Quilting."

161

CONGRUENT COUNTERTOPS

Connie wants new countertops in her three Polar Parlor ice-cream stores. Styles can vary from store to store, but the countertops for each store must be the same size and shape. Color the choices for each store that are congruent. Remember that shapes can slide, flip, or turn and still be congruent!

> If you need help, trace one figure on another sheet of paper. Then place the traced figure over the other figures and compare.

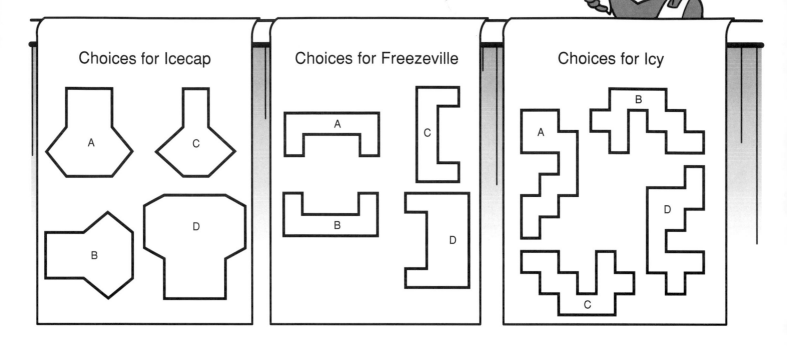

This is one of Connie's parlors. List as many examples of congruent figures shown in the picture as you can. One has been done for you.

the floor tiles _____

Bonus Box: On the back of this page, draw a picture that includes these shapes: two congruent squares, two congruent circles, and two congruent triangles.

©The Mailbox® • TEC44018 • April/May 2005 • Key p. 310

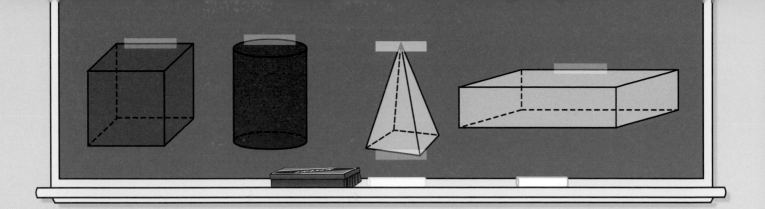

Fab Figures!

Activities for Exploring 3-D Shapes

NAME THAT SOLID!
Describing attributes of 3-D figures

Take the guesswork out of finding out how much your students know about 3-D figures with a matching activity that gets them up and moving around! Make enough copies of the cards on page 164 so that each child will have a card. Having more than one matching set of cards for each 3-D figure is fine. Cut the cards apart. Without letting students see the cards, tape a card securely to each child's back. Make sure that for every word card a student has, another student has the matching picture card. (If you have an odd number of students, include yourself in the activity.) Once everyone has a card, have each child walk around the room asking his classmates for a clue about what is on his card until he has correctly identified it and found the classmate(s) with the matching card(s).

These cool activities for exploring 3-D figures will take learning to a whole new dimension!

with ideas by Melissa Bryan, Valley Forge Middle School, Wayne, PA

3-D DESIGNS
Using the shapes of solid figures to make models of everyday objects

What do you get if you combine students' creativity, the shapes of 3-D figures, and a little clay? A new look for an everyday object! Write on the board the name of an object, such as *table*. Next, give each child or small group of students a supply of paper towels and modeling clay. Have each designer or group create a model of the object using rectangular prisms, spheres, cubes, cylinders, cones, or square pyramids. As a visual aid, display this issue's poster on 3-D figures for students to refer to as they work. When the models are finished, students will be amazed to discover the different 3-D figures used to create the same object!

Both tables are made with cylinders and rectangular prisms.

Activity Cards
Use with "Name That Solid!" on page 163.

cylinder	cube	cone	square pyramid	sphere	rectangular prism

It's in the Cards!

Look at the pictures.
Fill in the chart.

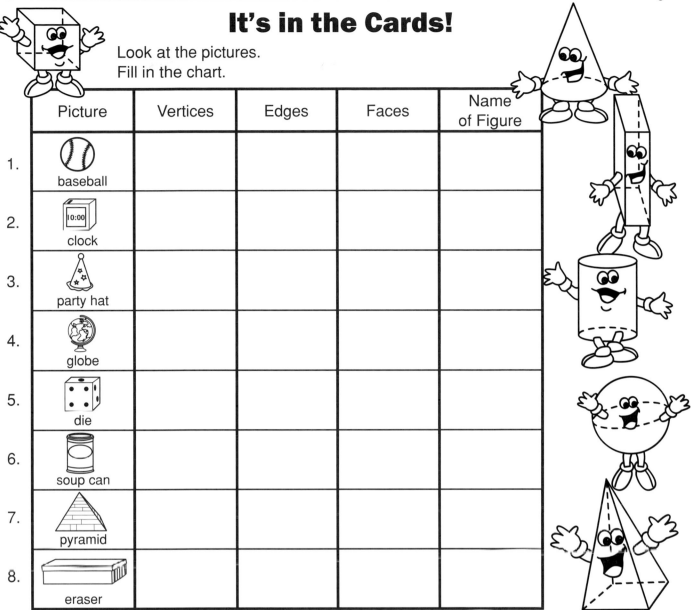

	Picture	Vertices	Edges	Faces	Name of Figure
1.	baseball				
2.	clock				
3.	party hat				
4.	globe				
5.	die				
6.	soup can				
7.	pyramid				
8.	eraser				

Why did the bald guy paint rabbits on his head?

To solve the riddle, color each game card below that has a matching answer in the chart above.
Then read the uncolored cards in order.

0 he	7 Because	8 likes	1 to	3 they	4 look	0 do	0 art
0 can't	6 see	0 the	12 top	8 of	8 come	0 his	sphere head
1 brush	5 so	3 like	0 she	0 color	13 hares	12 by	12 not
9 from	0 and	rectangular prism neck	6 next	2 ear	cylinder again	cone my	cube one
8 or	6 to	4 far	square pyramid close	5 five	sphere eyes	cube man	10 away

Nailing Down Area

If your students are having trouble understanding area, these activities will help them nail it!

by Shawna Graham, Degan Elementary, Lewisville, TX

Same Area, Different Shape
Finding the area of regular polygons

A picture is worth a thousand words, especially when it makes finding the area of regular polygons easier to understand! Display a centimeter grid transparency on which you have outlined four different squares or rectangles that each have an area of 16 square centimeters (see the examples). After reviewing the meaning of area with the class, have everyone count the squares inside the first polygon. Number the squares and record the area in square units below the polygon as shown. Invite three different students to repeat the process to find the area of each remaining shape. When finished, write each polygon's length, width, and area in a chart such as the one shown. Guide students to use the chart to determine the formula for finding the area of a square $(A = s^2)$ or rectangle $(A = l \times w)$. Follow up by giving each child a sheet of centimeter graph paper and ten minutes to outline as many figures as he can that each have an area of 24 square centimeters. To extend the activity, have students include outlines of irregular figures that have areas of 16 and 24 square centimeters.

Figure	Length	Width	Area
1	4	4	16
2	8	2	16
3	2	8	16
4	1	16	16

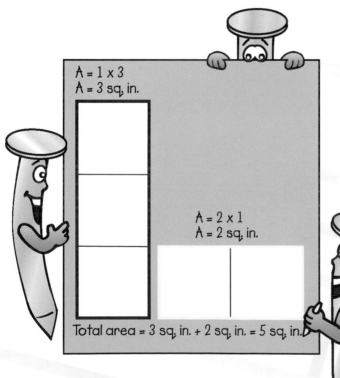

A = 1 x 3
A = 3 sq. in.

A = 2 x 1
A = 2 sq. in.

Total area = 3 sq. in. + 2 sq. in. = 5 sq. in.

Designer Letters
Finding the area of irregular figures

Put new designs on finding the area of irregular figures with this letter-perfect idea! Cut ten two-inch paper squares for each student and ten two-inch squares from transparency film for yourself. After reviewing the formula for finding the area of a square or rectangle with students, give each child a ruler, colored markers, and ten squares. Direct her to use the ruler and formula to find the area of any one of the squares *(four square inches)*. Next, arrange five transparency squares into an *L* on the overhead. Help students conclude that the formula for the area of squares and rectangles does not work with irregular figures. But demonstrate that they can use the formula if they divide the *L* into two rectangles and add the two areas together as shown. Then have each child construct the letters *T* and *E* with her squares, trace them with markers on paper, and then find the area of each one. Check by forming the letters on the overhead with the transparency squares, dividing the *T* into two rectangles, dividing the *E* into four rectangles, and then adding the areas of each letter's parts together.

Finally, have each child pretend to be a carpenter who must design five letter-shaped rooms: *I, F, O, H,* and *J.* Instruct her to trace her squares on paper to form each room. Then have her trade papers with a partner and find the area of each room so it can be carpeted!

Top It With a Triangle!

Finding the area of triangles

This top-notch activity is perfect for finding the area of triangles! Draw a triangle on a centimeter grid transparency. Demonstrate how to count and label the triangle's whole and partial squares to find the area. Repeat the process with two more triangles; then check the answers using the formula for finding the area of a triangle: $A = \frac{1}{2} \times (b \times h)$. Next, outline the shape of a house on the transparency. Guide students to find the house's area two ways: (1) by counting the whole and partial squares and (2) by dividing the house into two shapes (a triangle and a square) and using formulas. Follow up by giving each child a ruler, colored pencils, and a sheet of centimeter grid paper. Instruct him to outline a shape (regular or irregular) that includes two or more squares or rectangles and is topped by at least one triangle. Then have him find the figure's area both by counting and by dividing it into its individual shapes and using formulas.

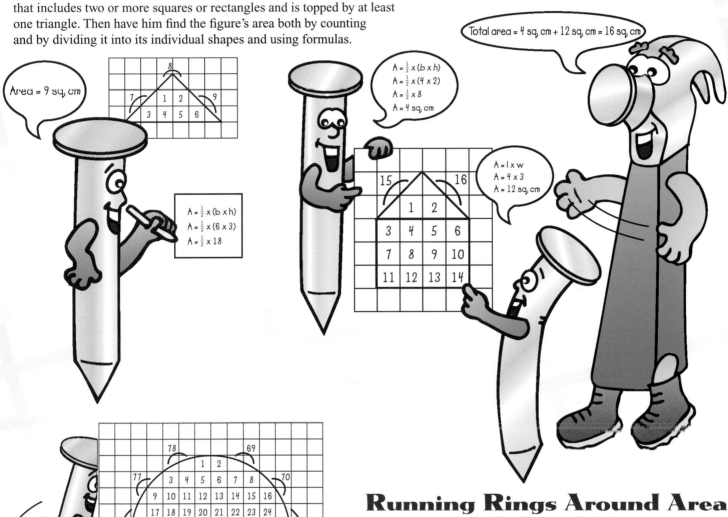

Area = 9 sq. cm

$A = \frac{1}{2} \times (b \times h)$
$A = \frac{1}{2} \times (6 \times 3)$
$A = \frac{1}{2} \times 18$

$A = \frac{1}{2} \times (b \times h)$
$A = \frac{1}{2} \times (4 \times 2)$
$A = \frac{1}{2} \times 8$
$A = 4$ sq. cm

Total area = 4 sq. cm + 12 sq. cm = 16 sq. cm

$A = l \times w$
$A = 4 \times 3$
$A = 12$ sq. cm

Estimated area = 78 sq. cm

$d = 10$ cm
$A = 3.14 \times r^2$
$A = 3.14 \times (5^2)$
$A = 3.14 \times 25$
$A = 78.5$ sq. cm

Running Rings Around Area

Finding the area of a circle

Students will be putting the lid on the area of a circle with this fun-to-do activity! Ask students to bring in clean, circular lids from coffee cans, pickle jars, oatmeal containers, soda bottles, etc. Once you have a class supply, display a centimeter grid transparency on which you have traced a circle. Have students help you count and label the circle's squares to estimate the area. Then ask students whether the formulas for finding the area of a square, rectangle, or triangle could be used to find the area of a circle *(no)*. After discussing a circle's unique traits that require it to have a different formula, measure the displayed circle's diameter with a ruler. Review how to find the radius and explain that pi (π) is approximately 3.14; then use the formula $A = 3.14 \times r^2$ to find the actual area. Help students understand why the two findings are different.

Next, give each child a different container lid, a ruler, and a sheet of centimeter grid paper. Instruct her to trace the lid on the paper, estimate the circle's area by counting, and then use the correct formula to find the circle's actual area. After students share their findings, display the papers on a bulletin board titled "We're Running Rings Around Area!"

Playing Around With Area

Great news! Each playing surface at Playground Area Park is being repaved! Arnie, the person in charge of the paving, must find the area of each surface. Help him complete this task. Each square for problems 1–3 measures 1 ft. x 1 ft. Each square for problems 4–6 measures 1 yd. x 1 yd.

1.
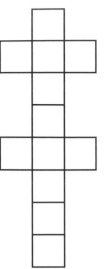

hopscotch area
A = _____ sq. ft.

2.
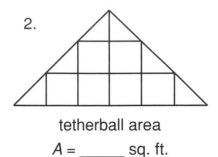

tetherball area
A = _____ sq. ft.

3.
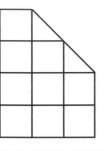

jump rope area
A = _____ sq. ft.

4.
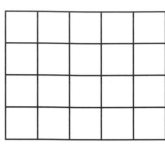

volleyball court
A = _____ sq. yd.
A = _____ sq. ft.

5.
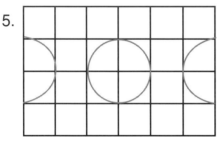

basketball court
A = _____ sq. yd.
A = _____ sq. ft.

6.
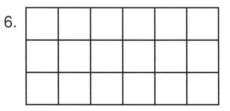

tennis court
A = _____ sq. yd.
A = _____ sq. ft.

7. 52 ft. x 95 ft. area for bleachers _____ sq. ft.

8. 27 ft. x 54 ft. area for snack stands _____ sq. ft.

9. 36 ft. x 48 ft. area for covered picnic shelter _____ sq. ft.

10. 44 yd. x 60 yd. parking lot _____ sq. yd. _____ sq. ft.

Bonus Box: Find the total area in square feet for problems 1–10. If the pavers charge $8.00 per square foot, how much will the paving cost? Show your work on the back of this page.

©The Mailbox® • TEC44017 • Feb./Mar. 2005 • Key p. 311

Name

Carpeting Clarence's Cabin

Clarence wants to carpet the floors of his cabin. Use the measurements on the floor plan to help you find the area of each room or space. Don't worry! His rooms do have doors. He just didn't show them on the drawing.

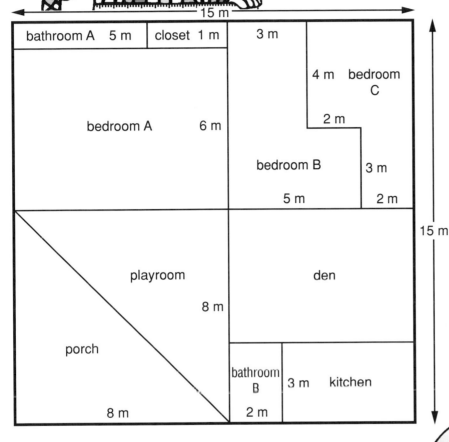

1. bedroom A = _____ sq. meters

2. bathroom A = _____ sq. meters

3. closet = _____ sq. meters

4. bedroom B = _____ sq. meters

5. bedroom C = _____ sq. meters

6. den = _____ sq. meters

7. kitchen = _____ sq. meters

8. bathroom B = _____ sq. meters

9. playroom = _____ sq. meters

10. porch = _____ sq. meters

11. Which room has the largest area? _____

12. If carpet costs $7.00 per square meter, how much will it cost Clarence to carpet the den? _____ Bedroom A? _____ The entire cabin? _____

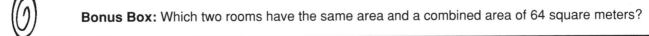

Bonus Box: Which two rooms have the same area and a combined area of 64 square meters?

169

Icing Carla's Cakes

Carla must ice five mini cakes in a hurry for her best customer. She needs your help! First, estimate the area of each cake top by counting the squares. Then use each cake top's diameter and the formula $A = 3.14 \times r^2$ to find the actual area.

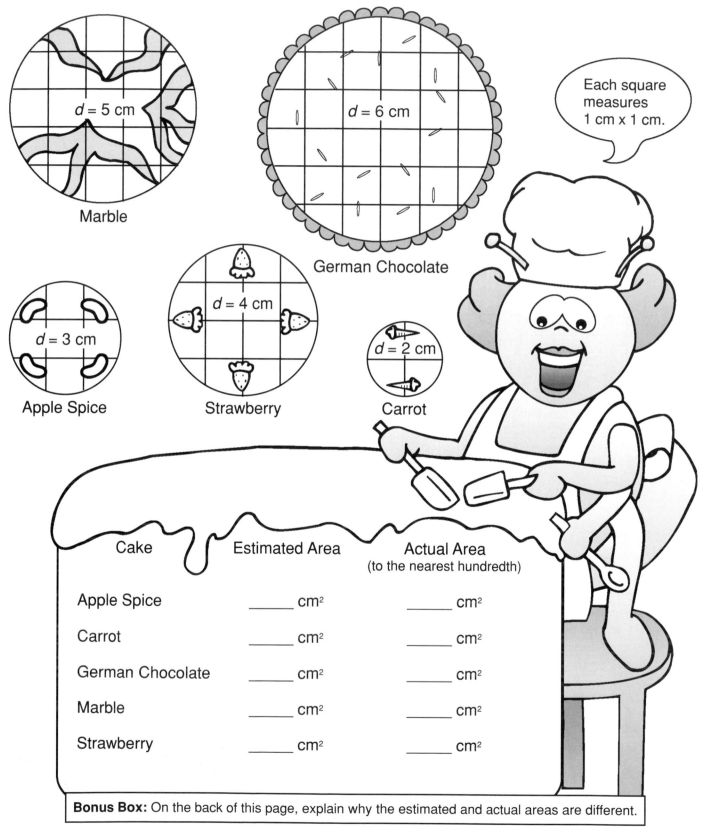

Marble — $d = 5$ cm

German Chocolate — $d = 6$ cm

Each square measures 1 cm x 1 cm.

Apple Spice — $d = 3$ cm

Strawberry — $d = 4$ cm

Carrot — $d = 2$ cm

Cake	Estimated Area	Actual Area (to the nearest hundredth)
Apple Spice	_____ cm²	_____ cm²
Carrot	_____ cm²	_____ cm²
German Chocolate	_____ cm²	_____ cm²
Marble	_____ cm²	_____ cm²
Strawberry	_____ cm²	_____ cm²

Bonus Box: On the back of this page, explain why the estimated and actual areas are different.

©The Mailbox® • TEC44017 • Feb./Mar. 2005 • Key p. 311

On the Lookout for Perimeter

Perimeter means the distance around an object.

If you've been looking far and wide for activities that can help your students really get what perimeter is all about, you can stop right here!

by Liz Harrell, Sacred Heart School, Highland Falls, NY

Pools of Perimeter

Finding perimeter of regular and irregular shapes

Dive right in to perimeter with this hands-on activity! Pair students. Give each duo four 9" x 12" sheets of paper (two gray, two blue), scissors, glue, a ruler, and two 48-inch lengths of yarn. Direct one partner to cut a straight-edged shape from blue paper and glue it to a gray sheet. Have him measure each edge and then record the measurements and perimeter as shown. Instruct the other partner to cut a curved shape from blue paper and glue it to the remaining gray sheet. Have her outline her shape with yarn, measure the yarn's length, and record the perimeter as shown. Finally, have each partner cut a length of yarn equal to his or her shape's perimeter and glue it around the shape as an accent. Display students' projects on a bulletin board titled "Pools of Perimeter."

Paco's Pool
6½ in.
4½ in.
P = 32 in.
3 in.
9½ in.
5 in.
3½ in.

Penny's Pool
P = 28 in.

Protect the Perimeter!

Developing a formula for finding perimeter

Motivate students to find perimeter using this real-life scenario. Tell students that they have been hired to provide pest control services to a new neighborhood of homes. Explain that their task is to find the perimeter of the houses and then determine the number of termite traps each one will need. Divide students into groups of four. Give each group a ruler. Direct the students in each group to choose four rectangular items from their desks to represent houses. Have group members take turns finding the perimeter of each house and recording it in a chart such as the one shown. Instruct the students to figure one termite trap for every two inches of perimeter. When the reports are completed, have students discuss any patterns they noticed. Finally, guide the groups to use what they've learned to write a formula for finding perimeter.

Pest Control Report

House	Length	Width	Perimeter	Number of Traps
sticky note	3 in.	3 in.	12 in.	6
textbook	11 in.	9 in.	40 in.	20
crayon box	4 in.	3 in.	14 in.	7
pencil box	9½ in.	7½ in.	34 in.	17

The Decorator's Edge

Using models to find perimeter

Cook up excitement about perimeter by transforming students into bakers! Give each child six centimeter cubes, grid paper, a 6" x 9" piece of construction paper, glue, scissors, and markers. Direct the student to arrange her cubes to create as many different cake shapes as she can within an allotted time. Have her record each shape on grid paper (allow irregular shapes). If desired, give each student four additional cubes and have her also create shapes built with ten cubes. When she's finished, instruct each child to find and record each cake's perimeter as shown. Check her calculations. Then have the student decorate her cakes, using the markers to outline them with colorful icing. Finally, invite each baker to cut out her cakes, group them by perimeter, and glue them to a nifty construction paper tray for display. Yum!

P = 10 units
P = 12 units
P = 14 units
P = 14 units
P = 14 units
P = 16 units

Mini Bulletin Boards

Reviewing perimeter

Showcase your class's knowledge of perimeter with a mini display that maximizes understanding! Make a poster board pattern of each polygon listed. Give each pair of students a 9" x 12" sheet of colorful construction paper, paper scraps in various colors, a 1½" x 24" piece of white sentence strip, a centimeter ruler, scissors, glue, and markers. Explain that each twosome will create a mini bulletin board about perimeter. Then guide the partners through the steps shown. Conclude by having each pair share a formula for finding the perimeter of each polygon on its board.

Steps:

1. Select a sheet of construction paper to use as the board's background color.
2. To create a decorative border, draw a curved (or angled) line down the center of the sentence strip piece. Cut along the line, creating two long strips. Cut each long strip in half. If desired, color the strips or add a design.
3. Glue the strips to the board's edges, overlapping the corners. Trim the extra part of the strips.
4. Choose four or five different poster board polygons. Trace each shape on a different color of construction paper. Cut out the tracings.
5. Find the perimeter of each cutout and record it on the shape.
6. Glue the cutouts to the board in an attractive arrangement. Add a title.

Polygon Perimeters

P = 12 cm
P = 20 cm
P = 15 cm
P = 15 cm
P = 15 cm

Polygons

3 cm square
4 cm x 5.5 cm parallelogram
2 cm x 8 cm rectangle
5 cm equilateral triangle
2.5 cm hexagon
1.5 cm octagon
4 cm rhombus
3 cm x 3 cm x 3 cm x 6 cm trapezoid
2.5 cm pentagon

Polly's Portal

Do you like my new door?

One entrance to Polly's burrow has a new door! To find out which entrance it is, calculate the perimeter of each polygon. Then write the letter of each answer in its matching blank at the bottom of the page.

1.
6 ft.
5 ft.
$P =$ _____ ft.
(P)
6 ft.

2.
$P =$ _____ ft. (D)
2 ft.
5.5 ft.

3.
4.5 ft.
$P =$ _____ ft.
(O)
4.5 ft.

4.
$P =$ _____ ft.
(E)
5.5 ft.

5.
$P =$ _____ ft.
(R)
2 ft.

6.
$P =$ _____ ft.
(A)
6.5 ft.

Which one is it?

7.
3.25 ft.
$P =$ _____ ft.
(Z)

8.
$P =$ _____ ft.
(T)
2.75 ft.

9.
4 ft.
2 ft.
$P =$ _____ ft. (I)
2 ft.
5.5 ft.

Polly's entrance is the

____ ____ ____ ____ ____ ____ ____ ____ ____ .
16.5 ft. 16 ft. 19.5 ft. 17 ft. 22 ft. 13 ft. 18 ft. 13.5 ft. 15 ft.

Bonus Box: Polly wants to increase the size of her entrance. Find the new perimeter if she adds two feet to each side of her door.

Name _____

Our Very Own Places on the Prairie

Patty, Perry, and Prissy have their own special burrows on the prairie. Find the perimeter of each one. Then outline each burrow's grid in the color that tells which prairie dog it belongs to.

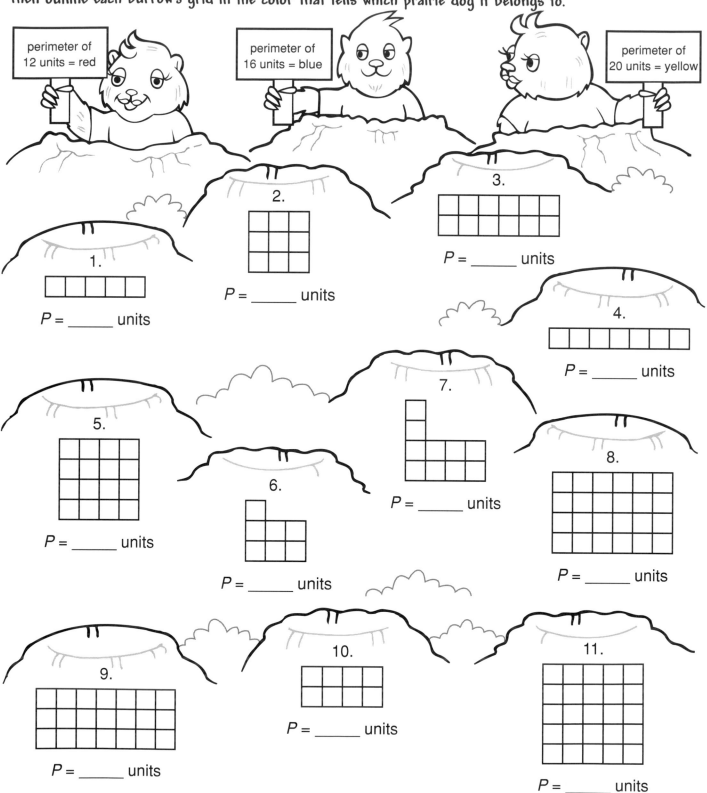

perimeter of
12 units = red

perimeter of
16 units = blue

perimeter of
20 units = yellow

1.
P = _____ units

2.
P = _____ units

3.
P = _____ units

4.
P = _____ units

5.
P = _____ units

6.
P = _____ units

7.
P = _____ units

8.
P = _____ units

9.
P = _____ units

10.
P = _____ units

11.
P = _____ units

Bonus Box: Pokey, their cousin, prefers burrows that have perimeters of 24 units. On the back of this page, draw a grid box that has a perimeter of 24 units.

Note to the teacher: Each student will need three crayons to complete this page: red, blue, and yellow.

Playful Prairie Dogs

Paula wants to design new rectangular play
areas for her pups. But she needs your help!

Directions:
1. Find the missing length of each rectangular play area.
2. Use the four measurements to write an addition sentence to find the perimeter of each area.
3. Write another addition sentence that shows the perimeter as the sum of two products.

1.
8 m
_____ m
$P = 28$ m

P = _____

P = _____

2.
_____ ft.
12 ft.
$P = 74$ ft.

P = _____

P = _____

3.
10 m
_____ m
$P = 30$ m

P = _____

P = _____

4.
_____ ft.
26 ft.
$P = 76$ m

P = _____

P = _____

5.
_____ ft.
36 ft.
$P = 108$ ft.

P = _____

P = _____

6.
_____ m
5 m
$P = 26$ m

P = _____

P = _____

Bonus Box: What do you know about the length of the opposite sides of a rectangle that allows you to use the formula $P = (2 \times \text{length}) + (2 \times \text{width})$ to find perimeter? Explain your answer on the back of this page.

©The Education Center, Inc. • *The Mailbox®* • TEC44015 • Oct./Nov. 2004 • Key p. 311

Note to the teacher: If desired, allow students to use calculators to complete this page.

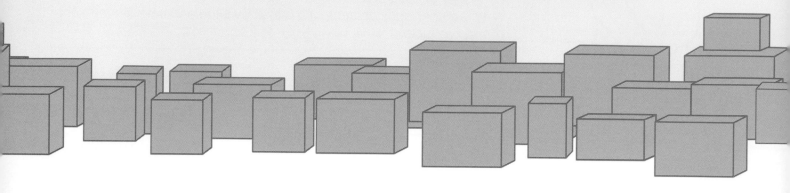

Stock Up!

Activities to Measure Volume

$3 \times 4 \times 3 = 36$ | $1 \times 3 \times 12 = 36$ | $3 \times 2 \times 6 = 36$

VOLUME VALLEY
Using concrete models

Discover the formula for volume with this model-building activity! Gather a supply of base ten unit cubes or one-inch wooden blocks or plastic cubes. Then divide students into groups. Assign each group a particular number, such as 36 or 24. Explain that each group will have a set amount of time to build as many rectangular prisms containing its assigned number of cubes as it can. When time is up, have students view the towers built by other groups and then come up with a formula for finding the volume of each tower *(multiply length times width times height)*. To test the formula, have each group find the product of each of its towers' dimensions to see whether it matches the group's assigned number!

If your storehouse of volume activities needs replenishing, then restock your shelves with these fun-to-use ideas. At inventory time, students' skills are sure to measure up!

by Melissa H. Bryan, Valley Forge Middle School, Wayne, PA

$V = l \times w \times h$
$V = 9 \times 3 \times 13 = 351$ in.^{3}

Calculator, library book, textbook, dictionary, notepad, composition notebook, filing cabinet, chalkboard eraser, cardboard box, box of crayons, pencil box, ream of paper...

IT'S WHAT'S INSIDE THAT COUNTS!
Using concrete models

Basing a package's volume on its size will be a thing of the past with this eye-opening exercise! Ask students to bring in one each of several different kinds of empty cereal boxes. Number the boxes with sticky notes; then arrange the boxes in numerical order along a chalk tray. Ask students to predict which box has the greatest volume and which has the least volume and tally each child's response on the board. Next, divide students into groups of two or three. Give each group a cereal box, a ruler, a paper strip, a marker, and tape. Direct the group to measure its box's length, width, and height to the nearest inch to find its volume. Then have the group record its work on the sentence strip, tape it near the box's top, and return the box to the chalk tray. Once the boxes have been returned, have a child from each group share the group's box's dimensions and volume with the class so students can check their predictions and identify the boxes with the greatest and least volume.

CLASSY VOLUME
Using real-life objects

Everything needed to make this class book about volume is right in your classroom! Ask students to brainstorm classroom objects that are rectangular prisms. List the objects on the board. Next, assign each child (or pair of students) a different object. Instruct him to measure his object's length, width, and height. Also have him illustrate the object on unlined paper, label the object's dimensions, and find its volume. Compile the completed pages into a book titled "Volume: Volume 1." For homework, have each child repeat the task using an object from home to make Volume 2!

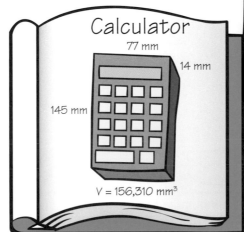

Calculator
77 mm
14 mm
145 mm
$V = 156,310$ mm^3

Scrumptious Servings

Find the volume.

One serving is one cubic inch.

Brownies
1 in.
6 in.
6 in.

V = _____ in.³, or _____ servings

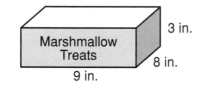

Marshmallow Treats
3 in.
8 in.
9 in.

V = _____ in.³, or _____ servings

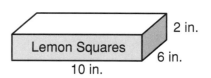

Lemon Squares
2 in.
6 in.
10 in.

V = _____ in.³, or _____ servings

Chocolate Bars
1 in.
2 in.
5 in.

V = _____ in.³, or _____ servings

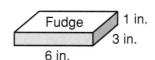

Fudge
1 in.
3 in.
6 in.

V = _____ in.³, or _____ servings

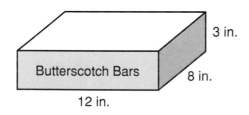

Butterscotch Bars
3 in.
8 in.
12 in.

V = _____ in.³, or _____ servings

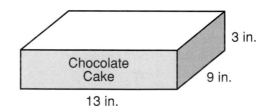

Chocolate Cake
3 in.
9 in.
13 in.

V = _____ in.³, or _____ servings

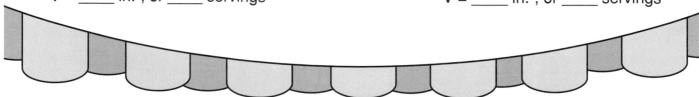

Bonus Box: Find the total number of servings the caterer will have for the party.

Which Tank Is My Home?

Find the volume.
Use the letters to put each fish in the correct tank.
Color each fish as it is put in a tank. One fish will have to wait on a tank.

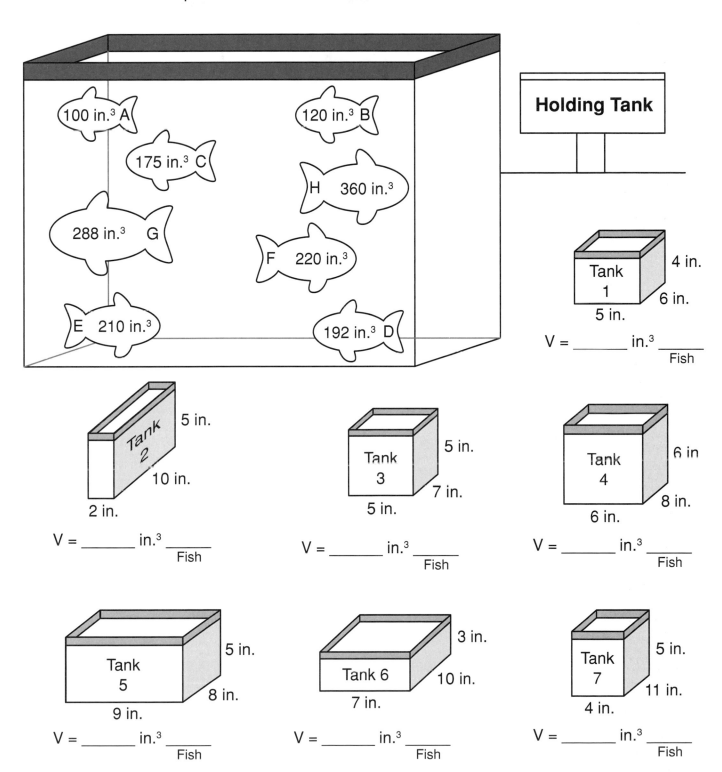

100 in.³ A

120 in.³ B

175 in.³ C

H   360 in.³

288 in.³   G

F   220 in.³

E   210 in.³

192 in.³ D

Holding Tank

Tank 1   4 in.   6 in.   5 in.

V = _____ in.³ _____
Fish

Tank 2   5 in.   10 in.   2 in.

V = _____ in.³ _____
Fish

Tank 3   5 in.   7 in.   5 in.

V = _____ in.³ _____
Fish

Tank 4   6 in   8 in.   6 in.

V = _____ in.³ _____
Fish

Tank 5   5 in.   8 in.   9 in.

V = _____ in.³ _____
Fish

Tank 6   3 in.   10 in.   7 in.

V = _____ in.³ _____
Fish

Tank 7   5 in.   11 in.   4 in.

V = _____ in.³ _____
Fish

Bonus Box: Based on the number on the homeless fish, it will need a tank just a bit larger than the one belonging to fish _____ and just a bit smaller than the one belonging to fish _____.

Note to the teacher: Each student will need a crayon to complete this page.

Wanted: More Storage Space

Find the current volume.
Find the new volume.
Subtract to find the gain in volume.

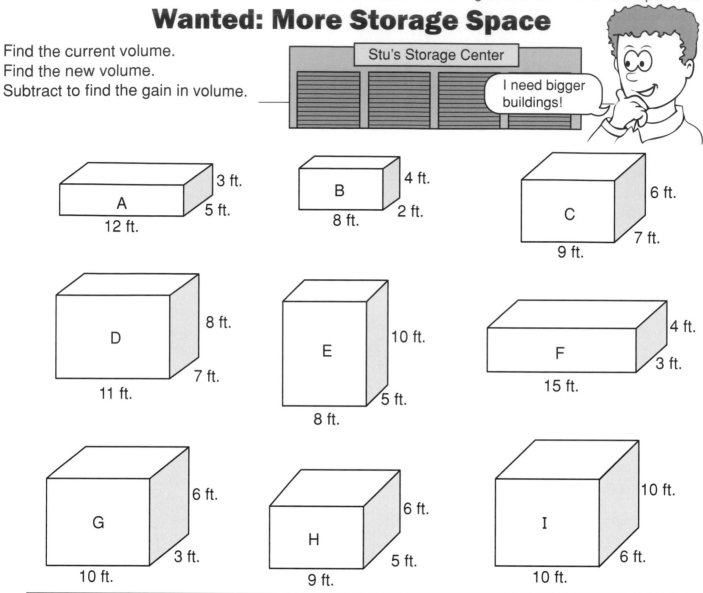

Stu's Storage Center

I need bigger buildings!

	Building	Current Volume of Building	Change to Make in the Building	New Volume	Gain in Volume
1.	A		2 feet wider and 3 feet taller		
2.	B		1 foot wider and 5 feet longer		
3.	C		8 feet longer		
4.	D		2 feet wider and 3 feet taller		
5.	E		1 foot wider and 5 feet longer		
6.	F		8 feet longer		
7.	G		2 feet wider and 3 feet taller		
8.	H		1 foot wider and 5 feet longer		
9.	I		8 feet longer		

Note to the teacher: If desired, allow students to use calculators to complete this page.

Social Studies Units

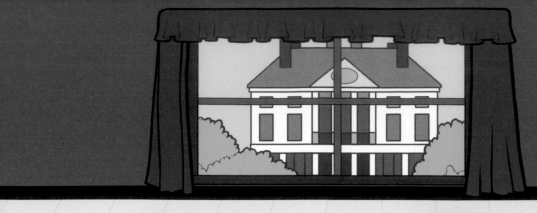

Adding On
Amendments to Our Constitution

FIRST AMENDMENT SCENARIOS
Understanding the first amendment

How well do your students understand the first amendment? Here's how to find out! Obtain a supply of yarn and make and color five copies of the traffic light pattern on page 184. Cut out the traffic lights and mount them on a bulletin board, each under a different heading of the following freedoms: speech, assembly, press, religion, and petition. Next, divide students into groups of five and give each group six index cards and a copy of page 185. Discuss the first amendment on page 185; then assign each group a different freedom from the display. On each of three cards, have the group describe an example of its assigned right being respected. On each of the remaining cards, have the group describe an example of that right being abused.

When everyone is finished, instruct the groups to trade cards, read the examples, and sort them into three groups: respected, abused, not sure. Then have each group connect its cards with yarn to the corresponding traffic light so that those connected to a red light represent abuses of the right, those connected to a green light represent respectful exercising of the right, and those connected to a yellow light are ones the group is unsure about.

Freedom of Speech

A popular disc jockey uses bad language on the air.

Someone threatens to harm another person.

A student calls another student a bad name.

Someone sends out an email reminding people to vote in an upcoming election.

A TV station refuses to show a commercial for beer.

A man does not like how the president is handling an issue, so he writes the president a letter.

Understanding our constitutional rights and freedoms is
guaranteed with these thought-provoking activities!

by Simone Lepine, Gillette Road Middle School, Cicero, NY

THEN AND NOW
Interpreting the first three constitutional amendments

Step back in time to help students understand more about the first three constitutional amendments. Discuss with the class the different rights and freedoms guaranteed by these three amendments and how students think the interpretation of each one might have changed over time. Next, have each child choose a topic from the list shown and write it as the title of a T chart he draws and labels, as shown, on a sheet of drawing paper. Then have him add illustrations showing what he thinks the writers might have had in mind when the amendment was first added to the Constitution and what the amendment means today. When everyone is finished, display the pictures and have the class discuss what the founding fathers might think of how the amendments are being interpreted today!

Freedom of Speech
Freedom of the Press
Freedom of Religion
Freedom of Assembly
The Right to Bear Arms
Freedom From Quartering
  Soldiers in Your Home

Amendment Categories

Bill of Rights: 1, 2, 3, 4, 5, 6, 7, 8, 9, 10

Citizenship and Voting: 12, 13, 14, 15, 19, 23, 24, 26

Rights of the Accused: 4, 5, 6, 7, 8

Running the Government: 10, 11, 12, 16, 17, 18, 20, 21, 22, 25, 27

FOUR-CORNER RIGHTS
Reviewing the amendments

Corner an understanding of our constitutional amendments with a fun review game that gets students up and moving! Post one of the following signs in each corner of the room: Bill of Rights, Citizenship and Voting, Rights of the Accused, and Running the Government. Explain that you will count to ten, giving each player time to go to a corner of her choice. Further explain that once you reach ten, everyone must stay in place. Begin counting. When you reach ten, read aloud one of the amendments on page 185. Instruct everyone standing in a corner related to that amendment to sit down (see the list shown). Then begin counting to ten again and have the students who are still standing select a new corner. This time when you reach ten, read aloud a different amendment. Continue eliminating players in this manner until only one student is left standing!

183

Traffic Light Pattern

Use with "First Amendment Scenarios" on page 182.

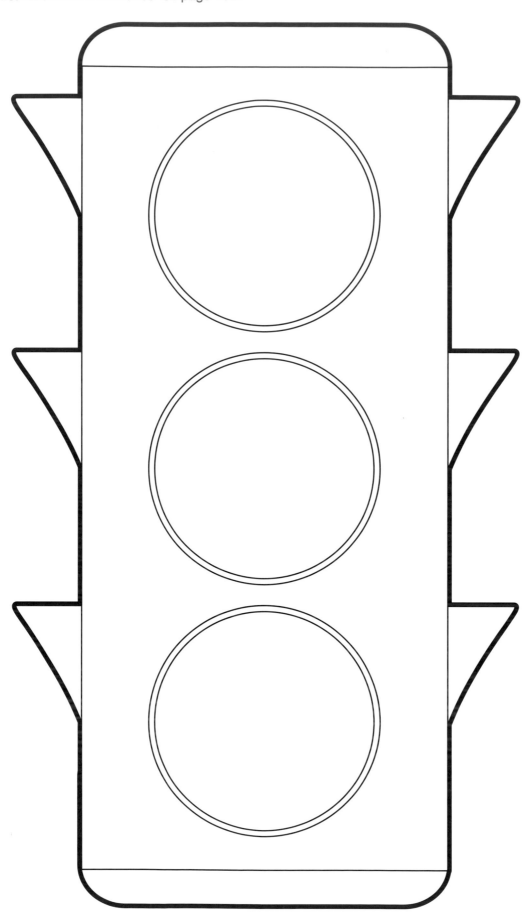

The Constitutional Amendments

1 — People have the freedoms of religion, speech, and the press. They also have the right to meet together peacefully and to bring a matter of concern to the government's attention.

2 — People have the right to own guns and protect themselves.

3 — The government cannot force people to keep soldiers in their homes.

4 — People or their property cannot be searched or seized without a warrant based on a good reason.

5 — People accused of crimes have certain rights. They can't be held for a crime without an indictment from a grand jury. They can't be tried twice for the same capital or other serious crime. They don't have to testify against themselves in court.

6 — People accused of crimes have the right to have fair trials and have a lawyer defend them.

7 — In civil cases, a person is guaranteed a trial by jury.

8 — People accused of crimes cannot be treated cruelly. Excessive fines, excessive bail, or cruel and unusual punishment are not allowed.

9 — People have many other rights not listed in the Constitution.

10 — States have powers not belonging to the national government.

11 — A citizen from one state cannot sue another state, nor can a citizen of another country sue a U.S. state.

12 — The candidate with the greatest number of electoral votes becomes president.

13 — Slavery is unlawful.

14 — All citizens have rights.

15 — No citizen can be kept from voting because of race.

16 — The government has the right to collect income taxes.

17 — People have the right to elect state representatives to the federal senate.

18 — It is illegal to make, sell, or transport alcoholic beverages.

19 — Women have the right to vote.

20 — A president's term in office begins at noon on January 20. Congress shall meet at least one time each year.

21 — The 18th Amendment is repealed, making alcoholic beverages legal.

22 — A president cannot serve more than two terms.

23 — Residents of Washington, DC, have the right to vote in a presidential election.

24 — A person cannot be denied the right to vote for failing to pay a tax.

25 — If the president becomes sick, leaves office, is removed from office, or dies, the vice president takes over. If the position of vice president becomes vacant, the president will nominate a new vice president, who is then voted on by Congress.

26 — The minimum voting age is 18.

27 — Pay raises for members of Congress are delayed until after the next congressional election.

 denotes amendments that make up the Bill of Rights

Note to the teacher: Use with "First Amendment Scenarios" on page 182 and "Then and Now" and "Four-Corner Rights" on page 183.

Insights on the Industrial

Many technological, economic, and cultural advancements occurred in America during a time period that spanned from about the early 19th century to the early 20th century. Guide your students to a greater appreciation of these changes—also known as the Industrial Revolution—with the following creative activities.

by Julia Ring Alarie, Pierce Memorial School, Huntington, VT

Where Would I Be Without You?
Understanding the role of inventions in everyday life

Investigate the importance of inventions with this appreciative poem activity! Write on the board a list of inventions from the Industrial Revolution, such as the ones shown. Explain that each item was invented during the Industrial Revolution. Have each child choose one invention and research its importance. Then instruct the student to imagine how life would be different if that item had never been invented. Have him use his thoughts to write a poem about his invention titled "Where Would I Be Without You?" Direct him to conclude the poem with the sentence "Where would I be without the [invention]?" When students have finished writing, invite the poets to share their rhymes with the class. Then post the poems on a bulletin board titled "Where Would I Be Without You?"

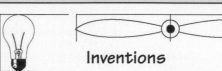

Inventions

electric lightbulb	typewriter
film camera	reaping machine
rotary printing press	barbed wire
electromagnet	cable car
telegraph	ice machine
steamboat	vulcanized rubber
screw propeller	rotary steam engine
transatlantic	air brake
telegraph cable	telephone
practical sewing	phonograph
machine	steel plow

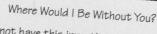

Where Would I Be Without You?

If I did not have this invention,
My days would drag on and on.
What would my friends think
If I didn't call them with this thing I own?

They'd get mad at me for sure,
And I would mope and moan,
But that would make my parents mad!
Where would I be without the telephone?

Homework Helper

Dictionary · Calculator
Thesaurus · Help
Encyclopedia
Telephone

Production Proposals
Understanding the impact of the Industrial Revolution, thinking creatively

Put new designs on creative thinking with this inventive idea! Have each child think of a task or chore she finds challenging. Next, have her invent a machine or system that could make the task easier. Instruct her to write a description of her invention that could persuade a manufacturer to produce it. Remind her to include an explanation of how the machine works and how it could improve people's lives. Have her also include a drawing of her machine. If desired, provide the student with a variety of craft materials and have her make a model of her creation. When students are finished, invite your industrious inventors to present their proposals (and models) to the class.

Revolution

Alexander Graham Bell

Commemorative Corners
Recognizing the contributions of important industrialists

Pay tribute to individuals who influenced the Industrial Revolution with commemorative corners that students construct themselves! Have each student (or pair of students) choose a person from the list shown. Instruct the child to research her chosen person's contribution to the time period. Next, give her a 4½-inch square of white construction paper, scissors, markers, glue, and a copy of page 188. Have her use the materials to complete page 188 as directed. Then display the completed commemorative corners on a tabletop or bookshelf with a banner or tent card titled "Giants of the Industrial Revolution."

Famous People of the American Industrial Revolution

Cornelius Vanderbilt
Robert Fulton
Eli Whitney
Samuel F. B. Morse
Henry Ford
Thomas Alva Edison
John D. Rockefeller
Eugene V. Debs
George Eastman
Andrew Carnegie

Jane Addams
George Westinghouse
Andrew W. Mellon
Alexander Graham Bell
Elijah McCoy
John Pillsbury
James B. Duke
George Pullman
Gustavus Swift
Philip D. Armour

YIKES! Barbed wire!

HAPPY BIRTHDAY

Assembly Line Analysis
Analyzing the impact of mass production and division of labor

Use this creative activity to explore the impact of shifting from goods being produced by a tradesman in a home or village store to one driven by mass production! Gather various craft materials, such as light-colored construction paper, crayons, stickers, glue, tape, glitter, and colorful paper scraps. Have each child use the materials to create a greeting card for an upcoming event or holiday. When the cards are finished, divide students into groups of five. Announce to the groups that they are now workers in a greeting card company that you own. Look over each group's cards and choose one for each group to mass-produce in assembly line fashion.

Next, direct each group to create a division-of-labor plan so that each group member has a specialized job. Explain that the group should make as many cards as possible in the time it will have to work and that each card made should be identical to the original. Then announce how much time the workers will have and instruct them to begin. When time is up, have each group display its original card and its mass-produced ones and share thoughts about the positive and negative factors of the assembly line system with the class.

Commemorative Corner Pattern

Use with "Commemorative Corners" on page 187.

Finished Sample

Alexander Graham Bell

Directions:

1. Cut out the pentagon below, making sure not to cut through the directions.

2. Bring A/B to E/F so that the triangle is folded along the solid line onto rectangle HGDC. Fold the rectangle in half to form two squares.

3. Unfold the shapes and cut along the dotted line.

4. Turn the pentagon so that the triangular part points downward. Use crayons or markers to draw on square HEIC a picture showing how your person influenced the Industrial Revolution.

5. On white construction paper, draw a full-length picture of your person. Cut out the figure and glue it to square FGDJ. Write your person's name next to the cutout.

6. On triangle ACI, write a sentence explaining how your person's contribution changed people's lives.

7. Bring A over to D and glue in place over triangle BJD.

8. Glue B to C.

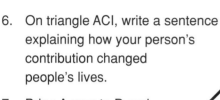

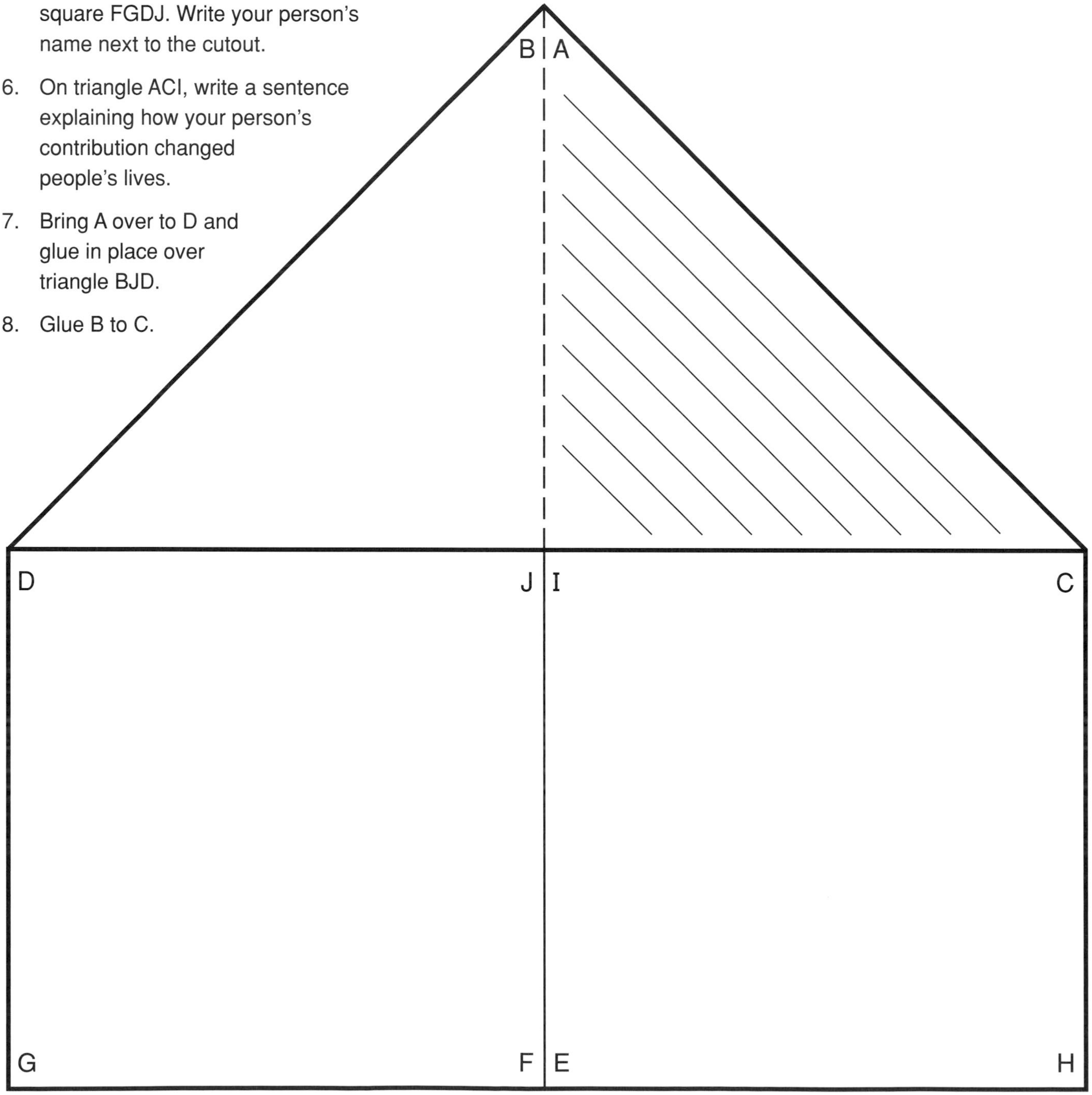

B | A

D   J | I   C

G   F | E   H

Name _____

It's About Time!

Create an Industrial Revolution timeline! Solve each problem below to find out when each invention was developed. Then write the item's name and its date in the correct place on the timeline below.

1. Families started taking lots of photos when the film camera was invented. 5,924 − 4,036 = _____

2. The improved power loom made creating cotton cloth easier. 3,628 ÷ 2 = _____

3. Transportation improved with the creation of the first successful steamboat. 1,285 + 522 = _____

4. Having lightbulbs with filaments made it possible to work without candles. 2,388 − 508 = _____

5. Communication improved when the telegraph was invented. 25,718 ÷ 14 = _____

6. The sewing machine made making clothing much faster. 2,833 − 987 = _____

7. The ice machine led the way to having air conditioning and refrigerators. 617 x 3 = _____

8. The typewriter made office work go much faster. 1,218 + 649 = _____

9. After the reaping machine was patented, farmers could harvest wheat faster. 1,106 + 728 = _____

10. The vulcanizing process kept rubber elastic in all types of weather. 613 x 3 = _____

1800	1820	1840	1860	1880	1900

Bonus Box: The air brake was an invention that helped trains stop more safely. To find the year it was patented, multiply 623 times 3.

Note to the teacher: Allow students to use calculators to complete this page if desired.

Getting a Bird's-Eye View of Map Skills

Give students a different perspective on map skills with this high-flying collection of activities!

by Beth Gress, Highland Central Elementary, Sparta, OH

How Much Farther?
Reading a mileage chart

Show students how much mileage they can get from a road map by examining two different types of mileage charts! Make and display a transparency of two mileage charts: one rectangular and one triangular (for examples, see page 192). Explain that a mileage chart gives distances between cities. Use the directions shown to demonstrate how to use each chart. Point out that the number in the cell where the fingers meet represents the distance between the two cities. Call on different students to find the distance between two given cities or to name cities that are a specified distance apart. Help students recognize that a rectangular chart contains duplicate information while a triangular chart lists the mileage between each pair of cities only once. For more practice, have each child complete a copy of page 192 as directed.

How to Read a Mileage Chart

Rectangular: Place your left index finger on a city on the left side of the chart. Place your right index finger on a different city at the top of the chart. Move the left finger right and the right finger down until they meet in a cell.

Triangular: Place each index finger on a different city. Move the left finger down and the right finger left until the two fingers meet in a cell.

New Hampshire

New York

Massachusetts

Ohio's hills make its rivers flow either south into the Ohio River or north into Lake Erie.

Michigan

Lake Ontario

Lake Erie

Maumee River

Cleveland

Indiana

Ohio

Great Miami River

Columbus

Muskingum River

Ohio River

West Virginia

Kentucky

Virginia

"Water" We Learning About Maps?
Using maps to interpret data

Clear up any misconceptions students may have about where rivers begin and end with a map scavenger hunt! Pair students; then give each twosome a detailed physical map of the United States and of your state. Have students use the maps to trace a river in your state back to its source. Explain that a river's source may be its highest point of elevation and that from there it can flow north, south, east, or west to lower and lower elevations until it reaches a larger river, lake, or ocean. Next, have each duo trace a river to its mouth. Also have students determine whether all rivers in your state flow into the same large body of water. Then explain that the Continental Divide is an imaginary line that separates Atlantic-flowing and Pacific-flowing rivers. Conclude by reading aloud *Paddle-to-the-Sea* by Holling Clancy Holling, a book in which an Indian boy puts a small carved wooden canoe with a passenger into a Canadian river. The canoe travels through the Great Lakes to the Atlantic Ocean.

Homeward Bound!

Creating a map

Keep map skills close to home with this personalized cartography project! Announce that each student will make a road map of his route home from school. Give students several days to pay close attention to landmarks, street names, and any turns made along the route. On mapmaking day, briefly discuss the streets and landmarks near the school. Next, draw an example of a map on the board to show students how to orient their maps with north at the top. Suggest a map scale. Then give each child a 12" x 18" sheet of light-colored construction paper on which to draw and color a map that includes the following items: compass rose, street names (or road numbers), and drawings and names of landmarks. After students share their completed maps, display them on a bulletin board titled "Homeward Bound!"

Inventing an Imaginary Island

Using a coordinate grid to create a map

Hone students' mapmaking skills with an activity that reviews landforms as well! Make and display a transparency of the steps below. Also give each student a copy of page 193. Then guide the child through the steps to create an imaginary island. When she's finished, have her color her map with colored pencils.

Steps:

1. Draw the outline of a fish on your grid so that the mouth is in C2, the upper and lower body extend from the top of B4 to the bottom of D4, and the tail fin is in B6, C6, and D6. (Demonstrate this step by drawing a general outline on the transparency.)
2. Draw a compass rose in F5 and label it with cardinal and intermediate directions.
3. Redraw the fish's mouth to form a bay. Label it "Bass Bay."
4. Redraw the top of the fish in B4 to form a pointed fin that extends into A4. Label the fin "Cape Carp."
5. Redraw the bottom of the fish in D4 to form a long, slender fin that extends into E4. Label it "Pike Peninsula."
6. Label the area between the lower fin and tail "Great White Gulf."
7. In C3, draw a star and circle it. Label the symbol "Coral City."
8. Draw an archipelago that spreads through C1, B1, B2, and A2. Label it "Bubble Chain Islands."
9. Draw a mountain range through C3 and C4. Label it "Gill Mountains."
10. Draw a desert in D4. Label it "Scales Desert."
11. Draw a river that begins in the western Gill Mountains in C3 and ends in C2 as a delta in Bass Bay. Add a south tributary to the river.
12. Draw another river that begins in the eastern Gill Mountains in C4 and ends in C6 as a delta at the center of the tail fin. Add three tributaries that feed into this river.
13. Draw a lake in B4. Label it "Fin Lake."
14. Add symbols for natural resources and products of your choice somewhere on the map.
15. Complete the legend by drawing and coloring symbols for the capital, mountains, desert, natural resources, and products. Then color the rest of the map.

191

Are We There Yet?

On the family's road trip, Jay Bird does not want his sons, Red and Blue, asking, "How much farther is it?" So he's given them copies of the mileage charts shown. Use the charts to answer the questions.

1. How far is it from Deadwood to Hot Springs?

_____

City	Belle Fourche	Custer	Deadwood	Hill City	Hot Springs	Mount Rushmore	Rapid City	Spearfish	Sturgis	Wall
Belle Fourche		84	29	92	118	84	60	11	32	111
Custer	84		57	14	32	21	49	73	70	104
Deadwood	29	57		37	89	32	41	15	13	91
Hill City	92	14	37		43	13	23	81	54	77
Hot Springs	118	32	89	43		48	55	104	102	124
Mount Rushmore	87	21	32	13	48		18	76	49	72
Rapid City	60	49	41	23	55	18		46	28	55
Spearfish	11	73	15	81	104	76	46		18	102
Sturgis	32	70	13	54	102	49	28	18		79
Wall	111	104	91	77	124	72	55	102	79	

2. Is it farther from Custer to Deadwood or from Custer to Rapid City?

_____

3. Which distance is shorter: from Monterey to Palm Springs or from San Diego to San Francisco?

_____

4. How far is it from Las Vegas to Monterey and then to Los Angeles?

_____

California mileage chart:

```
Fresno
Lake Tahoe, South
388
408  466   Las Vegas
251  479  314   Long Beach
222  456  302   29   Los Angeles
 55  194  446  308  277   Merced
 93  156  484  344  315   37   Modesto
152  266  504   64  335  118  153   Monterey
181  195  567  432  403  126   86  111   Oakland
333  435  276  112  111  388  426  448  514   Palm Springs
329  249  840  580  551  274  236  325  214  652   Redding
165  107  567  416  387  110   72  185   87  498  164   Sacramento
281  436  228   69   59  336  374  394  462   52  610  446   San Bernadino
338  542  332  105  116  393  431  451  519  139  667  503  105   San Diego
190  192  568  441  412  135   97  115    9  523  223   87  471  528   San Francisco
145  197  524  395  357  114   82   71   40  478  254  114  426  483   45   San Jose
137  197  414  229  200  192  230  135  227  311  441  301  259  316  232  187   San Luis Obispo
242  492  354  124   95  297  335  240  332  206  546  406  154  211  337  292  105   Santa Barbara
151  229  524  402  373  118  114   45   72  484  266  148  432  489   77   32  180  285   Santa Cruz
240  199   10  491  452  185  147  155   59  573  251  103  521  578   50   95  282  357  127   Santa Rosa
 82  335  408  265  236  137  175  234  263  347  411  247  295  352  272  227  174  267  233  322   Sequoia Park
120  131  510  371  342   65   27  140   75  453  209   45  401  458   84   69  256  361  101  134  202   Stockton
 93  133  435  344  315   81  119  199  207  426  355  191  374  431  216  195  230  335  199  266  175  146   Yosemite
```

5. Which two cities on each mileage chart are the closest together? _____

_____ Farthest apart? _____

Bonus Box: Use the mileage charts above to help you write two more problems for a partner to solve. Write the problems on the back of this page.

©The Education Center, Inc. • *The Mailbox*® • TEC44015 • Oct./Nov. 2004 • Key p. 312

192 **Note to the teacher:** Use with "How Much Farther?" on page 190.

Using a coordinate grid to create a map

Fish Island

	1	2	3	4	5	6	7
A							
B							
C							
D							
E							
F							

Legend

©The Education Center, Inc. • *The Mailbox*® • TEC44015 • Oct./Nov. 2004

Note to the teacher: Use with "Inventing an Imaginary Island" on page 191.

Amblin' Across

Gear students up for a
historical backpacking adventure
across your state!

by Kim Minafo, Cary, NC

Sweet 'n' Sour "State-mints"

Research, forming opinions

Leave a sweet taste in students' mouths about studying your state's history! Give each child six four-inch circles. Next, announce that your state is developing a new kind of candy called "state-mints." Explain that each piece will feature a fact from your state's past. Further explain that each mint's flavor will be sweet or sour, depending on whether he thinks the fact represents a positive or negative event in your state's history. Direct each child to find a different historical fact to write on each of his circles. Next, have him lightly color each positive event with a red swirl and each negative event with a green swirl. If desired, instruct him to wrap each candy in clear plastic wrap and tie the ends with ribbon as shown. Invite students to share their "state-mints" with the class; then post the candies on a bulletin board titled "[Name of your state] 'State-mints.'"

> North Carolina became the 12th state on November 21, 1789.

> In 1590, John White returned to Roanoke Island and found the English settlement deserted.

In the Spotlight

Studying famous people, oral expression

Shine the spotlight on famous people in your state's history! After studying past and present residents who made contributions within or beyond your state's borders, divide students into groups of four or five. Then have each group complete the steps below to spotlight deserving individuals.

Materials for each student: 2" x 4" sheet of white paper, crayons, scissors

Materials for each group: 12" x 18" sheet of black construction paper, 4¼" x 11" sheet of white paper, glue, yellow crayon, black crayon, brad

Steps:

1. Direct each group member to select a different famous state resident and research facts about the person's contribution to the state.
2. Have the child draw and color her chosen person on the 2" x 4" piece of paper. Then have her cut out the picture and glue it to the black paper as shown.
3. Instruct the group to draw and color a spotlight and light beam on the white paper and then cut it out and attach it with the brad to the black paper as shown.
4. Invite groups to present their famous people to the class, shifting the spotlight to each person, in turn, as they do so.

My State

Hiking the Immigration and Migration Trails

Investigating immigration and migration, summarizing

As students traipse across the state, help them reflect on how immigration and migration have influenced your state's history. Give each child a copy of page 196. Then have him think about one of the following questions:

- How did immigration affect our state's history?
- How did migration affect our state's history?

After the student investigates that question, direct him to write his answer on the patch shape on page 196. On each remaining shape, have him write a detail that supports his answer. Next, give the student a lunch-size paper bag, scissors, glue, and access to a stapler. Have him follow the directions on page 196 to make a lunch bag backpack. When he finishes, instruct him to cut out the shapes on page 196, glue the patch to the backpack, as shown, and place the remaining gear inside. After students share their work with the class, arrange the completed backpacks on a table with a tent card labeled "Hiking Along the Immigration and Migration Trails."

Migration has brought a lot of interesting people to our state.

Footprints in History

Research, creating a timeline

Hike through history with this "boot-iful" timeline! First, have each student research a different event from your state's history. Then give her an oaktag cutout shaped like a boot print. Direct the student to label the boot print's sole with the place where the event occurred and the heel with the event's date. On the back of the cutout, have her describe the event as if she had arrived just in time to see it happen. When all of the boot prints are finished, have students pin them in order to a bulletin board or clothesline titled "Footprints in History."

Kitty Hawk, NC

December 17, 1903

I looked across the sand and saw a machine that looked like a glider. It had wings and an engine. I could see a man inside. Then the machine started to move. It began to move faster and faster. Soon it lifted off the ground! It didn't stay up very long. I couldn't believe my eyes! The man and his machine had flown through the air!

Backpack Patterns

Use with "Hiking the Immigration and Migration Trails" on page 195.

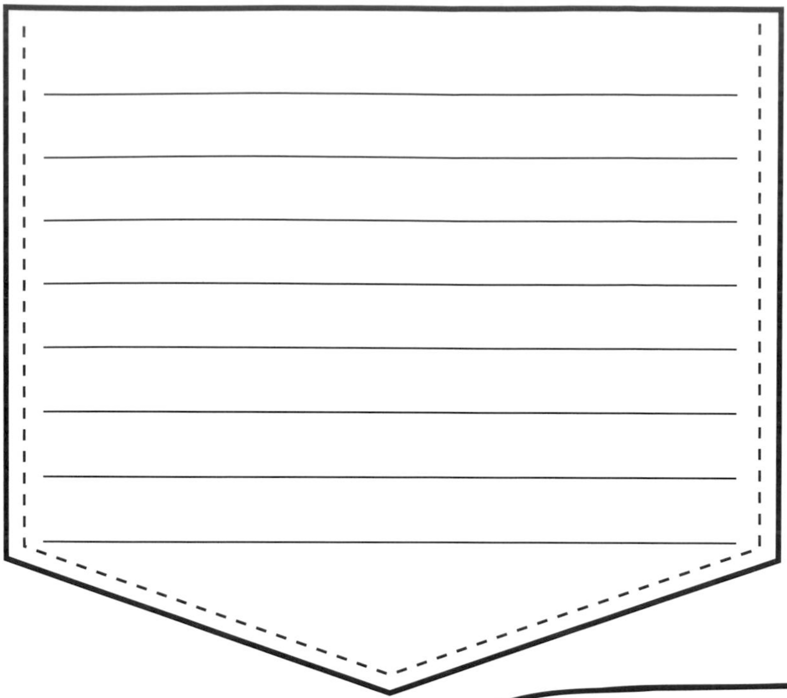

Directions for Making a Lunch Bag Backpack:

1. Beginning at the top left corner of the notched side, cut down four inches. Then cut across the left side, unnotched side, right side, and up to the top right corner, as shown, to create a flap.
2. Fold about three inches of the flap forward across the bag's opening.
3. To make straps, cut the piece you removed into two long strips. Loop each strip and staple it to the backpack, as shown, being careful not to staple the bag shut.

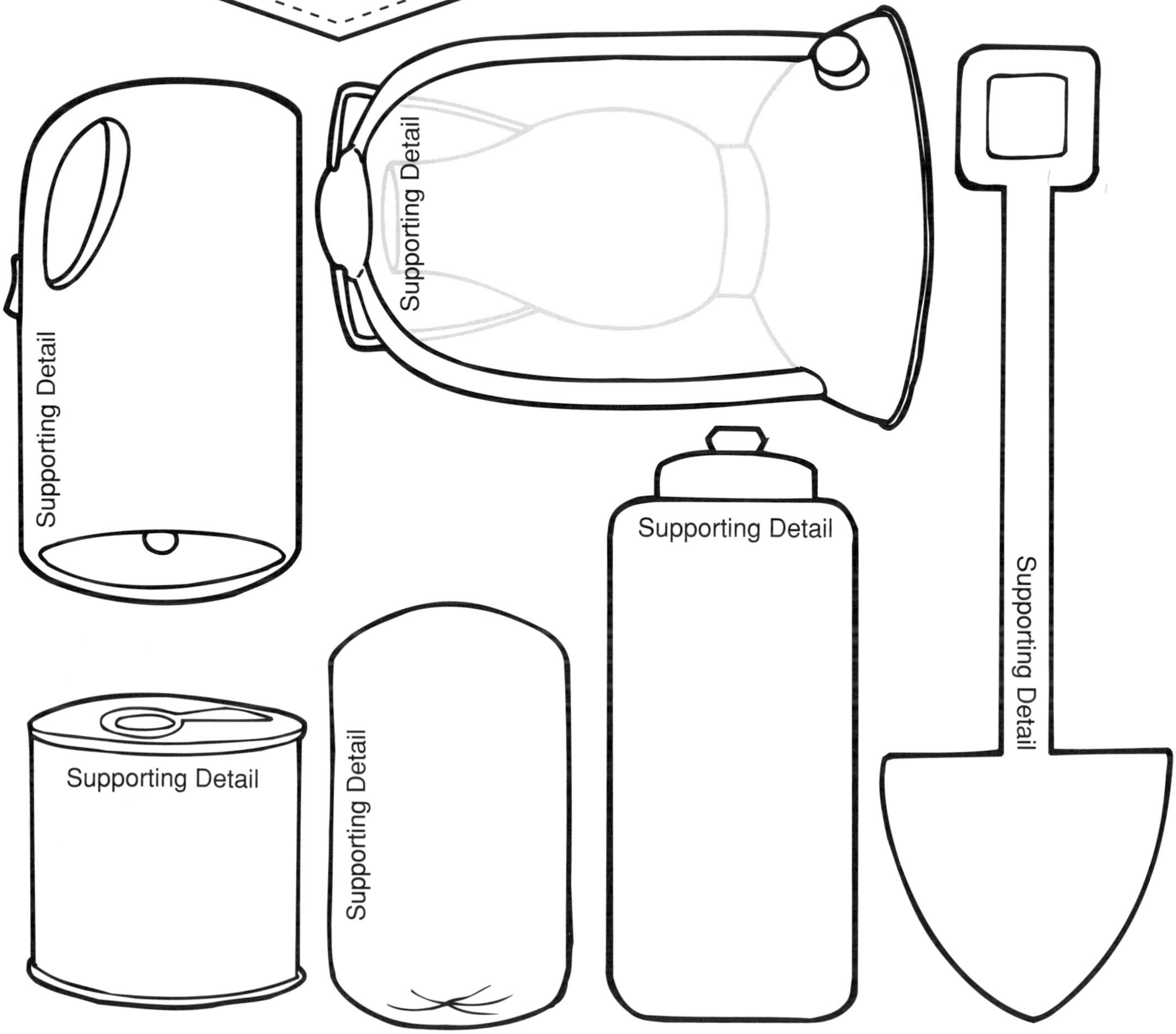

Supporting Detail

Supporting Detail

Supporting Detail

Supporting Detail

Supporting Detail

Supporting Detail

Supporting Detail

Exploring Your State's Native Americans

Native Americans are an important part of your state's history. Respond to each item below to learn more about the Native Americans in your state.

1. What was life like for Native Americans in your state before other people moved there?

_____
_____
_____
_____
_____

2. How did your state's Native Americans get along with the first immigrants who moved there?

_____
_____
_____
_____
_____

3. How did your state's Native Americans react as more and more people moved into your state?

_____
_____
_____
_____
_____

4. How have the actions of Native Americans changed the history of your state? _____

_____
_____
_____
_____
_____

5. Name the Native American group(s) living in your state before others moved there.

_____
_____
_____
_____

6. Name three Native Americans who have made an impact on your state's history.

_____
_____
_____
_____

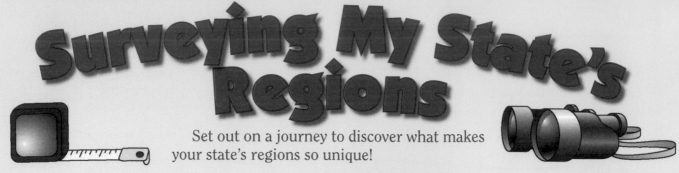

Surveying My State's Regions

Set out on a journey to discover what makes your state's regions so unique!

ideas by Amber Barbee, Wharton, TX

Touristy Tees
Researching your state's regions

Show pride in the uniqueness of your state's physical regions by featuring them on paper T-shirts designed to appeal to tourists! Give each child the materials listed and have him follow the directions shown to make a shirt highlighting either an assigned state region or the one in which he lives. Invite students to share the information on their shirts with other classes using a runway format similar to a fashion show. Then display the completed shirts on a bulletin board titled "Terrific Tees."

Materials for each child: brown paper grocery bag, scissors, markers, access to reference materials

Steps:

1. Cut three holes in the bag: one in the bottom large enough for your head and one in each side for your arms.
2. On the shirt's front, draw an outline map of your state and label it with the following information: state name, capital, name of each region. Draw an arrow that points to your assigned region.
3. Label the shirt's back with the following information about your assigned region: landforms, bodies of water, industries, crops and/or natural resources.

North Carolina
Capital: Raleigh
Regions: mountains, piedmont, coastal plain

Landforms: mountains, valleys, gorges
Rivers: Nantahala, Little Tennessee, Tuckasegee
Lakes: Fontana, James
Indus... farming, mining, ...em, manufacturing
...appl.., Christmas trees

Piedmont Region

Hats Off to State Regions!
Investigating a region's location, landforms, and bodies of water

Students will look sharp after making and donning dapper hats about the attributes of their state's regions! Give each child the materials listed and have him follow the directions shown to create a hat. Then invite students to wear their completed hats and share them with the class before pinning them to a bulletin board titled "Hats Off to Our State's Regions!"

Materials for each child: 12" x 18" sheet of light-colored construction paper, markers, ruler, access to reference materials

Steps:

1. Fold the paper in half horizontally. Turn the folded paper so that the unfolded edges are closest to you.
2. Fold the outer corners of the folded edge inward toward the center.
3. Form the brim by folding up each bottom flap twice to make two one-inch folds.
4. Label both sides of the brim with the name of the region you are featuring.
5. Label one side of the hat with an illustrated description of your region's location and its major landforms. Label the other side of the hat with at least three facts about the region's lakes and rivers.

Regions Pop-Up Book

Identifying a region's crops and/or natural resources

A region's major products or natural resources will be popping up everywhere with this fun book-making project! Give each pair of students the materials listed; then guide the duo through the steps shown to make a pop-up book about any one of your state's regions. When all of the books are completed, invite each twosome to present its book to the class. Finally, post the completed books on a bulletin board titled "Look at What's Popping Up in Our State's Regions!"

Materials for each pair: 2 sheets of 9" x 12" construction paper, scrap paper, ruler, scissors, markers, glue, access to reference materials

Steps:

1. Fold one sheet of paper in half horizontally. Cut two two-inch slits one inch apart in the center of the folded edge as shown.
2. Fold the center section down, creasing it at the bottom of the cuts; then bend the section back to its original position.
3. Push the center section to the inside of the folded paper. Crease the folds again so that they bend in opposite directions, making the center section pop out like a table.
4. Place the other sheet of paper behind the first; then glue it in place to make a book cover. Write on the cover the title of your book, your name, and your partner's name.
5. Lay the book flat. Label the left side with the names of crops grown in the region. Label the right side with the region's natural resources.
6. On a piece of scrap paper, draw one or more pictures or symbols that represent the region's products or natural resources. Cut out the picture and glue it to the pop-up section.

Name a body of water found in the region.

Regional Checkers

Reviewing your state's regions

This variation of a popular board game is the perfect culminating activity! Collect old sets of checkers. Next, make a copy of page 200 for each region in your state. As you teach each region, create an answer key by completing the page. After the class completes its study of each region, divide students into groups of three. Give each trio a blank copy of page 200, a copy of the key, a checkerboard, and checkers with each red and black set labeled with the letters from *A* to *L*. Then guide each threesome through the directions shown.

To play:

1. One player in each trio becomes the answer key holder. The other two players each choose a color and set up the checkerboard.
2. Players go in alphabetical order by first or last name, taking turns in the traditional way until one player is ready to jump another player's checker.
3. To jump an opponent's checker, a player must answer the prompt on the game card that matches the letter of the checker he wants to jump. The answer key holder reads the prompt aloud and uses the answer key to check the player's response. If correct, the player jumps the piece and captures it. If incorrect, he loses his turn.
4. Play continues in this manner until one player gains all of his opponent's checkers.

Game Cards

Use with "Regional Checkers" on page 199.

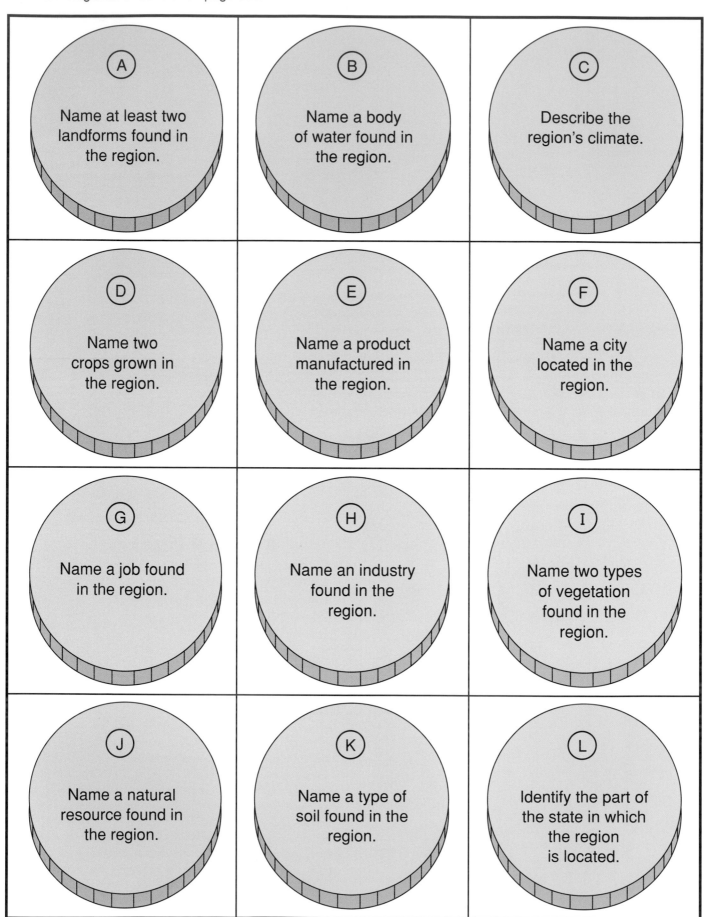

A — Name at least two landforms found in the region.

B — Name a body of water found in the region.

C — Describe the region's climate.

D — Name two crops grown in the region.

E — Name a product manufactured in the region.

F — Name a city located in the region.

G — Name a job found in the region.

H — Name an industry found in the region.

I — Name two types of vegetation found in the region.

J — Name a natural resource found in the region.

K — Name a type of soil found in the region.

L — Identify the part of the state in which the region is located.

Moving to Your Region

A friend is moving to your region. Clue him in to the types
of clothes he'll need to bring along!

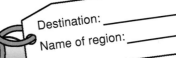

Destination: _____

Name of region: _____

This region's climate is _____
_____.

The weather here In the spring is _____
_____.

You should pack these types of clothes for spring:

1. _____   2. _____   3. _____

4. _____   5. _____   6. _____

The weather here in the summer is _____
_____.

You should pack these types of clothes for summer:

1. _____   2. _____   3. _____

4. _____   5. _____   6. _____

The weather here in the fall is _____
_____.

You should pack these types of clothes for fall:

1. _____   2. _____   3. _____

4. _____   5. _____   6. _____

The weather here in the winter is _____
_____.

You should pack these types of clothes for winter:

1. _____   2. _____   3. _____

4. _____   5. _____   6. _____

Note to the teacher: Each student will need access to reference materials to complete this page.

Taking a Closer Look at Landforms

Eye Earth's ever-changing landforms with
the following creative investigations!

with ideas by Liz Harrell, Highland Falls, NY

How'd We Get Those Mountains?
Folded and fault-block mountains

How are folded mountains formed? What about fault-block mountains? Have mountains of fun discovering the answers with this hands-on activity! Pair students. Give each pair two craft sticks and a small amount of clay. Then guide each duo through the directions below to help them see that a folded mountain is formed when two tectonic plates collide and force rock upward and that a fault-block mountain is formed when masses of rock move up or down along a fault.

To make a folded mountain:
1. Divide the clay in half and shape the halves into flattened blocks of the same approximate size.
2. Press one side of a square onto one stick. Repeat with the remaining block of clay and craft stick.
3. Place the blocks about four inches apart on a flat surface.
4. Slide the sticks together until the blocks meet and the clay folds as shown.

To make a fault-block mountain: Repeat steps 1–3 of the directions for making a folded mountain. Then hold one stick so that its clay block remains still. Push the other block toward it until one block rises above the other as shown.

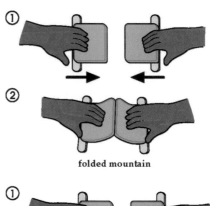

folded mountain

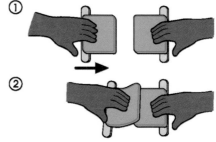

fault-block mountain

Water at Work
Water as an agent of erosion, acid rain

Nothing changes landforms like moving water! List landforms such as the following on the board: mountains, beaches, cliffs, canyons, deltas, valleys, lakes, and islands. Then divide students into small groups. Guide each group through the steps below to help them see water at work!

Materials for each group: copy of page 204, aluminum pie pan, damp soil, sand, gravel, small rocks, 5 oz. paper cup, pushpin, ½ c. water, pencil

Steps:
1. Shape the soil, sand, gravel, and rocks in the pie pan to form an island large enough to represent five of the landforms listed on the board.
2. Draw your island on the recording sheet. Label each landform. Then answer questions 1 and 3 on the sheet.
3. Use the pushpin to poke five small holes in the bottom of the paper cup. Hold the cup over your island and pour in half of the water. Shake the cup so that the drops rain gently on your island. Then answer question 2 on the sheet and draw how the island looks.
4. Use the pencil to enlarge the cup's holes. Hold the cup over your island and pour in the remaining water. Then answer question 4 on the sheet and draw how the island looks.

I'm Getting That Sinking Feeling!
Erosion, chemical weathering

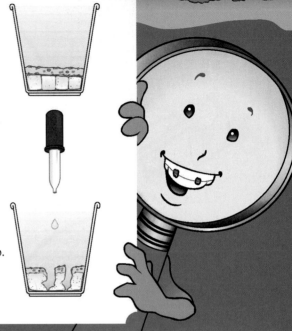

Students have probably seen stories on TV about huge sinkholes opening up in the earth. Give your young scientists a better understanding of how something like this can happen by guiding them through the following steps to model a chemical change that can cause sinkholes.

Materials for each group: eyedropper, 5 oz. paper cup, 7 sugar cubes, ⅛ c. cookie crumbs, 2 tbsp. white vinegar

Steps:
1. Place the sugar cubes in one layer in the cup's bottom to represent underground limestone rock.
2. Pour the cookie crumbs over the sugar cubes. Press them down so that there are no holes between the sugar cubes, and the crumbs form an even layer on top to represent the ground.
3. Fill the eyedropper with vinegar to represent acid rain. Hold the dropper above the cup. Squeeze the vinegar over the crumb surface. Repeat until all of the vinegar is used.
4. Observe the cookie crumb surface. *(Like limestone, the sugar cubes dissolve easily. Vinegar seeps through the crumbs, dissolving the sugar. The cookie surface collapses, creating a sinkhole.)*

The Winds of Change
Wind erosion, weathering

Expose your students to the landform-changing effects of the wind with interactive dioramas to demonstrate how sand dunes form!

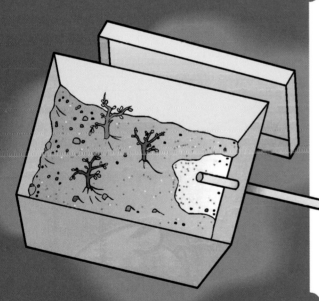

Materials for each group: shoebox with lid, clay, 3 to 5 twigs, dry soil, small rocks, sand, tape, a straw for each student

Steps:
1. Set the box's lid aside. Use a pencil to poke a hole in one end of the shoebox.
2. Push each twig into a small ball of clay. Stand the twigs on the floor of the box.
3. Place thin, even layers of soil and sand on the bottom of the box. Scatter rocks on top of the soil.
4. Place the lid on the box and tape it closed.
5. Push one end of a straw into the hole and blow once into the box. Have each group member repeat this step with her own straw.
6. Without jostling the box, remove the lid and observe the soil's surface. *(Wind can erode soil and sand, forming new landforms, such as dunes, where plants or rocks slow the wind down.)*

Chocolate Cake Mudslides
Physical weathering and erosion

Understanding mudslides is a piece of cake with this simple simulation! Bring in a 9" x 13" pan of unfrosted chocolate cake cut into squares (one square for each pair of students). Give each twosome a small cup of water and a cake square in a paper bowl. Direct one child to stand the cake square on its side and hold it, as shown, to represent the steep sides of a canyon. Have the child's partner slowly pour water on the top of the cake square until parts of it collapse and slide down. Then discuss what happened, explaining that mudslides can cause landforms to change rapidly.

Water at Work

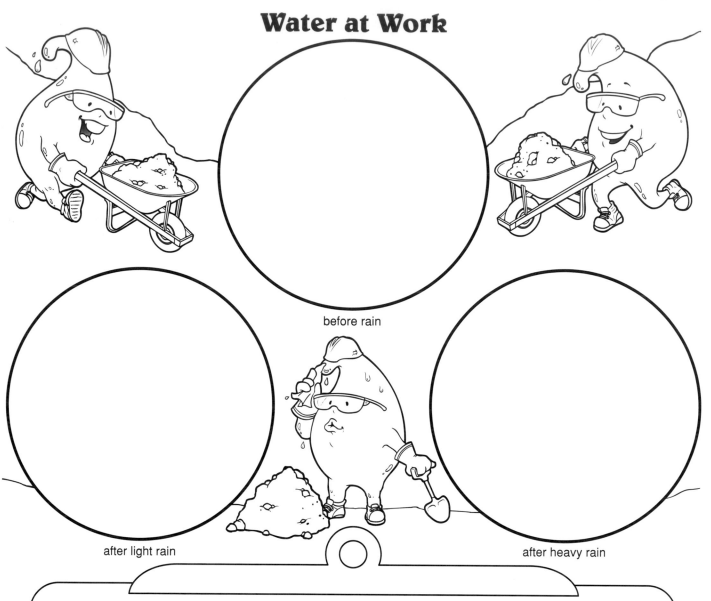

before rain

after light rain

after heavy rain

1. What do you think will happen to the landforms after a light rain?

    _____

2. What happened?_____

    _____

3. What do you think will happen to the landforms after a heavy rain?

    _____

4. What happened? _____

    _____

©The Education Center, Inc. • The Mailbox® • TEC44014 • Aug./Sept. 2004 • Key p. 312

Look Out Below!

Read each definition below. Find its matching term on a rock. Then write the matching letter in the blank. Use your science book or a dictionary if you need help.

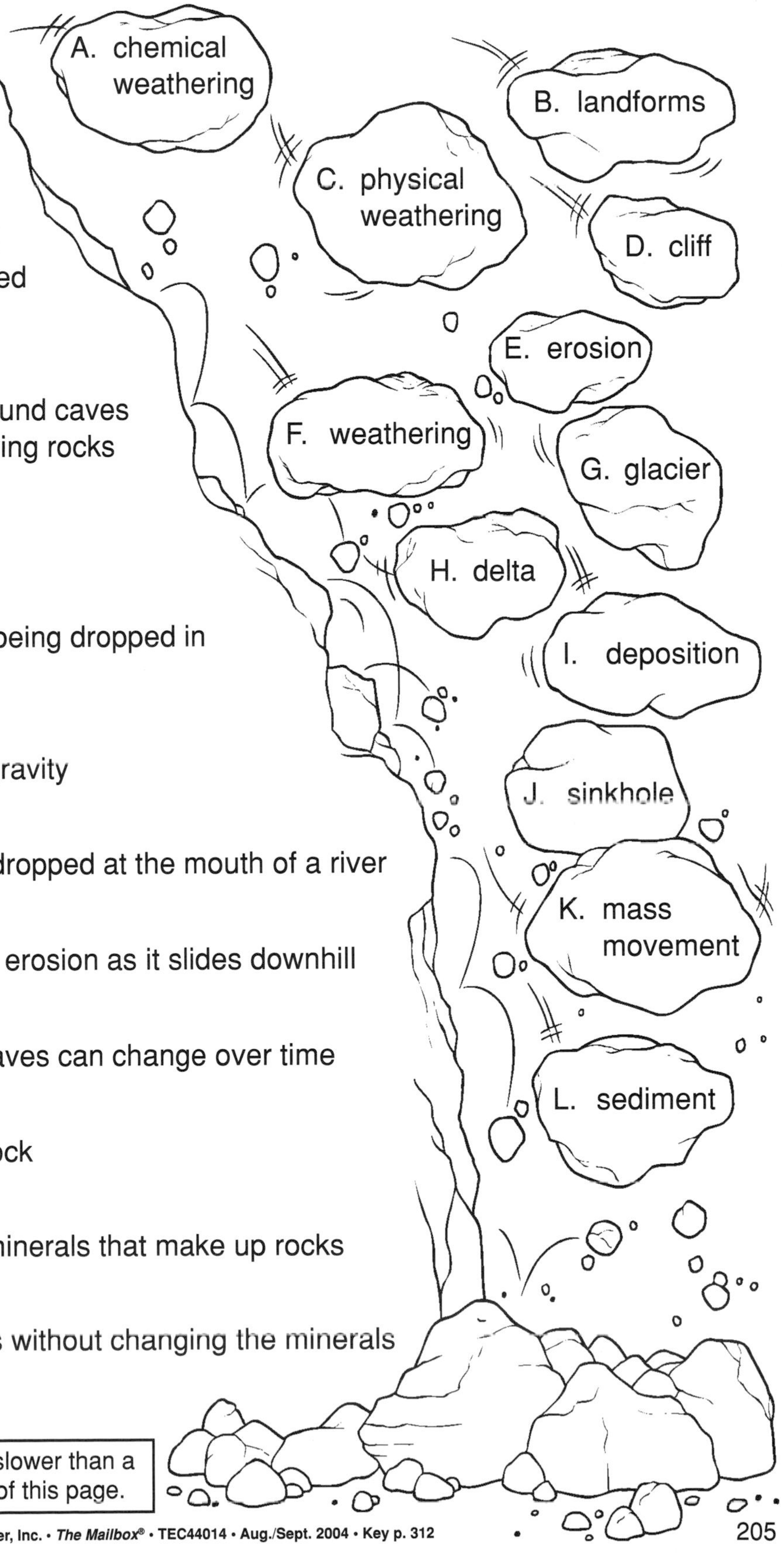

A. chemical weathering

B. landforms

C. physical weathering

D. cliff

E. erosion

F. weathering

G. glacier

H. delta

I. deposition

J. sinkhole

K. mass movement

L. sediment

1. ____ rocks being broken down into soil and sand

2. ____ the process of soil, sand, and tiny pieces of rock being moved by wind, water, or glaciers

3. ____ a large hole formed when ground caves in because of weak or dissolving rocks

4. ____ the earth's physical features

5. ____ the process of soil and sand being dropped in a new place

6. ____ rock and soil that fall due to gravity

7. ____ new land where sediment is dropped at the mouth of a river

8. ____ thick sheet of ice that causes erosion as it slides downhill

9. ____ a very steep landform that waves can change over time

10. ____ tiny pieces of broken-down rock

11. ____ a process that changes the minerals that make up rocks

12. ____ a process that changes rocks without changing the minerals they are made of

Bonus Box: Why does a mudslide move slower than a landslide? Write your answer on the back of this page.

Path to the Presidency

Invite students to stroll along a path of thought-provoking activities that not only examine the process of electing a president but peer into a candidate's personal qualities as well!

with ideas by Simone Lepine, Fayetteville, NY

Presidential Hats
Presidential roles

Make students aware of the important duties a president performs with an activity that shows how many different hats he has to wear! Cut out five construction paper hats and five paper hat bands. For patterns, go to www.themailboxcompanion.com. Label each hat band with a different role from the chart shown and glue it to a hat. Accordion-fold a 2" x 3" strip of paper and glue it to the back of each hat. Staple the folded strip and brim of each hat to a bulletin board titled "Which Hat Is the President Wearing?" Also copy the duties for each role shown on separate strips of white paper. Next, pair students and divide the strips among the pairs. Have the partners decide how to match the strips to the hats. As students share their decisions with the class, give assistance as needed to correct any incorrect matches. Then have the pairs staple their strips under the appropriate hats.

Presidential Duties

Chief Executive
- enforces federal laws
- plans the country's budget
- nominates Supreme Court judges and cabinet members

Foreign Policy Director
- meets with diplomats from other countries
- names ambassadors to other countries
- works on treaties with other nations

Commander in Chief
- appoints the highest military officers
- helps decide how large the armed forces should be
- is responsible for defending the United States during war

Chief of State
- gives awards to war heroes
- visits other countries to represent the United States
- may throw out the first ball of the professional baseball season

Legislative Leader
- gives a State of the Union address
- can veto bills passed by Congress
- affects how new laws develop

Chief Executive

nominates Supreme Court judges and cabinet members

plans the country's budget

Exploring Eligibility
Presidential requirements

Can just anyone become president of the United States? Have students explore this question with a persuasive letter-writing activity that has them consider not only the constitutional requirements to be president but other attributes as well. Remind students that the president is often thought to be the most powerful leader in the world. Share that the Constitution requires that a presidential candidate must be at least 35 years old, be a natural-born U.S. citizen, and have lived in the United States for at least 14 years. Also discuss some of the president's duties (see "Presidential Hats" on this page). Next, discuss with students the qualities they think a president should have. Record their responses on the board. Then give each child a copy of the pattern on page 208. Direct her to choose a quality listed on the board and write a letter on the pattern urging Congress to amend the constitutional requirements for president to include that quality. After students share their letters, have the class vote on the most important quality. Display the letters on a bulletin board titled "Exploring Chief Executive Eligibility."

Electoral College 101
Electoral College

Introduce students to the workings of the Electoral College with this quick simulation. First, select a state whose number of electoral votes equals about half the number of your students. For example, if you have 24 students, you could choose Massachusetts, which has 12 electoral votes. Divide students into two groups. Have one group represent the chosen state's Republican electors and the other group its Democratic electors. Next, write sample election results on the board in a chart. Ask students which candidate received more popular votes. Explain that that candidate should also gets the state's electoral votes. Then have the winning party's student electors write their votes in the chart. Repeat with other states as time allows.

Massachusetts	Popular Vote	Electoral Vote
Republican candidate	1,546,238	0
Democratic candidate	2,218,079	卌 卌 ll

Eyeing Electoral Votes
Electoral College

Examine why candidates strive to win certain states with this exciting collection of pick-and-choose activities!

- Use this quick coloring activity to show students which states have the least and most electoral votes! Give each student a copy of page 209, a blank U.S. map, and colored pencils. Then have each child title his map "Electoral College Votes," add the map key shown at the right, and color the map according to the key.

- Give students a graphic idea of the Electoral College with this activity! Give each child a copy of page 209, a sheet of graph paper, and a ruler. Have her use the map key's categories as her graph's labels to create a bar graph that shows how many states have a few votes and how many have a lot!

- Here's a quick game to help students get the total picture of the Electoral College! Pair students and give each pair a copy of page 209 and scissors. Have the pair cut out its cards and place them in a lunch-size paper bag. Then instruct the partners to take turns drawing a card from the bag and recording its number of votes. Continue playing in this manner, having each partner keep a running tally of his votes until all cards have been drawn. Declare the player with more votes the winner!

- This day-after-the-election activity has students mapping out the results! Gather election results from each state and give each student a copy of page 209, two envelopes, a blank U.S. map, scissors, and colored pencils. Have the child label each envelope with a main candidate's name and cut apart the Electoral College cards. Next, read aloud each state's election results and have each student place the corresponding card in the winning candidate's envelope. Then have the student use the sorted cards to color her map to show which candidate won each state's electoral votes.

- Let students see how the election stacked up with this double-bar graph! Post the election results from each state. Then pair students. Give each pair a copy of page 209, blue and yellow markers, scissors, a 12" x 18" sheet of construction paper, and glue. Direct the pair to color each state's electoral card blue if the Democratic candidate won that state and yellow if the Republican candidate won. Finally, guide each pair to glue the colored cards for each category on the construction paper as shown. Display the completed graphs on a bulletin board titled "Election [year]: How It All Stacked Up!"

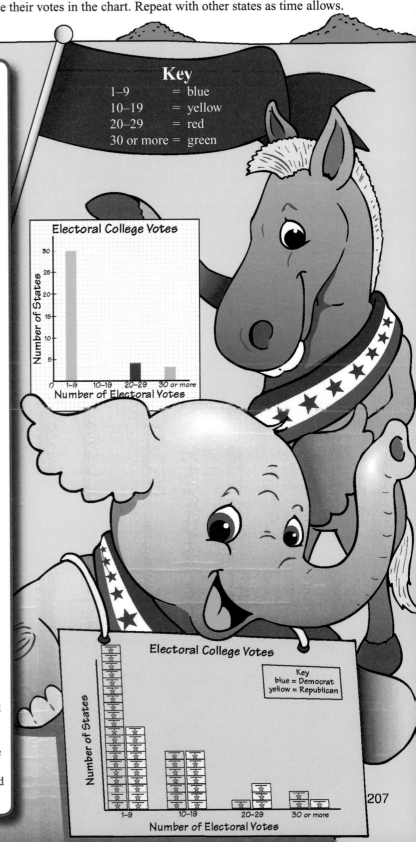

Key

1–9	= blue
10–19	= yellow
20–29	= red
30 or more	= green

207

The Importance of a Vote

Voting rights

Impress on students how important the right to vote can be with this unforgettable activity! Gather a class supply of index cards. Program three or four cards each with the following categories: "under 18 years old," "not a U.S. citizen," "in jail or on probation for committing a felony," "chose not to vote," "forgot to register," "registered voter," and "absentee ballot." Also select either a pro-girl or pro-boy issue, such as girls should not have homework or boys should have an extra recess. Next, explain to students that a voter must be an American citizen and at least 18 years old. Afterward, announce the voting topic and randomly give each child a programmed card and a slip of paper. Instruct the student to read his card. Then allow only the students whose cards say "absentee ballot" or "registered voter" to vote. After counting the ballots and sharing the results, have students discuss how they felt about having only a few voters decide the outcome.

For more election information, contact your local
- county's board of elections office
- chapter of the League of Women Voters
- newspaper to see whether it can provide educational materials
- political parties' headquarters

Eagle Pattern

Use with "Exploring Eligibility" on page 206.

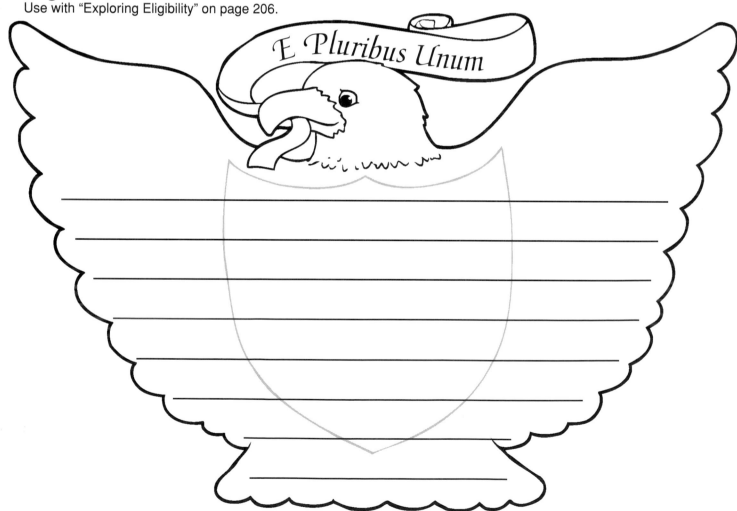

E Pluribus Unum

				Alabama 9
Alaska 3	Arizona 10	Arkansas 6	California 55	Colorado 9
Connecticut 7	Delaware 3	District of Columbia 3	Florida 27	Georgia 15
Hawaii 4	Idaho 4	Illinois 21	Indiana 11	Iowa 7
Kansas 6	Kentucky 8	Louisiana 9	Maine 4	Maryland 10
Massachusetts 12	Michigan 17	Minnesota 10	Mississippi 6	Missouri 11
Montana 3	Nebraska 5	Nevada 5	New Hampshire 4	New Jersey 15
New Mexico 5	New York 31	North Carolina 15	North Dakota 3	Ohio 20
Oklahoma 7	Oregon 7	Pennsylvania 21	Rhode Island 4	South Carolina 8
South Dakota 3	Tennessee 11	Texas 34	Utah 5	Vermont 3
Virginia 13	Washington 11	West Virginia 5	Wisconsin 10	Wyoming 3

Presidential "Term-inology"

The White House press corps needs help! The reporters forgot what the Latin phrase on the president's seal means! Help them find out. Use the words on the microphones to complete the statements. Then write the bold letter of the matching answer in its numbered blank below.

Microphones: cabinet | oath of office | vice president | State of the Union address | inauguration | term | Oval Office | veto | first lady

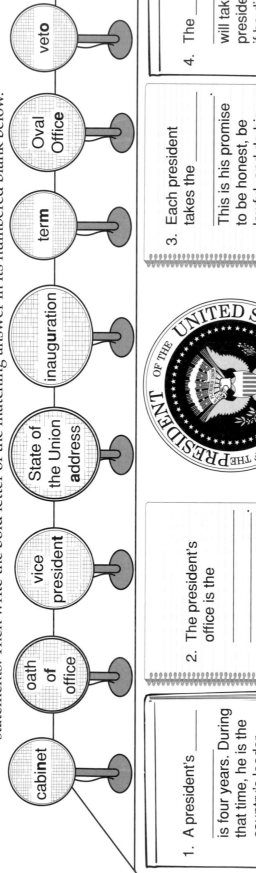

1. A president's _____ is four years. During that time, he is the country's leader.

2. The president's office is the _____.

3. Each president takes the _____. This is his promise to be honest, be lawful, and do his best for the country.

4. The _____ will take the president's place if he dies or quits.

5. The president can _____ or reject, a bill passed by Congress.

6. The president's wife is the official hostess of the White House. She is called the _____.

7. The president chooses the people in his _____. They help him run the government.

8. The new president takes the oath of office at the _____. Then he officially becomes the president.

9. The president's _____ tells Congress how the country's last year was. It also tells about the president's plans for the next year.

E pluribus unum means "___ ___ ___ , ___ ___ ___."
5 8 4   5 3 1 9 7 6 , 5 7 2

©The Education Center, Inc. · *The Mailbox*® · TEC44014 · Aug./Sept. 2004 · Key p. 312

Science Units

Horsin' Around With Human Body Systems

Use this roundup of creative activities to enhance your students' knowledge of human body systems!

So that's why chewing is so important!

That's How the Cookie Crumbles!
Understanding the digestive process

Treat students to a digestive system simulation that delights their taste buds! Gather two clear wide-mouth jars with screw-on lids, two containers of water, and two more than a class supply of chocolate chip cookies. Divide the class into two groups and give each group a cookie, a container of water, a jar, and a lid. Have Group 1 put its cookie in the jar, add a small amount of water, and screw on the lid. Instruct Group 2 to do the same but to first break its cookie into pieces (to represent chewing). Next, direct the members of both groups to take turns shaking their jars for ten minutes (to represent the stomach's action). Then have students compare the two mixtures and respond in their science journal to questions such as the following: Where does the body begin to break down food? Why is chewing important? What does your stomach do? As each child works, reward him with a cookie to munch on. Mmm, good! *Julie Eick Granchelli, W. P. Towne Elementary, Medina, NY*

Much better!

Crucial Cartilage and Ligaments
Understanding the importance of cartilage and ligaments

Show students the importance of cartilage and ligaments with this eye-opening demonstration! Gather four two-inch clay pots, a thin piece of foam, glue, scissors, and a rubber band. Remind students that bones have cartilage and ligaments. Then explain that cartilage acts as a cushion for bones and that ligaments connect bones. Ask students to imagine the skeletal system without cartilage or ligaments. Continue by holding up two clay pots and telling students that each clay pot represents a bone. Put the pots together end to end (as shown) to demonstrate a joint and then rub the pots together. Explain that bones would rub against each other each time they moved without cartilage to cushion them. Next, trim the foam to fit the bottom of one pot and glue it in place as shown. Rub the pot with the foam bottom against the bottom of the other pot to simulate how cartilage cushions the bones. Then wrap the rubber band around the pots to show how ligaments hold bones together. *Karen Freres, Morrison, IL*

212

Wanted: Circulatory Specialists!

Understanding the roles of the parts of blood

Drive home the importance of different parts of the blood with this group activity! Divide students into four groups and give each group a sheet of 11" x 14" light-colored construction paper, markers, and scissors. Next, assign each group one of the following blood parts: red blood cell, white blood cell, platelet, or plasma. Direct group members to draw and cut out a construction paper shape of their assigned part. Then have them write a help wanted ad on the shape that describes the blood part's duties and responsibilities and also lists the qualifications needed to do the job well. Invite groups to share their completed ads with the class; then post the cutouts on a bulletin board titled "Help Wanted: Circulatory System Specialists."
adapted from an idea by Debra Johnston, St. Joseph School, Stratford, WI

From Cells to Systems

Understanding how cells, tissues, and organs combine to make body systems

Mold students' understanding of how cells relate to tissues, organs, and body systems with this creative hands-on activity! Draw on a sheet of butcher paper a large outline of the human body. Also glue to a labeled 3" x 5" index card a picture of each body organ students are studying. Next, prepare for each child a resealable plastic bag filled with several marble-size balls of play dough (cells). Divide students into as many groups as you have organ cards. Then give each child her bag and give each group a card. Then guide the groups through the steps shown to complete the activity. *Ashley Carpenter, McBride Elementary, Muscle Shoals, AL*

Steps:
1. Remove the cells from your bag. Press them together into a larger ball to form tissue.
2. Combine your tissue with those of your group members to create a model of your group's assigned organ. Use the picture on the index card as a guide.
3. Present the completed organ to the class and explain its role in a body system.
4. Place the organ on the human body outline to show its location in the body.

213

Comparing heartbeat rates, multiplication

Heartbeat Roundup

Whose heart beats more times in a year? That's what the two friends below want to know. To help out the cowboys, count the number of beats your heart makes in 15 seconds. Use that number to help you solve the first problem below. Then use the answer to help you solve the second problem, third problem, and so on.

My small heart beats 150 times in 15 seconds.

Bird Heart

1. $\underline{\hspace{1cm}150\hspace{1cm}}$ $\times 4 =$ _____ beats per minute
   beats in 15 seconds

2. _____ $\times 60 =$ _____ beats per hour
   beats per minute

3. _____ $\times 24 =$ _____ beats per day
   beats per hour

4. _____ $\times 7 =$ _____ beats per week
   beats per day

5. _____ $\times 52 =$ _____ beats per year
   beats per week

Human Heart

1. _____ $\times 4 =$ _____ beats per minute
   beats in 15 seconds

2. _____ $\times 60 =$ _____ beats per hour
   beats per minute

3. _____ $\times 24 =$ _____ beats per day
   beats per hour

4. _____ $\times 7 =$ _____ beats per week
   beats per day

5. _____ $\times 52 =$ _____ beats per year
   beats per week

Bonus Box: On the back of this page, write two tips for keeping your heart healthy.

©The Mailbox® · TEC44018 · April/May 2005 · Written by Julie Eick Granchelli, Medina, NY · Key p. 312

Note to the teacher: Give each student a calculator to complete this page.

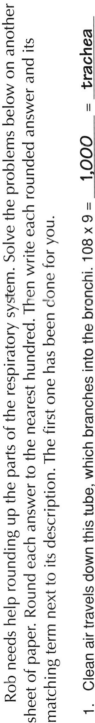

Respiratory Roundup

Rob needs help rounding up the parts of the respiratory system. Solve the problems below on another sheet of paper. Round each answer to the nearest hundred. Then write each rounded answer and its matching term next to its description. The first one has been done for you.

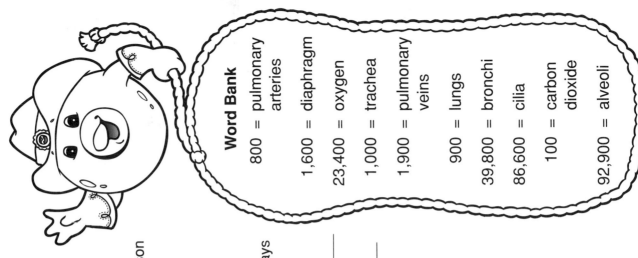

Word Bank

800 = pulmonary arteries

1,600 = diaphragm

23,400 = oxygen

1,000 = trachea

1,900 = pulmonary veins

900 = lungs

39,800 = bronchi

86,600 = cilia

100 = carbon dioxide

92,900 = alveoli

1. Clean air travels down this tube, which branches into the bronchi. 108 x 9 = ___1,000___ = ___trachea___

2. The pulmonary arteries carry blood that contains this gas. It's a waste product that is released when a person exhales. 312 ÷ 3 = ___ = ___

3. These are tiny air sacs at the ends of the small tubes inside the lungs. 89,012 + 3,874 = ___ = ___

4. These tiny hairs line parts of the respiratory system. They push along dust and dirt and help keep the airways clear. 124,621 − 38,025 = ___ = ___

5. Each of these two large air tubes lead into a lung. 2,654 x 15 = ___ = ___

6. The lungs sit on this dome-shaped muscle. 8,125 ÷ 5 = ___ = ___

7. These structures transport blood from the heart to the lungs. 458 + 347 = ___ = ___

8. These two objects are the major organs of the respiratory system. 6,874 − 5,926 = ___ = ___

9. This gas moves through the alveoli and into red blood cells. 521 x 45 = ___ = ___

10. These structures move oxygen-rich blood from the lungs to the heart. 25,914 ÷ 14 = ___ = ___

215

©The Mailbox® · TEC44018 · April/May 2005 · Key p. 312

Now Hear This!

Activities for Investigating Sound

BOTTLE BAND
Discovering how water level affects sound

Hear the sounds of familiar melodies with this "bottle-rific" activity! Round up eight identical clear glass bottles or glasses. Also gather food coloring and a metal spoon. Fill the bottles with different levels of water. Tap on the bottles with a spoon above the water line until they make a musical scale when tapped in order. Then mark the water lines on the bottles with a fine-tip permanent marker, making them easy to refill. Also add food coloring to each bottle to make the water level easier to see. Tap on one bottle at a time and have students think about how the water level affects the sound. Discuss why the bottle with the least amount of water has the highest pitch and the bottle with the most water has the lowest pitch. *(A sound is heard when the bottle vibrates. As more water is added, the bottle vibrates more slowly and produces a lower-pitched sound.)* Then number the bottles from 1 (most water) to 8 (least water) and place them at a center along with the spoon and a copy of the tunes on page 218.

Students can play Name That Tune, create their own tunes, or even blow across the bottle tops to make musical sounds!

Tune in to sound with this terrific collection of fun-to-do activities. In addition to being all ears, youngsters will be filled with good vibrations!

ideas contributed by Jennifer Otter, Oak Ridge, NC

FIRING SOUND WAVES
Observing the effects of sound waves traveling through air

Fire up students' observation skills with this flaming demonstration! Cover the end of a toilet paper tube with plastic wrap and secure it with a rubber band. Cut out a thin cardboard circle to fit the other end of the tube. Use a pencil to make a ¼-inch hole in the circle's center. Then tape the circle to the tube as shown. Next, place a small lighted candle on a table in front of the room and hold the tube so that its small hole is about one inch away from the flame. Thump the plastic with your finger and have students observe what happens. *(Tapping on the plastic makes it vibrate. The vibrating plastic makes the air in the tube travel in waves through the tube and out of the hole in the circle to the flame, causing it to flicker. If the plastic is thumped hard enough, the flame will go out.)*

To follow up, have students predict what might happen if, instead of thumping the plastic, you clap your hands together rapidly at that end of the tube. Test the predictions by having a volunteer hold the tube while you clap. Then challenge the class to brainstorm other methods of firing sound waves at the candle!

Speed of Sound Through Different Substances	
Substance	**Speed (ft./sec.)**
air	1,116
water	4,908
brick	11,980
wood (maple)	13,480
glass	14,900
aluminum	16,000
steel	17,100

Sound Conductor Clues
1. Sound travels faster through solids and liquids than it does through gases.
2. Steel and air are the fastest and slowest conductors, but not necessarily in that order.
3. The same number of substances are listed before wood as after it.
4. Water ranks between brick and air.
5. Wood conducts sound faster than brick but slower than glass and aluminum.
6. Aluminum ranks four places faster than water.

SOUND CONDUCTOR RANKINGS
Comparing the speed at which sound travels through different materials

Does sound travel better through a solid, a liquid, or a gas? Send one student at a time to this cool center to find out! Arrange the following materials at a table: glass windowpane, block of wood (maple), stainless steel cookie sheet, plastic resealable bag of water, aluminum pie tin, brick, ticking clock. Also laminate the chart and clues on page 218; then cut them apart, as shown, and place them facedown on the table. Next, have a student listen to the clock's ticks traveling through the air. Then instruct her to place the clock behind the windowpane and listen to the ticking with one ear next to the glass and the other covered with her hand. Have her note on paper whether the ticking is softer or louder than it was through the air. Direct her to repeat this process with each item. Then, using the six clues for help, have her list the items in order to show how well they conduct sound. To check her answers, have her turn over the chart!

Song Sheet

Use with "Bottle Band" on page 216.

"Mary Had a Little Lamb"

4 3 2 3 4 4 4   3 3 3   4 6 6

4 3 2 3 4 4 4   4 3 3 4 3 2

"Twinkle, Twinkle, Little Star"

1 1 5 5 6 6 5   4 4 3 3 2 2 1

5 5 4 4 3 3 2   5 5 4 4 3 3 2

1 1 5 5 6 6 5   4 4 3 3 2 2 1

"London Bridge"

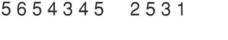

5 6 5 4 3 4 5   2 3 4   3 4 5

5 6 5 4 3 4 5   2 5 3 1

"For He's a Jolly Good Fellow"

1 3 3 3 2 3 4 3   3 2 2 2 1 2 3 1

1 3 3 3 2 3 4 6   6 5 5 5 4 2 1

"Row, Row, Row Your Boat"

1 1 1 2 3   3 2 3 4 5

8 8 8 5 5 5 3 3 3 1 1 1   5 4 3 2 1

"Ode to Joy"

3 3 4 5 5 4 3 2 1 1 2 3 3 2 2

3 3 4 5 5 4 3 2 1 1 2 3 2 1 1

Speed of Sound Chart

Use with "Sound Conductor Rankings" on page 217.

Speed of Sound Through Different Substances	
Substance	**Speed** (ft./sec.)
air	1,116
water	4,908
brick	11,980
wood (maple)	13,480
glass	14,900
aluminum	16,000
steel	17,100

Sound Clues Card

Use with "Sound Conductor Rankings" on page 217.

Sound Conductor Clues

1. Sound travels faster through solids and liquids than it does through gases.
2. Steel and air are the fastest and slowest conductors, but not necessarily in that order.
3. The same number of substances are listed before wood as after it.
4. Water ranks between brick and air.
5. Wood conducts sound faster than brick but slower than glass and aluminum.
6. Aluminum ranks four places faster than water.

Sensitive Sounds

Match each picture to its correct description.

Some sounds are too high or low for me to hear.

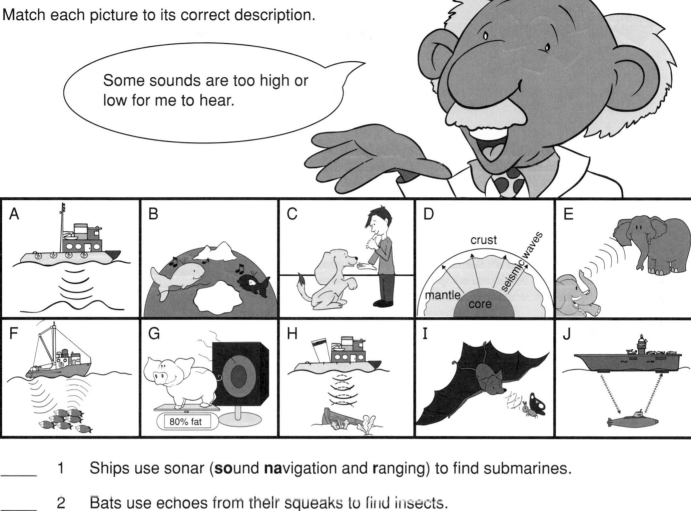

_____ 1   Ships use sonar (**so**und **na**vigation and **r**anging) to find submarines.

_____ 2   Bats use echoes from their squeaks to find insects.

_____ 3   Whales use low-pitched sounds to talk with other whales hundreds of miles away.

_____ 4   Farmers use echoes from very high sounds to check the amount of fat hogs have.

_____ 5   Echoes from sonar help map mountains and valleys on the ocean floor.

_____ 6   Elephants use low sounds to talk with other elephants miles away.

_____ 7   Fishermen use echoes from sonar to know the size of schools of fish.

_____ 8   Seismic waves help us know what the earth's core is made of.

_____ 9   Echoes from sonar help find sunken ships such as the *Titanic*.

_____ 10 Dog trainers use whistles that make very high sounds.

Bonus Box: A *hertz (Hz)* is the unit used to describe the frequency of sound waves. A cat's range of hearing is about 70 Hz to 60,000 Hz. If you blow a dog whistle with a frequency of 5,400 Hz, can a cat hear it? Explain.

Around the World With Adaptations

Hop aboard and explore how living things use adaptations to survive!

by Lauren Zavisca, Donovan Intermediate School, Lebanon, OH

Polar bears have fur and blubber to keep them warm in the Arctic.

Amazing Adaptations
Identifying adaptations that aid survival

Begin your adaptations journey with this brainstorming activity! Ask your media specialist to help you locate a book about plant or animal adaptations to read aloud to the class. Discuss the book with students, pointing out the adaptations that helped the organism(s) survive. Next, give each child an index card. Have him write about a part, an outer covering, or an ability that could help a living thing survive. Allow students to share their ideas as you list the adaptations on chart paper. Then have the class help you divide the adaptations into categories such as the following: avoiding predators, keeping warm, finding shelter, finding food. Post the list in the classroom for students to add to throughout the unit.

I've got a match!

I agree.

Pair It!
Matching plants to their adaptations

Challenge students to match plants to their adaptations with this great game! Give each student a copy of page 222. Pair students and have the partners set aside one copy to use as an answer key. Direct them to cut apart the cards on the second sheet, shuffle the cards, and place them facedown on a playing surface. To play, guide the twosome through the directions shown. Follow up by having students research other plants and their adaptations to create additional game cards.

Directions:
1. Player 1 turns two cards faceup.
2. Player 1 decides whether the cards are a match. A match occurs when a plant card is paired with the correct adaptation card. Player 2 uses the key to check. (Matching pairs are adjacent to each other.)
3. If the key shows that the cards are a match, Player 1 keeps the two cards, and Player 2 turns two more cards faceup.
4. If the cards do not match, the player replaces the cards facedown, and Player 2 turns two other cards faceup.
5. Play continues in this manner until all matches have been made.

Create a Creature!
Understanding survival and adaptation

What kind of structures help living things survive? Have students find out with this nifty activity! Create six different clue cards that describe different animals (see the example). Next, make a copy of the reproducible on page 223 for each student. Then divide the class into six groups. Give each group a clue card and each child a copy of page 223. Direct each group member to complete the page as directed to create an animal that could adapt to all of the situations listed in the clues. If desired, allow her to use craft materials to make a model of her creation. Then invite students to share their work with the class. After mounting the papers for each group on colorful paper, display them with the matching clue card on a bulletin board titled "Adaptation Zoo."

Your animal is a carnivore. It can swim, walk on land, and survive in cool and warm temperatures. To stay away from predators, it uses speed and camouflage.

Come Live in the Rain Forest!

Habitat Brochures
Adapting to survive in a habitat

Explore animal habitats around the world by transforming students into real estate agents! Begin by assigning each student one of the following habitats: desert, prairie, ocean, forest, rain forest, marsh, or mountains. Explain that each child will make a brochure highlighting the adaptations an animal living in that habitat would need to make. Next, have him research his chosen habitat's weather, the animals found there, and the adaptations they've made. Then give the student an 8½" x 11" sheet of white paper. Demonstrate how to fold the paper into thirds. Have him use his research and the guidelines at the right to create a habitat brochure. Allow students to share their completed brochures with the class.

Cover: Show a scene from the habitat with at least two animals that live there. Include the habitat's name.
Inside left flap: Explain how animals stay warm, stay cool, or maintain a comfortable temperature while living in the habitat. Add illustrations.
Inside center flap: Explain how animals use adaptations to find homes in the habitat. Add illustrations.
Inside right flap: Explain how animals adapt and find food in the habitat. Add illustrations.
Back right flap: Explain how adaptations are used to avoid predators in the habitat. Add illustrations.
Back center flap: Write your name and the date.

Game Cards

Use with "Pair It!" on page 220.

This plant's leaves have a leatherlike surface that causes water to run off. It also has air-filled ribs that keep the leaf afloat.

Habitat: wetlands

Water Lily

This plant has spines that keep grazing animals from eating it. The spines also reflect sunlight to keep the plant cool.

Habitat: desert

Cactus

This plant uses its long pitcher-shaped leaves to "swallow" insects. It attracts the insects with a sweet, sticky nectar.

Habitat: swamp

Pitcher Plant

This plant's seeds are attached to tiny fluffy parachutes that can be carried by the wind to help the plant reproduce.

Habitat: prairie

Dandelion

This plant has thorns that keep animals from eating it.

Habitat: prairie, forest

Dog Rose Flower

This plant can make food inside its bark. It can continue making food during the winter.

Habitat: forest, mountains

Aspen Tree

This plant has cuplike leaves that catch and hold water. It lives on a host plant but does not harm it.

Habitat: rain forest

Bromeliad

This plant has a rootlike base that can attach to rocks. It has no real stem, leaves, or roots.

Habitat: ocean

Seaweed

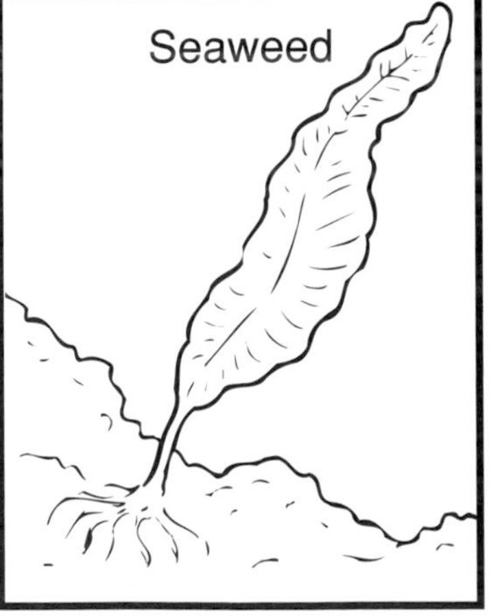

Create a Creature!

Use the clues your teacher gives you to create a creature that has all the adaptations it needs to survive. Answer the questions below to help you plan. Then draw and color your creature in the frame below.

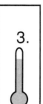

1. What body parts or abilities will your creature use to move? _____

_____

2. What body parts or abilities will your creature use to eat? _____

_____

3. What body covering or abilities will your creature have to keep cool or stay warm?

_____

_____

4. How will your creature protect itself from predators? _____

_____

5. How will your creature find or make a

home? _____

_____

_____

6. In which habitat would your creature

best survive? _____

Why? _____

_____

_____

_____
name of creature

Bonus Box: If your creature had to survive in another environment, what kinds of adaptations would it need to make? Write your answer in complete sentences on the back of this page.

Note to the teacher: Use with "Create a Creature!" on page 221.

Soaring Through the Solar System

Watch students' understanding of the solar system reach new heights with these stellar activities!

by Michelle Bauml, Houston, TX, and Jennifer Otter, Oak Ridge, NC

Scale It Down!

Understanding how the solar system is organized

Launch your space study with an outdoor activity that results in a scale model of the solar system! Gather the materials listed and take the class outdoors. Once outside, give nine different students a labeled index card and the corresponding object. Also give a meterstick to each of three students. Have the remaining students form a circle representing the sun. Designate one child in the circle to be the starting point for measuring. Next, have the students with metersticks take turns measuring the distances in the chart. As each distance is measured, have the child with the corresponding model hold it the measured distance away from the child designated as the sun. Explain that each centimeter in the model represents about 1 million miles. After returning to the classroom, challenge students to write and illustrate mnemonics to help them remember the planets' order!

Materials for the class: 3 metersticks, marble (Pluto), 2 Ping-Pong balls (Mercury and Mars), 2 tennis balls (Venus and Earth), 2 small beach balls (Neptune and Uranus), large beach ball (Saturn), Hula-Hoop toy (Jupiter), 9 index cards each labeled with a different planet's name, chart of the distances shown, access to an outdoor area at least 40 meters long

Mike's Very Enormous Moose Just Spotted Uncle Ned's Penguin!

Scaled Distance From the Sun (rounded to the nearest mile)
Scale: 1 cm = 1,000,000 miles

Mercury: 36 cm	Saturn: 8.9 m
Venus: 67 cm	Uranus: 17.8 m
Earth: 93 cm	Neptune: 27.9 m
Mars: 1.4 m	Pluto: 36.5 m
Jupiter: 4.8 m	

365 × 9 = 3,285 days
3,285 ÷ 225 = 14.6 years
Wow! I'd be a teenager on Venus!

Planet	Earth Days Needed for Orbit (rounded to the nearest day)
Mercury	88
Venus	225
Mars	687
Jupiter	4,333
Saturn	10,759
Uranus	30,685
Neptune	60,189
Pluto	90,465

Space Age

Understanding how long it takes a planet to orbit the sun

How old would your students be in Martian years? Plutonian years? Show them how to find out! Make and display a poster labeled with the information shown. Next, give each child a calculator and a ruler. Have her multiply her age in years by 365 to find her age in days. Then have her divide her age in days by the days needed to complete an orbit. Direct students to round their answers as follows: Mercury, Venus, and Mars to the nearest whole number; Jupiter, Saturn, and Uranus to the nearest tenth; Neptune and Pluto to the nearest hundredth. Students will be amazed to think that they could be their parents' ages on Mercury, only months old on Jupiter, Saturn, and Uranus, or a few days old on Neptune or Pluto!

Exploring Ellipses

Understanding that planets have elliptical orbits

Explore the shape of a planet's orbit with this hands-on activity! Ask a pizza parlor to donate unused cardboard circles (one for each pair of students). Also gather a sock and a tennis ball. Place the ball in the toe of the sock and twirl it in front of you as shown. Have students describe the ball's egg-shaped orbit. Next, pair students. Explain that for 20 out of every 248 years, Pluto crosses into Neptune's orbit and is closer to the sun. Then have the partners represent this interesting fact by giving them the materials listed and guiding them through the steps shown.

Materials for each pair of students: cardboard circle, 2 pushpins, pencil, sheet of half-centimeter graph paper, 12" length of string, 16" length of string, 3 colored pencils (yellow, red, blue), tape

Steps:

1. Label the graph paper's axes using increments of two; then tape the paper to the cardboard circle.
2. Using the yellow pencil, plot and connect the following coordinates to draw the sun: (21, 16), (23, 16), (24, 17), (24, 19), (23, 20), (21, 20), (20, 19), (20, 17), and (21, 16).
3. Form two loops of string by tying both ends of each string together.
4. Place one pushpin at (12, 18) and the other at (36, 18). Loop the 12-inch string around the base of the pushpins. Insert the red pencil in the loop, pull the string tight, and draw Neptune's orbit.
5. To draw Pluto's orbit, repeat Step 4, moving the pushpins to (12, 27) and (38, 3) and using the 16-inch string and the blue pencil.
6. Label the orbits.

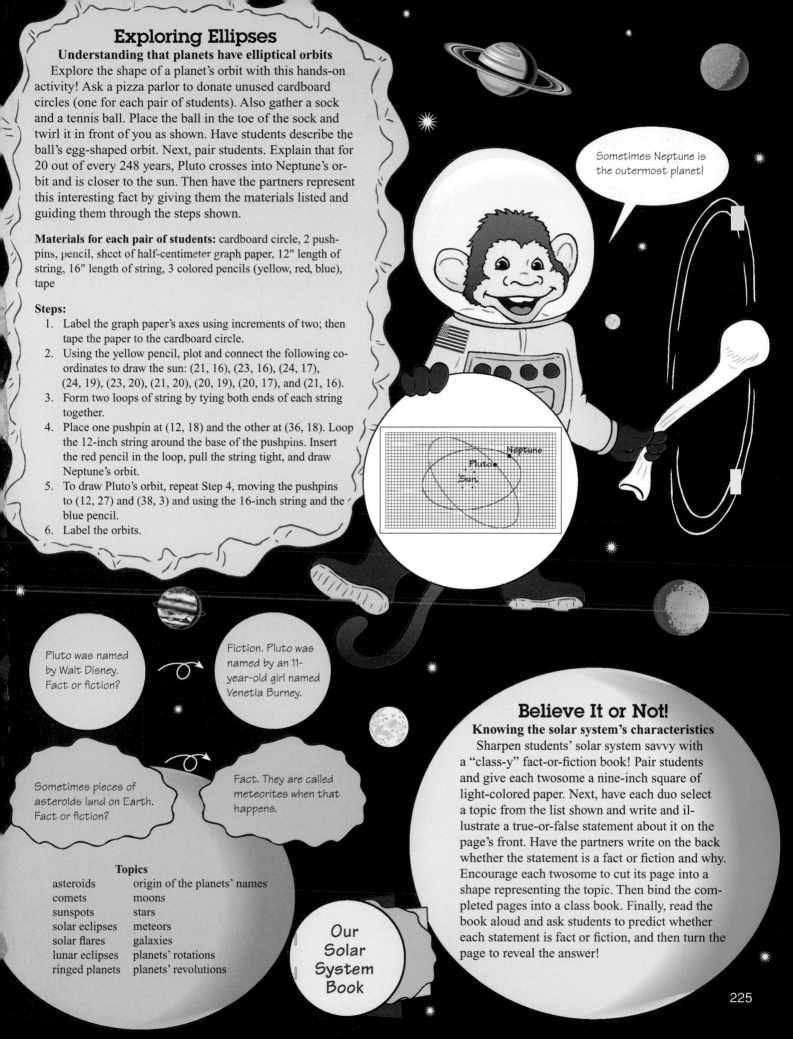

Sometimes Neptune is the outermost planet!

Pluto was named by Walt Disney. Fact or fiction?

Fiction. Pluto was named by an 11-year-old girl named Venetia Burney.

Sometimes pieces of asteroids land on Earth. Fact or fiction?

Fact. They are called meteorites when that happens.

Topics

asteroids	origin of the planets' names
comets	moons
sunspots	stars
solar eclipses	meteors
solar flares	galaxies
lunar eclipses	planets' rotations
ringed planets	planets' revolutions

Our Solar System Book

Believe It or Not!

Knowing the solar system's characteristics

Sharpen students' solar system savvy with a "class-y" fact-or-fiction book! Pair students and give each twosome a nine-inch square of light-colored paper. Next, have each duo select a topic from the list shown and write and illustrate a true-or-false statement about it on the page's front. Have the partners write on the back whether the statement is a fact or fiction and why. Encourage each twosome to cut its page into a shape representing the topic. Then bind the completed pages into a class book. Finally, read the book aloud and ask students to predict whether each statement is fact or fiction, and then turn the page to reveal the answer!

Name _____

"Weight" 'til You See This!

If you think Elmer is heavy on Earth, wait until you find out how much (or how little) he would weigh on the other planets!

Directions: Solve the problems to find Elmer's weight on each planet. Color the peanut with the matching answer. Some peanuts will not be colored.

① Mercury

13,000
x 0.39

② Venus

13,000
x 0.879

③ Mars

13,000
x 0.38

④ Jupiter

13,000
x 2.53

⑤ Saturn

13,000
x   1.1

⑥ Uranus

13,000
x   0.9

I weigh 13,000 pounds!

⑦ Neptune

13,000
x   1.14

507 lbs.

4,940 lbs.

32,890 lbs.

9,100 lbs.

910 lbs.

11,420 lbs.

14,820 lbs.

⑧ Pluto

13,000
x 0.07

5,070 lbs.

11,700 lbs.

14,300 lbs.

11,427 lbs.

Bonus Box: On which planet would Elmer weigh the most? The least? Write your answers on the back of this page.

Note to the teacher: Each child will need a crayon or marker to complete this page.

Planetary Puzzler

Each planet on the chart (except Earth) was named for a Greek or Roman god. Use the clues to match each planet to the god it was named for.

Directions: Put a ✔ in each box that is true and an X in each box that is false.

1. The planet named for the king of the gods has the same number of planets on either side of it.

2. The planet named for the messenger of the gods is at one end of the solar system. The planet named for the god of the underworld is at the other end of the solar system.

3. The planet named for the god of war is three planets beyond the planet named for the messenger of the gods.

4. The planet named for the god of the sea is four planets farther from the sun than the planet named for the god of war.

Planet	god of war	god of agriculture	god of the sky	messenger of the gods	god of the sea	god of the underworld	king of the gods	godess of love
Mercury								
Venus								
Earth								
Mars								
Jupiter								
Saturn								
Uranus								
Neptune								
Pluto								

5. The only planet named for a goddess is an inner planet. This means it is between Mars and the sun.

6. The planet named for the god of agriculture is between two planets. It's between the planets named for the god of the sky and the king of the gods.

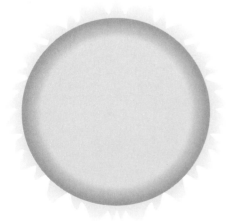

Rock

Hop into a study of rocks and minerals with these rock-solid activities and reproducibles!

by Jennifer Otter, Oak Ridge, NC

"Class-ic" Formations
Rock formation, rock classes

Put those old crayons to use for a fun activity and two quick demonstrations that show students how sedimentary, igneous, and metamorphic rocks are formed. Before beginning, direct each child to fold a sheet of lined paper into thirds and label each section with the name of a different rock class as shown. Follow up by having each student complete a copy of page 232 as directed.

Sedimentary Rock

Sandstone

Review with students how sedimentary rock forms. Next, divide students into small groups to form their own models of sedimentary rocks. Give each group member a different color of crayon and give each group two six-inch waxed paper squares, access to pencil or crayon sharpeners, and a textbook. Direct one child in each group to sharpen her crayon over the waxed paper, leaving a small layer of shavings. Then have each remaining group member add a layer of shavings. Guide the group to cover the shavings with the second waxed paper square and place the book on top. Have students take turns pressing on the book. Finally, have the group remove its book and the top sheet of waxed paper. Then direct each student to examine the model, draw a picture of it in the appropriate section of her folded paper, and add a paragraph explaining how sedimentary rock is formed.

Igneous Rock

Rhyolite

Before this demonstration, melt crayon pieces in an aluminum pie pan at 450° for five to six minutes. Carefully show students the hot, liquid wax and explain that igneous rock begins as magma deep inside the earth. Set the liquid down and explain that when magma cools, it hardens as igneous rock. Allow about 20 minutes for the wax to cool. Then direct each child to draw the model in the appropriate section of her paper and add a paragraph explaining how igneous rock is formed.

Metamorphic Rock

Slate

Use an iron to show students how heat and pressure can change sedimentary and igneous rocks into metamorphic rock. First, set up a heat-resistant surface and prepare the sedimentary and igneous models described at the left. Next, review with students how igneous or sedimentary rocks can be transformed into metamorphic rock. Then cover the sedimentary model with waxed paper and press a hot, dry iron (no steam) on it for two seconds. Display the result and guide students to describe how the model changed. Repeat with the igneous model; then display both models. Direct each observer to draw one model in the appropriate section of his paper and add a paragraph explaining how metamorphic rock is formed.

"Hop-py"

Name That Mineral!
Mineral properties

Here's a fun twist on the game 20 Questions that gives students some fast-paced practice with mineral properties! In advance, copy one more than a class supply of the properties table on page 230. Cut the extra copy into strips; then place the strips in a bag. Next, give each child a copy of page 230 and draw a strip from the bag. Explain that students can use the properties table as a guide to help them ask up to ten questions in an effort to identify the mineral listed on the paper strip. If the mineral is identified in ten or fewer questions, let the identifier draw the next slip and lead the next round. If not, read aloud the mineral's attributes one at a time until the class pinpoints the mystery mineral.

Grit

Bryce Canyon National Park

Rockhopper Penguin Rock Club

Tuff

Rock Stars
Rock formations

Students will be following the stars of the rock and mineral world with this stellar research project! Assign each pair of students a different famous rock formation to research (see the list of suggestions). Challenge the duo to find a picture of the formation and research how it was formed. Direct the twosome to also investigate the formation's size, rock makeup, and location. Next, have the pair display its findings on a large construction paper star as shown above. Then mount the projects on a bulletin board titled "Check Out These Rock Stars!"

Bingo Rocks!
Rock and mineral terms

Turn the familiar game bingo into a rockin' review! List on the board 16 important rock and mineral terms. Next, have each child draw a 4 x 4 grid on a sheet of paper. Direct her to randomly copy each term on the board in a different box of her grid. Explain that you will read a definition and each player will cover the matching term on her grid with a game marker. Also demonstrate the three unique patterns at the right to show how each player can win. Finally, pass out markers and randomly read aloud the clues. Check off each clue as you go so you can confirm the winner's answers!

Gneiss

Famous Rock Formations

Arches National Park	Giant's Causeway
Ayers Rock	Grand Canyon
Badlands National Park	Monument Valley
Bryce Canyon National Park	Painted Desert
Canadian Badlands	Rock of Gibraltar
Carlsbad Caverns National Park	Shiprock
Devils Tower National Monument	Stone Mountain
Garden of the Gods	Wind Cave National Park

Stonehenge
(any vertical column)

Rock Band
(a horizontal band in any row)

Rock Group
(a group of four spaces in any corner)

Mineral Properties Table

Use with "Name That Mineral!" on page 229.

Mineral Properties

Mineral	Color	Streak Color	Luster	Hardness
talc	gray, white, or greenish	white	pearly to greasy	1
silver	silver white	silver to light gray	metallic	2.5
gold	gold	yellow	metallic	2.5–3
halite	white, pale colors, or gray	white	pearly	2.5–3
magnetite	iron black	black	metallic	5–6
hematite	reddish brown to black	light to dark red	metallic	5.5–6.5
feldspar	colorless, white, or various colors	colorless or white	glassy	6
turquoise	blue-green	blue-green or white	waxy	6
pyrite	brass or yellow	greenish or brownish black	metallic	6–6.5
quartz	colorless, white, purple, pink, blue, or yellow	colorless or white	glassy or greasy	7.5–8
topaz	yellow, pink, bluish, or greenish	colorless or white	glassy	8
diamond	colorless, pale yellow, black, blue, brown, green, pink, purple, or red	colorless	brilliant or greasy	10

Dropped Rocks

Sid collects sedimentary rocks. Iggy collects igneous rocks. Mimi collects metamorphic rocks. They just bumped into each other. Now their rocks are all mixed up! To help them sort their rocks, read each tag. Then color the rock by the code.

Color Code
igneous = yellow
sedimentary = red
metamorphic = blue

1. Pressure changes layers of dead plants into **coal.**

2. Lava flows from cracks in the earth and hardens into **basalt.**

3. Layers of shell or coral sand and mud form **limestone.**

4. Heat and pressure change rocks inside the earth's crust into **gneiss.**

5. Hot lava filled with gas cools quickly and forms **pumice.**

6. Heat and pressure change limestone into **marble.**

7. Pressure changes layers of mud into **shale.**

8. Heat and pressure change sandstone into **quartzite.**

9. Layers of mud made mostly of tiny shells and calcite crystals form the soft rock **chalk.**

10. Magma cools slowly and hardens into **granite.**

11. Heat and pressure deep in the earth change shale to **slate.**

12. Hot lava on the earth's surface cools quickly to form **obsidian.**

Recycling Rocks

Rocks are always changing. Read each clue below and decide which stage of the rock cycle it describes. Then write the stage letter in the corresponding box of the column below.

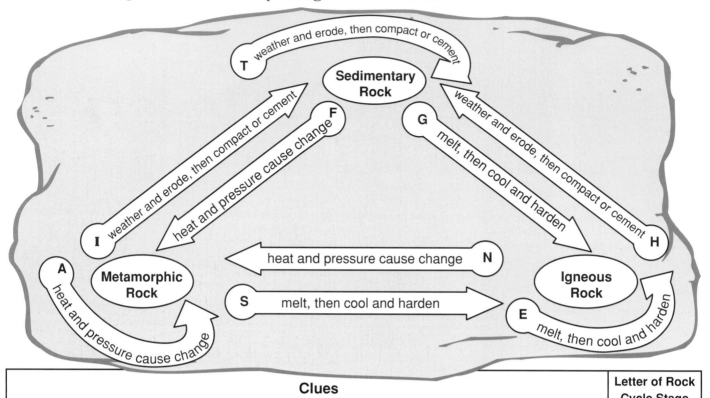

Clues	Letter of Rock Cycle Stage
1. Andesite, an igneous rock, melts to form new rock.	
2. Heat and pressure change sandstone, a sedimentary rock, into new rock.	
3. Bits of andesite, an igneous rock, are pressed together and form rock.	
4. Quartzite, a metamorphic rock, melts and forms new rock.	
5. Sandstone, a sedimentary rock, melts and forms new rock.	
6. Bits of weathered quartzite, a metamorphic rock, are cemented to form new rock.	
7. Compacted bits of sedimentary rock from the Grand Canyon weather and form new rock.	
8. Heat and pressure change granite, an igneous rock, into new rock.	
9. Heat and pressure change slate, a metamorphic rock, into new rock.	

What did Mimi say when she heard that a piece of granite (an igneous rock) had been changed into metamorphic rock? To find out, write the corresponding letter for each clue above in the matching numbered blank below. One letter will not be used.

___ ___ ___ ___ ___ , ___ ___ ___ ___ ___ ___ ___ !
7   3   9   7   4   5   8   1   6   4   4

Bonus Box: Which type of rock has a name that means "changed in form"? Which type's name means "formed from fire"?

LITERATURE UNITS

Literature That Looks at School

School experiences are a significant part of our lives. The people we meet in school and the events that happen there often influence who we are. Share some unforgettable school experiences with the memorable characters in these two remarkable books.

by Julia Ring Alarie, Pierce Memorial School, Huntington, VT

Prereading Activity
Identifying and understanding theme

Help students explore the theme of the two featured novels by having them examine their ideas of what makes a great school year. Direct the class to imagine that it's the night before the first day of school. Ask students what they hope the new school year will be like. Prompt them with questions such as the following:

- What kind of teacher do you hope to have?
- What kinds of activities and special events do you hope there will be?
- What kinds of friends do you hope to make?

Next, have each child use his ideas to write a recipe for a great school year. Give each student an index card or a preprinted recipe card. Instruct the child to write on the card the recipe's name, ingredients, and directions. Then invite each student to share his recipe with the class. Post the completed recipes on a bulletin board titled "Recipes for a Great School Year!"

A Super School Year

fun, caring teacher
24 kind classmates
5 interesting projects
4 fantastic field trips

scant cup of homework
pinch of mystery
large bunch of laughs
daily dose of recess

Combine all ingredients in a colorfully decorated classroom. Mix with respect, kindness, and cooperation. Divide into 180 delicious days. Makes one great school year!

You'll laugh until you cry, but even if you try, you'll never forget the Herdmans! These six siblings terrorize the students of Woodrow Wilson Elementary School and exasperate the whole town. Can the class's yearlong compliments project help everyone see the best in one another, including the Herdmans?

My Day on the Town
Exploring point of view

In chapter 2, the Herdmans go to the opening of the new laundromat and attempt to give their cat a bath in a washing machine. The cat gets out of the machine and streaks through town, upsetting folks at the laundromat, barber shop, and movie theater. Have the class consider this event from the cat's point of view. Encourage students to think about the cat's personality and imagine its previous experiences with its highly unusual family. Then pair students and direct partners to write a version of the episode from the cat's perspective. Have the pair choose to write its version as a comedy, tragedy, adventure, or drama. After each pair is finished, allow partners to share their stories with the class, using as much expression as possible. Then bind the stories into a class book.

My Trip to Laundry Land
by Claws Herdman

It's not every day that a cat like me gets to take a trip to a great place, but today was my lucky day! My family wanted to do something special for me because I'm such a great cat. So they decided to take me to the laundromat for a bath! I know what you're thinking—a bath isn't that fun! But with my family it is! We drove everyone out of the laundromat and tricked Mr. Santoro into calling the fire department. Plus, I got lathered at the barber shop, and on my way home, I managed to grab some free popcorn at the movies! All that fun, and I came home looking and feeling my best! What a great day!

Explain why you're upset.

Be brave and calm.

Ask the Herdmans to help you fix the problem.

Handling the Herdmans

Handling the Herdmans
Problem resolution

With the Herdmans, it's one wild event after another! No one seems to know how to handle this aggravating clan. Have students imagine that all six Herdmans live in their town and attend their school. Are the siblings' antics still hilarious and their pranks as entertaining? Next, divide the class into groups of three or four. Instruct each group to brainstorm positive ideas for dealing with the Herdmans and write its ideas on a sheet of paper. Direct the group to discuss the ideas and rank them from first effort to last resort. Then give each group a 9" x 12" sheet of colorful paper. Have the team fold it to create a pamphlet. Direct the group to list and illustrate its guidelines on the pamphlet's sections. Set aside time for each team to share its pamphlet with the class. Then post the completed pamphlets on a bulletin board titled "How to Handle the Herdmans."

If I Were Imogene...
Understanding how a character's traits influence the plot

Imogene Herdman seems to have an explanation for every situation and a solution for every problem. Help your students understand how this character trait of Imogene's affects the book's plot. Begin by having students list situations at school or at home that trouble them. Next, direct each student to choose one item from the list. Have the child pretend to be Imogene and imagine the kind of solution she would find. Remind students that Imogene's efforts appear to be sincere and helpful, which adds humor to the situations. Then give each student a 4½" x 12" strip of paper. Instruct her to divide the strip into three sections and label them as shown. Have her complete each box with a sentence and illustration that show how she thinks Imogene would solve the problem. After students share their strips, mount the projects on a wall or bulletin board titled "If I Were Imogene…"

The Year in Pictures
Using media to interpret text, writing narratives

Have students get in on the action of this hilarious story and present some of the book's funniest events. Divide students into nine groups and assign a different book chapter to each group. Instruct the group to choose a favorite scene from its chapter and write a narrative retelling the scene in an amusing and entertaining way. Next, explain that each group will present its narrative to the class and then pose as the scene's characters for a snapshot. Encourage students to bring in props and costumes for the photo and to ham it up. On the designated day, have each team read its narrative aloud to the class and pose for its picture. Also have the group mount its photo and narrative on a sheet of colorful construction paper. Bind the completed pages into a book titled "Our Picture Book of *The Best School Year Ever.*"

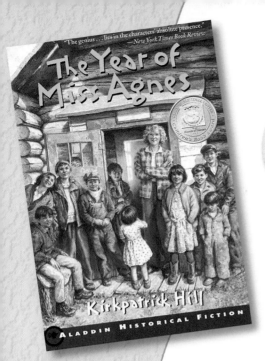

Every year a new teacher reluctantly comes to the small schoolroom in Fred's Alaskan village. Every year the students learn little and the teacher eagerly leaves, sometimes before the year is over. All this changes when Miss Agnes becomes the new teacher. After she arrives, school is never the same again!

Miss Agnes Will...
Making predictions

By the end of chapter 5, students have learned enough about Miss Agnes to make some predictions about the rest of the book. Direct each student to complete the provided sentences on a sheet of paper and to support his responses with evidence from the book. When students have completed their predictions, place the papers in a box until the class finishes the book. Then open the box and return each child's paper. Have the student check his predictions for accuracy.

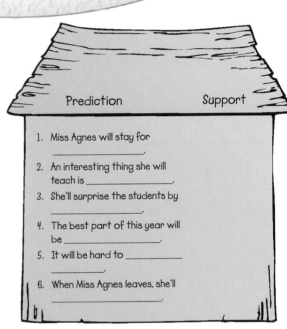

Prediction   Support

1. Miss Agnes will stay for _____.
2. An interesting thing she will teach is _____.
3. She'll surprise the students by _____.
4. The best part of this year will be _____.
5. It will be hard to _____.
6. When Miss Agnes leaves, she'll _____

Overcoming Obstacles
Making text-to-self connections, problem resolution

When Fred sees her sister Bokko go to school and learn to communicate through sign language, she realizes that people can overcome their obstacles. Fred says that "it's better to kick some instead of just sinking." Help students connect with this hopeful outlook by having them think about obstacles they wish to overcome or goals they want to achieve. Give each child a colorful mitten-shaped cutout and have her write the obstacle or goal on one side. On the other side, direct her to name and illustrate one way she can overcome the obstacle or reach the goal. Invite students to share their cutouts with the class. Then have each child follow the directions shown to make and attach to her cutout a pom-pom similar to the ones Fred and Bokko create to decorate the mittens Mamma makes. Afterward, have the student hole-punch the top left corner of her cutout and thread the ends of the yarn through it. Once she ties the ends of the yarn together to form a loop, allow her to take the cutout home and use it as a hanging reminder of her plan.

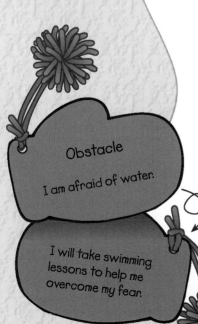

Obstacle

I am afraid of water.

I will take swimming lessons to help me overcome my fear.

Making a Pom-pom

Materials for each child: 3" x 3" square of heavy cardboard, 5-yd. length of yarn, two 9" lengths of yarn, scissors

Steps:
1. Wrap the five-yard length of yarn around the cardboard as shown.
2. Tie a nine-inch length around the middle of the yarn on one side of the cardboard.
3. Repeat the process on the other side of the cardboard with the second length of yarn.
4. Gently slide the yarn off the cardboard and tie the middles together.
5. Cut through the loops and fluff the yarn.

Walking in Someone Else's Shoes
Examining changes in a character

Show students that taking a walk in someone else's shoes can help them understand why a character's attitude might change. In chapter 4, Fred says that her mother "is not the laughing kind." Toward the end of the book Mamma's attitude seems to have changed. Help students explore Mamma's change of attitude by having them write two paragraphs on hole-punched index cards. In the first paragraph, have each child describe Mamma's outlook when Miss Agnes first arrives. In the second, have the student explain Mamma's attitude when she returns from fish camp. Remind students to support their ideas with evidence from the book. Then guide each child through the steps below to make a snowshoe. Post the projects on a bulletin board titled "Taking a Walk in Someone Else's Shoes."

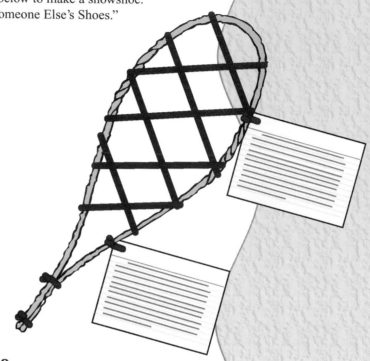

Making a Snowshoe

Materials for each child: 3 brown pipe cleaners, eight 8" lengths of yarn, four 3" lengths of yarn, scissors, programmed index cards from above

Steps:

1. Wire the pipe cleaners together, as shown, to form a snow-shoe frame.
2. Tie the pipe cleaners' ends together using two three-inch lengths of yarn. Trim the excess yarn.
3. Tie one eight-inch length of yarn diagonally across the snowshoe frame. Trim the excess yarn.
4. Repeat Step 3, tying the yarn lengths in a crisscross pattern.
5. Tie the index cards to the snowshoe using two three-inch lengths of yarn.

Miss Agnes's Gifts
Analyzing the effects of a character's qualities on the theme, recognizing symbolism

Miss Agnes has a profound effect on her students. To help students understand this, gather wrapping paper and a supply of small gift boxes (one per student). Remind the class that Miss Agnes gives her students many gifts, such as school supplies, encouragement, and understanding. Discuss with the class the difference between tangible and intangible gifts. Next, give each student a box, gift wrap, scissors, tape, and two index cards. Direct the child to wrap his box. Then have him choose a gift that Miss Agnes gives the entire class or one of her students. Instruct him to use one index card to make a small gift tag that names the giver and identifies the recipient. Direct him to use the second card to describe the gift and explain its importance. Then have him tape both the tag and the description to the gift and place it on a shelf or table titled "Gifts From Miss Agnes." Follow up by having students discuss what gifts Miss Agnes receives from her class.

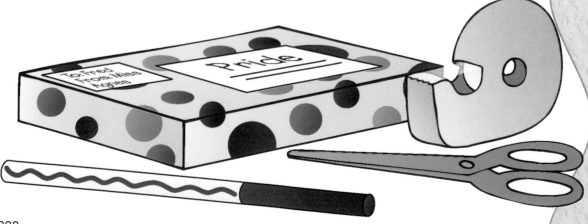

Swimming in the Same River

In *The Year of Miss Agnes,* Fred gives many details about her village and school in Alaska. How different is your town and school from hers?

Directions: List phrases that describe Fred's village and school in the fish at the top. In the fish at the bottom, list phrases that describe your own town and school. Then, in the middle, list the things that you and Fred have in common.

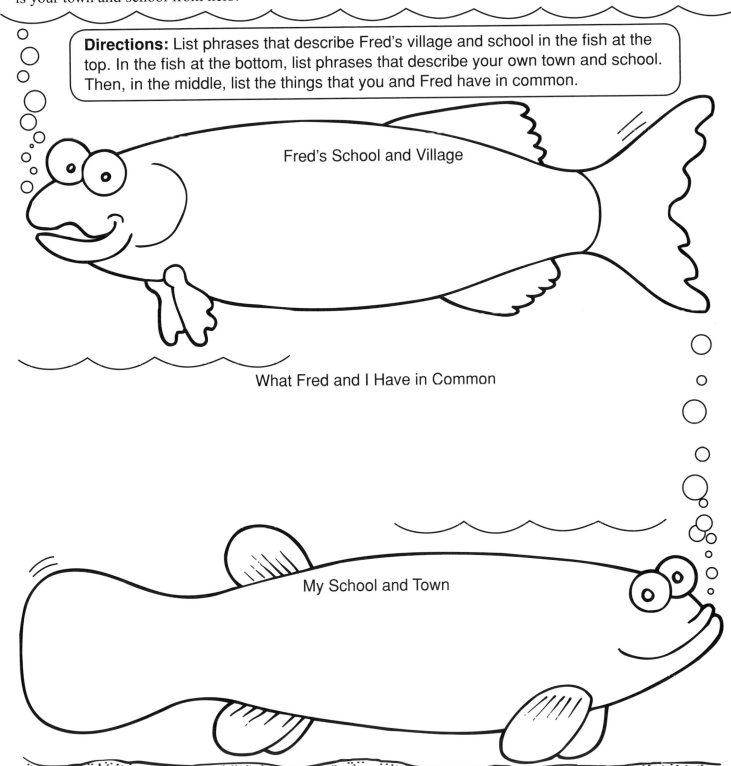

Fred's School and Village

What Fred and I Have in Common

My School and Town

Bonus Box: On the back of this page, explain what you think Miss Agnes means when she says there are lots of right ways to talk.

Note to the teacher: Use this page after students have finished reading *The Year of Miss Agnes.*

Literature That Looks at Chocolate

Rich and creamy, sweet and dreamy chocolate! This tasty treat does more than satisfy a sweet tooth. It's a terrific literature topic as well! Share a double helping of chocolate with two books that offer rich results!

by Kim Minafo, Cary, NC

Prereading Activity
Descriptive writing

This decidedly different descriptive-writing idea is a chocolate lover's dream! Collect several restaurant menus. Also gather for every four students a paper plate, a five-inch square of aluminum foil, glue, and a permanent marker. Next, divide the class into groups of four. Tell students that a new restaurant is opening and that its meals will combine old favorites, such as spaghetti, with chocolate. Explain that each group will redesign a favorite dish to include chocolate and then write a description of the dish for the restaurant's menu. After sharing examples of menu descriptions with the class, give each group its materials. Direct each group to cut a large chocolate-drop shape from its foil, write the item's name on the shape with the marker, and glue the shape to the plate as shown. Then have group members write on the plate a short description of their new food creation. Invite students to share the descriptive dishes with the class; then post the plates on a bulletin board titled "Sweet Sensations."

Pasta With Chocolate Cream Sauce

We cook angel-hair pasta to perfection. Then we mix creamy white chocolate and rich dark chocolate together, creating a cream sauce that's beyond compare. The sauce is drizzled over the pasta to top this mouthwatering dish.

•Robert Kimmel Smith•

CHOCOLATE FEVER

Can a boy really hatch from a chocolate bean? Of course not! But when a boy loves chocolate as much as Henry Green, folks begin to wonder. With the encouragement of his indulgent parents, Henry eats chocolate nonstop until he contracts Chocolate Fever. His unique condition, combined with a string of zany events, leads Henry to change his chocolate-eating ways.

Baby Splits From Banana!

Hatched From the Headlines
Descriptive writing, understanding symbolism

Concocting delightfully unbelievable tales that become headline news is what this activity is all about! Remind students that Henry Green's favorite food is chocolate and that some people say that he must have "hatched, fully grown, from a chocolate bean." Next, have each child make a short list of his favorite foods. Instruct him to choose one food from his list and create a headline about a baby's birth from the food; then have him write a newspaper article supplying all the details. Direct the student to draw his chosen item on a colorful sheet of construction paper as if the food had cracked open. Then have him cut out the shape and paste it to his news article. After students share their headline stories with the class, post the articles along with their shapes on a bulletin board titled "Baffling Births: Stories Too Delicious to be Believed!"

It's Alive!
Making predictions

Provide practice with making predictions with this chocolatey booklet-making activity! First, ask students to think about the following questions:
- What will life be like for Henry if he turns into a living, breathing body of chocolate?
- Will Henry take on a shape related to his illness?

Then have the class discuss the possible chocolate forms Henry might take and the related situations that could await him. Next, divide students into groups of four. Give each group four six-inch squares of white construction paper, scissors, two brown sheets of 9" x 12" paper, access to a stapler, and crayons or markers. Have the foursome predict what form of chocolate it thinks Henry could take and then cut the squares and colorful sheets into that form. Afterward, instruct each group member to illustrate on a white page a possible scenario that Henry might face in that form and include a caption describing the situation. Then have the group staple the papers together to make a booklet. When everyone is finished, invite the groups to share their chocolate-coated predictions with the class!

Henry walks home and tries to avoid the hot sun by holding a newspaper on his head.

Explain Yourself!
Analyzing point of view

Students can put themselves in the place of book characters with this point-of-view activity! After reading chapter 10, pair students and pose the following questions:

- How do you think Henry explains the situation to the police?
- What do you think Mac says?
- What do you think Louie says?
- What do you think Lefty says?
- How might one of the policemen explain the scene he finds?

Instruct each duo to choose a character to focus on and discuss what that character might have seen, heard, and felt during the hijacking and at the thieves' hideaway. Next, give each twosome a 12" x 18" sheet of white construction paper, scissors, and crayons or markers. Direct the twosome to illustrate its chosen character on one side of the paper and add as large a speech bubble as the paper will allow. Then have the partners write inside the bubble an explanation of the events from their character's point of view. Once that is done, have the pair cut out the character and its attached speech bubble and share the project with the class. What an eye-opening experience!

Sort and Stack
Exploring theme

Explore the book's theme with a sorting activity that could make students' mouths water! First, divide the class into groups of four. Have each group discuss the following questions:

- Are Henry's adventures ones that the average elementary student would experience?
- What do the events tell readers about the author's purpose for writing the book?
- How does the author convey humor?

Next, give each group 12 circle cutouts and four snack-size paper plates to label as shown. Explain that the circles represent pancakes. Then instruct the group mates to label each pancake with an example from the book that shows how the author uses characters, dialogue, actions/events, or images to show humor. Direct group members to label the other side of the pancake with the matching plate number. Once this is done, direct each foursome to shuffle its pancakes and trade them with another group. Have the group read each example, decide how to categorize it, and stack it on the corresponding plate. When all of the pancakes have been sorted, they can be flipped over one at a time and checked! Have the groups continue to swap and sort pancakes as time allows.

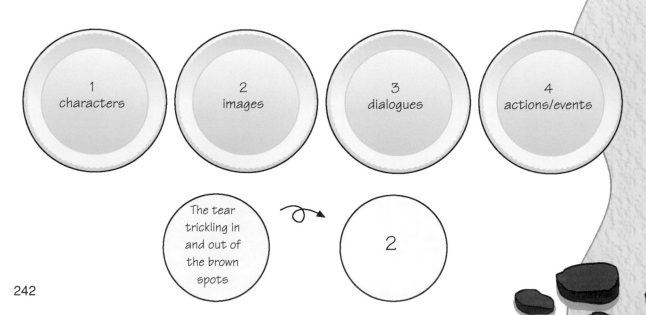

Reclusive Willie Wonka owns a large candy factory that no one has been allowed to enter for over a decade. When he suddenly decides to open its doors, he places golden tickets in the wrappers of five bars of chocolate. Each person who finds a ticket will be allowed inside for a day. Thousands of people begin buying bars, hoping to find a golden ticket. When a twist of fate helps Charlie Bucket purchase the last lucky bar, his life is changed beyond his wildest dreams.

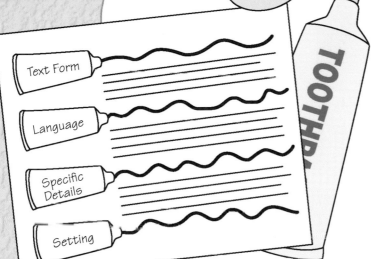

Uncapping the Purpose
Understanding the author's purpose

Squeezing everything you want to say into a chapter isn't easy for an author. After reading chapter 1, ask students what they think the author hoped to achieve in this chapter *(establishing Charlie as a likable fellow in tough circumstances)*. Draw a chart on a sheet of poster board and label it as shown. Next, divide students into groups of three. Have each group discuss how the author uses text form, language, specific details, and the setting to accomplish his purpose. Then invite each trio to share its ideas with the class. List the group's responses on the chart and keep it posted throughout the reading of the book. Revisit the chart periodically to keep students aware of the author's techniques.

Crating the Evidence
Using evidence to defend an opinion

To encourage students to defend an opinion, have them debate a sticky issue! After reading chapter 19, review with students how the Oompa-Loompas enter the country and begin working at the factory. Ask students if they think Mr. Wonka's actions toward the Oompa-Loompas are fair. Next, divide the class into small groups. Direct half of the groups to defend Mr. Wonka's actions and the other half to prove that his actions are unfair. Have group members gather evidence from the book to support their opinions. Give each group supporting Mr. Wonka's actions yellow sticky notes on which to record different supporting details and give the groups opposing his actions green notes. Once everyone has gathered evidence, pair each group with an opposing one for a brief debate. Then have each group decorate a sheet of newsprint to resemble a wooden packing crate and cut it out. After group members attach all their sticky notes to the cutout, add it to a display titled "Crating the Evidence."

243

Opening the Door to Prediction
Making predictions

Predicting a character's fate can be as easy as opening a door with this simple activity! Violet and Augustus each meet a fate that matches his or her disgusting behavior. Before reading chapter 22, ask students to predict what they think will happen to the remaining characters: Mike, Veruca, and Charlie. Assign each child one of these characters and give her a 9" x 12" sheet of construction paper and markers. Then guide her through the steps below to make a door on which to predict her character's fate based on what she knows about him or her thus far. Post the completed doors on a bulletin board titled "Opening the Door to Prediction." When Veruca's, Mike's, and Charlie's fates are revealed in the book, revisit students' predictions to see whether they match!

Steps:
1. Fold your paper in half vertically; then turn it so that the folded side is to your left.
2. Draw and color a doorknob on the front of the folded paper. Write your character's name at the bottom edge of the door.
3. Create a sign at the top of the door. Label the sign with the name of the room in which you think your character will face a challenge. Below the sign, add an illustration that represents the room.
4. Open the door so that the paper lies flat. To the right of the fold, write a paragraph telling how you think the challenge will occur. Illustrate your paragraph in the space to the left of the fold.

Songs for Charlie
Evaluating a character

Assess Charlie's character with a song-writing activity that helps you discover which of your students are poets and don't know it! As the book ends, readers will realize that every golden-ticket holder is serenaded except Charlie. Take a few minutes for students to review each character's song and to discuss the songs' similarities and differences. Then ask students what kind of song they think the Oompa-Loompas should sing about Charlie. Would it describe positive traits, negative traits, or a mixture of both? Next, pair students. Direct each twosome to list Charlie's character traits and write a supporting detail from the book next to each trait. Have the duo use its listed traits to write a song about Charlie that can be sung to a familiar tune. When all the lyrics are written, invite each duo to perform its song for the class!

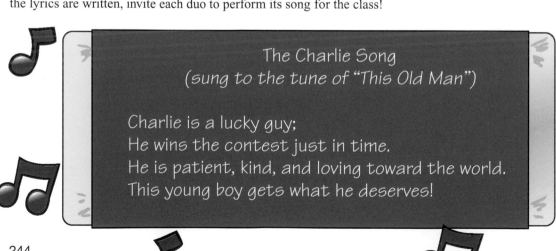

The Charlie Song
(sung to the tune of "This Old Man")

Charlie is a lucky guy;
He wins the contest just in time.
He is patient, kind, and loving toward the world.
This young boy gets what he deserves!

Confection Connections

Write the same word to complete each sentence pair. Color each candy as you use its word. Not all candies will be colored.

1) Eating anything made of chocolate is a _____ with Henry.
Henry's brother likes to _____ him on the head when they argue.

2) Henry's problem _____ up after he eats breakfast.
The last thing he _____ into his mouth is a chocolate cookie.

3) Henry notices that his arms look _____.
The class laughs at Henry's _____ answer.

4) Henry's situation is a _____.
Thankfully, Henry's appearance doesn't cause a _____ at school.

5) The school nurse doesn't want to make a _____ decision.
She isn't sure about treating Henry's _____.

6) Henry _____ out of the hospital.
Then he sneaks through a garage door that has no _____.

7) Everyone is trying to _____ Henry after he disappears.
Each brown _____ on Henry's body soon becomes a brown lump.

8) Dr. Fargo begins to _____ around the hospital room.
When Henry gets tired, he slows his running _____.

9) Henry _____ his mind about his problem.
After a few minutes he _____ down to rest.

10) There is a _____ of kids in the schoolyard.
They begin to _____ up on Henry when they see him.

ring

riot

funny

hit

rash

spot

gang

pace

pops

settles

bolts

file

Bonus Box: On the back of this page, write pairs of sentences that show different meanings for each uncolored word above.

©The Mailbox® • TEC44017 • Feb./Mar. 2005 • Key p. 313

Note to the teacher: Use after reading *Chocolate Fever* by Robert Kimmel Smith. Each child will need a crayon to complete this page.

Sweet Synonyms

Find your way through each lollipop maze. Follow the synonyms of
the word on each lollipop's stick to color a path to its center. For fun,
use a different color for each path!

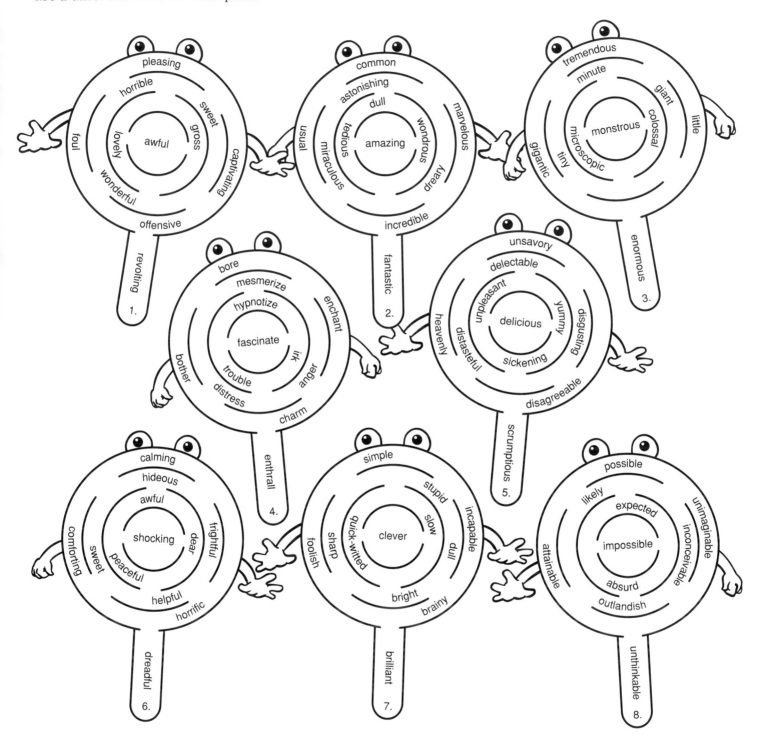

Bonus Box: On the back of this page, list the words on each lollipop that could be antonyms of the word
on the stick.

©The Mailbox® • TEC44017 • Feb./Mar. 2005 • Key p. 313

Note to the teacher: Use after reading *Charlie and the Chocolate Factory* by Roald Dahl. To complete this page, each child will need
crayons and access to a thesaurus or a dictionary.

Math Mailbag

Math Mailbag

Does Order Matter?
Understanding the commutative property

Everyone wins with this unforgettable activity about the commutative property! Gather a die; then write "__ + __ + __ + __ = ___" (or "__ x __ x __ x __ = ___" on the board for each student to copy. Next, divide students into groups of four. Roll the die and announce the number rolled. Have each player write the number rolled in a blank he thinks will make the greatest sum (or product) when added (or multiplied). After rolling the die three more times, have each player secretly find the product. Then call on one group's members at a time to share their answers with the class. Act shocked and exclaim, "Wow! Why is everyone's answer the same?" Allowing students to discover the order property themselves makes the activity even more memorable!

Kim Minafo
Cary, NC

My Decimal Booklet

Tenths!

Model	Fraction	Decimal	Word Name
	$\frac{1}{10}$	0.1	one-tenth
	$\frac{2}{10}$	0.2	two-tenths
	$\frac{3}{10}$	0.3	three-tenths
	$\frac{4}{10}$	0.4	four-tenths

Decimal Booklets
Understanding basic decimal concepts

Move students' understanding of basic decimal concepts from concrete to abstract with this booklet-making activity! Direct each child to make a four-page booklet by folding and stapling together two 9" x 12" sheets of construction paper. Next, give each child scissors, glue, crayons, and ten paper decimal models of tenths. Have the student divide each two-page spread into four columns and label them as shown. Model how to complete the first row. Then have each child add similar rows representing two-, three-, and four-tenths. Instruct her to use the next two facing pages for representing five- through eight-tenths and the last spread for nine-tenths and one whole. Once she decorates the cover, she'll have a handy reference! Later, students can make booklets for hundredths that include columns for percent and monetary value. For other decimal activities, see pages 137–141.

Sharon Fisher—Gr. 4, Orange Grove Elementary School, Charleston, SC

Deciphering Math Messages
Identifying place value

Place-value practice can be spelled F-U-N with this activity! Write on the board the number and answer blanks shown (without the letters) for each child to copy. Then give directions one at a time that instruct the student to fill a specific answer blank with a particular letter. For example, say, "Write the letter *U* in the tens place." Continue until a direction has been given for every place value in the number. If students record the letters correctly, a message will be revealed. Continue the fun by pairing students and having each child create a message for his partner to decipher!

Laura Hess, Providence School, Greencastle, PA

1 6 7 , 4 3 8 , 9 6 4
M A T H I S F U N!

Math Mailbag

Picture-Perfect Shopping
Creating and solving word problems

Turn students' excitement about holiday shopping into timely problem-solving practice! Have each pair of students cut out pictures and prices of popular toys from sales flyers and glue them to a sheet of paper. On another sheet of paper, have the duo write five word problems that could be solved using the pictures. For example, they could write "Jenny wants to buy her brother the basketball and the airplane. If she has $40, can she buy both gifts?" Have students skip lines between each problem and make an answer key. Next, place each set of problems and pictures back to back in a clear plastic sleeve with the answer key sandwiched between them. Then put the sets in a center with washable markers. Students can solve the problems right on the sleeve and then pull out the key to check!

Carrie Johanning, Shaner Elementary, Topeka, KS

	Player 1					Player 2			
	Estimated Length	Length	Difference	Points		Estimated Length	Length	Difference	Points
Round 1					Round 1				
Round 2					Round 2				
Round 3					Round 3				
Round 4					Round 4				
Round 5					Round 5				
Round 6					Round 6				
Round 7					Round 7				
Round 8					Round 8				
Round 9					Round 9				
Round 10					Round 10				
	Total Points					Total Points			

The Last Straw
Estimating and measuring to the nearest half inch

Make sure time spent at a center measures up with this cool game for student pairs! Gather nine plastic straws. Cut two straws into three parts each, making each part a different length. Cut each remaining straw into two parts, again creating different lengths. Put the parts in a plastic cup at a center along with pencils, rulers, and game sheets such as the one shown. Invite two students at a time to the center. For each round, instruct each player to select a straw from the cup, estimate its length to the nearest half inch, and record the estimate on the game sheet. Then have each player measure his opponent's straw to the nearest half inch. After he records the length, have him find and record the difference between his opponent's estimate and the actual length. The player with the smaller difference earns ten points. The player with the higher score after all the straws have been measured is the winner!

Kim Minafo, Cary, NC

Fraction Fun Kit
Finding equivalent fractions, comparing fractions

This make-and-use manipulative kit makes understanding basic fraction concepts oh so easy! On a sheet of duplicating paper, draw horizontal bars and divide them into the fractions you want students to use. Make a copy of the bars on white construction paper for each child. Next, give each child crayons, scissors, a resealable plastic bag, and a copy of the bars. Instruct her to color each row of bars a different color, cut the pieces apart, and place them in the bag. Then have students use the pieces to answer questions such as the following: How many fourths equal one half? Which is larger: $\frac{1}{5}$ or $\frac{1}{6}$?

Janice Schrag—Gr. 5, Christ the King School, Akron, OH

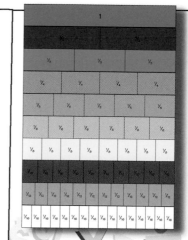

Math Mailbag

Fraction Fun
Finding the fractional part of a whole number
Finding fractional parts of whole numbers is something students will beg to do with this class game! Program each of a class set of index cards with a different problem such as ¾ of 16, ⅝ of 81, or ⅕ of 100. Next, spread the cards problem side down on a table and divide students into two teams. Have a child from Team 1 choose a card. Write the card's problem on the board for everyone to solve. After circulating to check students' answers, have the card's chooser record the correct answer on the board as his team's score for that round. Play additional rounds in the same manner, alternately having a child from each team choose a card. Then declare the team with more points the winner!

Kristi Titus, Leesburg Elementary
Leesburg, VA

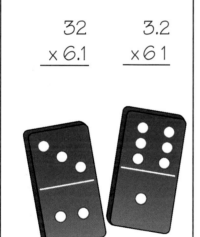

Domino Duel
Practicing addition and multiplication
Addition and multiplication are the operations of choice for this duel-to-the-end partner game! Direct partners to arrange a set of dominoes facedown on a table between them. Announce whether students are to practice addition facts or multiplication facts. Have each player simultaneously choose one domino and turn it faceup. Depending on the assigned task, each player adds or multiplies the two numbers her domino represents. The player with the higher sum or product gets both dominoes. Play continues until every domino has been captured. The player with more dominoes wins. For a greater challenge, have each player turn two dominoes faceup and then add or multiply on paper the whole numbers or mixed decimals her dominoes represent.

Terri Myers, Dalton, GA

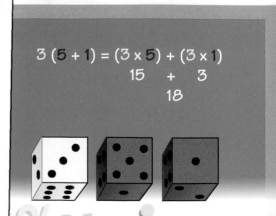

Distributive Breakdown
Understanding the distributive property
Show students how easy the distributive property is to understand when it's sliced and diced! Roll three dice: two of one color and one of a second color. Using the numbers rolled and colored chalk, if desired, write a problem on the board (see the example). Then solve the problem, explaining how to multiply the number in front of the parentheses by each number inside the parentheses. Next, give each pair of students similar colorful dice and, if desired, matching colored pencils. Have the twosome roll the dice and write problems as modeled until the duo has written ten different problems. Then have each partner take a turn solving a problem and explaining it to his partner until all ten problems have been solved.

Rebecca C. Waechter, Holy Spirit Episcopal School, Katy, TX

$$3(5 + 1) = (3 \times 5) + (3 \times 1)$$
$$15 \quad + \quad 3$$
$$18$$

Math Mailbag

Three-Way Match
Identifying matching forms of decimals, fractions, and percents

Recognizing matching forms of decimals, fractions, and percents is the winning combination for this small-group game! Label 42 index cards so that each set of three cards has a different matching decimal, fraction, and percent. For example, label one set "0.25," "25/100," and "25%" and another "0.20," "1/5," and "20%." Then have a group of three or four students arrange the cards facedown. Instruct one player at a time to turn three cards faceup to see whether they all make a match. If so, he collects the cards and takes another turn. If not, he turns the cards facedown again in the same spots, and another player takes a turn. When all the matches have been made, declare the player with the most matches the winner.

Teresa Campbell, Clark-Pleasant Middle School
Whiteland, IN

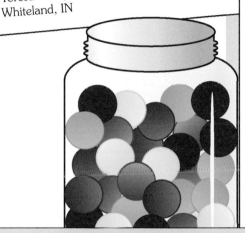

Benchmark Guesses
Using benchmark numbers to make reasonable estimates

Sweeten students' chances of estimating a number's size correctly with this guessing jar activity! Gather three different sizes of jars. Fill each jar with candy pieces such as gumballs, jelly beans, or candy corn. Make a note of the number of candies in each jar. Then display the jars. Announce that the student making the closest guess for each jar will win its contents. Next, use the steps shown to explain to students how benchmark numbers—familiar numbers such as 5, 10, 25, or 100—can help them make reasonable guesses without having to count. Then have each child use the steps to guess the number of candies in each jar and record each guess on paper. Invite the lucky winners to share their treats with the class!

How to estimate using a benchmark number:
1. Estimate how many items are in one section.
2. Estimate how many sections there are.
3. Multiply the items in one section by the number of sections.

Polygon Posters
Distinguishing between similar and congruent polygons

Find out how well students understand the difference between similar and congruent polygons by having them make nifty miniposters! Review similar and congruent figures with the class. Then give each child or pair of students a 9" x 12" sheet of construction paper, glue, markers, white and colorful paper scraps, scissors, and/or access to various scrapbooking punches of polygon shapes. Instruct the child to use the materials to design a three-section miniposter, with each section featuring two polygons glued in place to represent a different pair of figures: similar and congruent, similar but not congruent, neither similar nor congruent. The sizes and shapes the child displays will quickly demonstrate his understanding!

Kelli Higgins, P. L. Bolin Elementary, East Peoria, IL

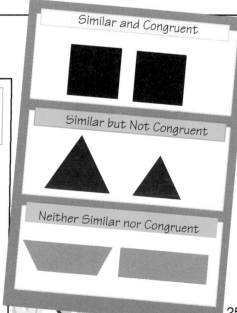

Similar and Congruent

Similar but Not Congruent

Neither Similar nor Congruent

251

Goal: 26

14	1	9	8
2	10	7	15
6	16	3	11
13	5	12	4

$10 + 16 = 26$

$3 \times 7 + 5 = 26$

$14 + 10 + 2 = 26$

$9 + 8 + 7 + 3 - 1 = 26$

$13 + 5 + 6 + 2 = 26$

$14 \times 10 \div 7 + 6 = 26$

$8 + 9 - 1 + 10 = 26$

Numo

Practicing number sense

Terrific as a time filler, this class game challenges students to represent numbers in different forms. Divide students into two teams and write on the board the goal shown. Also draw the grid shown. Explain that team members will be using at least one basic operation and two or more adjacent numbers in the grid to create number sentences that equal the targeted goal. Also explain that the order of operations will not apply and that an operation can be used as many times as needed. Announce that each team will start the game with three points; then begin the game. As soon as a player has a number sentence, have him call out, "Numo!" and state it for you to record on the board. If his sentence is correct, give his team one point. If it is incorrect, subtract a point. The first team to earn ten points wins. If a team's score falls to zero, the opposing team automatically wins. To play another round, randomly write the numbers from 1 to 16 in a new grid and announce a different goal!

John Bradley, Island Heights Grade School, Island Heights, NJ

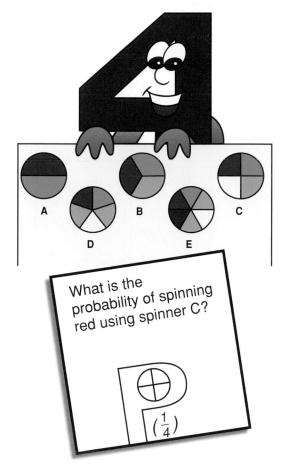

A B C
D E

What is the probability of spinning red using spinner C?

P$\left(\frac{1}{4}\right)$

Probability Power
Determining probability

Perfect as a center activity for two or more players, this "spinner-ific" game can strengthen probability concepts! Make a copy of the game cards and game pieces on pages 254 and 256. Color the game pieces; then laminate the pages and cut out the game pieces and game cards. Each player chooses a game piece and places it on Start on the ready-to-use gameboard on page 255. Then each player takes a turn rolling a die, moving her game piece forward the number of spaces rolled on the die, and answering a game card question drawn by her partner. If she answers correctly, she leaves her game piece in place. If she is incorrect, she moves her game piece back the same number of spaces she moved forward. When a Wild card is drawn, the player must answer a question her partner makes up about any spinner on the board. The first player to reach Finish wins!

Ashleigh M. Weaver, Toledo, OH

Fraction Figures
Representing fractions, equivalent fractions

Students can work out their wiggles with this interactive team game! Use masking tape to create on the floor two 4 x 6 grids with each square large enough for a student to sit in. Divide students into two teams. Have each team line up behind a different grid. Then call out a fraction. Have the first player on each team stand, sit, or lay across the squares of her team's grid to represent that fraction. Once a player is in place, do not allow her to move. If the squares she occupies represent the targeted fraction, allow her to stay in the grid. If not, send her to the back of her team's line. Then call out another fraction and have the second player on each team represent that fraction using his grid's unoccupied squares. Continue calling fractions in this manner. The first team to occupy all of its squares or the team with fewer unoccupied squares wins. To vary the game, have two or more players at a time from each team represent a fraction, with each player standing in a different square!

Miriam Krauss
Beth Jacob Day School
Brooklyn, NY

$^{1}\!/_{12}$

That's the same as $^{2}\!/_{24}$!

Game Cards

Use with "Probability Power" on page 253.

What is the probability of spinning green using spinner A? $\left(\frac{0}{2}\right)$	What is the probability of spinning blue using spinner A? $\left(\frac{1}{2}\right)$	What is the probability of spinning purple using spinner A? $\left(\frac{0}{2}\right)$	What is the probability of spinning red or blue using spinner A? $\left(\frac{2}{2}, or \frac{1}{1}\right)$
What is the probability of spinning blue using spinner B? $\left(\frac{1}{3}\right)$	What is the probability of spinning blue or green using spinner B? $\left(\frac{2}{3}\right)$	What is the probability of spinning green using spinner B? $\left(\frac{1}{3}\right)$	What is the probability of spinning orange or purple using spinner B? $\left(\frac{0}{3}\right)$
What is the probability of not spinning green using spinner C? $\left(\frac{3}{4}\right)$	What is the probability of spinning red using spinner C? $\left(\frac{1}{4}\right)$	What is the probability of spinning orange using spinner C? $\left(\frac{0}{4}\right)$	What is the probability of spinning yellow or green or blue using spinner C? $\left(\frac{3}{4}\right)$
What is the probability of spinning blue using spinner D? $\left(\frac{1}{5}\right)$	What is the probability of not spinning orange or red or blue using spinner D? $\left(\frac{2}{5}\right)$	What is the probability of spinning purple using spinner D? $\left(\frac{0}{5}\right)$	What is the probability of spinning orange or green or yellow using spinner D? $\left(\frac{3}{5}\right)$
What is the probability of spinning orange or green or purple using spinner E? $\left(\frac{3}{6}, or \frac{1}{2}\right)$	What is the probability of not spinning red using spinner E? $\left(\frac{5}{6}\right)$	What is the probability of spinning yellow using spinner E? $\left(\frac{1}{6}\right)$	What is the probability of spinning orange or purple using spinner E? $\left(\frac{2}{6}, or \frac{1}{3}\right)$

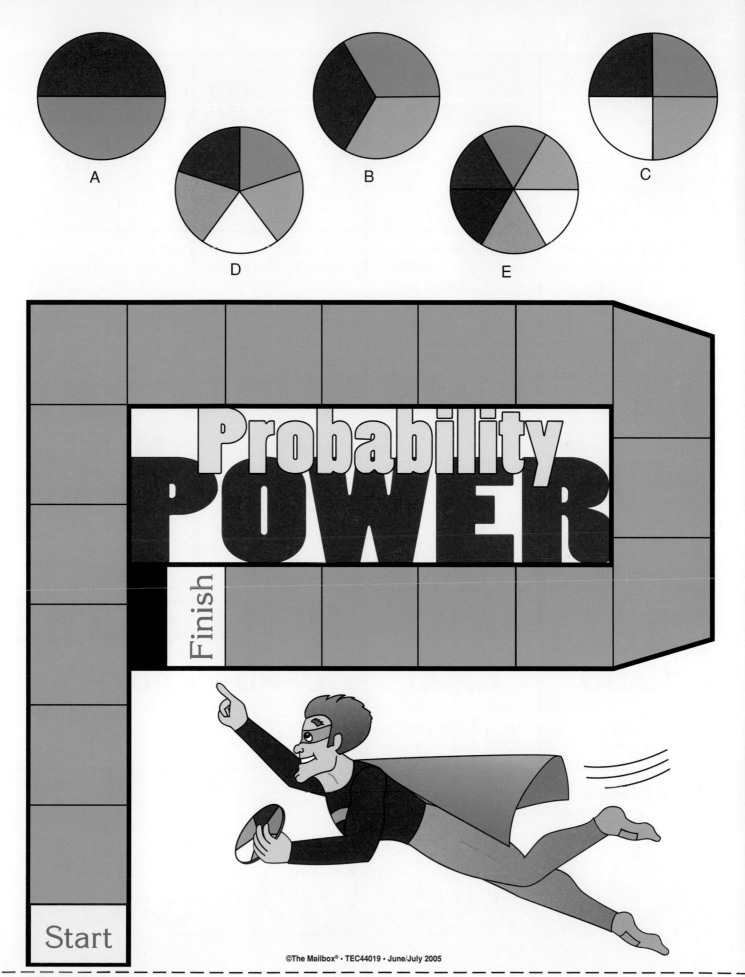

A

B

C

D

E

Probability POWER

Finish

Start

Game Cards

Use with "Probability Power" on page 253.

What is the probability of not spinning blue using spinner A? $\left(\frac{1}{2}\right)$	What is the probability of not spinning red using spinner A? $\left(\frac{1}{2}\right)$	What is the probability of spinning red using spinner B? $\left(\frac{1}{3}\right)$	What is the probability of spinning yellow using spinner B? $\left(\frac{0}{3}\right)$
What is the probability of spinning blue or red or orange using spinner C? $\left(\frac{2}{4}, \text{ or } \frac{1}{2}\right)$	What is the probability of spinning yellow or red or green using spinner C? $\left(\frac{3}{4}\right)$	What is the probability of spinning orange using spinner D? $\left(\frac{1}{5}\right)$	What is the probability of spinning green using spinner D? $\left(\frac{1}{5}\right)$
What is the probability of spinning blue or green or red or yellow using spinner E? $\left(\frac{4}{6}, \text{ or } \frac{2}{3}\right)$	What is the probability of spinning red or yellow using spinner E? $\left(\frac{2}{6}, \text{ or } \frac{1}{3}\right)$	**WILD CARD**	**WILD CARD**
WILD CARD	**WILD CARD**	**WILD CARD**	**WILD CARD**

Game Pieces

Use with "Probability Power" on page 253.

Write On!

Write On!

Ideas and Tips for Teaching Students to Write

The Me You See
Writing an informational essay

Make writing an informational essay easier for everyone with a get-to-know-you activity they'll zip right into! Give each student a resealable sandwich-size plastic bag. Instruct the child to fill the bag with actual items (or pictures) that represent him in some way. Next, have the student write a three-paragraph essay explaining what each item represents about him. Allow him to personalize his paper by decorating its margins. Then invite students to share their compositions with the class and show the contents of their bags. Finally, attach each bag to its essay and post them on a bulletin board titled "The Me You See."

Cynthia D. Davis
Bonaire Middle School
Bonaire, GA

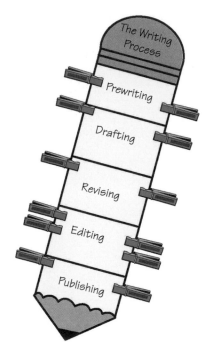

Writing Process Pencil
The writing process

Track your students through each step of the writing process with this get-it-at-a-glance activity! Create a large paper pencil and label it with the steps of the writing process. Laminate the pencil shape and hang it in an area accessible to students. Use a permanent marker to write each child's name on a separate spring-type clothespin. Attach each clothespin to the pencil's eraser. As a child progresses through the writing process, have her move her clothespin to the correct step on the pencil!

Angie Verano—Grs. 4–5
McKinley Elementary
Tacoma, WA

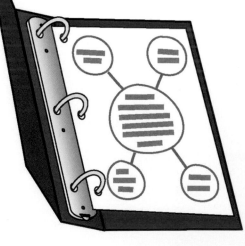

Writing Binders
Organizing students' writing

Keep students' writing organized throughout the year with this terrific tip! Include on your student supply list a 1½" ring binder, a two-pocket folder for binders, and dividers. To organize the binder, have each student create four sections and label the corresponding tabs as follows: "Brewing Stories," "Work in Progress," "Published Pieces," and "All About Writing." Instruct the child to file her prewriting papers in the first section and place drafts, edits, and revisions in the second section. When she publishes a story, direct her to put those papers in the "Published Pieces" section. Then have the student store general information, such as rubrics or definitions of writing terms, in the last section. Require students to keep their writing binders at school. Whenever a child needs to take papers home to work, have her carry them in the removable pocket folder. What a simple way to organize students' writing!

Naomi Konovitch—Gr. 5
Torah Academy for Girls
Far Rockaway, NY

Write On!

Ideas and Tips for Teaching Students to Write

I SAID
Parts of a personal narrative

Use this nifty mnemonic device to remind students of the components of narrative writing! Create and display a poster like the one shown. Discuss the information with students. Also read aloud a few examples of personal narratives. Review each example with the class, pointing out the elements of I SAID. Then assign a topic and direct students to begin brainstorming and writing, using the format as a guide.

Carrie L. Greene—Gr. 4
Oakfield-Alabama Elementary, Oakfield, NY

When Writing a Personal Narrative, Remember What

I – Write in first person (I, me, my, mine, we, us, our, ours).

S – Sound like yourself (use words you would normally use).

A – Include adjectives (descriptions, details).

I – Tell why the event is important.

D – Draw it all together with a closing.

Bare-Bones Sentences
Writing descriptive sentences

Say so long to bare-bones sentences with this idea! Write on the board a simple sentence, such as "Leaves are falling." Next, divide the class into groups of three or four. Give each group time to discuss ways to improve the sentence and then record it. Invite one group member to share the improved sentence with the class. Repeat the process throughout the year to keep students' sentence-writing skills sharp.

Isobel L. Livingstone, Rahway, NJ

Leaves are falling.

> Beautiful autumn leaves are falling, covering the ground with a colorful blanket.

> Now that autumn is here, leaves are falling in my grandmother's yard.

Writing Rhymes
Understanding the six traits of good writing

How well do your students understand the six traits of good writing? Find out by having them create rhymes! Review with the class what each trait means. Next, divide students into groups of four or five. Direct each group to write a poem explaining the six traits of writing (see the example). After groups share their rhymes with the class, display them as handy reminders!

Tammy Haas—Gr. 4
Northside Elementary
Larned, KS

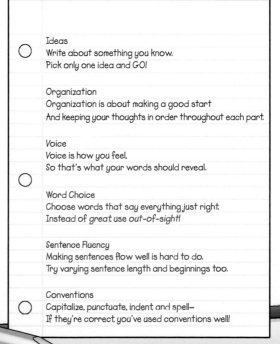

○ Ideas
Write about something you know.
Pick only one idea and GO!

Organization
Organization is about making a good start
And keeping your thoughts in order throughout each part.

Voice
Voice is how you feel,
So that's what your words should reveal.

○ Word Choice
Choose words that say everything just right.
Instead of great use out-of-sight!

Sentence Fluency
Making sentences flow well is hard to do.
Try varying sentence length and beginnings too.

○ Conventions
Capitalize, punctuate, indent and spell—
If they're correct, you've used conventions well!

Write On!

Ideas and Tips for Teaching Students to Write

Paragraph Presents
Writing paragraphs

Present students with a gift that can improve their paragraph-writing skills! Cut the following pieces from construction paper: two bows (one 3" x 6", one 1½" x 3"), eight squares (four four-inch, four two-inch), two strips (one 2" x 8", one 1" x 4"), and two rectangles (one 8" x 10", one 4" x 5"). Label the pieces as shown; then put the smaller of each piece in a small resealable bag. Next, review with the class the parts of a complete paragraph: topic sentence, supporting details, concluding sentence. As you do so, glue the larger of each piece to the larger rectangle to form a wrapped gift. Then have each child write a paragraph about the best gift he has ever received, using the visual aid as a guide. Place the aid and small bag at a writing center, explaining that students may take the smaller aid to their desks any time they write a paragraph to check for completeness. Now that's a gift that keeps on giving!

Suzanna Alde—Gr. 4 Paraprofessional
Mountain School
Los Alamos, NM

Fortune Cookie Fables
Writing dialogue

All you need for this fable-writing activity is fortune cookies! Give each child a fortune cookie and have her open it and read the fortune. Next, have her write a brief story that features animal characters and uses her cookie's fortune to teach a lesson or moral. When she is finished, have her staple the fortune to her paper. After students share their fables with the class, post the tales on a bulletin board titled "Fortune Cookie Fables."

Kara Sholes
Vinita, OK

Reindeer Wanted!
Writing a persuasive letter

Reinforce students' persuasive-writing skills by recruiting a new reindeer for Santa! Read aloud *Olive, the Other Reindeer.* by Vivian Walsh and J. Otto Seibold. The story is about a dog that helps Santa complete his mission. Next, tell the class that Santa wants another reindeer for his team. Help students brainstorm animals whose abilities would be useful to Santa. Then have each child choose an animal and write a persuasive letter from that animal to Santa asking for the job. Direct the student to include in the letter at least three of the animal's useful traits. Allow time for students to illustrate and share their letters. Then post them all on a display titled "Reindeer Wanted!"

Julie McPherson—Gr. 5
Sherman Elementary
Sherman, IL

Dear Santa,
If I could be your new reindeer, I would use my trunk to get the toys down the chimney.

Write On!

Ideas and Tips for Teaching Students to Write

Tag Team Revisions
Peer-editing

Passing a paper tag can turn revising students' story writing into a team effort! Make, label, and laminate several poster board tags as shown. When students are ready to revise their writing, divide them into groups of four. Give one student in the group a tag and have that student read her paper to her three group mates. After she reads, have her hand the tag to any child in the group. Direct the recipient of the tag to identify a part of the story that is unclear and then pass the tag to another group member. Have that child ask the writer to clarify something about the story and then pass the tag to the remaining group member. Instruct this student to suggest an improvement. The writer records each person's feedback and uses it to revise her story. This continues until each student has received feedback. Go team!

April Dennis, Meadowlane Elementary, West Melbourne, FL

T–Tell about a part of the story that is unclear.
A–Ask a question to clarify something.
G–Give a suggestion for improvement.

On Friday, I was resting inside Ms. Markland's desk when I heard her announce a field trip. I almost toppled over with excitement! Surely she would take me along and later put my pictures in a scrapbook. But then I thought, "What if she takes the digital camera instead and I miss all the fun?" So worried, my flash almost went off!

That's me!

First-Person Perspectives
Writing to show first-person point of view

What do you get when you mix mystery, a classroom object, and first-person point of view? A fun writing lesson! Ask each student to think of a classroom object and a situation that could involve the object. Then have the child write a paragraph or story about the event from the object's point of view without revealing what the object is. When everyone is finished, invite each writer to share his work while the class tries to guess the object's identity.

Heather Kime Markland, Chatham Park Elementary, Havertown, PA

SHOW Me a Summary!
Writing a summary

Make summarizing as easy as spelling S-H-O-W! Create a transparency of a brief newspaper article. (Enlarge the text if necessary.) Also make and display a poster of the acronym shown. Next, display the transparency and read the text aloud. Then summarize the article for the class, using the acronym as a guide. Follow up by having each child use the SHOW method to summarize a particular section from his social studies or science text or a short passage of his reading text. Who would have thought that four little letters could make a tough task so easy to do?

Sugar Thiessen, Grace Abbott Elementary, Omaha, NE

How to Write a Summary

S kim the article for the main idea.

H ighlight details that answer the five Ws.

O rganize your details.

W rite sentences in your own words in paragraph form.

Write On!

Grand Canyon Nightmare

My visit to the Grand Canyon is one I won't soon forget! My dad decided that we should camp there overnight. So we pitched our tent along the river.

At dusk, we heard the mosquitos beginning to buzz. Then they began to bite. We spent the night fighting them off.

The next day, we were miserable. We'd had no sleep, plus we spent the day scratching our mosquito bites. We thought the Grand Canyon was beautiful, but we could have done without the visit from the mosquitos!

"Bubble-rific" Adventures

Writing a narrative

Discover the sticky situations students will put themselves in with this adventurous narrative-writing activity! Make and cut apart enough copies of the natural wonders of the world cards on pages 263 and 264 so that each child will have a card. Next, give each child a piece of bubble gum. Have him chew the gum with his eyes closed until you have placed a card from page 263 or 264 on each child's desk. Then instruct him to open his eyes, pretend that the bubble gum has magically transported him to the place shown on his card, and write about an adventure he experiences while he's there. When he shares his narrative with the class, have him point out on a map the natural wonder's location. For a delightful display, have him draw an image of himself with puffed cheeks and tape his story to it. Then have him cut a small hole between the image's lips and insert a small inflated balloon through the hole to represent a bubble being blown!

Joan Sweeney, Stagecoach Elementary, Selden, NY

The Grand Canyon
Arizona

Celebrity Testimonials
Writing a persuasive testimonial, paraphrasing

Brainstorm with students examples of TV commercials in which popular Hollywood actors and actresses promote different products. Next, review that a *testimonial* is a persuasive technique that uses a well-known person to endorse an idea or product. Then give each child crayons or markers and a copy of the pattern on page 264. Direct her to decorate the pattern with facial features and details to make it resemble her favorite famous person and then cut it out. In the speech bubble, have her write a brief testimonial the celebrity might use to persuade the public to buy a particular product. On the person's shirt, have her write a sentence that paraphrases the celebrity's comments. After she shares her cutout with the class, display it on a board titled "What Persuasive Celebs!"

adapted from an idea by Stacey Galasso, Center School, Stratford, CT

Seashell Descriptors
Writing vivid descriptions

Bring a basket of colorful seashells to class. Then write on the board detailed examples of seashell descriptions from a guide book. Or create your own! Next, privately give each child or group a different numbered seashell. Allow students five minutes to describe the shell in a way that could help others distinguish it from all the other shells. When time is up, collect the shells and display them in front of the room. Then have each child or group share the written description aloud and allow the class to guess which shell is being described. The more detailed the description, the quicker the shell will be identified!

Barbara Richardson, Lone Oak School, Spartanburg, SC

Natural Wonders of the World Cards
Use with "'Bubble-rific' Adventures" on page 262.

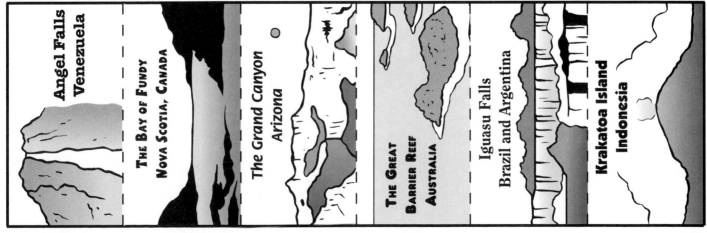

Natural Wonders of the World Cards

Use with "'Bubble-rific' Adventures" on page 262.

Person and Speech Bubble Pattern

Use with "Celebrity Testimonials" on page 263.

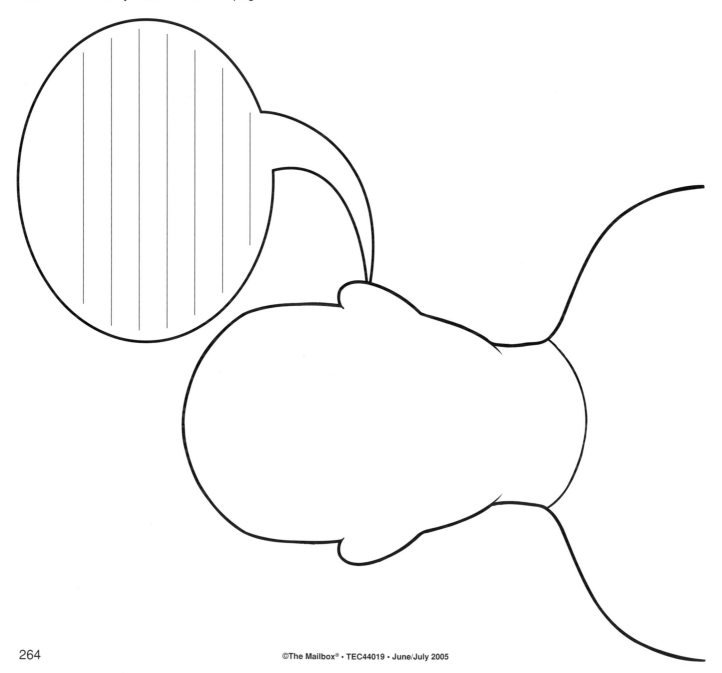

LanguageWorks

LANGUAGE WORKS

Activities for Teaching Grammar, Usage, and Mechanics

Spotting Subjects and Predicates
Identifying subjects and predicates

Make finding simple subjects and predicates buried among surrounding words easier to spot! Write a long, interesting sentence on sentence strips (see the example). For the sentence, use a number of words that equals the number of students in your class. Cut the sentence strips apart so that each word is on a separate piece of paper. Next, invite two students to come up and hold the pieces representing the sentence's simple subject and predicate. Ask the class to identify the subject *(dog)* and predicate *(eats)*. Distribute the remaining cards. Then have two or three students at a time join the two standing at the front at appropriate places to lengthen the sentence. After each addition, ask students to identify the simple subject and predicate. It won't take long for everyone to realize that the subject and predicate remain the same no matter how many words surround them.

To follow up, have pairs of students each write a long, interesting sentence to trade with another duo. Then have the partners find and underline their new sentence's simple subject and predicate and share the findings with the class.

Natalie Tanner
Adam Elementary
Houston, TX

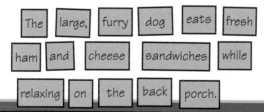

Shortcut Words
Using abbreviations

Here's a game that can make short work of words! Help students brainstorm a list of words and their abbreviations. Then give each child one or more colorful 2" x 9" strips of paper divided into boxes as shown. Challenge the student to write a chain of as many abbreviations as she can in the boxes making certain that the last letter of one abbreviation is the first letter of the next. Award points for the greatest number of boxes in a chain, the fastest time completing a chain, or creating the most chains in a given time.

Kim Minafo
Cary, NC

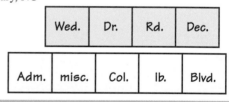

Wed.	Dr.	Rd.	Dec.

Adm.	misc.	Col.	lb.	Blvd.

In the autumn, we…

…jump in colorful leaves.
…eat pumpkin pie.
…wear interesting costumes for Halloween.

…_____
…_____
…_____
…_____
…_____
…_____
…_____
…_____

Autumn Action
Using action verbs

Inspire action verbs practice with an activity that's perfect for any season! After reviewing action verbs with the class, have each student use an action verb in an interesting way to complete the following sentence: "In the autumn, we…" Write each response on the board and have students identify the action word. Ask a volunteer to record the responses. Then copy the responses on a poster students can decorate!

Debra Wilham—Gr. 4
Mt. Pulaski Elementary
Mt. Pulaski, IL

LANGUAGE WORKS

Activities for Teaching Grammar, Usage, and Mechanics

Dashing Through the Text
Using dashes

Put students in the hot seat to demonstrate that dashes can be substituted for other punctuation marks! Review with students that writers sometimes replace commas, parentheses, and colons with dashes to emphasize a point or to provide additional information. Next, direct each child to find in his reading text several sentences in which a dash could replace the existing punctuation mark. Have him list the page number and paragraph of each example. Then choose a student to sit in a chair at the front of the room and call out one of his listings. Allow the first classmate to find the example to write it on the board using the dash. If correct, let him be the next person to sit in the hot seat and challenge the class!

Pat Twohey—Gr. 4
Old County Road School
Smithfield, RI

Two witnesses—Mr. Kelsey and his son—saw the car speed away.

Walk to the bookcase rapidly.

Walk to the door nervously.

Go stand beside the window.

Adverb Actors
Identifying adverbs

Transform students into temporary actors for this simple act-out-an-adverb lesson! Call up one student at a time and whisper to her a command that includes an adverb. Invite the class to tell what action the child acted out. Then have students identify how, when, or where the action was done. Can anyone guess the exact adverb that was whispered?

Natalie McGregor—Grs. 4–5
Grenada Upper Elementary
Grenada, MS

Paragraph Surgery
Revising and editing paragraphs

Train students to become sentence surgeons who bring poorly written paragraphs back to good health! In advance, create a poster labeled with text similar to the Hippocratic oath, which doctors take. Also write on a transparency a rough draft written by an unidentified child from another classroom. Display the poster and discuss it with students. Next, roll in the patient (the transparency) on an overhead projector and conduct a pre-op examination on the text from head (topic sentence) to toe (concluding sentence). Have students offer a diagnosis. Then guide them to fix or replace each unhealthy part of the text so that every sentence is ordered correctly and written clearly. Have the surgeons also remove tumors (misplaced or unnecessary details) and conduct cosmetic surgery where needed (to improve word flow). Finally, have students refer to their grammar textbooks to close the sutures (correct the spelling and grammar errors). After the operation, sum up the major corrections that were done. By the end of the year, paragraphs with sick sentences will be hard to find!

adapted from an idea by Lisa Zeff—Gr. 5
Signal Knob Middle School, Strasburg, VA

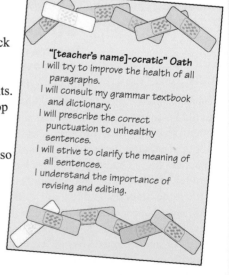

"[teacher's name]-ocratic" Oath
I will try to improve the health of all paragraphs.
I will consult my grammar textbook and dictionary.
I will prescribe the correct punctuation to unhealthy sentences.
I will strive to clarify the meaning of all sentences.
I understand the importance of revising and editing.

LANGUAGE WORKS

Activities for Teaching Grammar, Usage, and Mechanics

Picture-Perfect Idioms
Illustrating and explaining idioms

Reviewing idioms takes on a whole new perspective with this Pictionary-like game! Program a class set of index cards with different idioms, writing an idiom on each card front and its meaning on the back. Invite a volunteer to draw a card. Then have him go to the board and begin illustrating the designated idiom. Give the class one minute to identify the idiom and explain its meaning. Allow the first correct guesser to be the next artist! Continue in this manner as time allows.

Maranda A. McElwee
Redemptorist Catholic School
Crowley, LA

Verb Quilt
Identifying verb tenses

Patch up students' understanding of present, past, and future tense verbs with this simple quilt-making activity! Display a mixed, unlabeled list of verbs. Instruct each child to write any six of the examples on a sheet of paper. Next, give each student scissors, glue, markers, a sheet of drawing paper, and three sheets of construction paper (one red, one blue, and one yellow). Direct her to decide whether each verb on her paper is in present, past, or future tense. If it is in present tense, have her write it on a shape she cuts from red paper. If it is in past tense, have her write it on a shape she cuts from blue paper. If it is in future tense, have her write it on a shape she cuts from yellow paper. Then invite each child to glue her cutouts to the drawing paper and decorate the shapes with markers. After students share their designs, arrange them on a wall to create a unique and colorful quilt!

adapted from an idea
   by Lynn Dunklee
Danville School
Danville, VT

Musical Bloopers
Reviewing grammar rules, improving listening skills

Tune up students' grammar and listening skills with an activity that will be music to their ears! On Monday, discuss with the class the types of usage errors that could be found in musical lyrics, such as subject-verb agreement problems, double negatives, incorrect verb forms, or ambiguous pronouns. After setting guidelines about acceptable types of music and lyrics, invite students to listen for such bloopers until Thursday. Have each child list on a sheet of paper each error he hears and how to correct it, along with the song's title and the artist's name. On Thursday, collect the bloopers and recognize the student who finds the most. Invite the champ to bring an acceptable musical selection to class the next day as a treat. On Friday, have each child share his bloopers with the class and choose a classmate to correct the error in each one. After all examples have been shared, allow the champion to play his music selection!

Joy A. Kalfas, Palatine, IL

LANGUAGE WORKS

Activities for Teaching Grammar, Usage, and Mechanics

Stringy Sentences
Recognizing and correcting run-on sentences

Grab a large ball of yarn to demonstrate how run-on sentences can create a tangled-up mess! Review with students the characteristics of a run-on sentence. Then recruit a student to be the scribe. Next, read a short sentence aloud and randomly move with the yarn throughout the room, calling on students one at a time to add another sentence to yours. Have the scribe record each sentence. As each child contributes, loosely wrap yarn around his fingers and then go on to the next student. Once the entire class has contributed, the string should be very tangled up and the resulting run-on sentence should be very long. Ask the scribe to read the lengthy sentence aloud. Listen for students' reactions to it. Then untangle the yarn and have each child correct the way-too-long sentence by using simple and/or compound sentences to rewrite it!

Loydene Dyas Terry
Glen Rose Junior High
Glen Rose, TX

> I like my dog he is nice to me he plays with me I take him for walks he sleeps in my room...

Revise, Review, and Rejoice!
Using correct spelling, capitalization, and punctuation

Reward students who use correct spelling, capitalization, and punctuation by giving them a few clues about an upcoming test! Several days before the test, have each child write on an index card a question about the test's content. Ask her to use correct spelling, capitalization, and punctuation when writing her question. Then read through the questions and answer only those that are written correctly. As an added motivation, allow students to work in pairs or groups to double-check and revise each other's work before turning it in!

Kim Minafo, Dillard Drive Elementary, Raleigh, NC

> Which amendments do we need to know and understand?

> Do we have to know the year that North Carolina became a state?

Golden-Glove Adverbs

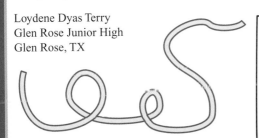

How? — quickly, carefully, slowly
When? — today, yesterday, tomorrow
Where? — here, there, everywhere

Adverb All-Stars
Recognizing adverbs and their purpose

Turn students into adverb all-stars with this interactive bulletin board! Make three copies of the baseball glove pattern and a class supply of the baseball pattern on page 67. Label the baseball gloves "How?" "When?" and "Where?" and mount them on a bulletin board titled "Golden-Glove Adverbs." Next, help the class brainstorm a list of adverbs. Then have each student write an adverb on a baseball cutout and post it on the board under the question it answers. Follow up by having each child use the adverbs to write creative sentences. Challenge students to add more adverbs to the board throughout the year as they find them in their reading and writing. Students will have a ball!

Angela Rood
Dyersburg Intermediate
Dyersburg, TN

Check out the great pronoun reproducible on page 270!

Jilly Bean's Candy Jar

Jilly Bean's teacher found the perfect way to find out whether Jilly knows her pronouns. Help Jilly decide what type of pronoun is written on each jelly bean. Color by the code. If you are correct, you'll see the grade Jilly made!

Pronoun Color Code

subject = blue
object = red
both subject and object = purple
possessive = green
both possessive and object = yellow

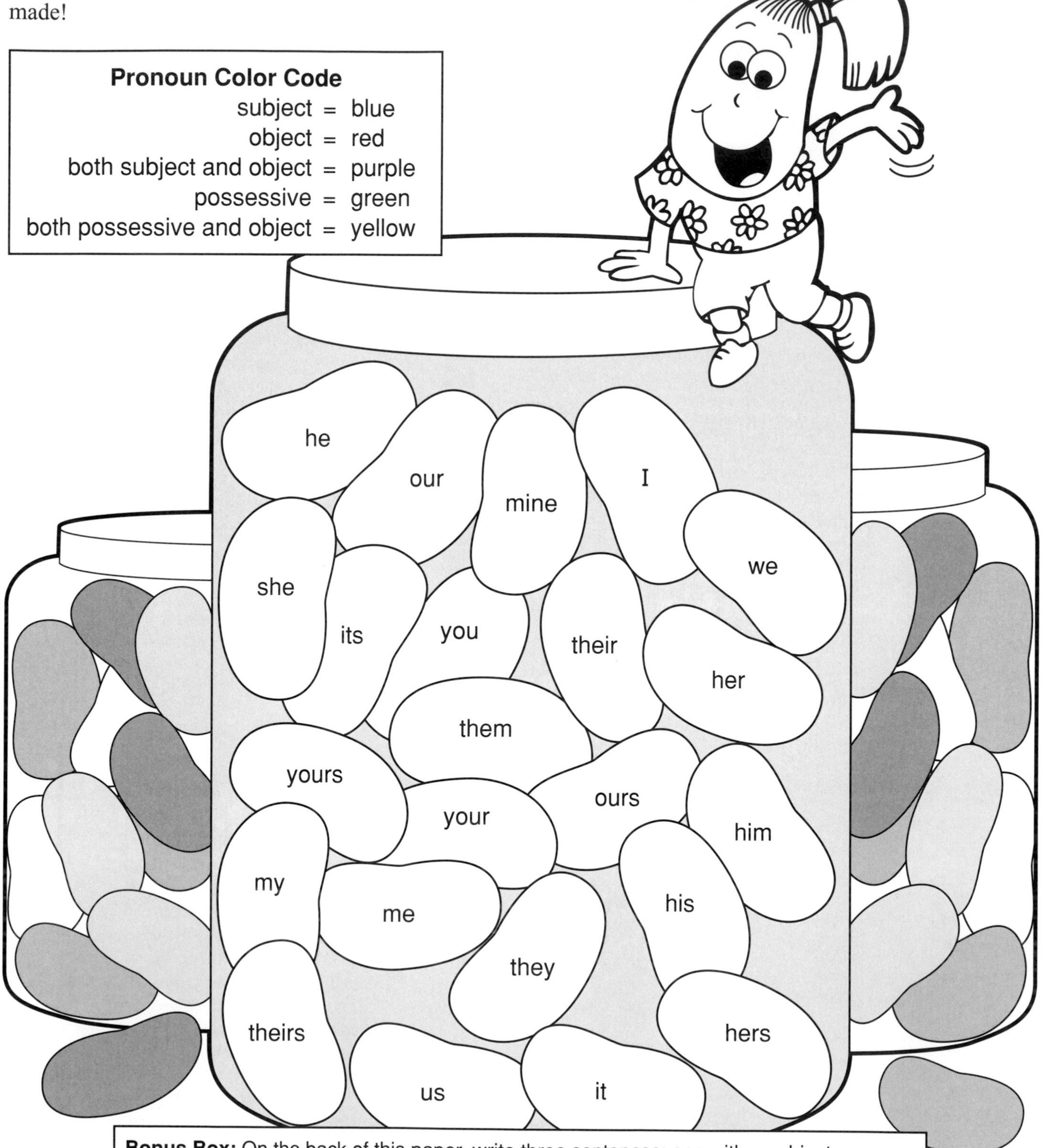

he

our

mine

I

we

she

its

you

their

her

them

yours

your

ours

him

my

me

his

they

theirs

hers

us

it

Bonus Box: On the back of this paper, write three sentences: one with a subject pronoun, one with an object pronoun, and one with a possessive pronoun.

Note to the teacher: Each student will need five crayons (blue, red, purple, green, and yellow) to complete this page.

Buzzy Prepositions
Identifying prepositions

A busy little bee can help students see that prepositions can describe direction, movement, or the way two ideas or words are related. Make a copy of the bee pattern shown. Then color the bee and cut it out. On a sheet of poster board, draw a person's head; then display the poster on the board. Place the bee cutout on the drawing's nose and say, "The bee is on the nose." Write "on" on the chart. Next, invite students to name other prepositions that describe the bee in relation to the head, such as "under the nose" or "between the eyes." Each time a child shares a preposition, add it to the chart and move the bee to act out the position. When the chart is full, display it as a ready reference for students. Bzzz!

Christine Veltri, Green's Farms Elementary
Westport, CT

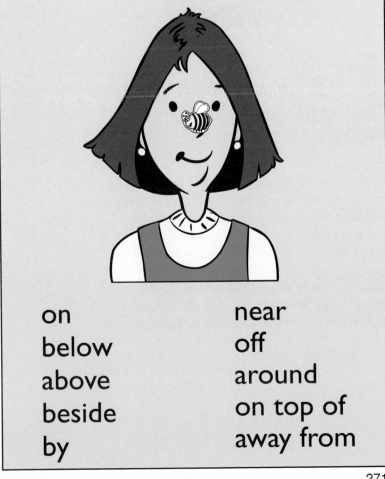

on	near
below	off
above	around
beside	on top of
by	away from

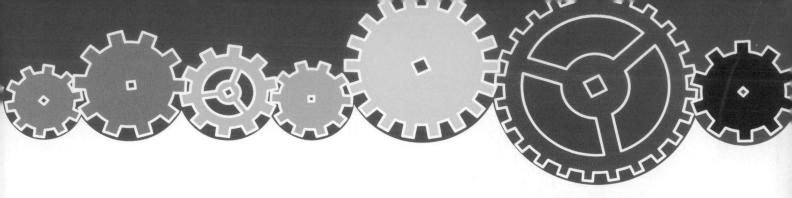

J
Action Verbs

~~jump~~
jog
join

J
Action Verbs

jaywalk
~~jump~~
jabber

War-of-Words Challenge
Parts of speech, vocabulary development

Review parts of speech with this vocabulary-building game! Divide students into small groups and provide each child with a sheet of paper and a pencil. Write on the board a letter of the alphabet and any part of speech you wish students to review. Give students 60 seconds to list as many words as they can of that part of speech that start with the assigned letter. When time is up, have the students in each group compare their lists and give themselves one point for each unique word. Explain that group members having the same word on their papers must cross out the word and receive no points for it. Play as many rounds as desired, using a different letter of the alphabet and/or a different part of speech each time. The player with the most points when play ends is the winner. What a vocabulary stretcher!

Bethany Butt, Alabama Christian Academy, Montgomery, AL

Quips, Quotes, and Thoughts
Writing and punctuating with quotation marks

Reminisce about the school year with this memorable punctuation review! Gather photographs you've taken of your class throughout the year. Next, divide students into small groups and give each group a photo taped to a sheet of lined paper. Instruct the group to write and punctuate correctly on the paper at least three sentences of dialogue that could represent what those pictured might have said or thought at the time the photo was taken. Require that students not use the word *said* but instead use synonyms for it. When everyone is finished, invite each group to share its sentences with the class.

Stephanie Contreras, Autrey Mill Middle School, Alpharetta, GA

"Hold steady, Mr. Pumpkin," Brian warned.

"Why are you taking our picture?" Alexis wondered.

"Looking at this pumpkin makes me want a piece of pumpkin pie!" joked Mandy.

BUILDING BETTER READERS

BUILDING BETTER READERS

Cause-and-Effect Challenge
Identifying cause and effect

Students will flip over this cause-and-effect activity! Give each child two index cards. Have him label one card with an event from a recent reading assignment. Have him label the front of the other card "Cause" and its back "Effect." Collect the event cards. Next, read aloud one of the events. Direct students to hold up their cards to show whether they think the event is a cause or an effect. Call on a student to justify his answer. If another child answered differently, allow him to defend his response. Then challenge the class to compare the answers to see whether both could be correct. Repeat until every event has been read. For more cause-and-effect activities, see pages 110–114.

Kathy Kopp
Lecanto Primary School
Hernando, FL

Cause

Grandma cried.

Effect

A Year's Worth of Reading
Motivating students to read

Can your students read a year's worth of pages during the school year? They can with this activity! Announce a goal equal to the year that the current school year ends. For example, if it will be the year 2005 when school ends, set the goal at 2,005 pages. Have each reader keep a chart of the pages she reads each day. Once a month, have her total her pages and enter the total in her reading log. Try to recognize every student's progress in some way, such as most pages read during the month, longest book read, type of book read, or most books read. As soon as a reader reaches the goal, reward her with a special certificate or small treat. It'll be worth it!

Michael Foster—Gr. 4
Heartland Elementary
Overland Park, KS

CONGRATULATIONS TO

Cathy

For reaching the class goal of reading 2,005 pages

Mr. Foster, Teacher

Great Job!

Magic Square Book Report
Reporting on a book

Here's a magical way for students to share books! Have each child fold a 12-inch construction paper square in thirds twice to make nine squares and then trace the folds with a marker. Direct him to label the center square "Book Title" and the remaining squares as follows: "Author," "Setting," "Characters," "Conflict," "Climax," "Theme," "Vocabulary," "Illustration." Then have the student complete the project by adding pictures and text to the appropriate squares. Every square will add up to a quick synopsis of the book!

Colleen Dabney
Williamsburg JCC Public Schools
Williamsburg, VA

Theme	Illustration	Setting
Climax	Book Title The Year of Miss Agnes	Characters
Vocabulary	Author Kirkpatrick Hill	Conflict

BUILDING BETTER READERS

Sequence Chains
Sequencing events

Use sequence chains to discover how well your readers connect main events! Read aloud several chapters of a class novel. Next, pair students and give each twosome glue and a supply of colorful 2" x 5" paper strips. Have the pair discuss the story's major events, write each one on a separate strip, and then connect the strips to form a paper chain. Explain that each listed event must be caused by the event before it and lead to the next one attached to it. After you read aloud several more chapters, have each duo repeat the process. Continue in this manner until the book is finished. Display students' chains on a bulletin board titled "Chain Reactions in [title of book]."

Diane Coffman—Gr. 5
St. Peter Catholic School
Deland, FL

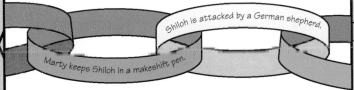

Shiloh is attacked by a German shepherd.

Marty keeps Shiloh in a makeshift pen.

Tell Me More!
Reading informational text

Before students tackle nonfiction text, give them a tool that makes the task easier! Display a poster like the one shown. Tell students that TMM stands for "Tell Me More." Explain each letter's meaning. Then encourage students to use the poster as a ready reference whenever they have informational articles, chapters in science or social studies texts, or the guide for a new computer game to read!

Kim Minafo
Cary, NC

TMM! (Tell Me More!)

T = Tell (What do the text's features—such as titles, headings, boldfaced print, labels, illustrations, diagrams, tables, and charts—tell you about the passage?)

M = Me (What experiences have you had with the topic of the passage?)

M = More (What else do you hope to learn about the topic from your reading?)

Briefcase Book Report
Reporting on a book

Add a bit of mystery to students' next book reports! Have each child write a brief book summary that concludes with a teaser, leaving the reader wondering how the book ends. Next, have each student fold a large sheet of brown construction paper in half and add two paper handles at the top to make it resemble a briefcase. Direct him to write his book's title and author on the front of his briefcase and then open it to lie flat. On the top half, have him illustrate four or five of the book's main events and write a clue next to each one. Then instruct him to staple his book summary to the bottom half. What a nifty way to inspire students to read!

Julie Kaiser—Grs. 4–5
Floyds Knobs Elementary
Floyds Knobs, IN

*Hatchet
by Gary Paulsen*

BUILDING BETTER READERS

Character Scrapbook
Reporting on a book, character analysis

For your next book-sharing project, capitalize on the scrapbooking craze! Have each child or small group of students design a scrapbook about a book's main character. Explain that the first page should show an illustration of and include important information about the chosen character. Require the remaining pages to focus on the character's interests or traits and the important events the character experiences (arranged in sequential order). Whether the scrapbooks are simple or elaborate, the final results will be fun to share! For fun-to-do character-analysis ideas, see pages 4–8.

Teresa Vilfer-Snyder—Gr. 4
Fredericktown Intermediate School
Fredericktown, OH

A Scrapbook
About Henry Green

from Chocolate Fever
by Robert Kimmel Smith

Beanbag Reading
Reading orally

To make oral reading something students anticipate rather than dread, grab a beanbag! Have each child in the group sit on top of his desk with his reading, science, or social studies book. Read aloud the selected passage's introduction and first paragraph. Next, gently toss the beanbag to someone in the group. Have him read aloud at least a paragraph but no more than a page. Then have him toss the beanbag to someone else. After this child has read aloud, have him toss the beanbag to another student who has not read. Explain that anyone who does not follow along or pass the beanbag gently will lose the right to sit on his desk. Use the time between tosses to discuss what was just read!

Brenda Tweed—Grs. 4–7
Pigeon Forge Middle School
Pigeon Forge, TN

Match Four!
Identifying main ideas and supporting details

Concentrate on main ideas and supporting details with this fun game! Give each pair of students a copy of the game cards on page 277, scissors, glue, and 20 index cards (five of one color and 15 of another color). Direct the duo to cut the game cards apart and glue each card with boldfaced type (main idea) to one of the five same-color index cards. Have the partners glue each card with lightfaced type (supporting detail) to one of the remaining index cards. Next, instruct the twosome to shuffle the cards and arrange them facedown in a 4 x 5 array, putting the five same-colored cards in the first column and the remaining cards in columns 2–4. Then have one partner turn four cards faceup (one from column one and three from the other columns). If they match, the player wins the four cards. If not, he turns the cards facedown again, and his partner takes a turn. Play continues in this manner until time is called. Declare the player with more cards the winner!

Tina Cassidy—Gr. 4, Ella Canavan Elementary, Medina, OH

There are many different types of transportation.

Planes are a convenient way to travel long distances quickly.

Trains crisscross the land to take people from place to place.

Boats carry people across water to other places.

There are many different types of transportation.

Boats carry people across water to other places.

Planes are a convenient way to travel long distances quickly.

Trains crisscross the land to take people from place to place.

A school's staff is very helpful.

The school nurse can check a student's eyesight every year.

The custodian cleans the halls thoroughly.

The cafeteria workers prepare healthy foods.

A school has many different places for students to learn.

The science lab can have microscopes that make small things appear larger.

The library has books on many different topics.

The computer lab is a great place to do online research.

Teachers use different kinds of equipment and tools to help them teach.

Chalkboards make it easy for the entire class to see what is being written.

Maps are useful for showing the location of different states and countries.

Overhead projectors allow a teacher to use see-through manipulatives.

Doctors use different types of equipment to help them care for patients.

A stethoscope makes it possible to hear a person's heart beating.

A thermometer tells whether someone has a fever.

Scales tell whether a patient has gained or lost weight.

BUILDING BETTER READERS

"Idea-l" Checklists
Reading informational text

Arm students with five tips that can help them become more effective readers of nonfiction! Give each child a copy of the bookmark pattern on page 279 to color and cut out. Next, guide her to accordion-fold the bookmark so that the first checklist, "Investigate the text," is faceup. Go over each of the five checklists, in turn, until all five have been discussed and the bookmark refolded. Then suggest that each reader use the bookmark as a guide whenever she reads nonfiction passages by folding it to the section she needs!

Kim Minafo
Cary, NC

Breezy Book Reports
Reporting on a book

Looking for a creative way for students to share books? Try these sensational windsocks! Have each child decorate a 12" x 18" sheet of construction paper with his book's title, author, and illustrations of the story's important elements. Next, have him glue the 12-inch sides together to make a tube. Then give each student six 2" x 18" colorful construction paper strips and guide him to list on separate strips elements such as the following: character and setting descriptions, the problem and solution, a story summary, five new words from the story, and examples of interesting dialogue. Instruct the child to glue each strip along his tube's bottom edge as shown. Finally, punch holes in the top of each project, tie yarn through the holes, and hang it for a breezy display!

Shari Miller
Northeast Elementary
Arma, KS

Stuck on Comprehension
Supporting answers with evidence from the text

Make your next lesson on supporting answers to comprehension questions one readers are sure to stick with! Before students read the assignment, ask them to look for particular story elements or answers to specific questions. Next, direct each child to read the text with those questions in mind. Every time he finds an answer, have him mark the page with a sticky note. Then, when the assignment is being discussed, he can quickly flip to the note-marked pages to share and justify his answers!

Jessica Schiery, Perrywood Elementary, Upper Marlboro, MD

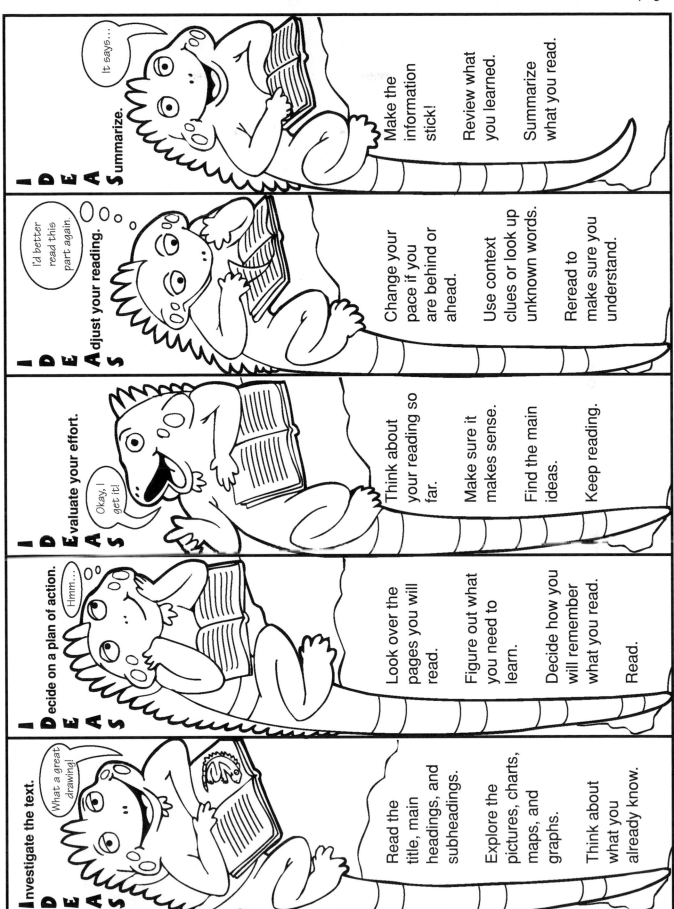

The Mailbox® • TEC44017 • Feb./Mar. 2005

BUILDING BETTER READERS

Biographical Book Characters
Reporting on a book

Students will be eager to do biography book reports when they get to make look-alikes of the subjects! Have each student fill one-third of an empty, two-liter plastic bottle with rice or sand. Have him also glue a small foam ball atop the bottle's mouth to represent the character's head. Next, have the student use scissors, glue, and various art supplies such as tissue paper, pipe cleaners, and fabric scraps to decorate the bottle to resemble the man or woman he read about. Once the student writes five facts about his person on a notecard and places it next to his bottle, his project is ready for display!

Kathleen Butler
Meadows Elementary
Millbrae, CA

Tiger Woods
1. Eldrick "Tiger" Woods was born on December 30, 1975
2. _____
3. _____
4. _____
5. _____

Read 'n' Initial Bookmark
Developing reading fluency

Reading can be more fun with the help of family, friends, and a colorful bookmark to document all the work! Create a bookmark similar to the one shown and photocopy it onto colorful paper to make a class set. Then laminate the bookmarks and cut them out. Next, assign students a reading passage. Have each student read the passage first to himself and then to the next two people listed on the bookmark. Have each listener, in turn, check and initial the bookmark. Once the student reads the passage to you, collect the bookmark. Repeat the activity as often as you like by wiping off the initials and redistributing the bookmarks. You'll be amazed at how fluent your readers will become!

Kristen Snable
Edgewood Elementary
Homewood, AL

Name: _____

☐ I read it to myself.
   _____
☐ I read it to a friend.
   _____
☐ I read it to a parent. _____
☐ I read it to my teacher. _____

Inference Stones
Making inferences

Cut a clear path when it comes to inference making with an activity that leaves no stone unturned! Discuss with students the importance of making inferences and the confusion that can occur when a reader makes an incorrect inference. Next, have students brainstorm several events or situations from a current read-aloud or class book that lend themselves to making inferences. Have each child pick one event from the list and then cut out three stone shapes from gray construction paper. Direct him to tape the cutouts together end to end as shown. On the first stone, have him write a sentence related to the first action of his chosen event. On the last stone, have him write the conclusion of that event. On the middle stone, have him fill in the missing details. Then invite each student to share his cutouts with the class.

Kim Minafo
Dillard Drive Elementary
Raleigh, NC

John woke up at 8 A.M.   He got dressed, brushed his teeth, and ate break   Then he went to school.

Management Tips
and Timesavers

Let's Have a Party!
Tips for Successful Classroom Parties

Chew on these choice suggestions to make sure your next classroom party is not only successful but also easy to manage!

by Chris Christensen, Las Vegas, NV, and Colleen Dabney, Williamsburg, VA

Games and Activities

• **The Mysterious Gift:** Fill a box with enough treats for the entire class. Wrap the box with several layers of seasonal paper. Have students pass the box to music. When the music stops, have the child holding the box remove the outer layer of paper. Continue in this manner until each layer is removed. Give the child who removes the last layer a special treat. Then have everyone share the treats in the box.

• **Picture That Song!** Label slips of paper, each with a different familiar song title related to the current season. Put the slips in a container; then divide students into two teams. Have a child from Team 1 draw a slip, read it silently, and hand it to you. At your signal, have him draw on the board clues that can help his teammates guess the correct song title. If his team guesses correctly within a set time, award two points. If not, allow the opposing team a chance to earn the points. After all the songs have been guessed, declare the team with more points the winner.

• **Mystery Word Scramble:** Write the letters that spell a mystery word related to the current season on separate paper squares. For example, use *chocolate* for Valentine's Day. Put the squares in a resealable plastic bag. Repeat until there is one bag for each group of four students. Give each group a bag. Direct the group members to form as many words with the letters as possible and record them on paper. Give teams one point for each word spelled correctly. Award a bonus point for spelling the mystery word!

• **Dodge the Sock!** Use a balled-up, mismatched sports sock instead of a ball for an indoor version of dodgeball. For a more fast-paced game, use two socks!

• **Sneak a Spoon!** Divide students into four groups. Give each group a deck of cards. Put plastic spoons in the center of each group (one spoon fewer than the number of students in the group). Explain the object of the game: to get four cards of a kind, such as four eights, and then remove a spoon. Direct one group member to deal four cards to every player and then a single card to the player on his right. Have that player decide whether to trade that card for one in his hand or to pass it to the player on his right. After the dealer takes his turn, have him put the card to be passed at the bottom of the deck and deal a new card to start the next round. Continue in this manner until one player has four of a kind and sneaks a spoon. Then allow the other players to grab a spoon. The player without a spoon is out of the game. Continue until only one person remains.

How to Involve Parents

- **Party in a Bag:** Ask parents to fill white lunch bags with individual packages of potato chips, pretzels, cookies, cakes, drinks, candies, or treats that match the current season. Add a ticket for a chance to win a book, gel pen, or homework pass. Cleanup will be a cinch!

- **Preplanned Parties:** Make it easier on parents who help with parties by having each one be part of a team that is responsible for only one party! For example, if there will be four parties during the year, divide the parents into four groups. Then assign each group a different party to plan.

- **Supervised Stations:** Invite parents to man stations on the playground at which small groups of students complete an activity, such as making free throws or jumping rope. Students earn a candy treat and then rotate to the next station. Great fun! *Brooke Beverly—Gr. 5, Julia Bancroft School, Auburn, MA*

Fun Alternatives to Class Parties

- **View a Video:** After the class completes a novel that is available on video, view it together and munch on popcorn. Afterward, have students compare and contrast the two versions.

- **Create a Craft:** Instead of having a party, spend that time completing a seasonal craft, such as decorating an apple as a turkey for Thanksgiving, that students can enjoy at home with their families.

- **Classy Choices:** With other teachers on your grade level, plan a different simultaneous activity for each classroom. For example, have a craft in one room, board games in a second, and academic games (small- or whole-group) in another. Limit the number of participants for each activity. Then allow each child to sign up for an activity of her choice.

- **Character Dress-Up:** Instead of a Halloween party, ask students, faculty, and staff members to come to school dressed as their favorite book characters. Those who like the same book could even team up and represent different characters from that book! *Vicki Christian—Gr. 5, Buford Academy, Buford, GA*

- **Winter Breakfast:** Instead of a Christmas party, plan to have a breakfast just before winter break. Invite parents to bring in foods such as sausage and egg casseroles, cereal, juice, hot chocolate, and milk. Some may even bring in latkes or offer to cook pancakes on the spot! *Rebecca Hayes—Gr. 5, Stern Enhancement School, Greenville, MS*

- **Multicultural Festival:** To celebrate different cultures, culminate a study of different countries by decorating the room with students' projects and having parents prepare dishes from those countries for students to sample. Group together all foods from countries on the same continent on a table with a map of that continent. For more fun, students can make passports that parents stamp (initial) as they visit each country (sample the food)! *Lisa Funk—Gr. 5, Hoover Elementary, Buffalo, NY*

Managing Makeup Work

If you're unsure about how to manage students' makeup work, there's no need to fret. Try these top-notch tips from our readers!

Use the buddy system.

- Assign each child a buddy. When a student is absent, her buddy collects the assignments and handouts, labels them with due dates, and clips them to a clipboard. Then the buddy places the clipboard on the absentee's desk along with any other necessary materials so they are ready for her return! *Kathleen Bulter—Gr. 5, Meadows Elementary, Millbrae, CA*

- Staple ten copies of a blank assignment sheet in a colorful folder for each child. Label each folder "[Child's Name]'s Makeup Work" and arrange the folders alphabetically in an accessible place. When a student is absent, have his makeup buddy put any handouts in that child's folder and record the day's assignments on the top assignment sheet. The returning student uses the folder to get his assignments and turn in the work. After you collect the makeup work and tear off the used assignment sheet, the folder is ready to use again! *Danielle Reynolds, Henry David Thoreau School, Milwaukee, WI*

Create a makeup work center.

- Write each student's name on a separate strip of masking tape. Affix each strip to a different pocket of an inexpensive, pocketed vinyl shoebag. When a child is absent, place a list of her assignments and any handouts in her labeled pocket. When the student returns, have her collect her makeup work from her pocket! *Vicky Fioravante—Gr. 4, PS16 Academy, Staten Island, NY*

Use sticky note reminders.

- Leave a sticky note on the absent child's desk reminding him to collect his handouts and assignments from an accessible folder when he returns. *Erin Silmser—Gr. 5, Odessa Public School, Odessa, Ontario, Canada*

Make the task a classroom job.

- Add "Makeup Work Monitor" to your list of classroom jobs! Have the monitor record the day's assignments and put any reproducibles and handouts for the absent students in separate folders. When each absentee returns, the monitor gives her the folder and answers questions about assignments. The monitor can also be the one to collect the makeup work and turn it in! *Terri Bey—Gr. 5, Ragsdale Elementary, Atlanta, GA*

Set up separate makeup folders for the different groups you teach.
- If your students change classes and you teach different groups of children during the day, create a folder for each group and label it with the homeroom teacher's name or room number. Mount the folders near your assignment board. During each class, label an assignment sheet and any handouts for each absentee and put them in the appropriate folder. When the student returns, he can go straight to his group's folder for his makeup work! *Karen Clements—Grs. 4–6, Brooklyn Middle School, Brooklyn, OH*

Room 1

Room 4

Room 5

Room 12

Include a note to parents.
- Along with handouts and an assignment sheet for the parent to sign when the work is complete, staple inside each child's colorful folder a letter to parents that explains your expectations about makeup work. Knowing that a parent must verify that the work is done can motivate the returning student to dig right in! *Jodi Keane—Gr. 4, Blaisdell Elementary, Bradford, PA*

File absentees' handouts by the date.
- Arrange in a milk crate 31 file folders whose tabs have been numbered from 1 to 31. When a student is absent, write his name on any handouts and place them in the folder with the matching date. The returning child can quickly locate his handouts using the date(s) he was out! *Kathryn Kincannon—Gr. 6, Locust Elementary, Marengo, IL*

Keep an assignment journal.
- Place a 200-page spiral notebook in a prominent place. On a different page each day, list (or have a student list) the date, the names of absent students, a brief description of the day's classwork, and any homework assignments. When a student returns to school, have him check the journal to find out what he needs to make up! *Kathryn Kincannon—Gr. 6*

Organize makeup work by subject.
- Label and staple six two-pocket folders to a bulletin board as shown. When a student is absent, place any handouts for him in that day's pocket and a dated list of assignments in the assignment pocket. When the absentee returns, instruct him to collect the handouts from the folder of the day he missed and copy that day's assignments from the assignment pocket. As he completes his makeup work, have him place each assignment in the corresponding subject folder. How's that for organization? *adapted from an idea by Stacey Pardue—Gr. 5, Coosa Valley Academy, Harpersville, AL*

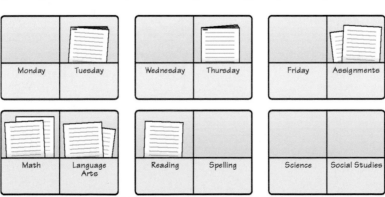

| Monday | Tuesday | Wednesday | Thursday | Friday | Assignments |
| Math | Language Arts | Reading | Spelling | Science | Social Studies |

Marvelous Ways to Motivate Students!

Keep your students yearning to learn with this stimulating collection of contributor tips and ideas!

Anything Is Possible!

This tall display guarantees recognition of your students' best work! Display on a wall colorful 24-inch-high construction paper letters that spell "ANYTHING IS POSSIBLE"; then assign each student a letter. If you have more students than letters, have two students share a letter. As you grade papers, mark each one that shows a student's very best work with "YDI," meaning "You Did It!" Each time a child finds "YDI" on a graded paper, invite him to sign his name on the appropriate letter on the wall. When a student has signed the letter ten times, cross off his signatures and give him a small treat or reward!

Sue Moore, Sumter Academy, York, AL

Homework Raffle

Students will be scrambling to turn in homework if each complete assignment means an entry in a raffle! Purchase a roll of raffle tickets (available at a party supply store). Also decorate a ticket jar and label it with the date of the drawing. Then display the jar and explain that each student who completes a homework assignment and turns it in on time will get a raffle ticket. When a child receives a ticket, instruct him to sign his name on the back and drop it in the jar. On the day of the monthly drawing, pull one ticket from the jar and award the winner a prize, such as a homework coupon or free-time pass. Then empty the jar and start all over! Students will soon realize that their chances of winning increase as they put more tickets in the jar. And that can lead to only one thing: more completed homework assignments!

Nicole McDonald
Arbor School
Piscataway, NJ

Video Rewards

Reward students who complete assignments on time with an educational treat parents will eagerly support! Obtain copies of fun, educational videos related to grade-appropriate topics of study. Then set up a video checkout system that is only available to a child who completes her classwork or homework on time. Your students will work harder, and parents will be thrilled that the videos their children bring home to view overnight can strengthen important skills!

Sherry St. Clair
Caneyville Elementary
Caneyville, KY

Homework Raffle
March 4th

Correct-Answers Contest

Here's an incentive that will motivate students to do their best work all the time, even on work that won't be included in your gradebook! Have students check the assignment and write the number of correct answers at the top of the papers. Next, randomly divide the class into two teams. Direct each team to use a calculator to find the team's total number of correct answers. Then declare the team with the higher number the winner and award each team member with a small treat.

Annette K. Salsburey, Laker Elementary, Pigeon, MI

Reading-Time Rewards

Compensate diligent readers with an incentive that also provides huge payoffs in math! Give each child a copy of a time sheet such as the one shown. Model how to use the sheet to track time spent reading at home. Announce that your goal is for each student to read 100 minutes each week. Then explain that each child will be "paid" $1.00 for each minute that she reads. If desired, offer each reader the chance to earn overtime, or $1.50, for each additional minute she reads. Every Monday, collect the completed time sheets and distribute new ones. Reward the readers who met their goals with a small treat. Set classroom goals of $25,000; $50,000; $75,000; or even $100,000! When each new goal is reached, reward the class with a popcorn party!

Mary Cochran, Osnaburg Local Schools, East Canton, OH

Reading Time Sheet

Name _____

	Monday	Tuesday	Wednesday	Thursday	Friday
Starting Time					
Stopping Time					
Minutes					
Parent's Initials					
Date					

Total Minutes = _____

Weekly Recognitions

Recognize student achievements—great or small—in any area with this easy-to-manage incentive. In advance, program an award certificate for each student. Then sign the awards and put them in a file folder. Each week, pull out one or two awards, fill in the reasons for the awards, and present the certificates to the deserving students. With just a glance, you'll know who has and has not received an award.

Amy Evans
Grace Christian School
Blacklick, OH

287

Great Ideas and Tips for Substitute Teachers

Set a course for smooth sailing when you're absent
with these helpful ideas from our contributors!

Welcoming Committee

Forming a student welcoming committee will not only make a substitute teacher feel comfortable but will also inform her about your classroom procedures! Brainstorm with students five important things any sub should know about your classroom. Next, choose six students—one to stand and introduce himself to the sub and prompt his classmates to do the same and five others to each explain a different procedure. At the beginning of each new quarter, train six new committee members! **Suzette Pfanstiel, Forest Park Elementary, O'Fallon, MO**

Suggestions for My Sub

Take roll.
Help students understand the procedure for the day.
Allow a little chatter. Kids are human!
Note any problems.
Keep students on task.

You can call on _____ for help.
Open the bag of treats in my desk drawer if the class is cooperative.
Use kid power to straighten the room at the end of the day.

Acrostic Assistance

Provide valuable tips for your substitute with the help of a unique acrostic bookmark! Label a 3" x 8" piece of oaktag as shown. Then laminate the paper and tie a length of yarn or ribbon through a hole punched in the top. Place the bookmark inside your substitute folder so it gets noticed as soon as the folder is opened! **Colleen Dabney, Williamsburg, VA**

Activity Binder

Rest assured that your sub will never run short of student activities by providing her with a backup binder! Make class sets of reproducible activities and games that can be completed at any time of year. Store each set in a different page protector; then sort the activities behind tabbed dividers in a three-ring binder and place it with your substitute folder. Whenever a substitute needs to fill time or wants to add a little pizzazz to the day, she can open the notebook and select an activity! **Kathleen Butler, Meadows School, Millbrae, CA**

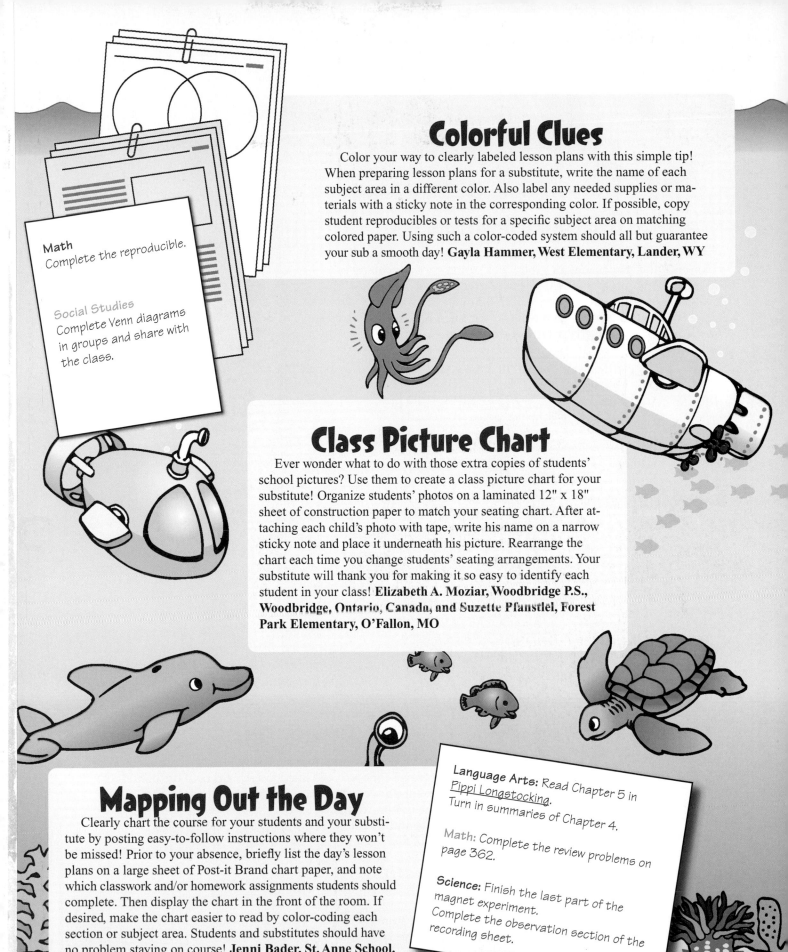

Colorful Clues

Color your way to clearly labeled lesson plans with this simple tip! When preparing lesson plans for a substitute, write the name of each subject area in a different color. Also label any needed supplies or materials with a sticky note in the corresponding color. If possible, copy student reproducibles or tests for a specific subject area on matching colored paper. Using such a color-coded system should all but guarantee your sub a smooth day! **Gayla Hammer, West Elementary, Lander, WY**

Math
Complete the reproducible.

Social Studies
Complete Venn diagrams in groups and share with the class.

Class Picture Chart

Ever wonder what to do with those extra copies of students' school pictures? Use them to create a class picture chart for your substitute! Organize students' photos on a laminated 12" x 18" sheet of construction paper to match your seating chart. After attaching each child's photo with tape, write his name on a narrow sticky note and place it underneath his picture. Rearrange the chart each time you change students' seating arrangements. Your substitute will thank you for making it so easy to identify each student in your class! **Elizabeth A. Moziar, Woodbridge P.S., Woodbridge, Ontario, Canada, and Suzette Pfanstiel, Forest Park Elementary, O'Fallon, MO**

Mapping Out the Day

Clearly chart the course for your students and your substitute by posting easy-to-follow instructions where they won't be missed! Prior to your absence, briefly list the day's lesson plans on a large sheet of Post-it Brand chart paper, and note which classwork and/or homework assignments students should complete. Then display the chart in the front of the room. If desired, make the chart easier to read by color-coding each section or subject area. Students and substitutes should have no problem staying on course! **Jenni Bader, St. Anne School, Columbus, GA**

Language Arts: Read Chapter 5 in *Pippi Longstocking*. Turn in summaries of Chapter 4.

Math: Complete the review problems on page 362.

Science: Finish the last part of the magnet experiment. Complete the observation section of the recording sheet.

Management Tips & Timesavers

Color-Coded Gradebook

For a get-it-at-a-glance way to check on **student performance**, color-code the grades in your gradebook! Enter each A in black ink, each B in blue, and each C or lower grade in red. If a child's grades are slipping, the pattern will stand out. It's also a great way to see which students are "in the black" for the A honor roll! *Patti Etchison—Gr. 4, Living Word Academy, Yorktown, VA*

Stephanie	82	78	85	90	
Brandon	95	94	97	100	
Sarah	85	79	72	64	

Colorful Tests

Students' **test papers** will be "color-ific" with this bright idea! Copy each test or quiz on colorful paper. Students will enjoy working on the colorful paper, and the tests and quizzes will be easy to spot in each child's work folder during parent conferences! *Sonya Floyd—Gr. 5, Mount Olive Elementary, East Point, GA*

Reusable Practice Pages

Conserve paper and spend less time at the copying machine with this **classroom management** tip! Purchase a plastic sheet protector for each child. Also copy a set of practice pages for each student and place it inside a sheet protector. Give each child her pages and a wipe-off marker to keep at her desk. When it's time to practice the skill, have the student move the page on which she will work to the front of the set and write her answers on the sheet protector. Once the page is checked and her progress noted, all she has to do is wipe off her answers and she's ready for the next practice page! *Laurel Nascimento—Gr. 4, St. Joseph Catholic School, Marietta, GA*

It's your turn to use the computer.

It's Your Turn!

Here's a unique way to rotate students' turns at your **classroom computers**. Collect promotional CDs until there is one for each computer. Using a permanent marker, label each CD as shown. Also post a class list near the computers. Then give a CD to the first student on the list. As each student completes his turn, have him check off his name and give the CD to the next classmate on the list. Students will get a kick out of passing the CD, and you can easily check that turns are being taken fairly. *Sharon Zacharda—Gr. 4, West View Elementary, Pittsburgh, PA*

Fingertip Files

Keep important **student information** right at your fingertips in an easy-to-transport folder! How? Tape a 5" x 8" lined index card near the bottom edge of an open folder. Tape a second card on top of the first one, matching its bottom edge to the last line of the first card. Continue adding cards in this manner until there is one for each child (use both sides of the open folder if necessary). Then label each card with a different student's name as shown. The cards flip over for a ready record of student data or anecdotal notes and keep other students' information out of sight! *Dot O'Donnell, John Lewis Childs School, Floral Park, NY*

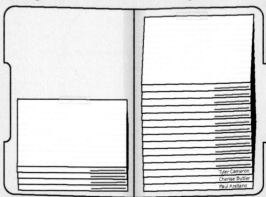

Management Tips & Timesavers

Hassle-Free Library Checkouts

Keep up with **classroom library checkouts** with this terrific tip. Write each book title on a different unlined index card. Next, glue a library pocket to the back of each book and place its matching index card in the pocket. Then write each student's name on a separate library pocket, glue the pockets to a poster board sheet, and display the sheet near your class library. To check out a book, a child removes the book's card and places it in his pocket on the chart. When he is finished with the book, he returns the card to the book. At a glance, you know who has which book! *Brooke Blake, Wentworth Elementary, Wentworth, NH*

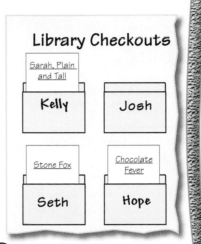

Library Checkouts

Sarah, Plain and Tall	
Kelly	Josh

Stone Fox	Chocolate Fever
Seth	Hope

Addressing Your Resources

Here's a quick way to label your personal **teacher resource books** so they'll find their way back to you when borrowed. Just stick a label with your name on it at the top of each book. There won't be any question about whose book it is! *Richard McCoy, Laquey R-V School, Laquey, MO*

Turnabout Seating

Do you sometimes have one student in a group facing the front and one facing the wall? Solve that problem with a weekly **desk rotation!** Every Monday, simply have the students in each group rotate their desks one turn as shown. Then everyone can start off the week with a bright new outlook! *Sheryl Hall, Davis Elementary, Austin, TX*

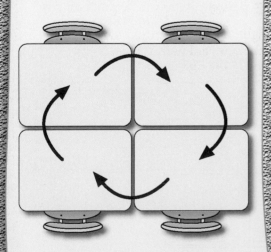

Classwork Sticks

Make it easier to tell who has finished **classwork** with this quick tip. Place a red cup and a blue cup beside the area where students turn in their work. Allow each student to personalize a craft stick and place it in the red cup. As each child turns in an assignment, have him transfer his stick to the blue cup. A quick check of the sticks lets you know who has finished the assignment and turned it in. Simple! *Cynthia Close, Warm Springs Middle School, Berkeley Springs, WV*

Research Project Organizer

This sturdy organizer gives students the ultimate tool for **organizing research notes!** For each student, glue 12 library pockets inside an open file folder as shown. Laminate the folder and cut open each pocket's slit. Have novice researchers add masking tape strips to the pockets and label each pocket with the information they need to gather. Then guide students to organize their 3" x 5" notecards in the pockets in the desired order or by topic. The cards will stay snugly in the pockets even if the folder is turned upside down when a student carries it with her to work in the library or at home. When students finish their reports, they peel off the masking tape and file the folders away for the next research project! *Lisa Funk, Hoover Elementary, Buffalo, NY*

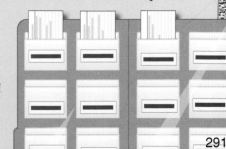

291

Management Tips & Timesavers

Silent Signals

Minimize **interruptions** by using sign language! Demonstrate for students that the sign for water is a *W* tapped against the mouth and that the sign for bathroom is an *R* formed in front of the body as shown. Once students have learned the movements, they can sign to you their need to visit the bathroom or to get a drink of water. Then you can just look at them and nod or point to let them go. Those who need a quiet work environment can enjoy the sweet sounds of silence! *Christine Grandinetti, Berkeley Intermediate School, Moncks Corner, SC*

BATHROOM
Point the right *R* hand forward and move it in a short arc to the right.

WATER
Touch the mouth with the index finger of the right *W* hand a few times.

Clip-Art Shortcut

Are you looking for a quick and easy way to create poster-size **clip art** from *The Mailbox®* magazine for classroom displays? Print each piece of selected art directly onto a transparency. Project the image onto a large sheet of bulletin board paper and trace the shape. Then color, cut out, and display the fabulous results! *Melissa McMullen, Saint Patrick School, Newry, PA*

Die-Cut Planner

Save time at the die-cut machine by creating a **die-cut planner!** Create a table, such as the one shown, that allows you to plan the colors and exact number of letters and punctuation marks you will need. In the top row, write in the colors that will be used. Then write in the appropriate color column the number of each letter or punctuation mark to cut. Every title will be covered from *A* to *Z*! *Carolyn Hart, Taylorsville Elementary, Taylorsville, NC*

Title: Spring's Just Fluttering By!							
Color	Black	Color	Black	Color	Black	Color	Black
A		S		a		s	2
B	1	T		b		t	3
C		U		c		u	2
D		V		d		v	
E		W		e	1	w	
F	1	X		f		x	
G		Y		g	2	y	1
H		Z		h		z	
I		1		i	2	.	
J	1	2		j		?	
K		3		k		!	1
L		4		l	1	" "	
M		5		m		,	1
N		6		n	2	:	
O		7		o		;	
P		8		p	1	( )	
Q		9		q		'	
R		0		r	2	$	

Catch-It Folders

Help students catch on to **organizational skills** with these easy-to-make folders. Have each child color and cut out an enlarged copy of the baseball glove pattern on page 67 and glue it to the outside of a file folder. Next, have him staple a sandwich-size resealable plastic bag atop the mitt. The student now has a folder in which to catch loose papers and a pouch in which to store markers, scissors, or pens until the items can be properly put away. *Kim Minafo, Dillard Drive Elementary, Raleigh, NC*

Strategic Filing System

It's easy to keep tabs on classroom ideas with this colorful **filing strategy.** Set aside sets of five file folders for each subject you teach. To the far-right edge of one folder in each set, attach a colorful tab labeled with the subject's name. Use different colors for each subject. Attach clear tabs to each of the four remaining folders for each set, spacing the tabs and labeling them as shown. Arrange the sets of folders in a file drawer so that the first folder in each set is the subject folder and the related folders for that subject follow it. You'll be able to find whatever you need with just a glance! *Jill Perry, Mason Corinth Elementary, Williamstown, KY*

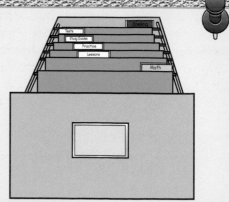

Management Tips & Timesavers

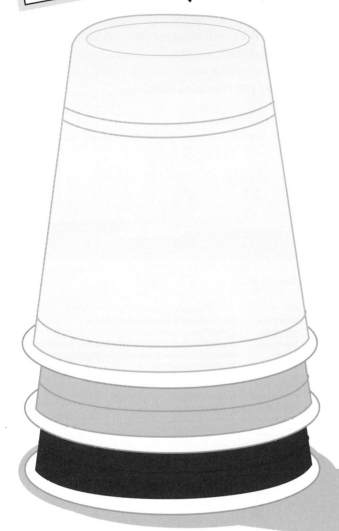

Testing Signals

This simple **testing tip** is sure to get the green light! Purchase a green, yellow, and red plastic cup for each student in your classroom. Before students take a test, give each child one cup of each color and have him stack them on a corner of his desk. Explain how the cups are to be used like traffic lights during the test to signal his need for help:

- Green means "I'm okay, and I know what to do."
- Yellow signifies "I'm stuck, but I can work on something else until you get to me."
- Red means "Please help me now."

Make sure the child knows to place the cup that signals his need on top of the stack. Test time will flow smoothly!

Kerin Stelgerwalt, Coopertown Elementary, Bryn Mawr, PA

Best-behavior Pockets

Can a pocketful of craft sticks motivate a student to be on her best behavior? You bet! Tape a laminated library pocket to each child's desk. Then have the student write her name on five craft sticks and place them in her pocket. If she breaks a classroom rule, remove a stick from her pocket. At the end of the day, collect the remaining sticks for a drawing to receive a special treat. Students will stick with good behavior every day!

Kim Fussell, Harding Academy of Memphis, Memphis, TN

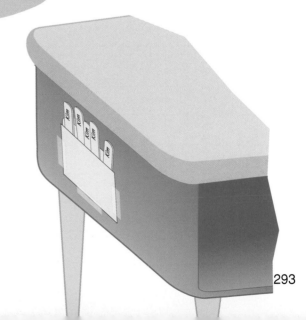

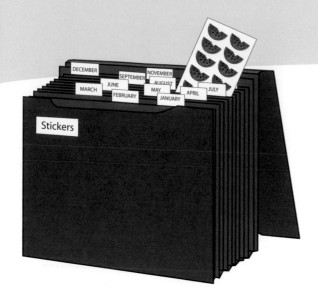

Sticker System

This organization tip can help you find the right sticker for students' papers in a snap! Purchase an accordion folder or an inexpensive tackle box. Label each section or compartment by month, season, or topic. Then place your stickers in the matching section. Now that's an idea you can stick with!

Mary Krause, St. Michael School, Indianapolis, IN
Paulette Porter, Random Island Academy, Clarenville, Newfoundland, Canada

Information at Your Fingertips

Need help organizing files and units? Use the Web site www.themailboxcompanion.com! Each time you gather ideas for an upcoming unit, search The Mailbox® intermediate edition index on the Web site. Print out the information and store it in a folder along with any other ideas and reproducibles for the unit. After completing the unit with your class, mark with a star the ideas that worked especially well. When preparing to teach the unit next year, you'll know at a glance which activities you want to use and where to find them in The Mailbox magazine!

Jennifer Davis, York Elementary, Wauseon, OH

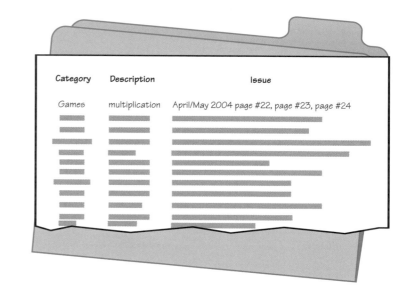

Category	Description	Issue
Games	multiplication	April/May 2004 page #22, page #23, page #24

Assignment Chart

Color your way to tracking students' assignments! Make a chart similar to the one shown, writing students' names down the grid's left side and listing each assignment and its due date across the top. As you grade an assignment, color the corresponding box beside each child's name if he turned in a paper. If he was present but did not turn in the assignment, make an X in the box. If he was absent, leave the box blank. Refer the student to the chart when he returns to get a list of the work he needs to complete. The chart is also handy during parent conferences!

Sharon Vance, Nash Intermediate School, Kaufman, TX

	Math, p. 254 (6/2)	Chapter 6 summary (6/3)					
Devon							
Shelly							
Kevin	X						
Marcus							
Andrea		X					

Our Readers Write

Our Readers Write

The Signs of Success

Encourage students to practice important **study skills** throughout the year with reminder signs they make themselves! Help the class brainstorm different signs found along highways and near buildings. Direct each child to choose one sign and think about how it relates to a skill he uses in class. Next, have the student draw the sign on a 9" x 12" sheet of light-colored construction paper and add a message explaining how he would use the sign in class. Then post the completed signs on a bulletin board titled "Signs of Success."

Kim Minafo, Cary, NC

STOP

Stop to read all the directions.

Stop to check your work.

Open House Programs

Make sure visitors don't miss a thing at your **open house.** How? With a simple program! Inside a folded sheet of 8½" x 11" paper, list the areas and displays you want parents to see. Include a checkoff box next to each entry. After making copies, decorate the front cover with a class picture, or have each child add his own artwork. Not only will your visitors have a productive visit, but they'll also have a keepsake to take home!

Kelli Higgins, P. L. Bolin Elementary, East Peoria, IL

Student Place-Value Chart

These sentence strip manipulatives make **place value** easy to understand! Have each student divide a sentence strip into sections and label them as shown. Also instruct the child to divide three index cards, as shown, and cut them apart to make three sets of numbers labeled from 0 to 9. Affix a piece of Velcro fastener to the back of each number and space on the chart. Have students store their charts in their math folders, ready to pull out whenever they need help finding the place values of whole numbers or decimals!

Doris Barker—Gr. 4, Mary Martin Elementary, Weatherford, TX

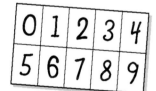

Millions	Hundred Thousands	Ten Thousands	Thousands	Hundreds	Tens	Ones		Tenths	Hundredths	Thousandths	Ten Thousandths
						0	.	1	7		

I Spy in the USA

Use this interactive classroom display to encourage students to learn more about **U.S. geography.** Post a large U.S. map on a bulletin board titled "I Spy in the USA." Attach a few magnifying glasses around the map along with several facts about states written on index cards. Place a supply of blank index cards next to the board. Then invite students to find other interesting facts about the states, write each one on a different card, and add it to the display!

Christina Ingram—Gr. 5, Delaware Academy Central School, Delhi, NY

Brain Boosters

Boost **critical-thinking** skills with this daily activity! Write on the board several items that have something in common. Next, challenge students to think about how the items are related. Encourage each child to find as many commonalities as possible and to be able to explain his reasoning. Then allow several volunteers to share their ideas with the class. What a simple way to keep reasoning skills sharp!

Diana Boykin—Gr. 4, DeZavala Elementary, Midland, TX

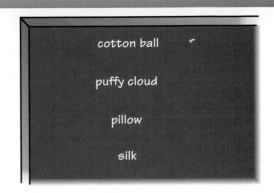

cotton ball

puffy cloud

pillow

silk

Lunch With Beaver

Looking for a **character education** activity that students are sure to tune in to? Obtain copies of episodes from the classic television series *Leave It to Beaver*. Then invite students to join you and Theodore "Beaver" Cleaver for lunch in the classroom. As each episode's predicament unfolds, stop the video and ask students what they would do. Then watch the rest of the video and discuss Beaver's dilemma and choices.

Lauren Westbrook—Gr. 5, Wharton Magnet School, Nashville, TN

Amy ate apples all afternoon.

Cole carries his toy cars in a case.

Alliterative Handwriting Practice

Searching for a fresh new way to practice **cursive writing?** Try combining it with alliteration! Have each student write and illustrate an alliterative sentence for each letter of the alphabet on separate half sheets of paper. Then bind each child's pages together to form a book. Display the completed books in your classroom. Or share them with students in a lower grade who are just learning to write in cursive!

Stacy Stetzel—Gr. 4, Swayzee Elementary, Swayzee, IN

New Teacher Shower

Welcome **new teachers** by showering them with classroom materials they're sure to use! Before classes begin, ask each returning faculty member to donate a teaching aid, such as bulletin board letters or a reproducible book. Then hold an afterschool gathering for the staff and serve snacks. Invite new teachers to choose two or three donated items for their classrooms. The newbies will soon feel right at home!

Patricia E. Dancho, Apollo-Ridge Middle School, Spring Church, PA

A Writing Smorgasbord!

Create a **writing display** that becomes a feast for the eyes! Make several placemats by fringing the ends of colorful sheets of 12" x 18" construction paper. Glue plastic utensils and a paper napkin to each placemat. Staple the placemats to a bulletin board titled "Dig In to a Smorgasbord of Writing!" When students are ready to publish their work, mount each piece on a different placemat. Update the board often. What a treat!

Tracy Cobb Paul, Veazie, ME

My Summer Vacation

Our Readers Write

The Sentences Cheer

This quick activity to reinforce the **four types of sentences** is something to cheer about! Teach your students the cheer shown, following the pattern for each type of sentence: declarative, interrogative, imperative, and exclamatory. Next, add motions such as a closed fist to represent a period for a statement, a shoulder shrug for a question, a pointed finger for a command, and raised arms for an exclamation.

Lindsay Cloud—Gr. 5, Randolph Howell Elementary, Columbia, TN

Teacher: When I say, "Declarative," you say, "Statement." Declarative!
Students: Statement!
Teacher: Declarative!
Students: Statement!

Switch!

Make **correcting students' work** fun with an activity that lets kids work some wiggles out! When you are ready to check a group assignment, have each child place his paper on his desk and then move one desk to the right. Call on a student to give the answer for the first problem. Direct each child to correct the answer at the desk where he is sitting. Then say, "Switch!" to signal students to rotate to the next desk and repeat the process to check the next answer. Continue switching until all answers have been corrected.

Lindsay Meloff—Gr. 4, St. Elizabeth Seton, Pickering, Ontario, Canada

The Keys to Problem Solving

Help students unlock the mystery of relating words in **story problems** to math symbols with this key idea! Make a key pattern for each child. Next, help students brainstorm important words used in addition problems, and list the words on the board. Then give each child a key pattern, four different-colored sheets of construction paper, scissors, a length of yarn, and access to a hole puncher. Direct the student to trace and cut out several keys from one sheet. Then have her write on a different cutout each clue, along with an addition symbol, as shown. Repeat the process to make keys for subtraction, multiplication, and division. When finished, each student puts her cutouts on a yarn keyring to use when solving word problems. What a simple solution!

Clidean Epps—Gr. 4, Mount Olive Elementary, Ft. Mitchell, AL

A Pocket Full of Vocabulary

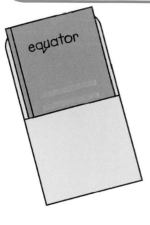

Say goodbye to lost **vocabulary cards** with a simple tip that also keeps students organized! Give each child an adhesive-backed library pocket to affix to the inside of his binder. Direct him to write each subject's vocabulary words and definitions on different sets of colorful 3" x 5" index cards. For example, designate yellow for reading, orange for social studies, blue for math, green for science, etc. When he needs to take the cards home to study, have him place them in the pocket!

adapted from an idea by Georgina Cole-McCarthy, Bennie Dover Jackson Middle School, New London, CT

Interesting Insect Rings

Culminate a study of **insects** with this jewelry-making project, which lets students wear a bit of science on their fingers! Gather a supply of plastic pull rings (with the seal still attached) from orange juice cartons. Have each child choose an insect and draw it on paper. Then give him the materials listed and guide him through the steps below to make a ring.

Materials for each child: plastic pull ring, craft foam scraps, glue, scissors, wiggle eyes, fine-tip black permanent marker

Steps:
1. Cut the body shape from foam scraps.
2. Glue the foam to the solid part of the pull ring.
3. Glue the eyes to the foam.
4. Add details with the marker.

Colleen Dabney, Williamsburg JCC Public Schools, Williamsburg, VA

Transparency Protector

What can keep your **transparencies** looking like new? A clear plastic sheet protector! Just slide a transparency inside the sheet protector and write directly on it. When placed on an overhead projector, it will look as though you're writing on the transparency!

Penny Morrison, KDS DAR Middle School, Grant, AL

The Great Adjective Swap

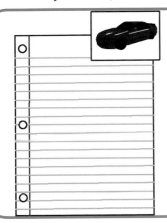

Reinforce **adjectives** with this picture-perfect idea! Cut out interesting magazine pictures and laminate them. Next, arrange students in a circle with paper and a pencil for each student. Then give each child a picture. Allow each student 15 seconds to list adjectives that describe her picture. When time is up, have her pass her picture to the classmate on her right. Then allow another 15 seconds for each student to write adjectives about her new picture. Continue the process until each child has written adjectives for every photo. Finally, invite students to share adjectives from their lists as you record them on chart paper. Post the list for students to use as a reference when they write.

Carrie Roux—Gr. 4, Wilson School, Manchester, NH

Measuring to the Quarter Inch

Make **measurement** easier with this "ruler-ific" idea! Find a picture of a ruler that has inches divided into fourths. Write fractions above the hash marks as shown. Make approximately eight copies of the ruler on a sheet of paper. Then make three to four transparencies of the page. Cut apart the rulers and give one to each student. With this see-through tool, measuring to the half or quarter inch is a breeze!

Barb Mores, Haines School, New Lenox, IL

Name Stamp

Use this simple tip to make **signing papers** and notes more efficient! Visit a copy store and have a self-inking signature stamp made. When you need to sign students' planners or folders, use your stamp to sign it in an instant!

Gayle Cadwell—Gr. 5 and Leigh Evans—Gr. 4, Palmetto Christian School, Palmetto, FL

Our Readers Write

Purposeful Poetry Project

Turn a top-notch **poetry** project into a gift that parents can enjoy throughout the year! Make a copy of next year's calendar for each child. Over a period of several days, have each student write 13 different types of poems (see the suggestions shown), typing and printing final horizontal copies with appropriate computer graphics and borders. If your school has a technology teacher, ask her to teach your students how to scan text over a special picture! Then have each child compile his calendar pages, gluing one poem to the cover and one above each month's page. What a great gift that will keep on giving!

Pam Sturtz—Gr. 6, Sellman Middle School, Cincinnati, OH

Types of Poems

ballad	limerick
free verse	epitaph
cinquain	shape poem
haiku	diamante
alphabet poem	ode
acrostic	clerihew

January can be quite cold,
But it's not so bad when there's a cup of Mom's hot cocoa to hold!
The warm drink tastes good after sledding.
Mom is great—she thinks of everything!

January

S	M	T	W	T	F	S
						1
2	3	4	5	6	7	8
9	10	11	12	13	14	15
16	17	18	19	20	21	22
23	24	25	26	27	28	29
30	31					

Cleanup Countdown

Signal cleanup time each day using a countdown that can make teaching **fractions** easier! Say, "One," and then continue counting down to zero using fractions with increasingly larger denominators, such as ½, ¼, ⅛, 1/16, 1/32, and 1/64. By the time you reach zero, students should be finished and quiet!

Jessica Portlock—Gr. 5, Clinton Public School, Clinton, NJ

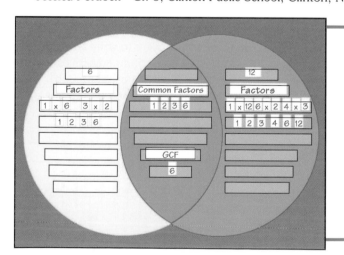

Factor Diagrams

Looking for a new way to use a Venn diagram pocket chart? What about finding **greatest common factors?** Have students write the number facts and factors of two given numbers on separate index cards and place them in the appropriate parts of the chart as shown. Once the common factors are moved to the shared part of the chart, the GCF (greatest common factor) is easy for everyone to see!

Kelly Schoettley—Gr. 4, Spring Elementary, Toledo, OH

Revolution vs. Rotation

There's nothing like a few lines of rhyme to help students remember confusing concepts! To distinguish the difference between **revolution and rotation,** help each child memorize jingles such as "Revolution is when the earth travels around the sun. After 365 days, it's done!" and "Rotation is when the earth takes a spin. After 24 hours, a new day can begin!"

Alicia Bush—Gr. 4, Mount Olive Attendance Center, Mount Olive, MS

Key Chain Hall Passes

Put promotional key chains to good use by turning them into durable **hall passes!** Just write your room number on the back and tie a necklace-length piece of yarn through the ring!

Monica Marino—Gr. 4, Shady Lane School, Deptford Township, NJ

Calendar Calisthenics

This **calendar math** activity resembles the popular Twister game and really s-t-r-e-t-c-h-e-s students' math muscles! Draw a calendar grid on a large plastic tablecloth or shower curtain. Label each day with a date; then spread the mat on the floor and have students sit in a circle around it. Call up two or three players. Have a seated student roll a die to identify the body part that Player 1 will use (even = foot, odd = hand). Have another student roll to determine which foot or hand she will use (even = right, odd = left). Then call out a direction, such as "Two weeks after the first Tuesday" or "Nine days before the last day of the month." Have the player use the designated hand or foot to touch only that date and no other part of the mat. If she does not, have her sit down. Repeat the process for the other players using different rollers and directions. Continue taking turns in this manner until one player wins. Then call up another group of players.

Amy Bruening—Gr. 4, Sacred Heart School, Yankton, SD

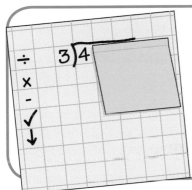

Division Rx

If your students have trouble with **long division,** this tip is for you! Have each child solve the problems on grid paper, using a small sticky note to cover all numbers in the dividend except the one(s) needed for each step. If necessary, have students add the symbols shown to help them remember the order of the steps. After completing each series of steps, the sticky note can be moved to uncover the next number in the dividend!

Patricia O'Leary—Gr. 4, Grandview Elementary, Connersville, IN

Conversion Song

Converting mixed numbers to improper **fractions** will be music to your ears when students sing this simple song! Write on a poster the sentences shown. Have students sing the words to the tune of "Tom Dooley." Before you know it, they'll have the process down pat!

Judy Hooks—Gr. 5, Manning Elementary, Manning, SC

> Write down your denominator.
> Multiply it by the whole.
> Add your numerator.
> Now you're on a roll!

Government Flip Booklet

Make understanding the roles of the **three branches of government** as easy to do as making a booklet! Give each child a 9" x 12" sheet of construction paper. Have her fold it in half, cut the top half into three strips, and label the strips "Executive," "Legislative," and "Judicial." Next, direct her to fold back one strip at a time and write on it two sentences: one explaining that particular branch's job and another explaining who or what is in charge of it. Across from each explanation, have her illustrate the building that represents that branch: the White House, Capitol, or Supreme Court Building. To review, all students have to do is flip the strips!

Anita Perez—Gr. 5, Laureles Elementary, Los Fresnos, TX

Ms. Wood's Posters

Poster Pockets

Looking for an easy **storage tip** for posters and bulletin board displays? Make a poster pocket! I seal the bottom edges of flat, unassembled cardboard boxes with packing tape and then slide my posters inside. For a personal touch, I invite my students to decorate the pockets with drawings that depict the posters inside.

Melissa Wood, Memorial Day School, Savannah, GA

Daily Book Critics

Thumbs-up, thumbs-down, what's the best book in town? Let your students decide with this easy **time filler!** Each day I randomly select two or three students to be the daily book critics. I then allow each critic a few minutes to tell the class about the book she is currently reading, and I have her make predictions about what might happen next. I also have each critic give her book either a thumbs-up or a thumbs-down vote. Then I post a list of the thumbs-up books to help students who want suggestions for future reading selections.

Teresa Vilfer-Snyder, Fredericktown Intermediate, Fredericktown, OH

Thumbs-Up Books
There's a Boy in the Girls' Bathroom
by Louis Sachar
The Trumpet of the Swan
by E. B. White
Where the Red Fern Grows
by Wilson Rawls
Hatchet
by Gary Paulsen
The BFG
by Roald Dahl
Superfudge
by Judy Blume

Mighty Math Time Filler

Stimulate students' minds during **free time** with an interactive math bulletin board! I start by dividing a bulletin board into four equal sections. I then title each section and attach an answer envelope as shown. I also provide a supply of blank paper slips. On Monday, I post in each section a different challenging problem. During a student's free time throughout the week, he solves a problem on a paper slip he labels with his name and places the solution in the matching answer envelope. At the end of the week, I reveal to the class the correct answer for each problem. Then I draw one answer from each envelope. If that student solved the problem correctly, he receives a mystery prize. To make use of the board again the following week, I simply replace the math problems and restock the paper supply.

Laura Weiss, West End Elementary, Industry, TX

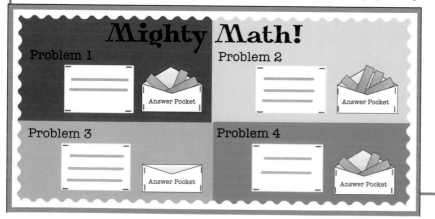

Quick Transparencies

Are you running short on **overhead transparencies?** I recycle excess laminating film from other projects and cut it into 8½" x 11" sheets, creating reusable overhead transparencies. I can write on the sheets with dry-erase markers and just wipe them clean when I'm done. This is clearly an economical solution!

Sally F. McGuire, Greensboro West Elementary, Greensboro, AL

Kid-Created Window Clings

Brighten up your classroom with homemade **window clings!** I buy clear ten-gauge plastic at a local fabric store and cut it into squares. Next, I photocopy several different simple pieces of seasonal clip art. I place the copies at a center along with the plastic squares and permanent markers. Then I have each student choose one piece of clip art, cover it with a plastic square, and use the markers to trace and color the shape onto the plastic. When he is finished, I have him place the plastic on the inside of a classroom window, where it sticks on its own throughout the season. The kids love it!

Joyce Hovanec, Glassport Elementary, Glassport, PA

Dry-Erase Board Eraser

My students love to use dry-erase boards, but I needed an **eraser alternative.** The answer to my problem was foam paintbrushes. They are inexpensive, reusable, and easy to clean. My students keep the brushes in their desks until they need them, and when they are done, they rinse them with water to clean them.

Shelia Walker, Reedy Creek Elementary, Charlotte, NC

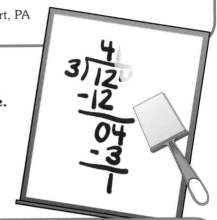

Showered With Kindness

I cultivate **character development** with this neat idea. First, I hang an umbrella upside down in my classroom. I also label a supply of paper slips with the text shown. I invite a child to fill out a slip each time she sees a classmate showing kindness. Then I have her fold the slip and place it in the umbrella. At the end of each week, I select a few strips to share with the class. Then I reward each recognized student with a small treat.

___ was showered with kindness by ___.
The kind gesture was ___ Date ___
Signed ___

Dana Bruegenhemke, Forest Park Elementary, O'Fallon, MO

Terminator Table

Turn the tables on ordinary **review games** with this fast-paced challenge! I place a call bell in the middle of a tabletop at the front of the room. Then I have two students stand on either side of the table, each with one hand flat on the tabletop and one hand behind his back. I ask a review question. The first player to ring the bell has five seconds to answer the question. If correct, he stays for another question, and his opponent is terminated. If incorrect, his opponent gets a chance to answer correctly and terminate him. If neither player is correct, they are both eliminated and replaced by new players. Play continues in this manner with each new question asked. The winner is the student who terminates the most players.

Patricia Rigueira, Southern Cross School, Beccar, Buenos Aires, Argentina

Calling All Readers!

Make **read-aloud time** less noisy with a class set of reading phones! To make each handset, I use one four-inch length of half-inch PVC pipe (most home improvement stores will cut the pipe for you) and two 90-degree elbows. After I attach an elbow to each end of the pipe, as shown, the handset is ready to use. When the student holds the phone up to his ear, he can read aloud to himself without distracting anyone else around him. Now quieter read-aloud time is just a phone call away!

Jill Reeves, Krisle Elementary, Springfield, TN

Our Readers Write

Tower Power

What's the object of this exciting review game? Building a tower that doesn't topple! I gather wooden blocks in different sizes, shapes, colors, and styles. Then I divide the class into three or more teams and have each team line up behind a desk piled with blocks. I ask Player 1 on Team A a question. If he answers correctly, he starts his team's tower either by placing a block flat on the desk or by standing the block upright. If his answer is incorrect, I give Player 1 on each remaining team, in turn, a chance to answer until one player answers correctly. If no team answers correctly, I share the answer. Then I start round two with Player 2 and a new question. Play continues as players add blocks to their towers. If a tower falls, that team cleans up its blocks and starts over in the next round after a team member gives a correct answer. Tower on!

Ann Marie Hand, Oostburg Elementary, Oostburg, WI

Handy Editing Symbols

Make editing and revising easier for students with this ready reference! I laminate several copies of a sheet of editing symbols. I also affix a strip of magnetic tape to the back of each copy. Then I adhere the sheets to a magnetic surface. During each writing session, a child can take one to his desk, as needed, and return it when finished!

Rifki Frieder, Masores Bais Yaakor School, Brooklyn, NY

Symbol	Meaning	Example
◯	Correct spelling	
ℓ	Delete or remove.	dogs
⌒	Close the gap.	
∧	Add a letter or word.	lives in tree
#	Make a space.	
∼	Reverse the order of a letter, a word, or words.	plant eats
∧	Insert a comma.	the crab an arthropod
⊙	Insert and punctuation.	Cats purr
∨	Insert an apostrophe.	a deers antlers
∨∨	Insert quotation marks.	She said, Look at the pig.
≡	Make the letter a capital.	birds eat seeds.
/	Make the letter lowercase.	a Snowshoe hare
¶	Start a new paragraph.	¶Some dogs have tails.

Number Line ABCs

Positive and negative integers can be troublesome for students. Need a trick for remembering that on a number line negative numbers are to the left of zero and positive numbers are to the right? I have my students recite the ABCs up to *P,* slowing down when saying *N* (negative numbers), *O* (zero), and *P* (positive numbers). It works every time!

Francine Camino, St. Margaret's School, Mattydale, NY

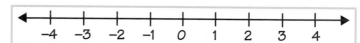

Nixing Linear Mix-Ups

Metric Club Members
millimeter
centimeter
decimeter
kilometer

Four-Letter Club Members
inch
foot
yard
mile

End confusion over whether a unit of length is metric or customary! I introduce my students to two clubs: the metric club and the four-letter club. Then I explain that units containing the word *meter* are members of the metric club and those spelled with four letters belong to the four-letter club. Simple!

Allison Adams, Grafton Village Elementary Fredericksburg, VA

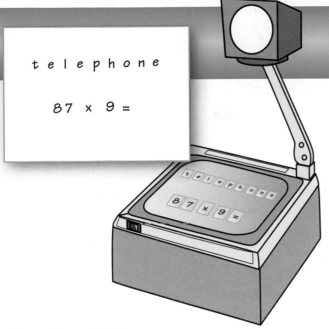

Overhead Tiles

Instead of buying expensive overhead manipulatives, make your own! I use a computer to print the letters of the alphabet (uppercase and lowercase) in the font and size I want. Then I make a transparency of the letters and cut them out. I create tiles for words, numbers, math symbols, and pictures the same way! What a savings!

Brooke Blake, Wentworth Elementary, Wentworth, NH

Catsup (Catch-Up) Center

Make catching up on assignments more appealing to students by designating a special place in the room for them to work. To identify the spot, I place a clean catsup bottle at a table along with a crate containing a labeled folder for each child. In each folder, I place any work from the previous day that a child needs to complete or correct. When a student finishes her regular assignments, she heads for that spot to work!

Christine Cooley, C. C. Meneley Elementary, Gardnerville, NV

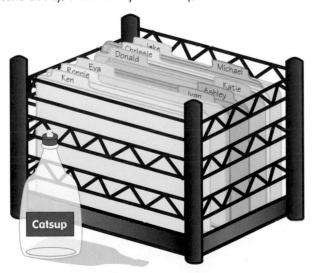

Picture-Perfect Book

A plastic photo album from a photo center makes a fantastic class minibook! I bring in the plastic album provided by my photo center each time I get my photographs developed. Next, my students make the book's pages by writing on and illustrating 4" x 6" index cards. Then they slide the completed cards in the album's plastic sleeves in order, making sure the first card with the book's title shows through the cover's front window. Each book becomes a class favorite!

Brandi Lampl, J. W. Arnold Elementary, Jonesboro, GA

Summertime SORT

This management tip helps me make the most of my summer so I can be ahead of the game when the new school year starts. How? I SORT (**S**hare, **O**rganize, **R**earrange, and **T**hink)! I go through workshop handouts and resource materials I've collected during the school year and decide which ideas to share with colleagues and which ones might be useful during the upcoming school year. Then, while the ideas are still fresh in my mind, I jot down in a special notebook the things I want to try.

Beth Carron, North St. Francois County Intermediate School, Desloge, MO

Summer Surfing

Summer is a great time for enjoying the beach, but this year spend some time surfing the internet too! I use the summer to bookmark Web sites that could enhance the units I teach. Once school starts and my kids arrive, that tidal wave of helpful sites "shore" comes in handy!

Colleen Dabney, Williamsburg JCC Public Schools, Williamsburg, VA

Answer Keys

Page 9
1. fact, yellow
2. opinion, orange
3. fact, yellow
4. opinion, orange
5. fact, yellow
6. fact, yellow
7. opinion, orange
8. opinion, orange
9. fact, yellow
10. opinion, orange
11. fact, yellow
12. opinion, orange

Page 10
Answers may vary. Possible answers include the following:

said—cried, shouted
won—captured, grabbed
stood—huddled, gathered
talked—cheered, chatted
hit—smacked, knocked
ran—sprinted, raced
had—dominated, controlled
made—slugged, knocked
was—happened, occurred
threw—hurled, launched
hit—punched, pounded
went—headed, traveled
ended—concluded, terminated
say—boast, proclaim

Bonus Box: Pictures will vary.

Page 11
1. O
2. W
3. O
4. S
5. O
6. R
7. B
8. K
9. M

He heard there were <u>BOOKWORMS</u>!

Bonus Box: 998,621; nine hundred ninety-eight thousand, six hundred twenty-one

Page 12
1. 24 + 7 = 31 students
2. 87 − 19 − 36 = 32 students
3. 19 + 19 + 19 + 19 + 11 = 87 students
4. 56 + 82 + 41 = 179 riders
5. 88 − 44 − 22 = 22 students
6. 24 + 35 + 18 = 77 students

Bonus Box: No, 23 + 37 + 46 = 106 fifth graders. This number of students will not fit on a 98-passenger bus.

Page 14
1. The *Mayflower* was a small ship (96.5 feet long and 26 feet wide) with an oak beam frame covered by oak planks. It may have had three masts and square sails.
2. Captain Christopher Jones commanded the ship and was part owner. A crew of 47 men accompanied him on the voyage. The ship was usually used to transport trade goods to and from other countries.
3. There were 102 passengers on the *Mayflower*. The ship was an unhealthy place to live because it was crowded, uncomfortable, and the Pilgrims were constantly wet from seawater.
4. The *Mayflower* sailed back to England in April of 1621 and was used for trade with France, Spain, and Ireland. After Captain Jones's death in 1622, the *Mayflower* was appraised and declared to be in ruins. It was most likely sold as scrap wood.

Page 16
1. 304 oz.
2. 128 oz.
3. 512 oz.
4. 224 oz.
5. 96 oz.
6. 176 oz.
7. 12 lb.
8. 30 lb.
9. 20 lb.
10. 8 lb.
11. 4 lb.
12. 25 lb.

Bonus Box: 240 oz., 15 lb.

Page 17
Answers may vary. Possible answers include the following:
1. Cory has 8 Candy Creeps (4 pkgs.) and 5 Popcorn Pythons.
2. Rita has 10 Gummy Ghouls (2 pkgs.), 4 Candy Creeps (2 pkgs.), and 11 Popcorn Pythons.
3. Hal has 25 Gummy Ghouls (5 pkgs.), 4 Candy Creeps (2 pkgs.), and 4 Popcorn Pythons.

Bonus Box: Answers may vary. Possible answers include the following:
Owen has 75 Gummy Ghouls (15 pkgs.), 20 Candy Creeps (10 pkgs.), and 5 Popcorn Pythons.

Page 19
(four) for
(plain) plane
(Ant) Aunt
(write) right
(too) to
(sea) see
(they're) their
(wee) we
(new) knew
(flower) flour
(knows) nose
(scene) seen
(peaked) peeked
(there) their
(herd) heard
(inn) in
(won) one
(eight) ate
(ore) or
(peace) piece

Bonus Box: Answers will vary.

Page 23
1. 44 min.
2. 26 min.
3. 1 hr. 22 min.
4. 35 min.
5. 29 min.
6. 1 hr. 3 min.
7. 1 hr. 19 min.
8. 37 min.
9. 2 hr. 9 min.
10. 28 min.
11. 52 min.
12. 2 hr. 28 min.

Bonus Box: 12 hr. 43 min.

Page 24
1. shirts
2. diaries
3. watches
4. footballs
5. mice
6. moose
7. backpacks
8. bookshelves
9. monkeys
10. boxes

Bonus Box: child, tooth, goose, dress, baby

Page 25
1. 32.111
2. 25.026
3. 15.005
4. 32.88
5. 28.902
6. 16.469
7. 45.141
8. 23.751
9. 30.9
10. 27.379
11. 20.614
12. 28.824

Bonus Box: A poinsettia costs more. Its value is 32.342. The value of a stocking is 30.415.

Page 26
1. K
2. L
3. O
4. E
5. J
6. B
7. D
8. C

Bonus Box: Adjectives and paragraphs will vary.

Page 30

1. 24
2. 16
3. 8
4. 5
5. 8
6. 5
7. $3.50
8. 36
9. 12
10. 14

Bonus Box: $2.40

Page 31

Puzzle 1: John Tyler
Puzzle 2: Andrew Jackson
Puzzle 3: John Adams and Thomas Jefferson

Bonus Box: John Adams

Page 32

The leprechaun is a smiling little elf who, according to legend, cannot be trusted. Ancient myths say that the leprechaun guards a pot of gold and keeps it hidden from humans. In one story, a leprechaun gets caught by an old Irishman who forces the elf to reveal that the gold is buried under a tree in the forest. After the Irishman ties a red handkerchief around the tree's trunk to help him remember the location, he leaves to find a shovel. When the man returns, he sees that the tricky leprechaun has tied a red handkerchief just like his own around every other tree in the forest!

Bonus Box: Stories will vary.

Page 33

1. blue
2. red
3. green
4. yellow
5. purple
6. blue
7. red
8. green
9. blue
10. yellow
11. purple
12. red

Bonus Box: 9 adjectives, 7 nouns, 4 verbs, 4 pronouns, 2 adverbs

Page 37

1. fi
2. ng
3. we
4. ed
5. ve
6. st
7. lo
8. ni
9. ha
10. Ma
11. ju
12. day
13. ch
14. sh
15. 31

Because we have just finished a long 31-day March!

Bonus Box: Yes, because the letter *s* comes after *l* and before *w* in the alphabet.

Page 38

Helpful actions: 2, 3, 4, 7, 10
Harmful actions: 1, 5, 6, 8, 9

Bonus Box: Answers will vary.

Page 39

Basketball
Mean = 9
Mode = 8.5
Median = 8.5
Range = 8

Baseball
Mean = 6.5
Mode = 7.5
Median = 6
Range = 9.5

Track
Mean = 5.5
Median = 6
Mode = 6.5
Range = 4.5

Tennis
Mean = 8
Mode = 10
Median = 8.5
Range = 9

Softball
Mean = 6
Mode = 4
Median = 6
Range = 7

Golf
Mean = 5
Mode = 5
Median = 5
Range = 6

Bonus Box: Answers will vary.

Page 40

1. 40
2. 2004
3. 75
4. 2002
5. 2003
6. 2000, 2003, and 2004
7. 5,500
8. 2002, 2003
9. 2004
10. 2002

Bonus Box: Graphs will vary.

Page 44

1. adjectives: old, their, camping
   adverb: safely
2. adjectives: large, drive-in, movie, their
   adverbs: there, silently
3. adjective: famous
   adverb: slowly
4. adjectives: big, blue, old, water
   adverb: briefly
5. adjectives: flat, ten
   adverbs: west, There, nose-down
6. adjectives: Route 66, two, roadside
   adverb: quickly
7. adjectives: elevator, cool, limestone
   adverbs: eagerly, down
8. adjective: nice
   adverbs: around, home

Page 45

1. VACATION
2. BEACH
3. BARBECUE
4. BIRD-WATCHING
5. ICE CREAM
6. FIREWORKS
7. SANDCASTLE
8. BASEBALL
9. SKATEBOARD
10. CAMPING
11. BOATING
12. SEASHELLS
13. SWIMMING POOL
14. SUNTAN
15. BATHING SUIT

IT MAKES HER FEEL "DI-STING-UISHED"!

Page 46

1. Friday
2. Tuesday
3. 6°F
4. 38°C
5. 108°F
6. See the thermometer.
7. 22°F
8. 100°C

Bonus Box: 122°F

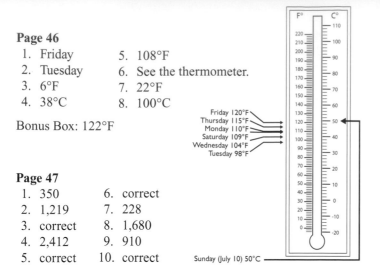

Friday 120°F
Thursday 115°F
Monday 110°F
Saturday 109°F
Wednesday 104°F
Tuesday 98°F

Sunday (July 10) 50°C

Page 47

1. 350
2. 1,219
3. correct
4. 2,412
5. correct
6. correct
7. 228
8. 1,680
9. 910
10. correct

Number not crossed off: 268

Bonus Box: 536

Page 73

1. I taught my dog Fifi a new trick, <u>but she won't do it if you are watching</u>.
2. <u>I have visited Vermont</u>, but I haven't been to the capital.
3. <u>Brad is the best writer in class</u>; he moved here from Dallas.
4. You may not believe this, <u>but I have never played a video game</u>.
5. <u>My brother is younger than I am</u>; he's in first grade.
6. Ally is my poodle, <u>and Elly is my calico cat</u>.
7. <u>We may go to the mountains</u>, or we may go to the beach.
8. <u>I want a new bike for my birthday</u>, so I have been dropping hints.
9. I'm going horseback riding Friday, <u>and this will be my first time on a horse</u>.
10. <u>I asked my dad if I could drive the car</u>, but he said no.

Bonus Box: Sentences will vary.

Page 74

1. Simple Sid
2. Complex Conrad
3. Compound Carla
4. Compound Carla
5. Complex Conrad
6. Complex Conrad
7. Simple Sid
8. Compound Carla
9. Complex Conrad
10. Simple Sid

Bonus Box: Sentences will vary.

Page 83

The correct order of the steps is 3, 5, 10, 1, 8, 4, 9, 6, 2, 7.

Page 98

My Trip to the Beach

by Marvin M. Mouse

Last June, my family went to Long Beach. We stayed at the Sands Hotel on Ocean Drive. We walked to the beach every day. One day, we were almost the only ones there. So, Dad said, "This is like having our own private beach!" We ate a lot of great food on the trip. We had cheeseburgers at B. J.'s Surfin' Grill. The Fishnet had great seafood. I loved the cheesy shrimp and grits! We had cheese sticks at Dana's Diner because Mom read about how good it was in *Beach Life*. Friday was our last day at the beach. We went for a ride on a boat called the *Luna*. The *Luna* had a glass bottom, so we could see the fish swimming under us! After the boat ride, we made sand castles. I heard that there is a sand castle contest at the beach every year on the Fourth of July. Maybe we can do that next summer!

Bonus Box: Sentences will vary.

Page 103

1. no
2. yes
3. no
4. yes
5. yes
6. no
7. yes
8. no
9. no
10. no
11. yes
12. no

He lost his "<u>BEAR-INGS</u>"!

Bonus Box

1. Bert bragged, "I've got the best bait ever!"
3. "It cost $5.00 a jar," Bert answered.
6. Bert checked his line and asked, "Are you sure?"
8. Bertha squealed, "Look at this! I've caught three fish!"
9. Bert asked, "What bait are you using?"
10. Bertha replied, "Worms from my garden."
12. Bert asked shyly, "Could I have one of your worms?"

Page 104

1. blue—We finished play practice early, so I still had time to ride my bike.
2. purple—Sandra, the best singer in the choir, will play the lead role.
3. red—Ty, did you find a costume?
4. yellow—We read over our lines, found our spots on stage, and began practice.
5. green—After practice, we had pizza.
6. yellow—We have to wear white shirts, black pants, and black shoes for the final act.
7. purple—Mrs. Jones, our drama teacher, said we are almost ready to perform.
8. red—Mrs. Jones, I found a costume!
9. green—During the first act, there are nine actors on the stage.
10. orange—Our first show will be November 13, 2004.
11. yellow—We will perform at the Smith Center on Thursday, Friday, Saturday, and Sunday.
12. orange—The Smith Center is at 2103 Cowan Road, Ogden, Utah.

Bonus Box: Answers will vary.

Page 109

1. bear
2. train
3. well
4. draw
5. lap
6. rock
7. pitcher
8. trip
9. sink
10. check

The unshaded chips are *fall* and *break*.

Bonus Box: Sentences will vary.

Page 113

Answers will vary. Possible answers are provided.

1. She got 30 extra minutes of TV time.
2. Damon spilled his cereal.
3. Dana's class got a treat.
4. Damon's team won the game.
5. Dana stepped in a mud puddle.
6. Damon had more time to play with his friends.
7. Dana studied for her math test.
8. Damon tripped over someone's foot.

Page 114

Plants are needed for life on Earth. They provide food for many living things. We need plants because they are a major part of our food chain. Animals at the bottom of the food chain eat plants. These animals can be eaten by other ones. We eat plants and animals.

Providing food is not the only way plants help us. Most plants make their own food. In order to do this, they use water, sunlight, minerals, and carbon dioxide. The process makes glucose and oxygen. The plant uses the glucose for food and releases the oxygen into the air. Therefore, humans and animals can breathe.

Many plants produce seeds. If the seeds scatter, then new plants can grow. For this reason, many seeds have special parts. Some have small hooks. The hooks stick to animal fur and the seed is moved from one place to another. Other seeds have parts that act like wings. As a result, these seeds can be carried by the wind. Some plants can only release their seeds in extreme heat. One effect of a forest fire is that some pine tree seeds burst from their cones. These features may be due to plants adapting to their climate and setting.

When a plant dies, it breaks down and returns nutrients to the soil. Thus, dying plants help new plants grow.

Page 125

1. These men are carved in stone // high above the fruited plain, // and visitors come to see them // from California to Maine.
2. Sweet bell of freedom, // now old and worn, // you cracked just as // our nation was born. // Years after repair, // you cracked again. // How you are now // is how you'll remain.
3. Just beside the harbor's door // stands a statue tall and sure. // She welcomes the tired, the weak, and the poor. // She lights the way to our country's shore.
4. A declaration told the king // that freedom waited in the wings. // It told him why and made it clear // that England's flag would not fly here.

1. Mount Rushmore
2. Liberty Bell
3. Statue of Liberty
4. Declaration of Independence

Bonus Box: Poems will vary.

Page 126

1. My younger brother wanted a pet. // He said he'd take anything that he could get. // But when I brought him a snake, // the kid started to quake // and fell to the ground in a sweat!
2. Consider yourself quite a fan? // Let me tell you about my neighbor, Dan. // He went opening day // and decided to stay. // Four months later, he's still in the stands!
3. Mrs. Wilson just visited Mars. // She brought us all back candy bars // that are made by wee folk // who sell eggs with six yolks // and carry their children in jars!
4. I once knew a man who had eyes // that got larger each time he told lies. // They started off small, // but in no time at all, // they'd grown to 50 times the normal size!
5. My sister plays music each spring. // She's loud and she makes my ears ring. // She's a rock and roll star, // and I'm sure she'll go far, // so long as she learns how to sing!

Page 136

Colored bubbles:

6 x 9 = 54	9 x 9 = 81	4 x 6 = 24
8 x 6 = 48	12 x 12 = 144	7 x 5 = 35
3 x 9 = 27	10 x 10 = 100	4 x 5 = 20
4 x 8 = 32	4 x 9 = 36	8 x 7 = 56
5 x 8 = 40	6 x 6 = 36	9 x 7 = 63

It was REALLY "FIN-TASTIC!"

Bonus Box: 8 x 9 = 72, 7 x 7 = 49, 4 x 7 = 28, 8 x 8 = 64, 6 x 7 = 42, 3 x 8 = 24, 4 x 4 = 16, 0 x 8 = 0, 3 x 7 = 21, 3 x 3 = 9

Page 139

Boxes that should be colored:
Row 1: 0.250, 0.25; 0.7, 0.70; 0.50, 0.5
Row 2: 0.20, 0.2; 0.03, 0.030
Row 3: 0.330, 0.33; 0.450, 0.45; 0.540, 0.54
Row 4: 0.08, 0.080; 0.07, 0.070; 0.80, 0.8
Row 5: 0.63, 0.630; 0.10, 0.1; 0.602, 0.6020; 0.750, 0.75

Bonus Box: Answers will vary.

Page 140

1. 13.36	5. 11.6	8. 11.016
2. 13.036	6. 11.06	9. 0.41
3. 6.033	7. 11.16	10. 40.01
4. 6.33		

Bonus Box: one and six hundredths, one and eight thousandths

Page 141

1. 0.430, T	8. 0.010, N	15. 0.004, E
2. 0.030, H	9. 0.03, T	16. 665.20, P
3. 1.94, E	10. 3.971, G	17. 0.008, O
4. 0.505, Y	11. 0.7, E	18. 31.13, I
5. 3.441, D	12. 0.002, T	19. 19.25, N
6. 31.92, I	13. 100.3, T	20. 2.32, T
7. 0.593, D	14. 74.39, H	

THEY DIDN'T GET THE POINT!

Bonus Box: Hattie won because the least time represents the faster runner.

Page 144

1. 16.6	4. 0.18
2. 0.36	5. 35.5
3. 0.90	6. 0.84

"DISC-O"

7. 6.15	12. 2.7
8. 13.398	13. 0.85
9. 0.72	14. 29.00
10. 2.4	15. 26.52
11. 57.0	16. 72.18

A "SAXO-PHONE"

Bonus Box: 72.18, 57.0, 35.5, 29.00, 26.52, 16.6, 13.398, 6.15, 2.7, 2.4, 0.90, 0.85, 0.84, 0.72, 0.36, 0.18

Page 147

1. ²⁄₉
2. ³⁄₇
3. ²⁄₉
4. ⁵⁄₈
5. ²⁄₇
6. ²⁄₆ or ¹⁄₃
7. A total of seven candies should be drawn. Three of the seven should be colored purple.
8. A total of 15 candies should be drawn. Two of the 15 should be colored green.
9. A total of ten candies should be drawn. Three of the ten should be colored yellow.
10. A total of nine candies should be drawn. Seven of the nine should be colored red.

Bonus Box:

7. ⁴⁄₇
8. ¹³⁄₁₅
9. ⁷⁄₁₀
10. ²⁄₉

Page 148

Group 1	Group 2	Group 3
Ann ⁷⁄₈	Kelly ⁵⁄₆	Kim ¾
Bob ⁴⁄₈	Emma ⁶⁄₈	Jake ⅔
Harry ³⁄₈	Jack ⅔	Billy ⁵⁄₈
Jill ²⁄₈	Erin ½	Katie ½
Lilly ¹⁄₈	Ryan ¼	Abby ⅙

Bonus Box: ⁷⁄₈, ⁵⁄₆, ¾. Since Ann (⁷⁄₈) ate the most pie, she came in first. Kelly (⁵⁄₆) came in second. Kim (¾) came in third.

Page 149

Mom's Favorite Chocolate Pie
⁷⁄₂ c. sugar
⁹⁄₈ c. egg yolks
⁴⁄₃ c. cocoa
⁷⁄₆ c. plain flour
⁷⁄₄ c. butter
¹⁹⁄₄ c. canned milk
¹¹⁄₈ c. egg whites
¹⁹⁄₈ tsp. cream of tartar
3 unbaked pie shells

Best Ever Banana Crumb Muffins
3¾ c. plain flour
2⅛ tsp. baking soda
1¼ tsp. baking powder
1¾ tsp. salt
7⅓ c. mashed bananas
2⅓ c. sugar
2 eggs
1¼ c. butter, melted
1½ c. packed brown sugar
1⅛ tsp. cinnamon

Bonus Box: Answers will vary.

Page 154

1. 300 + 400 = 700, 834
2. 500 − 200 = 300, 229
3. 6,000 − 700 = 5,300; 5,306
4. 40 x 60 = 2,400; 3,024
5. 1,000 x 4 = 4,000; 7,728
6. 300 x 50 = 15,000; 20,412

TWENTY

Bonus Box: Problem 3 is closest to the exact answer. Problem 6 is furthest from the exact answer.

Page 155

1. 300 ÷ 50 = 6, Mexico
2. 70 x 60 = 4,200; Europe
3. 20 x 50 = 1,000; Malaysia
4. 80 ÷ 20 = 4, Papua New Guinea
5. 450 ÷ 90 = 5, Australia
6. 120 x 30 = 3,600; South Africa
7. 240 ÷ 12 = 20, Brazil
8. 60 ÷ 20 = 3, Peru
9. 40 x 20 = 800, North America

The western pygmy blue

Bonus Box: Problems will vary.

Page 156

1. d
   15 + 10 = 25 and 5 + 5 + 15 = 25
2. f
   1,000 − 900 = 100 and 500 − 400 = 100
3. b
   200 + 50 = 250 and 100 + 150 = 250
4. e
   2,000 − 1,000 = 1,000 and 4,000 − 3,000 = 1,000
5. c
   150 + 50 = 200 and 100 + 100 = 200
6. a
   10 − 5 = 5 and 25 − 20 = 5

They will only eat milkweed leaves!

Bonus Box: 860,000 pounds (86,000 x 10)

Page 159

1.

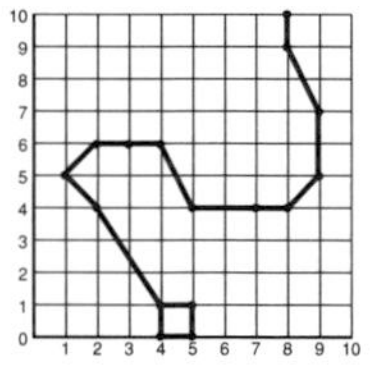

2.

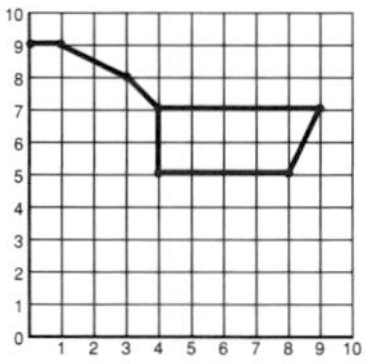

3.

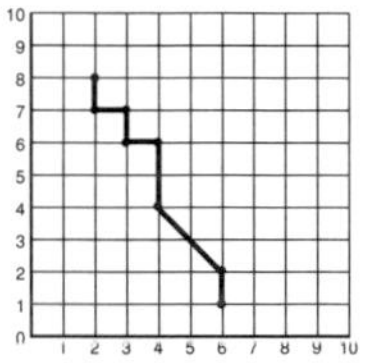

4. DRAGON
5. BIG DIPPER
6. LACERTA

Bonus Box: LIZARD

Page 162

Icecap: A, B
Freezeville: A, B, C
Icy: B, C

Examples of congruent figures may vary. Possible examples include the following: the floor tiles, the canopy's panels, the ice-cream posters, the ice-cream cones, the faucets, the stools, the chairs, the tables, the flower vases

Bonus Box: Pictures will vary.

Page 165
1. 0, 0, 0, sphere
2. 8, 12, 6, cube
3. 1, 0, 1, cone
4. 0, 0, 0, sphere
5. 8, 12, 6, cube
6. 0, 0, 2, cylinder
7. 5, 8, 5, square pyramid
8. 8, 12, 6, rectangular prism

Because they look like hares from far away.

Page 168
1. 12
2. 9
3. 10
4. 20, 180
5. 24, 216
6. 18, 162
7. 4,940
8. 1,458
9. 1,728
10. 2,640; 23,760

Bonus Box: Total area: 32,475 sq. ft.; total cost: $259,800.00

Page 169
1. 48
2. 5
3. 3
4. 27
5. 22
6. 35
7. 15
8. 6
9. 32
10. 32
11. bedroom A
12. $245.00; $336.00; $1,575.00

Bonus Box: playroom and porch

Page 170
Estimated area for each cake will vary.

Apple Spice = 7.07
Carrot = 3.14
German Chocolate = 28.26
Marble = 19.63
Strawberry = 12.56

Bonus Box: The areas differ because a formula can be used to find the actual area; however, to make an estimate, partial units must be put together to make wholes. How the partial units are combined to make wholes can vary.

Page 173
1. 17 ft.
2. 15 ft.
3. 18 ft.
4. 22 ft.
5. 16 ft.
6. 19.5 ft.
7. 13 ft.
8. 16.5 ft.
9. 13.5 ft.

Polly's entrance is the TRAPEZOID.

Bonus Box: $P = 21.5$ ft.

Page 174
1. $P = 12$ units, red
2. $P = 12$ units, red
3. $P = 16$ units, blue
4. $P = 16$ units, blue
5. $P = 16$ units, blue
6. $P = 12$ units, red
7. $P = 16$ units, blue
8. $P = 20$ units, yellow
9. $P = 20$ units, yellow
10. $P = 12$ units, red
11. $P = 20$ units, yellow

Bonus Box: Drawings of grid boxes may vary. Possible sizes drawn include the following: 3 x 9, 4 x 8, 6 x 6, 2 x 10, 1 x 11.

Page 175
1. 6 m; $P = 8 + 6 + 8 + 6$; $P = (2 \times 8) + (2 \times 6)$
2. 25 ft.; $P = 25 + 12 + 25 + 12$; $P = (2 \times 25) + (2 \times 12)$
3. 5 m; $P = 10 + 5 + 10 + 5$; $P = (2 \times 10) + (2 \times 5)$
4. 12 ft.; $P = 26 + 12 + 26 + 12$; $P = (2 \times 26) + (2 \times 12)$
5. 18 ft.; $P = 36 + 18 + 36 + 18$; $P = (2 \times 36) + (2 \times 18)$
6. 8 m; $P = 8 + 5 + 8 + 5$; $P = (2 \times 8) + (2 \times 5)$

Bonus Box: The opposite sides of a rectangle are equal in length.

Page 178
Brownies: 36, 36
Marshmallow Treats: 216, 216
Lemon Squares: 120, 120
Chocolate Bars: 10, 10
Fudge: 18, 18
Butterscotch Bars: 288, 288
Chocolate Cake: 351, 351

Bonus Box: 1,039 servings

Page 179
1. 120, B
2. 100, A
3. 175, C
4. 288, G
5. 360, H
6. 210, E
7. 220, F

Bonus Box: C, E

Page 180
1. 180 ft.³, 504 ft.³, 324 ft.³
2. 64 ft.³, 156 ft.³, 92 ft.³
3. 378 ft.³, 714 ft.³, 336 ft.³
4. 616 ft.³; 1,089 ft.³; 473 ft.³
5. 400 ft.³, 780 ft.³, 380 ft.³
6. 180 ft.³, 276 ft.³, 96 ft.³
7. 180 ft.³, 450 ft.³, 270 ft.³
8. 270 ft.³, 504 ft.³, 234 ft.³
9. 600 ft.³; 1,080 ft.³; 480 ft.³

Page 189
1. 1888
2. 1814
3. 1807
4. 1880
5. 1837
6. 1846
7. 1851
8. 1867
9. 1834
10. 1839

Bonus Box: 1869

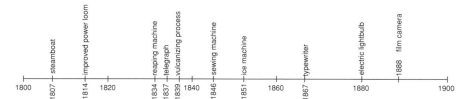

Page 192
1. 89 miles
2. Custer to Deadwood
3. Monterey to Palm Springs
4. 839 miles
5. closest together: Spearfish and Belle Fourche (rectangular chart), Oakland and San Francisco (triangular chart) farthest apart: Wall and Hot Springs (rectangular chart), Las Vegas and Redding (triangular chart)

Bonus Box: Problems will vary.

Page 204
1. Answers will vary.
2. Gravity made the water flow downhill. As the water flowed over the soil, it eroded landform surfaces, carrying away soil particles and depositing them in other places to create new landforms.
3. Answers will vary.
4. The heavier rain caused larger amounts of soil to move downward, creating mudslides that changed the landforms.

Page 205
1. F	4. B	7. H	10. L
2. E	5. I	8. G	11. A
3. J	6. K	9. D	12. C

Bonus Box: A mudslide moves slower than a landslide because its soil is saturated with water.

312

Page 210
1. term
2. Oval Office
3. oath of office
4. vice president
5. veto
6. first lady
7. cabinet
8. inauguration
9. State of the Union address

E pluribus unum means "out of many, one."

Page 214
Answers will vary for Human Heart.
Bird Heart
1. 600 beats per minute
2. 36,000 beats per hour
3. 864,000 beats per day
4. 6,048,000 beats per week
5. 314,496,000 beats per year

Bonus Box: Answers will vary.

Page 215
1. 1,000 = trachea
2. 100 = carbon dioxide
3. 92,900 = alveoli
4. 86,600 = cilia
5. 39,800 = bronchi
6. 1,600 = diaphragm
7. 800 = pulmonary arteries
8. 900 = lungs
9. 23,400 = oxygen
10. 1,900 = pulmonary veins

Page 226
1. 5,070 lbs.
2. 11,427 lbs.
3. 4,940 lbs.
4. 32,890 lbs.
5. 14,300 lbs.
6. 11,700 lbs.
7. 14,820 lbs.
8. 910 lbs.

The uncolored peanuts are 9,100 lbs., 507 lbs., and 11,420 lbs.

Bonus Box: Elmer would weigh the most on Jupiter and the least on Pluto.

Page 219
1. J
2. I
3. B
4. G
5. A
6. E
7. F
8. D
9. H
10. C

Bonus Box: Yes. The frequency 5,400 Hz is within the range of a cat's hearing.

Page 227

Planet	god of war	god of agriculture	god of the sky	messenger of the gods	god of the sea	god of the underworld	king of the gods	godess of love
Mercury	X	X	X	✔	X	X	X	X
Venus	X	X	X	X	X	X	X	✔
Earth								
Mars	✔	X	X	X	X	X	X	X
Jupiter	X	X	X	X	X	X	✔	X
Saturn	X	✔	X	X	X	X	X	X
Uranus	X	X	✔	X	X	X	X	X
Neptune	X	X	X	X	✔	X	X	X
Pluto	X	X	X	X	X	✔	X	X

Page 231
1. red
2. yellow
3. red
4. blue
5. yellow
6. blue
7. red
8. blue
9. red
10. yellow
11. blue
12. yellow

Page 232
1. E
2. F
3. H
4. S
5. G
6. I
7. T
8. N
9. A

THAT'S GNEISS!

Bonus Box: metamorphic, igneous

Page 239
Answers will vary. Possible responses are provided.

Fred's School and Village
Fred's school is smaller than mine.
Her school has several different grades and ages in one room.
Fred's village is small.
Fred's village is near the ocean.
Fred has had lots of teachers, and most of them don't stay long.

What Fred and I Have in Common
We both go to school.
We both help our moms.
We both like school.
We both have had good teachers.
We both like to hear our teacher read books aloud.

My School and Town
My school is larger than Fred's.
Our teachers usually stay longer.
Most people in my class are the same age.
Our school is divided into grades.
My town is bigger than Fred's.

Page 245
1. hit
2. pops
3. funny
4. riot
5. rash
6. bolts
7. spot
8. pace
9. settles
10. gang

Page 246
The path for each lollipop runs through the words shown.
1. offensive, foul, horrible, gross, awful
2. incredible, marvelous, astonishing, miraculous, wondrous, amazing
3. gigantic, tremendous, giant, colossal, monstrous
4. charm, enchant, mesmerize, hypnotize, fascinate
5. heavenly, delectable, yummy, delicious
6. horrific, frightful, hideous, awful, shocking
7. brainy, bright, sharp, quick-witted, clever
8. unimaginable, inconceivable, outlandish, absurd, impossible

Bonus Box: Words may be listed in any order.
1. wonderful, captivating, sweet, pleasing, lovely
2. dreary, usual, tedious, common, dull
3. tiny, little, microscopic, minute
4. bother, distress, trouble, anger, irk, bore
5. disagreeable, distasteful, disgusting, unpleasant, unsavory, sickening
6. comforting, sweet, helpful, peaceful, dear, calming
7. foolish, simple, stupid, slow, dull, incapable
8. attainable, possible, likely, expected

Page 270

blue	green
he	our
she	mine
I	its
we	their
they	yours
	your
red	ours
us	my
them	his
him	theirs
me	hers

purple	yellow
you	her
it	

Jilly made an A.

Bonus Box: Sentences will vary.